NEW DIRECTIONS IN ARCHAEOLOGY

Editors

Françoise Audouze *Director, Centre de Recherches Archéologiques, Meudon, France*

Richard Bradley *Professor of Archaeology, University of Reading*

Timothy Earle *Professor of Anthropology, University of California, Los Angeles*

Joan Gero *Assistant Professor of Anthropology, University of South Carolina, Columbia*

Patrick Kirch *Professor of Anthropology, University of California, Berkeley*

Colin Renfrew *Professor of Archaeology, University of Cambridge, and Master of Jesus College*

Jeremy Sabloff *University Professor of Anthropology and the History and Philosophy of Science, University of Pittsburgh*

Andrew Sherratt *Department of Antiquities, Ashmolean Museum, Oxford*

Norman Yoffe *Professor of Anthropology, University of Arizona*

ANCIENT ROAD NETWORKS AND SETTLEMENT HIERARCHIES IN THE NEW WORLD

Ancient road networks and settlement hierarchies in the New World

Edited by
CHARLES D. TROMBOLD

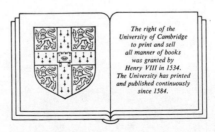

The right of the
University of Cambridge
to print and sell
all manner of books
was granted by
Henry VIII in 1534.
The University has printed
and published continuously
since 1584.

CAMBRIDGE UNIVERSITY PRESS
Cambridge
New York   Port Chester
Melbourne   Sydney

Published by the Press Syndicate of the University of Cambridge
The Pitt Building, Trumpington Street, Cambridge CB2 1RP
40 West 20th Street, New York, NY 10011, USA
10 Stamford Road, Oakleigh, Melbourne 3166, Australia

First published 1991

Printed in Great Britain by The Bath Press, Avon

British Library cataloguing in publication data

Ancient road networks and settlement hierarchies in the New
    World. – (New directions in archaeology).
    1. America. Human settlements. Archaeological
    investigation. 2. Landscape archaeology.
    I. Trombold, Charles D.   II. Series
    970.01

Library of Congress cataloguing in publication data

Ancient road networks and settlement hierarchies in the New
    World/edited by Charles D. Trombold.
        p.   cm. – (New directions in archaeology)
    ISBN 0 521 38337 4
    1. Indians – Roads. 2. Roads, Prehistoric – America. 3.
    Indians – Commerce. I. Trombold, Charles D.   II. Series.
E59.R6A53   1991
388.1′097′0902–dc20   90–33080   CIP

ISBN 0 521 38337 4 hardback

Contents

Illustrations

Plates (between pages 128 and 129)

Tables

Contributors

COLLEEN M. BECK
Desert Research Institute
University of Nevada
Las Vegas, Nevada 89120

THOMAS L. BELL
Department of Geography
University of Tennessee
Knoxville, TN 37996

THOMAS H. CHARLTON
Department of Anthropology
University of Iowa
Iowa City, IA 52242

WILLIAM M. DENEVAN
Department of Geography
University of Wisconsin
Madison, WI 53707

TIMOTHY EARLE
Department of Anthropology
University of California, Los Angeles
Los Angeles, CA 90034

WILLIAM J. FOLAN
Centro de Investigaciones Históricas y Sociales
Universidad Autónoma del Sudeste
Calle 14x55 No. 141
Campeche, Cam. CP 24000

LARRY J. GORENFLO
L.E.A.R.N.
2204 Chestnut St.
Port Townsend, WA 98368

SHIRLEY GORENSTEIN
Department of Anthropology
Rensselaer Polytechnic Institute
Troy, NY 12181

ROSS HASSIG
Department of Anthropology
Columbia University
New York, NY 10027

KENNETH HIRTH
Department of Anthropology
University of Kentucky
Lexington, KY 40506–0024

JOHN HYSLOP
Department of Anthropology
American Museum of Natural History
Central Park West at 79th St.
New York, NY 10024

JONI L. MANSON
Department of Anthropology
Southern Illinois University
Carbondale, IL 62901

FRANCES JOAN MATHIEN
National Park Service
Southwest Cultural Resources Center
P.O. Box 728
Santa Fe, NM 87504–0728

MARGARET SENTER OBENAUF
Bureau of Land Management
435 Montaño NE
Albuquerque, NM 87107

HELEN P. POLLARD
Department of Anthropology
Michigan State University
East Lansing, MI 48824

CARROLL L. RILEY
Department of Anthropology
Southern Illinois University
Carbondale IL 62901

ROBERT SANTLEY
Department of Anthropology
University of New Mexico
Albuquerque, NM 87131

KATHARINA J. SCHREIBER
Department of Anthropology
University of California, Santa Barbara
Santa Barbara, CA 93106

THOMAS SEVER
N.A.S.A.
Science and Technology Laboratories
Building 1100
Stennis Space Center, MS 39529

PAYSON D. SHEETS
Department of Anthropology
University of Colorado
Boulder, CO 80309–0233

CHARLES D. TROMBOLD
Department of Anthropology
Washington University
St. Louis, MO 63130

DAVID W. WAGNER
Department of Anthropology
University of Colorado
Boulder, CO 80309–0233

DWIGHT T. WALLACE
Department of Anthropology
State University of New York at Albany
Albany, NY 12222

THOMAS C. WINDES
National Park Service
Southwest Cultural Resources Center
P.O. Box 728
Santa Fe, NM 87504–0728

Editor's preface

This volume is the culmination of several distinct stages. Early in my studies of the northern Mesoamerican frontier I realized the importance of La Quemada, its settlement system and the causeways associated with it. This was mostly due to the influence of J. Charles and Ellen Abbott Kelley who at the time provided a lively forum for discussing many aspects of north-central and western Mexican archaeology. My initial fieldwork there in 1974 generated an anticipated number of questions. Some of these were fairly straightforward such as, in a complex society without draft animals or wheeled vehicles and few natural impediments to ordinary foot traffic, why was so much labor invested in causeways? Since the answer was not immediately evident, one solution might be to tackle the question on a cross-cultural basis. At the time I knew, though in retrospect rather dimly, that a small handful of researchers was involved in related studies in other areas. Thus with suggestions and encouragement from Karen Bruhns, Jane Stone, Jim Judge and David Browman, a symposium was organized for the 81st annual meeting of the American Anthropological Association to be held in Washington, DC.

Many papers presented at that symposium, entitled *Prehispanic Transport Networks in the New World*, now form the core of the present volume. The symposium was organized in three sections according to geographical area. The first focused on the Greater Southwest with primary emphasis on recent research in the Chaco Canyon region. Contributors to this section included Peter Dunham, Natalie Pattison, Chris Kincaid, Thomas Windes, Fred Nials, John Stein, Joan Mathien, Daniel Reff, Carroll Riley, and Joni Manson. The second section took account of recent Mesoamerican research and included myself, Shirley Gorenstein, Helen

Pollard, Robert Santley, Kenneth Hirth, and William Folan. The South American section included Colleen Beck, Dwight Wallace, Linda Spickard, and Patricia Lyon with Kathy Schreiber and John Hyslop as discussants. Cross-cutting the regional topics were considerations of discovery and verification procedures, survey strategies, uses of ethnohistorical accounts, and theoretical issues such as the extent to which roads could be used as an index of sociopolitical complexity.

The present volume is organized into three categories: Theoretical Considerations, Methodology, and Regional Studies. Although these categories are not mutually exclusive, the chapters within each category are meant to illustrate particular points. Hyslop's observations on South American roads, for example, are also appropriate for many other areas of the New World. Likewise, Beck's presentation is essentially regional in scope, yet her description of cross-cutting relationships is important for understanding relative chronology in any region with overlapping cultural landscape features. The remote-sensing papers by Sever and Wagner, and Sheets and Sever, give considerable information on Chacoan and Costa Rican routes as well as their cultural contexts. Their major importance in terms of methodology, however, lies in describing the uses of remote sensing in two vastly different physical settings.

Many chapters under the Regional Studies heading deal with theoretical issues, discovery, survey, the interpretive issues as well as new regional findings. Chapters in this category are intended to elucidate various subareas as well. Within the Greater Southwest, for example, Mathien discusses not only the history and present status of research in the Chaco Canyon region, but other portions of the Southwest such as Casas Grandes in Chihuahua and areas of California and Arizona. While Mathien provides a detailed overview, Windes focuses on particular aspects of description and analyses in the Chaco region. Contrasted with this is the chapter by Riley and Manson who use ethnohistoric data to reconstruct and interpret routes associated with the protohistoric statelets of Sonora. One important aspect of their paper is that "trade routes" may be visually identifiable in some cases. The Mesoamerican chapters likewise contain new information ranging over a wide geographic area, extending from the Chalchihuites cultural tradition of central northwestern Mexico to the Northern Maya of the Yucatan peninsula. These include many key cultural areas such as the Basin of Mexico (Teotihuacan and Tenochtitlan), the Tarascan heartland, Xochicalco and Coba. The South American portion is structured to describe three different geo-graphical situations where roads assumed considerable importance. The chapter by Denevan not only includes areas of Amazon basin and *Llanos* areas of Venezuela, but reviews early accounts of roads encountered in the Caribbean areas. Schreiber on the other hand discusses the history of Andean roads and their association with highly developed polities while Wallace focuses on a specific coastal port-of-trade situation with a view to their symbolic importance.

The studies contained in this volume are primarily meant to be representative. In this sense they are intended to bring an awareness to the scientific and lay community that formal routes exist in substantial numbers and that they can be used as a valuable research tool. The chapters presented here, then, are intended to show what progress has been made to date, and hopefully provide guidelines and impetus for future studies.

I would like to express my gratitude to Karen Bruhns, with whom I first discussed the possibility of organizing the symposium and who subsequently assisted in recruiting various participants, and to Jane Stone and Jim Judge for suggesting various participants for the South American and the Southwestern sections respectively.

Also important were George Gumerman and especially David Browman for their encouragement and suggestions throughout the symposium and publication stages. Finally, my gratitude to Harry William Henry III for his editorial comments.

1 An introduction to the study of ancient New World road networks

CHARLES D. TROMBOLD

The study of ancient roads, in both the Old World and the New World, is possibly best conceptualized under the theoretical orientation of landscape archaeology. Simply stated, landscape archaeology is the study of civilization's imprint on or modification of the natural environment. Its basic premise is that the cultural landscape reflects the interplay between technology, environment, social structure, and the values of the society that shaped it. The cultural landscape includes such features as roads, agricultural terraces, hydraulic works, field systems, settlement patterns, and any other man-made alteration of the natural terrain (Armillas 1971:654). This approach was refined by British archaeologists between about 1920 and 1950 primarily as a result of increased feasibility of aerial survey and technological advances in aerial photography developed during the two world wars. Roads are the focus of this particular facet of landscape archaeology because they are the only tangible evidence of a prehistoric population's structural organization across geographical space.

Although some data have accumulated on Old World roads, comparatively little attention has been paid to those of the New World. Part of this may be due to a very early realization that precolumbian technological development was markedly different from that of the Old World. Thus in the history of technology relating to transportation, most emphasis has been placed on the development of the wheel and innovations to harness the energy of draft animals. Associated with this is perhaps a feeling that roads are synonymous with wheeled vehicles. Since vehicles were not used in the New World before European contact, it followed that the few known precolumbian roads would be of little real significance, or curiosities at best. We are now discovering that they

Fig. 1.1. *Regions discussed in this volume.*

● **Chaco Canyon Region**
(Chapters 5, 6, 10, 11)

● **Sonoran Statelets**
(Chapter 12)

La Quemada Region
● (Chapter 13)

Lake Patzcuaro Basin ●
(Chapter 14)

● **Teotihuacan** (Chapter 15)
● **Tenochtitlan** (Chapter 16)
✕ **Xochicalco**
(Chapter 17)

● **Coba**
(Chapter 18)

Tilaran-Arenal Region
(Chapter 7)

● **Hato la Calzada de Paez**
(Chapter 19)

Chicama-Moche Region
(Chapter 8)

**Carhuarazo
Valley**
(Chapter 20)

Chincha
(Chapter 21)

● **Llanos de Mojos**
(Chapter 19)

were more widespread than previously realized and that in terms of construction techniques and engineering of comparable time periods, New World roads frequently showed a marked superiority over their Old World counterparts.

In this book we discuss New World road networks in a variety of regions (Fig. 1.1). One purpose is to delimit their underlying contexts in terms of political organization and social/economic complexity. In this sense we are attempting to identify regularities and peculiarities on a cross-cultural basis to account for functions and location, and to determine if (or to what extent) they can be used as an index of societal complexity.

The study attempts to go well beyond a simple classificatory scheme, however. Certain points on the landscape were connected by routes of one kind or another in all societies, regardless of complexity. What varies is the location of these routes and the social value that was placed on them at any given time. Seen holistically, the route system used by a particular culture or group should reflect something of its internal composition, value system (in terms of choosing to connect certain points and not others), and mode of adaptation to the cultural and natural environment. Thus if we are clever or fortunate enough to identify these routes as empirical entities, a potentially powerful tool will be at our disposal to decipher an important facet of regional prehistory.

Although it would be ideal to study an entire regional system, preservation does not permit this. We are therefore forced to deal with what is available as well as to seek innovative detection and analytical techniques. Thus while the following discussions deal primarily with formal prehispanic roadways, it is with the full realization that they are relatively rare, local or regional in scope (except for those pertaining to empires), and specialized instances of the overall spectra of transportation routes. As such they cannot be construed to be representative of a particular region's entire transport system, for as we shall see in the following chapters the formal systems, when present, almost invariably coexisted with the informal.

Formal and informal routes

There is a basic dichotomy between formal and informal routes. Formal routes are those that show evidence of planning and purposeful construction.[1] This is often reflected in straightness and non-duplication as well as construction of associated elements such as roadbeds, curbs, pavements, sidewalls, drainage culverts or bridges. Formal road systems, then, are characterized not only by evidence of labor in construction, engi-

neering,[2] and maintenance, but by an organizational apparatus responsible for their implementation. They are defined as tangible, physical evidence of a route of travel serving as a means of communication between points or activity areas. As such they usually have three basic characteristics: 1. a definable width, usually on the basis of architectural features such as border elements or roadbed preparation; 2. more than casual construction; and 3. normally, a failure to deviate in direction for minor topographic obstacles (*see also* Roney 1983:9). These may include a span or several aligned segments that may or may not have obvious termini; a network, consisting of a group of non-aligned linked segments; or a system consisting of a series of interconnected networks. There are two primary subdivisions of formal land routes: roads and causeways. This is based on structural criteria in that both retain the same definition given above, but causeways are roadbeds that are artificially raised above ground level.

Contrasted with this are informal routes that have minimal or no labor directed to their creation or maintenance. These for the most part would consist of paths, trails, and trade routes. As Earle points out, paths are usually highly redundant in that many have alternative routes and are usually the result of necessity. They also tend to be highly irregular in layout owing to their avoidance of natural obstacles.

As tidy as this dichotomy may seem at first glance, there is actually a substantial shadow zone between them. For example as several authors here note, roads built during one construction epoch may later degenerate into paths for lack of maintenance or change of purpose. Or, as Hyslop shows for the Inka, a route could vary from a road to a simple path on the same course within a few kilometers. Similarly, a question is raised as to whether simple route markings such as stakes or cairns constitute a path or a road. Denevan notes that a path or trail through a forest might involve construction in the sense of clearing foliage. It might also have to be maintained to some extent to keep it clear of subsequent growth. Thus although the dichotomy is usually quite clear, the reader should be aware that there are some cases where a simple distinction might not apply.

The evolutionary perspective

One of the primary reasons for distinguishing between roads and trails is that both may be seen in an evolutionary context. Earle, for example, shows that roads are generally only found in chiefdom and state-level societies while paths were used throughout all levels of the sociopolitical hierarchy. The crucial factor here is that roads were added to the cultural inventory to solve new needs of political integration while still retaining the informal routes for their previous purposes. Hassig, however, cautions that societal sophistication was not the only factor involved in the creation of specific types of routes. In this sense roads found in regions of easy terrain could be the products of societies possessing less developed technical skills because construction and maintenance costs would be within the means of a wider range of societies. Conversely, in mountainous or other difficult terrain, roads would be feasible only for a much narrower range of societies. Thus the presence of a road network in a given region does not automatically indicate a high level of societal complexity.

Schreiber and Hassig likewise remind us that not all polities had formal transport systems. Given this fact it is impossible to predict a road system on the basis of a polity's sophistication. This is amply brought to our attention by Charlton in his discussion of Teotihuacan. This center, probably the largest and most elaborate in the northern hemisphere of the New World, seems to have had very little in terms of a formal system outside of the city. At present, compared to other road networks discussed in this volume, the formal routes identified linking Teotihuacan with its hinterland seem quite insignificant.

Form and function

The evolutionary dimension is only one aspect of a formal route system. Also important is the role that a particular system played and what it can tell us of the regional organization of the people who built and used it. Insights in this regard come from an interplay between two perspectives: the particularistic or micro-morphological and the holistic or macromorphological. The former involves examination of specific elements in route construction that may have had cultural significance. Some of these elements include road width, roadbed preparation, architectural detail, continuity or discontinuity of construction style, and directness.

The macromorphological dimension, on the other hand, provides information on a different scale. It is focused on the extent of the network within or beyond a particular region, the function of points it connects (i.e., general habitation sites, administrative centers, way-stations, defensive positions), the contemporaneity of connected points, and the overall configuration of the system. The macro category is therefore concerned not so much with the physical attributes of the road as with inferences derived from syntheses of more multifaceted research. The two dimensions are complementary in that neither can give reasonably productive insights without the other.

Micromorphology

Aside from symbolic or ritual considerations, implicit throughout much of this volume is the fact that the form of the routes is greatly influenced by their use. An examination of some attributes found regularly among all formal routes may be particularly rewarding. One of the most basic is road width. Here there is a wide range of opinion on how much reliance should be placed on this criterion for forming valid inferences. Hassig takes the position that while local topography may dictate the maximum road width, actual use defines the minimum. He shows the differences between roads that would be used primarily for commerce and those that would be used for military purposes. Roads for the rapid deployment of an army, for example, would need to be much wider than those for commerce where traffic would probably not be more than about two individuals abreast and labor minimization would assume much greater importance. A military function for many wide roads also fits neatly with Earle's observations that roads were needed to solve new needs of more extensive integration in highly stratified societies.

Hyslop, on the other hand, cautions that at present the question of road width is both complex and poorly understood. For example, he mentions that with the Inka network the same road could vary considerably within a short distance. Some of the determining factors include natural topographic features such as steep slopes or rock surfaces. Others are cultural variables such as attempts to avoid valuable agricultural land, and accessibility of construction areas to laborers. Adding to the complications of using road width as an index of traffic volume is the fact that contemporaneous parallel road segments are found occasionally in some geographic areas. In certain respects, however, the distinctions between Hyslop's and Hassig's positions may not be so great. For example, a road 12 to 18 m wide with a variation of 6 m could still be used quite effectively by a small army as opposed to a road that was 2 to 3 m wide with a variation of 1 m. The most important factor in considering width would probably not be the range of fluctuation, since that would be expected to vary according to conditions mentioned previously. Rather, the average width in relation to the distance between the narrowest points would seem to be of primary importance since this would be a corollary to Hassig's maxim that actual use defines minimum width. The real issue, it seems, is in trying to distinguish between symbolic and other functions such as economic or military uses on the basis of micromorphology.

Two other morphological traits on this level include directness and roadbed preparation. The former, especially when it involves projecting a straight route alignment over topographic features that are not visible from one point to another, requires considerable planning and coordination of labor. If there is one attribute that characterizes New World road systems, it is straightness. Unlike roads in the Old World, those in the western hemisphere did not need to take into account problems of gradient that might have impeded vehicular traffic. The latter, roadbed preparation, is not only important in assessing the amount of labor, engineering and organization behind any given linkage, but in certain cases indicates the amount of energy a society or polity would expend to maintain year-long contacts within or between regions. This is especially evident if bridges or other support systems such as way-stations or garrisons were built. The causeways in the Llanos de Mojos region of eastern Bolivia and in the Barinas region of Venezuela discussed by Denevan are excellent examples of this. Here tremendous effort was expended in connecting settlements and other points in low-lying seasonally inundated areas. Beck likewise mentions causeways built near Chan Chan to protect roads from irrigation water as well as to make people (and presumably their intent) visible as they approached. Causeways need not always have been used to connect points on a year-round basis. At La Quemada, a massively fortified citadel on the northern Mesoamerican frontier, some of the more elevated causeways seem to have been designed as much for defensive advantage as to connect two points.

There are a number of construction styles that can vary both within and between regions. These are usually very general and include features ranging from simple clearing to pavements and retaining walls. As research on roads continues these may prove useful for analysis when taken into account with other data classes. At our present level of knowledge, however, it appears unlikely that they can aid in deciphering chronology or function. Beck underscores this point by listing five styles of road construction in the Moche valley that have an unbroken continuum of use for the last 2,000 years.

Architectural detail, however, holds somewhat more promise. This category of data includes features directly associated with the alignments but which are not necessarily considered termini or destinations of them. Some of these include ramps, bridges, drainage culverts and sidewalls. They may in some cases be minimally accept-

able for seriation, but their main use, when they show diagnostic criteria, is to confirm contemporaneity of the route with the points they connect. The usefulness of this class of data is demonstrated by Schreiber in identifying associations of architectural detail with known polities and distinguishing between "royal" and ordinary roads.

Macromorphology

As we see from the above, the microlevel data class provides information on specific form and potential function of any given road segment. It is from the macro or holistic perspective, however, that we begin to gain an understanding of their role in society. In this sense emphasis shifts from a focus on individual linkages to what they connect, where they lie in relation to what they connect and, beyond that, to the configuration of the entire system. When considered as a whole, two standards must be met. First, the routes must be contemporaneous with the points they connect. This criterion is often deceivingly difficult to establish because of problems sometimes created by periodic disuse or reuse. Hassig mentions that although roads had the potential for change to reflect new political, social, or economic situations, quite often they did not do so simply because it was usually more efficient to continue using a pre-existing route than to build another. Schreiber also notes that in some cases construction of a road may pre-date a period of political domination and although various empires built new roads, in most cases they upgraded previously existing ones. Similarly many continued in use after the fall of a particular polity. In this sense Hassig notes that those heavily invested with labor tended to have an inertial effect on changes in settlement pattern in that societies possessing more formal routes were proportionately "locked into" a particular network structure.

The second criterion is that the location of all or most segments of the network for a given geographical region must be known before meaningful analysis can begin. Individual isolated occurrences, though interesting, contribute little toward understanding the makeup of the system. This is especially evident when various locational models are employed such as those discussed by Gorenflo and Bell, Santley, and Gorenstein and Pollard.

Within this larger perspective the general purpose or importance of a route can often be gauged by what it connects. Schreiber again emphasizes this line of evidence in establishing associations between certain roads and states. A series of roads that connect sites representing political authority, for example, would probably be more representative of royal roads than roads connecting ordinary settlements of the local populace.

There is a potential problem in over-inferring the function of a road on the basis of what it connects, however. Often many smaller settlements, shrines, or activity areas such as mines are located on or near roads. Thus when there are many termini, the primary purpose of a given network may become obscured. Possibly one way to resolve this would be to consider the types of activities contained by the largest or most prominent settlements in direct association with the network. These could then be compared with the types of activities contained by other sites both on and off the roads. Positive as well as negative .evidence would then be effective in isolating road-associated functions. The success of this approach obviously depends on the degree to which the region is known archaeologically. Thus as Hyslop, Beck, and Schreiber note, a truly effective study of the road system can only take place after chronology, settlement pattern, and other detailed studies have taken place beforehand.

There are other inferences that can be drawn from the overall pattern of the network. Hassig mentions that multiple roads linking the same point may reflect local or multiple autonomous administrative bodies involved in construction. Likewise economic motivations may be a primary consideration both when roads link multiple settlements and when they utilize a minimum of labor and material. Political motivations for extending a road system may be evident, for example, when the hinterland of a particular administrative center is poorly connected or when roads are needed to connect widely dispersed regions. Interconnective road lattices between political centers may also be an indication.

Ultimately, however, the configuration of the system must be described and analyzed. This can be done to some extent verbally, but when quantitative factors such as distance, travel time, relative accessibility of termini, and other factors are involved, more explicit models become necessary. Most efficient from this standpoint are those that fall under the general classification of network analysis. Gorenflo and Bell provide an overview of the applications and potential of this approach in terms not only of networks, but of specific aspects of regional organization. Of particular importance in demonstrating various lines of investigation is their discussion of network simulation. Previously it was mentioned that form, particularly on the microlevel, was heavily influenced by function. On the macrolevel, however, the primary purposes of the routes are often not readily apparent because roads may link many

points containing a variety of activities. Thus on the macrolevel the same configuration could be generated by several different underlying processes. In the simulation studies discussed by Gorenflo and Bell we see that the researcher can propose underlying processes and compare the pattern that emerges to the empirically observed case. Although, as they point out, causality cannot be established through postdiction, probabilities of certain underlying factors can be ranked and subsequently tested.

While Gorenflo and Bell present an array of analytical techniques, Gorenstein and Pollard, and Santley use locational approaches to characterize specific systems. In the Tarascan core region, for example, Gorenstein and Pollard first analyze transport routes in relation to settlement role within the Lake Patzcuaro basin. For this they determined and ranked the relative accessibility of ninety-two settlements using matrix multiplication. The accessibility ranking was then compared to early ethnohistorical records to determine if a correlation existed between high accessibility and specific functions such as markets, administrative and/or religious centers, and elite settlements. The results, when compared with areas outside the core region, as well, showed that the Tarascan system was "solar" (see Fig. 16.1c) in that the direction of flow of goods and information was up the settlement hierarchy although horizontal flow, especially in the core region was more frequent. This situation both favored and consolidated Tzintzuntzan's role as primate center.

Similarly Santley examines Aztec regional economic organization at the time of the Spanish conquest. Unlike the Tarascan system, he shows that the Aztec system favored bulking and large-scale import–export enterprises. The system was dendritic in that it facilitated trafficking up and down the settlement hierarchy – not between centers of equal hierarchical rank. The latter he shows was possible, but generally only in close proximity to Tenochtitlan.

The symbolic dimension
There is one aspect of routes that at present defies rigorous analysis. This is the symbolic dimension. Not infrequently both cultural and natural landscape features were imbued with spiritual or abstract connotations. Forbes (1964:11), for example, mentions that when the modern Kpelle of West Africa wish to express the idea of an unused path becoming absorbed by the jungle, they say that "the road dies." Accordingly, if the route itself is represented by a spirit one might also expect ritual behavior to be directly associated with it,

such as insuring the well being of travelers or protection of villages against enemies.

Folan, Wallace, and Hyslop take special notice of the symbolic or cognitive aspects of routes as does Earle of the ritual significance. Folan notes that in the area of the Northern Maya, specifically at Coba and El Mirador, sacbes (causeways) and their associated architecture may have been laid out to represent a celestial map. Individual sacbes, for example, could have been aligned to the rising or setting of specific constellations. Mythological sacbes are also present and these may have helped conceptualize or define local and long-distance associations between other centers and regions. Wallace provides evidence for the symbolic aspect of Chincha roads on the basis of macrolevel synthesis of ethnohistorical and archaeological data. The roads there provided dual perspectives: from the outside they reinforced the image of centrality and monumentality of a neutral port of trade, while from within they reiterated the prestige of a great ritual center that had links to other major routes outside the region. Routes associated with the great fortress/ceremonial centers of Xochicalco and La Quemada in Mexico almost certainly had considerable political and ritual symbolism. Among other functions, they may have been intended to impress both visitors and local inhabitants of military prowess as well as the legitimacy of their respective elites. Hyslop notes the potential variability in symbolic functions throughout much of Andean Peru. These routes were often used to define spatial divisions, conceptualize cultural geography, and reflect elite status, and, as with the Nazca lines, probably served ritual purposes. Despite our speculations, the cognitive or symbolic aspect without aid of ethnohistorical data will remain one of the more elusive aspects of routes. This realization should serve to make us more aware that roads were not always perceived as utilitarian in our present-day sense.

Discovery and verification

All the discussions regarding theory, analytical techniques and network configuration are quite useless unless the networks can be known empirically. Likewise there is little real value in discussion of "trade routes" unless their exact location can be described. It follows, then, that discovery and verification techniques rank high in the study of ancient roads and landscape archaeology in general.

One of the earliest and still most effective discovery techniques employed in landscape studies is the use of aerial perspective. Its systematic use was pioneered during World War I by O. G. S. Crawford who noted

distinctive patterns from the air that were not readily apparent on the ground. Subsequently as aerial survey and photography became more feasible, it rapidly became popular in archaeological studies in Europe (e.g. Crawford 1929, 1953; Deuel 1969; Bradford 1957), the Near East (e.g. Schmidt 1940), and the New World (e.g. Morley 1946; Willey 1953). That this tradition continues to be an integral facet of discovery procedures is shown by its extensive use by many of the present authors. Obenauf in particular devotes an entire chapter to describing the role of aerial photography in the discovery and mapping of roads in the Chaco Canyon region of New Mexico. The techniques she describes, some of them specifically geared to studies of low-relief features, are also applicable to a wide range of other geographic areas that are not obscured by vegetation. Possibly most important, these methods are highly cost-effective and within the means of most researchers.

Taking the aerial perspective further are two chapters, one by Sever and Wagner and the other by Sheets and Sever, dealing with digital remote sensing. The versatility of this approach is evident in dealing with two extremes of environmental conditions, especially when used in conjunction with complementary conventional black-and-white and color infrared photography. Although far less accessible to most researchers at present, recent developments in remote sensing as demonstrated here have the potential to revolutionize landscape archaeology on a scale equal to that of conventional aerial photography two or three generations ago.

The effectiveness of remote sensing in arid regions is demonstrated by Sever and Wagner. In chapter 6 they describe the results of a 1982 N.A.S.A. project in the Chaco Canyon region using T.I.M.S (thermal infrared multispectral scanning) and lineament enhancement. This technique, which measures heat differentials between subsurface features and the surrounding terrain, showed the locations of trash middens, subterranean walls, a prehistoric agricultural field, and roads. Many of these features would have been invisible or unrecognizable using conventional aerial photography and ground survey.

Contrasted with this is the use of remote sensing in a tropical rainforest of northwestern Costa Rica. Here Sheets and Sever used a combination of digital radar and color infrared aerial photography. Penetration of the tree canopy by radar permitted a precise definition of topographic relief, but it was through the use of color infrared photography that the various paths were discovered. Ground verification and dating through small-scale excavations involved a fortunate combination of volcanic ash deposition and erosional processes. Possibly the most important message of this chapter is to point out that even such frail features as prehistoric footpaths can be detected, verified, and dated given favorable conditions and innovative research strategy.

Verification

It is one thing to identify an alignment from the air, but quite another to verify it as a prehistoric feature on the ground. This is especially true if nothing visible remains from a surface perspective, as is usually the case. Where intact segments or linear concentrations of rubble link sites or activity areas known to be prehistoric, the problem of verification is not so acute. However, when little remains of the original roadbed and there is little or no associated architecture, the task is made much more difficult.

Ground verification of roads generally involves two procedures. The first is intensive survey to detect intact segments or to plot artifact scatters, sites or other cultural features that are in direct association with the alignment of the basis of aerial imagery. The second is subsurface testing. Naturally there are a variety of survey strategies depending on local conditions and degree of preservation. In the La Quemada region, for example, the entire area was intensively surveyed and all visible sites, terraces, roads and other features were plotted. Another intensive survey specifically to discover roads missed previously was then conducted between sites thought to have been road-associated on the basis of maps produced early in the nineteenth century. In the second, a survey corridor approximately 75 m wide, centering on and parallel with the projected alignment, was examined between suspected points. Initially survey teams zig-zagged between the limits of this corridor with the purpose of crossing any vestige of the road at a near right-angle. When an intact portion or linear concentration of rubble was encountered, the corridor perimeter could be narrowed accordingly. This method proved to be highly effective because it often showed differences in rubble concentrations and occasionally minor features that were missed during the first survey.

Studies in the Chaco Canyon region regarding verification problems have been especially innovative. Many of these were addressed by the U.S. Bureau of Land Management during the first phase of the Chaco Roads Project. They are noteworthy because the procedures developed there are also applicable to many other geographical areas where aerial identification of routes is far easier than ground verification. The reader is encouraged to consult Kincaid (1983) for a detailed discussion of methods, descriptions, and suggestions for standardizing architectural and morphological terms.

Conclusion

Although many New World roads were noted and described by naturalists and prehistorians of the last century, it is only with the refinement of discovery techniques such as aerial photography and remote sensing that their value as an analytical tool is realized. Long viewed as an antiquarian curiosity, their importance now lies in the fact that they can provide tangible evidence of cultural links across geographical space. As links, they touch on a variety of cultural manifestations in both a physical and a figurative sense. Physically, they are evidence for the formalization of a particular space between two or more points. This formalization reflects both the value of joining these locations and the ability or willingness of a particular society to do so. Figuratively, the study of roads, as with archaeological studies anywhere, must touch on a variety of related fields, including architecture, chronology, settlement pattern, physical environment and ethnohistory. The study of ancient roads, then, provides a focus that can structure research around itself, yet at the same time contributes to the whole of regional archaeology.

We have outlined a number of factors to be considered in this study. Among these are the extent to which route formalization can be used as an index of sociopolitical complexity and the degree to which morphology on both the micro- and macro level might reflect the purpose of the network. Also reviewed are discovery procedures, verification and analytical techniques, and problems regarding symbolic functions. The purpose of discussing these represents an attempt to identify and address what we feel are key issues that should provide a foundation for future research.

Notes

1 Navigable canals might also fall into this category but will not be discussed in this volume.
2 There is a dichotomy between construction and engineering. Construction includes any intentional modification of the land for the purpose of creating a route of travel. Engineering involves planning, design, and technical implementation. This would also apply to any features such as curbs or walls found in direct association (Nials 1983:6–26).

References

Armillas, Pedro
1971 Gardens on Swamps. *Science* 174(4,010): 653–61
Bradford, John
1957 *Ancient Landscapes.* G. Bell and Sons, London
Crawford, O. G. S.
1929 *Air Photography for Archaeologists.* Ordnance Survey Professional Papers n.s. 12. London
1953 *Archaeology in the Field.* Phoenix House, London
Deuel, Leo
1969 *Flights into Yesterday: The Story of Aerial Photography.* St. Martins Press, New York
Forbes, R. J.
1964 *Notes on the History of Ancient Roads and Their Construction.* Adolf M. Hakkert, Amsterdam
Kincaid, Chris (ed.)
1983 *Chaco Roads Project, Phase I: A Reappraisal of Prehistoric Roads in the San Juan Basin.* United States Department of the Interior, Bureau of Land Management, Santa Fe and Albuquerque
Morley, S. G.
1946 *The Ancient Maya.* Stanford University Press, Stanford
Nials, Fred
1983 Physical Characteristics of Chacoan Roads. In Kincaid 1983: chapter 6
Roney, John
1983 Glossary. In Kincaid 1983:1–12
Schmidt, Erich
1940 *Flights over Ancient Cities of Iran.* University of Chicago Press, Chicago
Willey, Gordon
1953 *Prehistoric Settlements in the Viru Valley, Peru.* Smithsonian Institution, Bureau of American Ethnology Bulletin 155, Washington, DC

2 Paths and roads in evolutionary perspective

TIMOTHY EARLE

Paths and roads provide an unusual opportunity to discover archaeologically the structure and function of prehistoric society. To Wallace (chapter 21), road networks are a "tangible paradigm" of a prehistoric society. The networks on the landscape are both a physical print of repeated economic and sociopolitical interactions and a model of proper order in society.

A point made repeatedly in this volume is that road systems are multifunctional (see especially Hirth, Santley, Folan, Hyslop, and Wallace). Roads provide routes for the transport of goods and labor in economic systems of exchange and in political systems of tribute collection. They provide ways along which people move and interact. Furthermore, roads are important ceremonial ways which social and political institutions use to symbolize and to make manifest their structural charter.

Paths and roads combine economic, social, political, and ritual functions. But this should not be surprising to us. Organizations in non-industrial societies are by their very nature multifaceted (see for example Dalton 1977 and Earle 1987). While analytically we separate out the different functions for study, ultimately the intertwining and mutually reinforcing nature of the functions is a hallmark of such societies (Earle 1987).

A typology of human ways seems overdue in archaeology, and the contributors to this volume accept in large measure the dichotomy between paths and roads adopted recently by Hyslop (1985). Paths are informal routes beaten by repeated individual movements of people across the landscape. Such routes tend to be highly irregular in layout as they twist to avoid obstacles that would require large-scale construction. Paths are characteristically redundant, with many alternative routes, each of low volume; their construction is unplanned, growing with the immediate needs and utilities of individual travelers. Roads, in contrast, are formal routes characteristically laid out by planners and requiring organized labor in construction. The construction overcomes obstacles such as streams and slopes and creates a network which is less redundant and, in the long term, less costly for transport. Such planning and construction requires organized direction.

Between these ideal types exists incredible variety in routes that result from overlapping and changing patterns of interaction and planning. Paths are upgraded into roads, and roads through disrepair degraded to paths. The actual network of routes through a region is often an intricately intertwined set of paths and roads maintained at different levels or organization and used for different functions.

Rather than attempt a refined typology of routes that would out of necessity be very complex, I wish to identify critical dimensions of routes that should be described:

1. network pattern in terms of such variables as connectivity (Santley, Chapter 16) and centrality (Plog 1977);
2. magnitude of transported volume as measured by width and wear of routes;
3. types of facilities constructed, including roadbeds, steps, ramps, bridges, causeways, and drainage culverts;
4. labor invested in improvements.

Variability in routes is expected to be determined by several classes of variables. First is the nature of the terrain traversed, including topography, surface conditions (roughness), hydrology, etc. Second is the economics of transport, including types of goods/personnel being moved, technology of transport, and volume. Third is the organization of society, important both for the functions of the roads and the mobilization and coordination of labor in their construction.

Paths and roads are expected to vary with the level of societal integration, and I will now concentrate on this expected relationship. To do this I will summarize some of the road systems described in this volume and elsewhere as they relate to a basic evolutionary typology – family level, local group, chiefdom, and state (Johnson and Earle 1987).

The family level

Family-level societies are low density and informally organized. A model of the family level comes from Steward's (1955:53–4) work on Shoshonean gatherers.

Because a dispersed population avoids local resource depletion, through much of the year families exist apart and more opportunistically so as to minimize costs of making a living. Families come together to form ephemeral camps that exist only as long as they benefit the participating families. Beyond the camps, families establish social networks important for security, mating, and trade, but these networks involve only infrequent contact between small groups. Ceremonialism is *ad hoc*, when groups come together, and is not elaborated.

The low density of populations, the small size of temporary groups, and the infrequency of intergroup contacts suggest that recognized pathways will be minimally established. Paths, crisscrossing the landscape, would form and disappear according to shifting patterns of movement. Paths should form redundant and overlapping networks, without centrality and with only low volume. Among the !Kung, for example, paths are apparently only ephemeral and are not mentioned in the basic ethnography (Lee 1979). Among Californian Indians, trails apparently existed (Davis 1961), probably because the mountainous topography channeled traffic along natural routes (valleys, passes, and the like). "Myriads of Indian trails crisscrossed each other in the valleys of California. Early travelers were often confused by the multitude of choices; they needed and used Indian guides to show the correct paths ... the trails in the sierra regions followed natural passes. Many trails were wide and worn a couple of feet deep from long use" (Sample 1950:1–2, quoted in Kincaid 1983:2–1). Archaeologically, such networks of paths would be difficult to recognize although cairns were sometimes used to mark them.

The local group

Local groups of several hundred people form under conditions of higher population density, especially where warfare exists as a result of resource competition. Local groups, i.e., villages and hamlet clusters, are politically autonomous, each defending its own territory. Extensive interfamily and intergroup relationships are established for marriage, exchange, security, and especially military alliance (Dalton 1977). This regional web of relationships is *not* organized politically and is not centralized; it does, however, involve frequent interaction and intergroup ceremonialism.

In societies organized as local groups, intricate networks of paths exist at two levels. At the level of the local group, paths connect houses with locations of resource exploitations (fields, springs, etc.), with other houses, and with special ceremonial locations. Generally the nature of the path network should be similar to that described for the family level (redundant and overlapping), but some changes can be expected. Higher population density and increased sedentism would result in a proliferation of trails and in heavy repeated use of some of these. Because families cluster into villages, the paths entering the villages are traveled frequently, and village work-teams may improve their ease of use and defense. Trails used repeatedly by families, for example to get to their fields, may also be improved to lessen the daily drudgery of transport. An excellent example of this pathway pattern is the famous Sweet Track in Somerset, England, dating from the Neolithic (Coles and Coles 1986). An elaborate weaving and intertwining of branches was constructed to build up walkways leading out from settlements through surrounding marshy land. Trails generally served as well in group activities, especially related to the frequent ceremonies associated with clans and local groups. These trails may be improved with some group labor coordinated by head men and big men as part of ceremonial preparations. At the regional level, a network of paths joins together the local communities that interact repeatedly with each other. Hughes (1977:203–6) describes the trails in Highland New Guinea as follows. The pattern of paths is not centralized, although some trails are clearly more important than others because of more frequent movement reflecting patterns of resources, exchange, and natural routes of movement. The lack of a regional political organization suggests that such intercommunity trails would be primarily the result of repeated use and would not involve much group labor. Construction of bridges is mentioned; although many were simply felled trees, some at least suggest considerable planning and labor investment.

Since the pathways of societies organized as local groups typically involve little construction, they are difficult to recognize archaeologically. As seen in the American Southwest, paths may occasionally be identified by features such as steps leading into defensive cliff dwellings and by extensive wear on soft rock surfaces. Between settlements, paths have been identified archaeologically by cairns, by linear arrangements in which rocks have been cleared from the desert pavement, and by associations with artifact clusters scattered along the routes (Kincaid 1983:2–2). "These concentrations have all the appearances of having once been vessels which were dropped while being carried by someone using the trail" (Breternitz 1957:13, quoted in Kincaid 1983:2–2).

Chiefdoms

Chiefdoms are regional polities which organize comparatively large populations (in the thousands). Typically, the population of a chiefdom is spread out regionally around a center, where the paramount chief resides and where major rituals of the chiefdom take place. Chiefdoms are overarching political institutions created by embedded multiple local populations. This is done by creating generalized institutions in which chiefs are the social, political, and religious leaders of the region. They are supported by goods mobilized from their dependent population. Chiefdoms are stratified societies.

At the level of the local community, the basic pattern of pathways described for local groups would continue to operate. Intricate pathways connect houses with fields, neighboring houses, and local shrines. Additionally, the regional institution of the chiefdom often develops a formal road system to facilitate the integration of its polity. Although this integration has the explicit function of controlling the region economically and politically, its form is characteristically ritual, emphasizing the sacred charter that legitimizes the political system of regional and group domination.

An excellent historical example of such ways is seen in the Hawaiian chiefdoms. Within the local community, an intricate pattern of pathways linked the dispersed households and gave them access to their fields, uplands, and the seashore (Apple 1965). Paths followed the embankments of irrigation canals (Vancouver 1798:360–5) and are visible archaeologically through uplands where they appear as discontinuities in the field walls (Rosendahl 1972). In addition, the island-wide chiefdoms constructed and maintained a simple road that encircled the island. These roads were about 1 m wide, frequently paved with water-worn cobbles to create a smooth walking surface. Although these roads probably facilitated the movement of goods and people between coastal communities, the coastal road's primary function was linked to the annual Makahiki ceremonial procession. During the Makahiki, the god Lono, embodied in a draped stick figure, and an accompanying procession of chiefs and priests moved along the road from community to community. As the procession approached a community, the sea and fields were tabooed and all work went into assembling the annual tributary gifts of food, feathers, and other material. The gifts were offered to Lono and his chiefly retinue and evaluated at a special shrine positioned where the road entered the local community. This ceremonial procession and its special roadway served two functions critical to the chiefdom.

First, the Makahiki signified the chiefdom with its system of social differentiation and privilege as part of a natural order. The god Lono, who was responsible for the rain and the fertility of soil and its people, was represented on earth by the paramount chief. Life's very process was thus shown to be dependent on the natural order of chiefly domination (Peebles and Kus 1977). Second, the ceremony was an event in which staples were collected for the support of the ruling chiefs, and special materials, such as rare bird feathers, were collected for the manufacture of wealth. Regional ceremony was essential to the Hawaiian chiefdoms both to legitimize their rule and to collect goods for their finance (D'Altroy and Earle 1985). The road system is the primary archaeological evidence for this ceremonial and tributary system.

The ceremonial roadways of chiefdoms are clearly visible archaeologically. Unlike the pathways of simpler societies, these roadways were laid out in a formal pattern and involve considerable labor in construction. For example, Chacoan roads radiate as straight lines from their centers. These roads are defined by parallel mounds that serve no obvious function other than to distinguish the road from the landscape. The Epiclassic roads at Xochicalco, Morelos (Hirth, Chapter 17) would seem to be similar. The settlement of Xochicalco was a major center covering over 2 km², 38 per cent of which consisted of civic/ceremonial architecture. Hirth has documented 6 km of flat stone pavement radiating from the center; these roads were probably used during rituals as described for the Hawaiian chiefdoms. Other archaeological examples of road systems probably involved in the ceremonial integration of chiefdoms include the straight-line clearings of Nazca (Reiche 1968), the causeways of Poverty Point, Louisiana (Webb 1968), and the grand avenues of Avebury in Wessex, England that were lined with upright megaliths (Smith 1965). The directions of at least some of these processional roads appear to have symbolically significant orientations to compass directions, astronomical points, or topographic features. They also required considerable mobilization and coordination of labor. A Neolithic cursus in Dorset, England, for example, would have required more than a million man-days to move the dirt used to construct the parallel earthen banks that defined a ceremonial way or enclosure 9.8 km long (Bradley 1986).

The early road systems with their careful planning and construction would not have served primarily as a means of transport of goods or people. Simple paths would have served as well. Rather the roads served most prob-

ably as central props in large-scale ceremonies that legitimized the order of chiefdom and may have involved mobilization of goods to finance the chiefdom.

As a footnote, the tropical-forest causeways described by Denevan (Chapter 19) were probably also associated with chiefdoms. These causeways served more mundane functions of transport across a seasonally inundated terrain. In this case, the leaders of the chiefdom probably organized the construction of these public works that benefited the daily life of the population and also permitted a smoothly operating economy that supported the chiefly superstructure.

States

States are regional and interregional societies incorporating populations in the hundreds of thousands to millions. Typically, regional statelets, equivalent to chiefdoms, are united through conquest into multiregional and often multiethnic polities. The extended organization of empires especially requires elaborate new institutions of integration and control. States are strongly stratified. With increasing scale, institutions become specialized in administrative, military, and religious functions. The interconnection and dependence of the different functions are, however, of continuing importance in early states.

At the level of the local community, informal pathways continue to serve most daily movement by the many households. These are rarely identified archaeologically but we can surmise their presence from the ethnography of contemporary peasant societies. At the regional level, formal roadways continue to function as critical props in state ceremonies of legitimization. Several of the cases from this volume illustrate such formal road networks that served regionally, while, at the same time, they were linked into a broader interregional system. The Mayan network of causeways, for example, is similar to the chiefly road systems of the Chacoan society (Folan, Chapter 18). The formal causeways in the Maya lowlands were impressive roads – 3 to 20 m wide and up to 99 km long; constructed as rock-filled beds with pounded calcareous sand; and incorporating special features such as elaborate ramps. These roadways connected civic/ceremonial centers with satellite centers, and provided a system of integration on a twelve-month basis, despite the seasonal rains. Folan, however, argues convincingly that the roads served an essential symbolic function making manifest the cosmological order of the world. The causeways radiated from centers towards cardinal and perhaps astronomical directions. As in the Hawaiian case, formal roadways probably served for large ceremonial occasions that were put on to make manifest the mythological charter of the society. The symbolic and implied political significance of these roadways would seem to be the best justification for their formal layout and high labor investment.

States, expanding through conquest, created widely integrated interregional polities. The formal road systems constructed by the early empires are certainly one of the most impressive indications of the state's political integrity and contrast with the much more limited road systems of chiefdoms and component statelets. Such large road complexes are described for the Inka (Hyslop 1985 and Chapter 4), for the Aztec (Santley, Chapter 16; Gonzalez A. 1973), for the Roman Empire (Chevallier 1976; Isaac and Roll 1982; Greene 1986; Crumley and Marquardt 1987), and by implication for the Wari empire (Schreiber, Chapter 20). These imperial road systems are impressive for their extent and labor investment. For the Inka roads, which in many places stand intact 450 years after the empire's collapse, Hyslop (1985) estimates over 20,000 km. At many different locations, the irregular terrain of the Andes required high retaining terraces, causeways, grading and paving, flights of steps, drainage culverts, and bridges. The primary functions of the Inka roads were most certainly political and military. They linked directly a chain of administrative centers along the mountains and coast. These roads provided for communication with a rapid messenger service, for tours of administrative inspection, and for rapid military deployment. Hyslop (Chapter 4) also emphasizes the symbolic significance of the road linking the administered regions to the capital of Cuzco. The annual ceremonies held in the districts partly to legitimize the empire's dominance probably made use of these important imperial facilities. It seems reasonable to suggest that regional and interregional exchange encouraged or permitted by the state used these same roads.

The network analysis by Santley (Chapter 16) provides a creative insight into the function of the similar Aztec road system. This analysis shows that, with the exception of the area immediately surrounding the capital of Tenochtitlan, the network is neither well connected (with low scores for circuitry) nor easily accessible. Such a pattern of linkages emphasizes external contacts of settlements with the capital of Tenochtitlan, rather than internal contacts between settlements of a region. This pattern of roads fits well with Carol Smith's (1976) dendritic model in which the vertical movement of goods from a hinterland into an urban center dominates the economy. As Chevallier (1976:205) summarizes the similar European example, "the main unifying factor

was the political one, summed up in the famous dictum: 'All roads lead to Rome.' " Such an organized and centralized road system was certainly constructed to facilitate movement of troops and administrative information. If the formal system had functioned to facilitate market exchange, a pattern of higher connectivity would be expected regionally. Such connections were probably provided by informal and pre-existing paths not constructed or maintained by the state (see Crumley and Marquardt 1987).

A final level of state roads involves external relationships important in trade outside the boundaries of the state. States are concerned with external trade as a source of taxable economic activity and as a source of needed foreign goods. Wallace (Chapter 21), in his discussion of Chincha, believes that this statelet served as a port-of-trade for trans-shipment of goods obtained by seafaring Chincha entrepreneurs and headed inland to a large land-locked population. The linking of Chincha's formal valley road network with routes of external movement seems reasonable support for this position. Often states develop on the periphery of high-density agrarian states. The agrarian states represent a large consumer demand for goods that encourages long-distance trade. Peripheral (or trade) states develop, financed by this trade, either as a neutral port-of-trade or as owner of major routes. The sub-Saharan trade states of West Africa developed in part with the revenue from trade with the Mediterranean world. Such trade states actively seek control of trade routes through conquest and then improve the route to encourage trade. The network of roads through Sonora (Riley and Manson, Chapter 12) probably represents the economic basis for the statelets of this area. We know little about these roads, but they appear to be much less formal than imperial roads. The twisting-and-turning layout of the Sonoran roads suggests rather an improved network of paths that may have functioned something like the caravan routes in the Old World. Such trading routes would not involve the overall planning and intensive outlays in construction seen in imperial road systems.

Conclusions

From this brief evolutionary overview, I would like to highlight two conclusions. First, the evolutionary development described involves largely the addition of new ways and the upgrading of existing ways. Replacement of one kind of system with another is economically costly and not targeted to the specific needs of ways. Therefore, pathways handle much of the daily local movement in all societies. The development of formal roadways in chiefdoms and states is to solve new needs of larger-scale political integration, specifically the legitimization of inequality in regional chiefdoms and complex administration and tax collection in interregional imperial states.

Second, the primary justification for the construction and maintenance of formal roadway systems in chiefdoms and states is political, and not economic. The roadways of the chiefdoms would not be justified by the volume of goods and technology of transport known for these societies. Rather they appear as ceremonial routes in chiefdoms and represent physical paradigms of order in these societies. The economic function of roads in early states, such as the Aztec and Inka, would have been to facilitate not market exchange but tribute collection necessary for institutional finance. The trading function of many routes, however, may offer alternative opportunities for institutional finance. The advantage of controlling and fostering exchange along these routes would be clear.

References

Apple, Russell
1965 *Trails: From Steppingstones to Kerbstones.* Bernice P. Bishop Museum Special Publication 53. Honolulu

Bradley, Richard
1986 *The Social Foundations of Prehistoric Britain.* Longman, London

Breternitz, David
1957 A Brief Archaeological Survey of the Lower Gila River. *The Kiva* 22:2–3

Chevallier, Raymond
1976 *Roman Roads.* University of California Press, Berkeley and Los Angeles

Coles, Bryony, and John Coles
1986 *Sweet Track to Glastonbury.* Thames and Hudson, London

Crumley, Carole, and William Marquadt
1987 *Regional Dynamics: Burgundian Landscapes in Historical Perspectives.* Academic Press, Gainesville, FL

Dalton, George
1977 Aboriginal Economies in Stateless Societies. In *Exchange Systems in Prehistory*, edited by T. Earle and J. Ericson, pp. 191–212. Academic Press, New York

D'Altroy, Terence, and T. Earle
1985 Staple Finance, Wealth Finance, and Storage in the Inka Political Economy. *Current Anthropology* 26:187–206

Davis, J. T.
1961 Trade Routes and Economic Exchange among the California Indians. *University of California Archaeological Survey Report* 54:1–71

Earle, Timothy
1987 Chiefdoms in Archaeological and Ethnohistorical Perspectives. *Annual Reviews in Anthropology* 16:279–308

Gonzalez A., Luis
1973 *Plano reconstructivo de la region de Tenochtitlán.* Instituto Nacional de antropología y Historia, Mexico City

Greene, Kevin
1986 *The Archaeology of the Roman Economy.* University of California Press, Berkeley

Hughes, Ian
1977 New Guinea Stone Age Trade; The Geography and Ecology of Traffic in the Interior. *Terra Australis*, 3

Hyslop, John
1985 *The Inka Road System.* Academic Press, Orlando

Isaac, B., and I. Roll
1982 *Roman Roads in Judea.* British Archaeological Reports 141

Johnson, Allen, and T. Earle
1987 *The Evolution of Human Society.* Stanford University Press, Palo Alto

Kincaid, Chris (ed.)
1983 *Chaco Roads Project, Phase I: A Reappraisal of Prehistoric Roads in the San Juan Basin.* United States Department of the Interior, Bureau of Land Management, Santa Fe and Albuquerque

Lee, Richard
1979 *The !Kung San.* Cambridge University Press, Cambridge

Peebles, Christopher, and S. Kus
1977 Some Archaeological Correlates of Ranked Societies. *American Antiquity* 42:421–48

Plog, Fred
1977 Modeling Economic Exchange. In *Exchange Systems in Prehistory*, edited by T. Earle and J. Ericson, pp. 127–40. Academic Press, New York

Reiche, Maria
1968 *Mystery on the Desert. Vorbericht für eine Wissenschaftliche Deutung der vorgeschichtlichen Bodenzeichnungen von Nazca, Peru and Einführung in ihr Studium.* Vaihingen, Stuttgart

Rosendahl, Paul
1972 Aboriginal Agricultural and Residence Patterns in Upland Lapakahi, Island of Hawaii. Ph.D. dissertation, University of Hawaii

Sample, Laetitia
    1950 *Trade and Trials in Aboriginal California*. Reports of the University of California Archaeological Survey 9
Smith, Carol
    1976 Exchange Systems and the Spatial Distribution of Elites. The Organization of Stratification in Agrarian Societies. In *Regional Analysis*, edited by C. Smith Vol. II, pp. 309–14. Academic Press, New York
Smith, I. F.
    1965 *Windmill Hill and Avebury*. Oxford University Press, Oxford

Steward, Julian
    1955 *Theory of Culture Change*. University of Illinois Press, Urbana
Vancouver, George
    1798 *A voyage of discovery to the North Pacific Ocean and around the World*, Vol. II. London
Webb, Clarence
    1968 *The Poverty Point Culture*. School of Geoscience, Louisiana State University, Baton Rouge

3 Roads, routes, and ties that bind

ROSS HASSIG

Roads seem to be concrete phenomena. Yet it is difficult to reconstruct why roads were built and what their impact was in the precolumbian context. This is due, in part, to the incompleteness with which these roads are known. But the difficulty also lies in how the archaeological and historical data are interpreted. In hopes of clarifying some of the ambiguities, this paper examines some of the problems in such retrospective analyses and looks at possible alternatives.

Analytical approaches
The nature and significance of roads are not givens in any analysis. Rather, they are shaped by the different strategies by which they are analyzed. As an exercise in reconstruction, the study of precolumbian roads may appear to be best pursued by an historical approach; but as a single approach, this is inadequate. For example, historical approaches may attempt to establish why a road was built, but the reasons given by the builders are often either conscious or unconscious rationalizations of their actions or are limited in their perspective. Frequently more fundamental processes underlie the builders' avowed purposes or may act to thwart them. Consequently, to go beyond the explanations available in contemporary accounts, the historical approach must necessarily rely on the insights of other types of analyses in assessing the reasons for those changes.

Functional approaches, which consider roads in the current cultural situation, typically adopt economic-cum-transport models for assessing the utility of roads (e.g. Kansky 1963), and can be applied where there is little or no written historical documentation. These methods go a long way toward redressing the deficiencies of historical evidence. However, their main shortcoming lies in the primacy they accord economic motivations – an assumption based largely on Western societies. Although this economic focus nicely accounts for many transport factors and permits the evaluation of road network efficiency, there are problems. First, without knowing the constructing culture's understanding of what constitutes economic efficiency, functional approaches do not and cannot address the motivations behind the construction of those roads – even by measuring the disparity between actual roads and an assumed economic ideal. For example, where there are political motives, such as the desire to integrate a region through economic ties, the road system may only secondarily reflect economic concerns and give little or no hint of their political purposes. Second, these economic approaches rest on a consensual view of society and may well capture the economic concerns of the society's decision-makers, without reflecting the economic interests of all social groups (Barwell *et al.* 1985:127; Rimmer 1978:78–83). Thus, economic approaches to roads not only are based on our notion of economy, but also assume a consensus that reflects the dominant stratum rather than its totality (Barwell *et al.* 1985:2). Nevertheless, the economic-cum-transport approach can be used in the absence of historical data or to augment the scant historical evidence available, by at least providing an assessment of the economic impact of the road system as we understand it. But there are many alternative types of economies with their own distributional pattern and characteristic road system. Because there is no ideal economy in any abstract sense, there is no ideal road system, so no specific road system can be used to judge those found archaeologically. However, each road system does reflect something about its nature and the purpose of its builders – or at least of the decision-makers.

Roads serve purposes other than economic, of course, such as maintaining religious and social ties, but these are likely to be secondary. That is, roads serve these functions but the primary motivations for their construction are economic and political, and they can be more readily and convincingly analyzed in these terms. However, economic assumptions drawn from Western economic systems cannot be incorporated wholesale. Instead, analysis of indigenous New World road systems requires an initial consideration of transportation mechanics.

Building from the ground up
Pursued archaeologically and ethnohistorically, roads in the precolumbian Americas require consideration of what they are, where they are, and what they mean. No simple examination of their physical remains is adequate because roads that appear physically similar can have radically different uses and significance in different times, places, and societies.

At their simplest, roads increase the efficiency of transportation, thereby collapsing social space and effectively drawing distant places nearer (Janelle 1969:351). Roads are not merely creations of earth, stones, or concrete: they bind areas more tightly together. But this does not happen uniformly. Just as places are brought closer by the roads connecting them, places not so connected are correspondingly removed. Thus roads are selective in the ties they create and are the result of conscious, though often unplanned, decisions. In short, roads can profoundly affect the social world, but they do not do so uniformly.

How culturally valued resources – be they peoples, places, or objects – are linked is a direct reflection of a society's values and transport technology. Because roads do not exist in isolation, they cannot be fully examined in isolation. Where they go and how they are constructed are ultimately tied to the type of transport using them (Richards 1984:1). Histories of transportation often stress technological progress as the standard that marks development. Thus, the history of roads in the West is recounted as a string of innovations and technological developments from the earliest forms of foot transport through the invention and refinement of the wheel and its accompanying road surfaces, harnesses and draft animals, the road system of Imperial Rome, the emergence of toll roads, canals, railroads, and, finally, the automobile and its extensive road networks (e.g., Childe 1954; Cole 1954; Goodchild and Forbes 1957). However, each improvement in transportation does not necessarily bring a direct increase in efficiency, whether that improvement is one of pack animals over human feet, wheeled vehicles over pack animals, or automobiles over animal-drawn vehicles (Deglopper 1980:161).

This is because each transportation system has its own advantages and limitations (Jones 1966:216; Vidal de la Blache 1926:349–75). For example, rather than emphasizing ease of gradient to avoid topographical obstacles, human foot traffic emphasizes the directness of a route and thus often passes through rugged terrain relatively directly (Hassig 1985:32; Rees 1971:21–2). Pack animals require greater concern for terrain; and wheeled vehicles require the most, favoring longer but gentler routes. Nevertheless, the longer routes that commonly accompany terrain sensitivity are usually, though not invariably, offset by an increase in hauling capacity that makes these longer journeys more efficient than the previous means. Each of these successive means of transportation may be more efficient than its predecessor in terms of weight hauled per calorie expended, but each is also more sensitive to adverse terrain (Hassig 1985:218).

Also, technological progress is neither constant nor uniform. Emphasizing technological progress often ignores or slights areas left underdeveloped by these advances, or periods of relapse to simpler forms of transportation (e.g., Barwell *et al.* 1985). Even after a more efficient system of transportation has been introduced, less efficient systems may be favored under certain circumstances. Thus, one system rarely displaces another completely: competing systems often become complementary as they specialize in the terrain and/or social circumstances that favor them, as can readily be seen in the development of major transportation lines and their feeder systems. Different transportation "niches" foster a variety of transport systems, often hierarchically arranged (Hassig 1985:218–19).

Since changes in transportation systems have a direct impact on roads, where multiple systems coexist, a uniform system of roads is neither necessary nor expected. Although roads are the most salient characteristic, and often the most recoverable archaeologically, they are merely one part of a transportation *system* composed of roads, means of transport, and support facilities (such as inns). And it is the availability of *all* these elements that dictates the creation of roads: a road will not be built where support cannot be supplied no matter how feasible its construction may be.

Thus, rather than focusing on the sequence of technological developments, roads must be examined in this fuller context to appreciate the impact of unequal development of roads and of their demise (Barwell *et al.* 1985; Marchand 1973). Roads may exist between permanent settlements in patterns suggestive of the economic flows of that society, but these patterns do not, *ipso facto*, reveal the nature of the roads. To analyze why indigenous New World roads were built, and what their purposes were, three interrelated factors must be considered: the linkages created by roads, the physical nature of the roads themselves and their support systems, and the size of the roads.

Road linkages

An economic analysis of systems says much about the nature of roads, particularly if the focus is not simply on settlements and their spatial distribution (Christaller 1972), but on interconnecting road networks.

Roads signify a certain stability – if not of towns, then at least of regions. A society without settled communities

has little to connect in a permanent fashion, and its regional conduits are usually trails following natural terrain features. But with the advent of settled communities roads become feasible and, indeed, necessary; not with isolated communities, but with interconnected ones. And regional analysis offers one approach to such systems (e.g., Skinner 1964–5; Smith 1976).

Regional analysis is composed of a variety of models of regional economic integration based on market patterns, ranging from *laissez faire* to monopolistic, and assumes that the nature of economic interactions in a region dictates the traffic between towns and, by extension, the placement of roads. The classic, but not only, model used in regional analysis is the central-place pattern. Put simply, Central Place Theory assumes the existence of: 1. a free-market system; 2. homogeneous income and tastes; 3. an evenly distributed population; 4. equal knowledge of market conditions; and 5. a topographically featureless plain (Smith 1976 1:8, 12). Thus, nodal settlements are assumed to arise as a function of basic retailing dynamics, which are best expressed in terms of commodity threshold and range.

Threshold is the amount of business a retail firm needs to remain viable; that is, the minimum number of necessary consumers based on a given per capita demand and usually expressed in terms of the area within which that population is found. For example, if a corn vendor must sell 100 pounds of corn per day to reap sufficient profit to remain in business, and if people purchase an average of 2 pounds of corn per day, 50 people must buy from the vendor each day: the number of necessary consumers defines the vendor's threshold. Range is the distance beyond which consumers are unwilling to travel to secure a particular good. If, for instance, 5 miles is the greatest distance people are ordinarily willing to travel to purchase corn, that is its range. Since a firm's range must exceed its threshold, in this example, 50 or more people must live within a 5 mile radius of the vendor if his business is viable: if there are fewer people, it is not.

Under ideal conditions, central places are located to maximize customers by minimizing their travel distance. Thus, settlements arise and dominate their surrounding radial hinterlands to the exclusion of other settlements. Dividing the minimal overlap, the complete occupation of the area under this scheme results in a landscape marked by a hexagonal grid of settlements and hinterlands. Such a pattern places each settlement equidistant from six surrounding settlements with the result, for our purposes, that six radial conduits extend from the center and connect the hinterland and the hierarchy of settlements in a network of roads that facilitates the economic flow (see Fig. 3.1).

This model is, of course, an ideal that varies in practice as the underlying assumptions are modified by circumstances. So where the basic assumptions of *laissez-faire* economics do not hold, neither does this pattern. For example, under some conditions of monopolistic trade, as in some cases of cash-crop production, equivalent-level centers do not trade with each other because they produce the same goods or their surpluses are siphoned off for external consumption: trade links are not formed to distribute goods locally. Rather, trade flows vertically, up and down the system, each town being tributary to only one higher-level center in a pyramiding manner. Such a pattern facilitates extraction of local production by pulling it up the system while simultaneously providing a counterflow of consumer goods from outside. Because such a system offers producers one and only one market for their goods, each level of the hierarchy is systematically disadvantaged in both sale and purchase of its goods. This dendritic system leads, then, to a markedly different road pattern, one that branches as it goes from larger to smaller settlements, but which has minimal horizontal connections (see Fig. 3.2).

There are many other marketing patterns, but these two examples adequately illustrate the point that basic economic processes shape regional interaction and thus the number, location, and use of roads. This suggests

that regional economic models can be used to work back from a given road system to the purposes for which it was developed. However, the usefulness of regional analytical models rests on the underlying assumption that roads reflect the flow of goods between centers. And this is not always true. Because roads serve to drain resources from the area in return for excessively expensive goods, local communities in a dendritic system may not have a major interest in creating roads. Under those conditions, roads may be an outgrowth of external interests or of middlemen higher up the system. But under more *laissez-faire* conditions, roads may be stimulated locally because of their resultant advantages.

Road construction does have some direct benefits for local communities. The greater the distance a commodity is shipped, the greater the proportion of its market price is consumed by transportation costs. As a result, goods with relatively low initial values (e.g., bulk commodities such as grain) cannot be shipped very far before the transportation costs take up such a large proportion of the purchasing price that the commodity becomes prohibitively expensive. This, of course, varies by good, primarily on the basis of its value in relation to its bulk – high value/low bulk items travel the farthest and low value/high bulk items travel the shortest distances (see Fig. 3.3). Although the relationship between transportation and market range remains constant, any change in the transportation system (and, in our case, roads) that increases speed decreases travel time. And it is time, not distance, that is the key variable in costs. If a two-day trip costs two days' labor (whether it represents 10 miles or 50), a better road reduces the time required for travel (though not the distance), so any given com-

Fig. 3.1. K-3 central-place pattern.

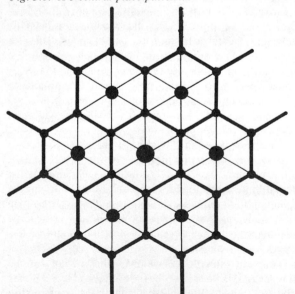

Fig. 3.2. Dendritic pattern.

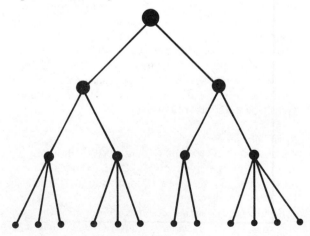

modity can be traded at greater distances because it can be shipped farther at the same cost.

The net effect of road building is that trade is generated between areas that previously had little or none. And with the growth of better transportation links, each area can now engage in more efficient production – economies of scale. As each area gains access to a larger marketing area, instead of producing a full range of locally needed commodities it takes advantage of its particular economic strengths – such as specific soil types or available raw materials – and increases its productive specialization. Products no longer produced locally can be purchased more cheaply from the complementary area, increasing the regions' overall wealth (Janelle 1969:351–5; Leaman and Conkling 1975; Taaffe 1962; Taaffe and Gauthier 1973).

Seeing the construction of roads as leading to economies of scale and complementary production implies that the purpose of regional ties is economic and is reflected in the roads. However, roads may also be built for primarily non-economic purposes, such as political control. Nevertheless because roads of whatever sophistication do alter social relations, all routes reflect something of the nature and degree of linkages between the points connected.

Roads can generate economic benefits in a region, but it is by no means clear that these benefits are shared equally. They are likely to vary by the social status of the participants and by their relative locations *vis-à-vis* markets, towns, and local resources. Even without knowing these factors, some evaluation of the sig-

nificance of roads may still be feasible if the analysis focuses on the elaboration of the roads, not on the flow of goods. Thus, the assessment requires further analysis of road construction and purpose.

Road construction

The construction of roads reflects the traffic they are to support. In societies lacking wheeled vehicles or draft animals of substantial size, the demands placed on roads are relatively simple (Goodchild and Forbes 1957). Because vehicles requiring roads to match their operational characteristics did not exist in the New World, roads were built primarily for foot traffic, stressing distance over gradient or turns (Rees 1971:21–2).

The construction of roadways – ranging in sophistication from mere route markers, to simple earthen roads, to elaborately engineered stone highways – was within the technological capacity of many New World societies, but the more elaborate systems were unnecessary for the available means of transportation. What was needed was a transportation *system* that not only demarcated a route but also fed and housed travelers.

The construction of roads was not simply a function of economic need or political dictate: technology also played a pivotal role. But although what a given society was technically and socially capable of doing was certainly one factor in the construction of roads, climate and terrain also affected what was possible and what was necessary. For example, in flat desert areas with only slight climatic variation, roads could be simple demarcated lanes requiring little construction or subsequent maintenance. Such roads required little technological sophistication, but under the conditions mentioned above, they were also the type most likely to be built by more complex empires. However, where mountainous terrain made construction more difficult, and where adverse weather such as frosts could damage the road surfaces and raise maintenance costs, these higher social costs made such roads feasible for a much narrower range of societies – the more sophisticated ones. It was not simply because of the greater technological requirements. Thus, the nature of roads and what they say about the societies that built them is, in part, a function not only of societal sophistication, but also of local terrain and climate: the greater the investment required to construct and maintain roads, the simpler they tend to be generally; and the greater the investment required, the likelier it is that roads will be built by more sophisticated societies. In short, under more favorable terrain and climatic conditions, construction can be simpler and the roads may be the products of less complex societies, while under harsher conditions, construction

Fig. 3.3. Exchange model.

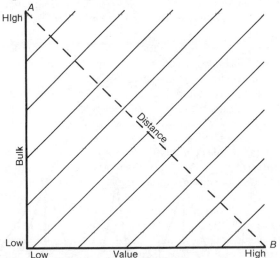

must be more sophisticated and roads are the products of more complex societies.

The existence of a road does not mean that its terminals are permanently connected. Seasonal variations in road accessibility and use can be caused by breaks in the road itself or by disruptions in support facilities. For example, routes that follow river valleys may be passable only when the water is low, or roads that remain physically passable may lack year-round support, as is the case during the dry season in arid areas.

Seasonal road disruptions can, however, be overcome. Greater planning can route roads through more favorable areas, such as temperate woodlands; solutions can be designed and roads can be built to minimize climatic difficulties by, for example, building bridges over seasonally swollen rivers; and all-weather roads can be built to shed water and minimize climatic disruptions. Again, the ability to do this varies with societal capacity and the degree of difficulty required. Thus, the greater the obstacles to be overcome, the narrower the range of societies possessing the capacity to adopt the necessary solutions.

Disruptions in support facilities can likewise be overcome. Food, shelter, and security cannot be maintained everywhere with equal ease year-round. Often this is because these services are tied to the economic capacity of the society – usually to its productive cycle. Thus, in agrarian societies, support is most feasible immediately following harvests. To provide such support thereafter requires a level of social planning foreign to simple societies. As a result, even areas of physically easy transit may be only intermittently accessible if food and shelter are unavailable. And as with roads, support disruptions are tied to societal complexity. The more pronounced seasonal variations are, the greater the organizational effort required to overcome them which is, in turn, increasingly likely with societal complexity.

Because altering the physical construction of roads also alters the social world by changing the purpose and the degree to which termini are bound together, shifting from a dirt road that may be impassable during the rainy season to an all-weather stone road means that the distance is shortened year-round, and the social (and other) ties are not periodically disrupted. And the same is true of the support facilities available on roads. Where these have been increased in quantity or quality, or made available for a greater portion of the year, the ties between the termini are accordingly strengthened, with all the consequent implications for the regional economy.

Road size

Knowing what roads link, and how (and when) they were constructed goes a long way in analyzing pre- or protohistoric roads. But traffic volume is also a consideration. Roads permit the movement of peoples and goods. But the specific dimensions of the roads dictate the magnitude of the flow. Roads need to be only wide enough to accommodate the flow of traffic.

For purposes of trade in much of the Americas, roads had to be the width of a person carrying a load with a tumpline and, in Andean South America, also provide space for a llama and pack. Roads dedicated primarily to trade could be quite narrow – only wide enough to allow single-file traffic, or possibly double-file to accommodate movement in both directions. Anything larger was unnecessary: building and maintaining a larger road was an extraneous expense unlikely to be freely undertaken by the local populace. Thus, while topography dictated maximum potential road size, actual usage defined the minimum. Roads built larger than necessary for economic intercourse could still be used for trade, but the reasons they were constructed cannot be readily addressed simply by recourse to economic analyses.

Increased trade may lead to wider roads to accommodate the increased traffic, but not typically. Increased economic volume is most easily accommodated by increasing traffic to the single-file flow. Instead, where wider roads are found, their most obvious use is political or, more to the point, martial. The mass movement of soldiers can be crucial to the exercise of political power.

Most preindustrial armies moved on foot and the roads over which they traveled affected their mobility as much as their walking speed. First-hand data on how fast indigenous New World armies marched are not available, and rates calculated from marches recorded in early chronicles too often yield unrealistically high or otherwise unreliable estimates. However, examples drawn from analogous preindustrial infantries do offer a basis for argument by analogy.

Xerxes' army required at least nineteen days to cover 280 miles during the invasion of ancient Greece. Resting one day in seven, the army marched at a maximum rate of 16.5 miles per day for each marching day, or slightly less than 15 miles per day for all the days of the march (Maurice 1930:212). Alexander the Great's army achieved a maximum march rate of 19.5 miles per day (Engels 1978:20). Hannibal's rate was 10, and in the time of Queen Elizabeth I the average was 15 miles per day (Neumann 1971). In 1760, Lascy marched on a road for ten days, averaging 22 miles per day, while in the early nineteenth century Napoleon, Blücher, and Frederick the Great all averaged 15 miles per day for ten days (Clausewitz 1943:276–7). By the early nineteenth century, the standard distance for a day's march was 15 miles, which fell to 10 miles for long-distance marches while mountainous country added approximately 20 percent more time than a march on level terrain (Clausewitz 1943:275). In general, the rate of march for premodern infantry varied from 5 to 20 miles per day (Neumann 1971).

Even today, the United States Army march rates fit comfortably within the averages for preindustrial armies: 4 km (2.5 miles) per hour on roads, or a total distance of 20 to 32 km (12.4 to 19.8 miles) in a normal 5- to 8-hour march per 24-hour period. (The actual speed of march used in U.S. Army calculations is 4.8 km [3 miles] per hour, figured at a pace of 76 cm [30 inches] and a cadence of 106 steps per minute, with a 10-minute rest halt per hour included.) The pace decreases marching uphill or on steep downslopes, and slows to 2.4 km (1.48 miles) per hour cross-country, rests included. Night marches are not very efficient and average 3.2 km per hour on roads and 1.6 cross-country (United States Army 1971a:11). (Forced marches are no faster: they cover greater distance by marching for more hours, but such marches impair the fighting efficiency of the army and are generally avoided [United States Army 1971a:16].) Based on analogous examples, and considering the inconsistent quality of New World roads, the rate of march probably varied between the modern cross-country and on-road rates – ranging from a low of 2.4 km per hour to a high of 4 km per hour, yielding a day's march of 19.2 to 32 km (11.9 to 19.8 miles).

These march rates are not given to show how far armies could march, but to show how roads constrain them. While premodern armies usually did not formally march en route – and there is little evidence to suggest that New World armies formally marched – some march discipline must have been observed to keep the army from fragmenting. The U.S. Army normally figures a distance of 2 m between men. (The distance is actually 2 to 5 m, but the maximum distance is used to avoid excessive casualties in the event of a modern explosive projectile attack, a factor that need not be considered for the precolumbian Americas [United States Army 1971b:C–2].) This is the same distance recorded for the Roman imperial army (Dupuy and Dupuy 1970:97). Furthermore, each soldier occupies a square meter (Sekunda 1984:23).

With these march characteristics, a single-file column, even for as small an army as 8,000 men, would stretch 24,000 m (15 miles), not including the accordion effect that normally occurs when marching. (The 8,000-man figure, the standard size of an Aztec army unit, will be used to illustrate the argument throughout, but the rates and spacing given above can be used to calculate the dynamics of whatever units are desired.) This means that, depending on the march rate, the end of the column would not begin moving until 6 to 10 hours after the march began, which would spread the army out, making the campaign longer and more costly. The primary method of avoiding this problem and decreasing the army's march time is to increase the number of men marching abreast.

As with the march rates, there are no reliable direct data on indigenous American army formations. But these march configurations can be indirectly calculated by drawing on military examples from elsewhere. Thus, for example, the imperial Roman army calculated approximately 1 m between columns (Dupuy and Dupuy 1970:97), which seems appropriate in the New World case as well. Armies do not need roads to march, but marching cross-country drastically reduces the speed they can travel, lengthens the campaign, and significantly increases the logistical costs. Marching on roads is faster, safer, and cheaper, but the roads' physical characteristics – principally width – dictate the number of columns that are feasible.

If the roads being used were built primarily for trade and were thus single-file in each direction, the army would be limited to a column of twos and would stretch 12,000 m (7.4 miles), adding 3 to 5 hours to the time required for the army to assemble at the end of the march, which effectively reduces the total marching time available to the army. This lag time can be reduced by shortening the column, but this requires an increase in the number of men marching abreast. This, in turn, depends on the width of the roads, and wide roads were not usually built for solely economic or local purposes. Since wide roads primarily facilitate the rapid movement of large numbers of men, their presence in a state or imperial system indicates a military purpose.

There are alternative strategies for moving armies. For example, troops might be permanently stationed in far-flung areas of the polity so the need to dispatch them quickly is reduced. Alternatively, troops can be sent along several narrow parallel roads simultaneously. But, in either case, the road system patterns the use of military force. Imperial systems that did not rely on troops garrisoned throughout the empire probably relied on the perception of their power (usually backed by some impressive prior military display) because they could not exercise force directly and promptly. Imperial systems that could exercise force directly and promptly did so either by dispatching troops rapidly (requiring wide roads), or by permanently garrisoning them throughout the empire (Luttwak 1976). Which option was selected was probably a function of the structure of the political system (e.g., Hassig 1985:92–102).

Wide roads do not necessarily reflect militaristic regimes nor does their absence mean that a society is pacific. But since wide roads are necessary for the rapid movement of large armies, their presence or absence does reflect something of the political constraints under which the polity acted, and probably its political structure.

Consequences
The above considerations have been examined as isolated topics to highlight decisive characteristics that affect the interpretation of roads. But the major factors – road linkages, road construction and support, and road width – will be reviewed in relation to each other before turning to the remaining considerations.

Economic organization does affect road patterns, as can be seen from the discussion of regional analysis. But not all integration is economic. In many instances, the types of roads constructed, their degree of elaboration, and the termini they connect cannot be explained solely by reference to economic criteria. Frequently, roads are built that far exceed the demands of economic intercourse in terms of permanence, size, and route. Roads and road systems also integrate large areas politically and are thus most easily understood for states and empires. The nature of a road system cannot be predicted on the basis of a polity's political sophistication, but the reverse may be feasible: the characteristics of a road system do set at least the minimum standards for the political organization in which they are found.

Much of the political nature of roads can be recognized by their regional patterns. Multiple roads linking the same towns reflect local concerns, and probably the existence of multiple autonomous bodies involved in their construction. And where roads link numerous towns, particularly when they require a minimum of material and labor, they integrate more towns into the regional network and they thus reflect economic motivations (Lopez 1956:23), although political considerations may dictate the placement of roads built for ostensibly economic purposes (Wolfe 1962). But centralized planning and political purposes are indicated where there is no duplication of roads between centers and the roads are straight and radiate from important centers. For example, the Romans built sturdy, all-weather roads running relatively directly from major centers to

administrative centers and points of strategic importance and were not primarily concerned with commerce (Lopez 1956:17).

While this may be true when the roads link equivalent-level centers, it is not necessarily the case when dealing with different-level centers. Straight roads linking peripheral settlements to the center, but not to each other, do not preclude economic motivations in road construction. But these economic purposes are mediated by political concerns since this pattern benefits the center over the peripheral towns. Because traffic flows in both directions, the center is disproportionately benefited by being the terminus of many roads while the other towns are the termini of single roads.

After taking economic incentives into account, the extant road system will play a major role in the specific way the state or empire is organized. For instance, wide all-weather roads permit large numbers of soldiers to be dispatched to enforce the imperial will at any time. In the absence of these roads and the political control they permit – and unless some non-coercive tie is central to the polity, such as enlightened self-interest, commercial interdependence, or religious unity – an alternative coercive organization must be adopted (Hassig 1985:70–1, 99–100). One alternative is to disperse imperial forces throughout the empire to deal with local problems as they arise. However, the profligate way this strategy consumes the limited manpower available restricts imperial growth. Another alternative is to dispatch centralized forces using inferior roads, but send them along multiple parallel routes, which ameliorates, but does not completely solve, the time constraints of military campaigns. These two alternatives can also be combined. Nevertheless, the presence of narrow and seasonal roads suggests that the empire does not place priority on its ability to wield great and immediate force.

Support systems often indicate more about the intended uses of roads than does the mere existence of roads. The lack of a support system (or its intermittent presence) can occur in the absence of a strong and centralized political system and, if a state is present, suggests its lack of interest in maintaining regional ties. Whether a support system indicates a strong centralized polity depends on the effort or organizational control required to create and maintain it: while a low-maintenance support system says little about its political system, the necessary sophistication of the supporting polity increases with the effort required by the system. And the level of sophistication increases further when the system is continual rather than seasonal.

Equally suggestive of the nature and sophistication of

the political system are the roads' physical character-istics. Simple roads indicate little about the polity where natural conditions require little formal road construction and maintenance. But the nature of the road surfaces can be seen as evidence of the polity's concerns where conditions are adverse. Thus, year-round all-weather roads indicate an interest in maintaining ties between centers, while their absence suggests the opposite.

Some economic integration of a region is expected even in the absence of a state, but narrow and seasonal roads are not expected where there are states or empires as the lack of year-round access markedly reduces the flexibility of the polity's control. Thus, wide all-weather roads and road planning are hallmarks of the empire – in part, for economic purposes, but primarily for political ones – because roads affect the empire's growth and nature, and define its policies.

A road system's complexity also reflects the social organization available to construct and maintain it. Local communities can maintain the narrow one- and two-person roads needed for trade. But more elaborate and all-weather roads are unnecessary for exchange, are an added financial burden, and are not explicable economically. Where construction costs are small and maintenance is minimal, large roads may be built in the absence of a state, as, for example, in some desert conditions, but under most adverse ecological circumstances, large construction and maintenance costs indicate centralized political control.

Despite the general correlation between political sophistication and complex road systems, transport and regional interaction – whether political, economic, or social – can and does exist in the absence of roads and support facilities. But road travel is significantly faster than travel cross-country, even without vehicles. Roads do facilitate regional traffic but they also create points where the polity can exercise control. Off-road forms of transport, not depending on roads, are less vulnerable to state manipulation or control, but the inherent limitation in this traffic is both a motivation for the creation of road systems and a funnel for existing travel.

Whatever the constraints, many of the problems encountered with roads can be ameliorated where alternative transportation systems exist. Even in the transportation-poor New World, multiple simultaneous systems operated – most notably, water-borne transport (ocean, lake, river, and canal) used in conjunction with foot traffic. Water transport not only linked road transport, it frequently shortened routes and served where roads did not, or could not, exist. Moreover, it could

potentially link political, social, and economic regions separated by hostile, empty, or barbaric areas. However, in most cases, water transport is constrained by natural water sources, not all of which are usable year-round.

In precolumbian Andean South America, light beasts of burden were also employed, linking both foot and water traffic. Each system was differentially efficient: although they all traveled at roughly the same speed, each could carry different quantities and types of goods and, where there was overlap, each moved along different conduits to serve different regions (Evans 1981; Hassig 1985:187–219). Because of their differential efficiency – water is the most efficient, then animals, and then humans – they integrate regions to varying degrees, with the consequent impact on their economies.

Even transport systems that do not (or cannot) integrate wide areas may be effective in particular circumstances in circumscribed areas. For example, in valleys, roads may be relatively wide (barring competing land use such as agriculture; see Hyslop 1984:230) and require little construction or maintenance. Thus, that area may be both economically and politically integrated with relative ease, whereas between regions, choke points easily restrict the flow, markedly limiting interregional political, if not economic, integration.

One problem in this functional approach to the interpretation of roads arises from reuse. Roads that pre-date their present use pose a potential difficulty because transportation systems do not necessarily remain stable once they have been created. Many factors alter them, including their links to other transportation systems, changes in the existing transportation system itself, and the shifting political, economic, and social situation.

Societies with very formal and elaborate road systems are far less responsive to change than those possessing less formal roads (Lopez 1956:23). This is a simple result of the effort already expended: the less formal the road (i.e., the less construction involved in it), the cheaper it is to alter and the more responsive the system will be to economic, political, and social changes. The less formal the road system, the less the society is locked into it and the less the economic status quo is perpetuated.

Reuse is more common when the prior roads also served the same terminals (Lopez 1956:20) and is opportunistic. (The issue of whether towns create roads or roads create towns is debated. See Burghardt 1969 for the former position and Taaffe, Morrill, and Gould 1963 for the latter.) As artificial creations, roads can be changed to reflect the current political, social, and economic situation, but often they were not. Many roads were important because of their prior use, so even if better routes could be created, the continued use of an existing road might be more efficient than building a new one.

In sum, there is an inevitable overlap in functions between political and economic purposes for roads, regardless of the initial reason for which they were built. For example, wider roads do enable armies to march rapidly. However, if roads were widened for political purposes (to permit a wide column and thus reduce the time the entire army was in transit), one would also expect the roads to be all-weather (to answer a political challenge whenever it arises) and straighter (further reducing the travel time). Economic (i.e., trade) roads, on the other hand, tend to be narrower (and hence cheaper), multiconnected, and less direct (to maximize the number of centers connected to the economic network). Direct roads indicate centralized planning and execution, while indirect roads suggest local concerns and little centralized planning.

As noted at the outset, this paper has not dealt directly with all possible explanations for the construction and use of roads. Concentrating on economic and political explanations is not intended as a blanket indictment of the omitted approaches, such as ritual or symbolic explanations. But if the more material explanations outlined above can adequately account for the role of the extant roads, recourse to other explanations may be unnecessary.

References

Barwell, I. J., G. A. Edmonds, J. D. G. F. Howe, and J. de Veen
1985 *Rural Transport in Developing Countries*. Intermediate Technology Publications, London
Burghardt, Andrew F.
1969 The Origin and Development of the Road Network of the Niagara Peninsula, Ontario, 1770–1851. *Annals of the Association of American Geographers* 59:417–40
Childe, V. Gordon
1954 Wheeled Vehicles. In *The History of Technology*, edited by C. Singer, E. J. Holmyard, and A. R. Hall, Vol. I, pp. 716–29. Oxford University Press, Oxford
Christaller, Walter
1972 How I Discovered the Theory of Central Places: A Report About the Origin of Central Places. In English and Mayfield 1972:601–10
Clausewitz, Karl von
1943 *On War*. Random House, New York
Cole, S. M.
1954 Land Transport Without Wheels. In *The History of Technology*, edited by C. Singer, E. J. Holmyard, and A. R. Hall, Vol. I, pp. 704–15. Oxford University Press, Oxford
Deglopper, Donald R.
1980 Lu-kang: A City and Its Trading System. In Knapp 1980:145–65
Dupuy, R. E., and T. N. Dupuy
1970 *Encyclopedia of Military History*. Harper and Row, New York
Engels, Donald W.
1978 *Alexander the Great and the Logistics of the Macedonian Army*. University of California Press, Berkeley and Los Angeles
English, Paul Ward, and Robert C. Mayfield
1972 *Man, Space and Environment*. Oxford University Press, New York
Evans, Francis T.
1981 Roads, Railroads, and Canals: Technological Choices in 19th-Century Britain. *Technology and Culture* 22:1–34
Goodchild, R. G., and R. J. Forbes
1957 Roads and Land Travel. In *The History of Technology*, edited by C. Singer, E. J. Holmyard, A. R. Hall, and T. I. Williams, Vol. II, pp. 493–536. Oxford University Press, Oxford
Hassig, Ross
1985 *Trade, Tribute, and Transportation: The Sixteenth-Century Political Economy of the Valley of Mexico*. University of Oklahoma Press, Norman
Howe, John, and Peter Richards, eds.
1984 *Rural Roads and Poverty Alleviations*. Intermediate Technology Publications, London
Hyslop, John
1984 *The Inka Road System*. Academic Press, New York
Janelle, Donald G.
1969 Spatial Reorganization: A Model and Concept. *Annals of the Association of American Geographers* 59:348–64
Jones, Emrys
1966 *Human Geography*. Praeger, New York
Kansky, K. J.
1963 *Structure of Transportation Networks: Relationships between Network Geometry and Regional Characteristics*. Chicago, Department of Geography Research Paper 84
Knapp, Ronald G., ed.
1980 *China's Island Frontier*. University of Hawaii Press, Honolulu

Leaman, J. Harold, and E. C. Conkling
1975 Transport Change and Agricultural Specialization. *Annals of the Association of American Geographers* 65:425–32

Lopez, R. S.
1956 The Evolution of Land Transport in the Middle Ages. *Past and Present* 9:17–29

Luttwak, Edward
1976 *The Grand Strategy of the Roman Empire*. Johns Hopkins University Press, Baltimore

Marchand, Bernard
1973 Deformation of a Transportation Surface. *Annals of the Association of American Geographers* 63:507–21

Maurice, F.
1930 The Size of the Army of Xerxes in the Invasion of Greece 480 B.C. *Journal of Hellenistic Studies* 50:210–35

Neumann, C.
1971 A Note on Alexander's March-Rates. *Historia: Journal of Ancient History* 20:196–8

Rees, Peter W.
1971 Route Inertia and Route Competition: An Historical Geography of Transportation between Mexico City and Vera Cruz. Ph.D. dissertation, University of California, Berkeley

Richards, Peter
1984 The Economic Context of Rural Roads. In Howe and Richards 1984:1–17

Rimmer, Peter J.
1978 Redirection in Transport Geography. *Progress in Human Geography* 2:76–100

Sekunda, Nick
1984 *The Army of Alexander the Great*. Osprey Publishing, London

Skinner, G. William
1964–5 Marketing and Social Structure in Rural China. *Journal of Asian Studies* 24:3–43, 195–228, 363–99

Smith, Carol A., ed.
1976 *Regional Analysis*. 2 Vols. Academic Press, New York

Taaffe, Edward J., and Howard L. Gauthier, Jr.
1973 *Geography of Transportation*. Prentice-Hall, Englewood Cliffs, NJ

Taaffe, Edward J., Richard I. Morrill, and Peter R. Gould
1963 Transport Expansion in Underdeveloped Countries in Comparative Analysis. *Geographical Review* 53:503–29

Taaffe, Robert N.
1962 Transportation and Regional Specialization: The Example of Soviet Central Asia. *Annals of the Association of American Geographers* 52:80–98

United States Army
1971a *Foot Marches*. Field Manual No. 21–18, Department of the Army, Washington, DC
1971b *The Infantry Battalions*. Field Manual No. 7–20. Department of the Army, Washington, DC

Vidal de la Blache, Paul
1926 *Principles of Human Geography*. Henry Holt, New York

Wolfe, Roy I.
1962 Transportation and Politics: The Example of Canada. *Annals of the Association of American Geographers* 52:176–90

4 Observations about research on prehistoric roads in South America

JOHN HYSLOP

In South America the study of roads as part of pre-historic culture is in its infancy. Roads are late-comers to the repertory of archaeological data for a number of reasons. Often the ancient routes are poorly preserved, with only small segments of once-important thoroughfares still visible. The fragmented preservation of roads has made it difficult, if not impossible, to follow them for any distance. Even if some roads are well preserved, most archaeologists are not equipped to survey them, lacking the facilities and knowledge of effective road-survey techniques. The emphasis in the last forty years on regional settlement patterns has directed attention to archaeological sites and their locations, but rarely concerned itself with the links – the paths and roads – that must have connected sites of the same culture and period.

Nevertheless, prehistoric roads have not been neglected completely. Occasional mention of them is made in the larger and more complete reports of travelers and natural scientists in the nineteenth century, and in the twentieth century there are many archaeological studies that cite the presence of an ancient road segment here or there. That information is rarely sufficient to contribute to a more complete understanding of the working of prehistoric culture, and thus references to, or brief descriptions of, prehistoric roads have generally remained as interesting curiosities in the literature. An exception is the Inka road network which has been reconstructed mainly through detailed research with early historical sources (Regal 1936; Strube Erdmann 1963).

As road studies progress, they can be expected to contribute much in various fields of understanding. For example, they will help define the relationship of sites within a settlement pattern. They will point to special areas (mines, shrines, storage areas, quarries, control points, and so forth) that frequently are not detected by rapid site surveys. Field surveys on ancient roads may allow archaeologists to detect types of small sites often poorly represented in settlement pattern studies. They will also raise a new set of questions that other types of archaeological research may, or may not, clarify. Roads constructed in extraordinary ways may reflect ritual or symbolic concerns. Since roads have been built and used by peoples for thousands of years in South America, one might expect that varied construction techniques are indicators of different cultures and time periods. Research has hardly begun to make such distinctions, or to understand why such changes occur. A related question is why certain ancient roads are abandoned, and why others continue in use over long periods of time.

My experience with prehistoric roads developed during a survey of twelve segments of Inka roads in the Andes between 1979 and 1981 (Hyslop 1984). During that time I traversed hundreds of kilometers of Inka roads, and learned a number of basic points that, in retrospect, seem almost self-evident. Before the survey began, they were not at all clear. The following pages will discuss some of these points. The observations below are based on a survey of roads used by the Inka Empire, and may not be valid for the roads used by American cultures at other times and in other places.

Roads and paths

Of some importance are certain distinctions that should be made about the difference between formally constructed "roads" and other routes simply defined as "paths." By "formally constructed" I mean a route marked by one or a number of construction techniques such as curbs, pavements, sidewalls, retention walls, and so forth. A "path" is defined by any surface indication that people traversed a given route, but that labor was not invested in building its course. Paths are often defined simply because the passage of many people, and in some cases animals, created a visible route through wear on the land's surface.

It is clear to me that no simple distinctions should be made about the level of societal organization associated with "roads" as against "paths." States and empires are not the only road builders, and simpler societies are not confined to using paths. Both roads and paths are present in the remains of prehistoric societies of many different levels of social complexity, at least among sedentary cultures. The Inka Empire used both, and in many cases the same route could vary from a formally

constructed road to a simple path within a few kilometers. There are several reasons for this, but it is sufficient here to note that the Inkas often did not bother to build a road where a path was sufficient. Several of the Inka road surveys found that a route would be "constructed" when it was necessary to alter the surface of the earth to create a feasible and effective passageway. When surface conditions permitted easy passage, no road was built, and a path was used.

It may be misleading to discern great cultural implications in the distinction between roads and paths. We know too little about how prehistoric roads were made to apply that simple typology with certain results. For example, is a route that is "marked" a road or a path? Some of the routes of the Inka Empire were marked with wood stakes, each one visible from the next. Apart from this, no construction techniques were used. Still other routes were indicated by piles of stones at frequent intervals. Other Andean routes appear to have been marked by petroglyphs (Núñez A. 1976), and it would seem that natural phenomena (a river, a mountain pass) would have been sufficient to "mark" a course transited by prehistoric peoples. Thus there are many types of routes that do not fall easily within the distinction between "formally constructed road" and "path." Since so few prehistoric American routes have yet been surveyed, I suggest that archaeologists continue to expand through fieldwork the range of physical manifestations exhibited by ancient roads. Only when more is known about the wide range of ways that routes are physically expressed, built, or marked will it be possible to define road typologies that might have useful cultural content.

Road width

Before beginning the Inka road survey, I hoped that it might be possible to study the amount of traffic, or flow, on certain Inka routes on the basis of their width. That is, as in our modern society, broader roads might be expected to carry greater amounts of traffic, and narrower roads would have a lesser flow. The survey found that the question of road width is both complex and, in some cases, still poorly understood. Using road widths to study a network's traffic could be undertaken with limited success, and only after weighing many other factors.

In the Inka network the same road could have many widths within a few kilometers. The width often seems to have been determined by a number of natural factors, such as topography, and culturally related factors, such as whether a road passed through valuable agricultural land or not. Landscapes such as steep slopes and rock surfaces clearly appear to have encouraged road builders to diminish the width of a road that was otherwise much wider. In other cases, a wide road passing through pasture, desert, or unused *puna* would be built with a narrower width when it entered cultivated areas. The width of Inka roads was doubtless affected by other factors such as: 1. the access to and distance from the labor necessary to build and maintain the roads; 2. whether a road had been built before the Inkas and reutilized by them; and 3. a wide range of symbolic and/or religious concerns. Interestingly, Inka roads were not usually built with increased width as they entered, or departed from, cities or other sites along their course.

Symbolic influences

Because many factors affect a road's appearance other than the flow of traffic on it, road construction might well inform us about other aspects of prehistoric culture. One of the most intriguing of these is the construction of roads with symbolic or ritual considerations in mind. The most spectacular roads in the Andes appear to have been built in part for ceremonial reasons. Some of the great "trapezia" and rectangles on the desert plains of Nazca on Peru's south coast were used for the passage of peoples (Morrison 1978). These "roads" are not yet clearly understood, but it is probable that they were invested with considerable symbolic importance in times well prior to the Inka Empire.

Sixteenth-century historical sources make it clear that Andean roads often had meanings and conceptual uses not found in our society. They were used to conceive cultural geography and define Andean spatial divisions, and many points on them were used for ritual activities. On the Peruvian north coast some single- and triple-lane roads which enter irrigated valleys have widths exceeding 25 m. These segments are never very long, but "announce" one's arrival in a valley after having traversed a segment of desert. One early historical source details how they were used in a special way by Inka royal progresses (Hyslop 1984:261–3). Once in a populated valley, the same road has a much diminished width. Thus it is possible that some of the roads of the Inka Empire were built with characteristics beyond those necessary to move people, goods, and animals about effectively. I have suggested that such is the case for certain segments of the great Inka road which linked the Inka capital, Cuzco, with its northern territory called Chincha Suyu. One of our surveys in the central Andes found lengthy segments of that road, far from population centers, built with a very broad width of 16 m, often paved. That width, greater than our two-lane high-

ways for vehicles, may well have been determined by engineers who decided to express the importance of that route by building it with a "grandeur" exceeding the practical needs of the traffic. Since Inka roads were a symbol of the state throughout the Andes, great roads could have symbolic significance in a "political" sense.

Much more can be said about the relationship between roads and the way symbolic concerns affected them in the Andes. However, such relations are one of the hardest things to determine with truly prehistoric cultures where there is no or little ethnohistory to guide one. Examples from the Andes should warn archaeologists that roads are not always strictly utilitarian devices in a twentieth-century sense. Attempts to interpret all aspects of prehistoric roads in purely materialist terms are bound to fail. We may never know why unique construction and engineering was lavished on certain parts of some prehistoric routes, since the reasons may be embedded in ritual concerns. In such cases, the archaeologist may be detecting only the tips of symbolic icebergs.

Recovering a prehistoric network

The point discussed here is that studies of ancient roads will be of limited value unless archaeologists develop ways of understanding how to locate visible segments, and to link them into a cohesive network that is more than a set of discontinuous lines on a map. Reports of road segments in an area are certainly important news, but they are only a stepping stone towards "anthropology" unless that data can be molded into information about how prehistoric cultures used them.

Many factors have worked to demolish prehistoric road systems to the point that only isolated segments of the roads still exist. As with many other types of archaeological remains, the older the road system, the less likely it is to be preserved to any extent. It goes without saying that ancient roads are often fragile structures, easily destroyed by changing patterns of land use, erosion, modern construction, and other causes. In some cases prehistoric roads are preserved only in the form of boundaries between fields, or lines of bushes or trees. Sometimes modern thoroughfares have been built on top of an ancient road.

As a student of Inka roads, I was more fortunate than some other archaeologists who have attempted to study prehistoric roads. Some of the roads of the Inka Empire can be located and followed by using information in sixteenth- and seventeenth-century historical sources. Also, some Inka roads remain in use today, and local people know where they are. Quechua toponyms help guide the survey archaeologist along the route. Scholars who study roads of earlier cultures do not have historical sources to guide them, nor is there usually a living memory of where very ancient roads are.

Regardless of whether one attempts to research recent or very ancient prehistoric roads, the fact remains that their preservation is fragmentary, and one can rarely follow a segment for any length without its disappearing. Thus a road survey in the field might well be undertaken only after a number of other activities such as a settlement pattern study, an aerial photographic analysis, and a map study of environmental and topographic conditions.

The settlement pattern study is important since one can be sure that roads or paths of some sort must have entered sites where people lived. Once a number of contemporary sites in a zone have been located, one can assume that they were connected. There may be exceptions to this assumption, but it is a good working premise. Often the site plans themselves give good clues concerning where roads entered and left the site, and one can work from the site out. In other cases, particularly if a site is poorly preserved, the roads leading to and from it might be located only some distance from the site where conditions for preservation are better, such as zones with no modern development or agriculture. As one attempts to determine the route between two nearby sites of the same period, careful attention must be paid to the best topographic maps available. A study of the contours and topography will hint at feasible routes, and allow one to rule out others because of environmental obstacles.

The great usefulness of aerial photography for road survey cannot be overrated. The road research in South America by Beck, Wallace, and Denevan in this volume would have been nearly impossible without the use of aerial photographs. Low-level aerial photographs allow one to see even faint paths, fieldlines, and other surface indications of roads, or features that may once have been roads. Perhaps the greatest advantage of aerial photographs is that they permit one to judge which visible segments may once have connected. This does not mean that segments necessarily form a straight, or nearly straight, line, but that, given the location of sites and topographic obstacles, the segments appear to link together. When studying aerial photographs it is especially useful to examine areas where preservation of the surface is good, and has not been disturbed. Likewise, one should pay special attention to areas where roads may have passed (slopes, passes, swampy terrain), and where it would have been useful to modify the

terrain to create an effective route. It is precisely the modifications that make the route visible. For example, the causeways observed in some parts of lowland South America are modifications of wet terrain to make a stable roadbed. Often such roads appear as discontinuous segments in aerial photographs because the route was not a formal construction on higher terrain between the causeway segments, or because the causeways are destroyed in some areas.

If one follows the above procedures, one may start to understand the road network in a zone. At that point surface survey becomes indispensable, or one is left with "segments" and hypotheses. Once in the field one will learn much about why segments appear, or disappear, in the aerial photographs. One can begin to make a registry of the different types of road construction techniques, and learn what environmental characteristics make for the good preservation or the destruction of roads.

It is important to remember that the same road may be built in many different ways along its route, given the nature of the terrain and other factors. It would not be unusual to find that a well-constructed road takes on the form of a simple path in flat, dry, isolated, unobstructed areas.

After surface survey has permitted one to see a variety of prehistoric routes, one can return to the aerial photographs and probably detect other road segments not previously noted. Some possible roads noted on the first photographic inspection will doubtless be discarded because surface survey has demonstrated that they are surface configurations that look like roads, but are not. There is an interplay between a settlement pattern site survey, an aerial photographic analysis, a topographic study, and a field road survey that will clarify aspects of each.

Dating a prehistoric road

If one cannot date a prehistoric road, and associate it with other prehistoric evidence of the same time, one knows almost nothing at all. Thus detailed studies demonstrating roads' associations with datable sites, canals, terraces, and other roads are particularly important. Beck's and Schreiber's articles (chapters 8 and 20) in this volume give examples of how roads may be dated through associations.

Investigators in South America have had little luck defining road construction and engineering techniques that are indicative of a specific time period. It is noteworthy that Beck (1979) found very few differences in road construction techniques used during 2,000 years in and near the Moche Valley of Peru. I, too, sense that forms of road building have changed little. I have noticed that many construction techniques used (on pedestrian roads) by Andean communities today do not vary from those used at the time of the Inka Empire.

Thus the justifiable question arises whether the physical appearance of prehistoric roads will be of any use for placing them in a time sequence. I am not particularly optimistic that roads will be seriated as effectively as pottery or architecture. Undoubtedly some aspects of their construction will be found to have chronological significance, but whether such traits will be commonly observed or easily detected is yet uncertain. One reason for this is that prehistoric roads are rarely totally abandoned, and such routes are frequently repaved, filled, stabilized, and widened (or narrowed) by annual maintenance efforts by neighboring communities. Thus many prehistoric routes are in a state of continual physical change determined by local use and maintenance, and other more "natural" factors such as erosion.

Dating prehistoric roads is complicated because many routes have continued in use for a very long time. It is noteworthy that some routes in the Andes have continued in use through many centuries although cultures and settlement patterns have changed. The continued usage of very ancient routes has a number of explanations. First, such routes are often strongly influenced by environment, and they continue in use simply because there is no other feasible passage between traditionally populated areas. Also, it must often have been easier to use a pre-existing route rather than build a new one. Nevertheless, it is also true that some prehistoric routes have been abandoned. To me, the question why a road was abandoned is as significant as why it may have continued in use. Such studies will not be easy to make unless we improve our capacity to determine when specific routes were used.

It is clear that some prehistoric roads have been developing, or changing, for hundreds of years or even millennia. I fear that we may tend to date these roads by some of their more obvious surface associations, and ignore or neglect the more limited evidence that argues for a greater antiquity. The remodeling and continued maintenance of any road may well destroy evidence of use by earlier and simpler societies. One might question whether the excavation of road segments will help to date them. There has been almost no excavation of roads in South America so it remains to be determined whether digging will be an effective technique for making chronological distinctions (see Keatinge 1975:217–19).

For the present, and in most areas, it appears that the best single technique for determining the age of a road segment is by surface survey which associates it with datable sites. A sequence of datable sites on a road gives a clearer indication of age than just one or two sites. The surveyor of a route may also be fortunate in finding pottery fragments, occasionally in considerable quantity, on a road's surface. Beck demonstrates how crosscutting relationships may be used to date roads. She notes, and I agree, that such an approach is useful only where a great deal of archaeological research in an area has preceded a road study.

Reporting standards

After reviewing much printed information about prehistoric roads in the Andes, I am convinced that archaeologists must adopt more rigorous methods for recording information about and reporting roads. Often the most fundamental types of information are lacking in publications. For example, some articles discussing roads lack a map, and expect a reader to understand a very localized geography. Most publications are not at all clear about the fundamental point of just what the author saw in the field, or whether data on a road came mainly from aerial photographs, or from informants. In the future authors must define explicitly what they themselves saw, under what conditions, and at what distance. The data derived from informants and aerial photographs is often very different, and should be separated clearly from field-survey information. There should be a greater use of photographs which depict the roads not only in "excellent" condition, but in their "average" state. Site plans and ceramic collections should be published to show the nature of the association with the road. Until the data on prehistoric roads are reported in a rigorous, thorough, and systematic way, the greater task of understanding their contribution to prehistory cannot begin.

References

Beck, Colleen M.
  1979 Ancient Roads on the North Coast of Peru. Ph.D. dissertation, University of California, Berkeley
Hyslop, John
  1984 *The Inka Road System*. Academic Press, Orlando
Keatinge, Richard W.
  1975 Urban Settlement Systems and Rural Sustaining Communities: An Example from Chan Chan's Hinterland. *Journal of Field Archaeology* 2:215–27
Morrison, Tony
  1978 *Pathways to the Gods*. Harper and Row, New York

Núñez A., Lautaro
  1976 Geoglifos y tráfico de caravanas en el desierto chileno. *Anales de la Universidad del Norte* 10:147–201
Regal, Alberto
  1936 *Los Caminos del Inca*. Sanmarti, Lima

Strube Erdmann, Leon
  1963 *Vialidad imperial de los Incas*. Serie Histórica 33, Instituto de Estudios Americanistas, Facultad de Filosofía y Humanidades, Universidad Nacional de Córdoba, Argentina

5 Photointerpretation of Chacoan roads

MARGARET SENTER
OBENAUF

Introduction

Photointerpretation of aerial photography is indispensable in the search for Chacoan roads. Although some of these roads were known long before aerial photographs became a tool of the archaeologist, it was only when the roads were seen from an aerial perspective that the network became apparent.

The roads are not easily seen on the ground. A few segments stand out distinctly at dawn or dusk and a few appear as a line of changed vegetation, but most are invisible from the ground. The situation is quite different from a vantage point above the roads. On aerial photographs the roads appear as straight, dark lines, while modern vehicular roads tend to have a curvilinear or erratic pattern which comes from avoiding topographic and vegetational obstacles. Most of the road segments were mapped with the aid of a stereoscope since stereoscopic viewing exaggerates the slight depressions of the roadbeds, making them easier to map.

Imagery

Gwinn Vivian and Robert Buettner's 1970 discovery that features previously thought to be related to water control were in fact part of a prehistoric roadway network laid the foundation for all future work on the roadway system. Several of the major road systems in the vicinity of Chaco Canyon were mapped through a combination of excavation and photointerpretation during this pilot project. The photography available for this project was primarily Soil Conservation Service (S.C.S.) aerials flown in the 1930s at scales of about 1:30,000 covering the Chaco Canyon area.

The National Park Service took up the project in 1971. Under the direction of Thomas Lyons, a number of

University of New Mexico graduate students experimented with various types of aerial photographs and methods of viewing them. The Park Service purchased S.C.S. aerials covering not only the immediate Chaco Canyon vicinity, but also the intervening distances between Chaco Canyon and the projected destinations of Vivian and Buettner's road systems. In addition, they purchased U.S. Geological Survey (U.S.G.S.) photography for an even larger area surrounding Chaco Canyon. They also contracted to have the entire Chaco Canyon National Monument flown at scales of 1:30,000 and 1:6,000 in black-and-white and color. Some hand-held color infrared slides were taken by members of the project.

Using a range of equipment to view the different sets of photographs, the Park Service found that the U.S.G.S. imagery, flown in the 1950s and 1960s at scales of about 1:30,000, was useful for mapping the roads, while the 1930s S.C.S. imagery at similar scales provided a valuable time depth. Taken before grazing was prohibited in the area, and before much of the other development which obscures prehistoric roadways took place in the Monument, it presents a very different landscape on which some of the roads are much more prominent than on more recent imagery, even though image quality is poor.

The U.S.G.S. imagery was originally compiled for use in mapping the area photogrammetrically on U.S.G.S. topographic maps. Some of it is suited to photointerpretation of prehistoric roads, while some of it has serious flaws. Most of it was flown between the hours of 10:00 am and 2:00 pm to avoid shadows which would obscure the topographic features to be mapped. Unfortunately, visibility of the Chacoan roads is often enhanced by the shadows cast by their slight depressions and some known roads are almost invisible on the U.S.G.S. imagery. Much of this imagery was photographed in late fall or winter, again for enhanced mapping visibility; on such imagery roadways may not be visible since vegetative differences account for visibility of at least some of the roadways.

Some possible roads were visible on the large-scale photography flown on contract for the Park Service; however, the scale turned out to be *too* large – the roads tend to dissolve into the landscape. This was almost as much of a problem on the color sets as on the black-and-white and the Park Service concluded that the additional expense of the color photography was not justified by the information returned. The Park Service project experimented with several kinds of video enhancement equipment including an edge enhancer and a color density

slicer and concluded that the additional roads visible did not justify the expense of the equipment or the large amounts of time spent using it.

The Bureau of Land Management (B.L.M.) began a Chaco Roads Project in 1981 to determine how to treat the roads when leasing coal in the San Juan Basin (Kincaid 1983; Nials, Stein, and Roney 1987). This project was based in part on a master's thesis (Obenauf 1980) which had utilized the N.P.S. archive to examine the areas between Chaco Canyon and the known Chacoan outliers, and between the outliers for roads. In addition, the B.L.M. purchased S.C.S. coverage of the entire San Juan Basin. This project also acquired B.L.M. imagery of the San Juan Basin, in both black-and-white and true color, taken at 1:31,680 in the fall of 1973. While image quality was high, the B.L.M. photography had many of the same drawbacks as the U.S.G.S. imagery – it was taken at midday to avoid shadows, and in the fall to avoid obscuring vegetation. In addition, the black-and-white prints had been dodged to reduce contrast across the prints, reducing the visibility of a number of known roads.

Marietta Wetherill, widow of Richard Wetherill who did early archaeological work at both Mesa Verde and Chaco Canyon, told Gordon Vivian in 1948 that "north of Alto in certain lights you can still see what appears to be a wide roadway running down to the Escavada" (Lyons and Hitchcock 1977:130). Several members of the N.P.S. Chaco Project noticed that this is still true, that at sunrise and sunset the Great North Road is much more visible than at midday. As an experiment, the B.L.M. Chaco Roads Project contracted to have low-sun-angle photography flown of the entire Great North Road and of the Pueblo Alto area (Figs. 5.1 and 5.2). Because the subtle depressions of the road segments threw shadows in the early morning sun, the road was consistently more visible than on other imagery, and many previously unknown segments, including several previously unknown parallel segments, were discovered on this photography.

Later, the B.L.M. flew further low-sun-angle photography in the southern periphery of the San Juan Basin following the routes of several known or suspected roads. This imagery strengthened the belief that photography acquired specifically for a project, under the lighting and seasonal conditions most conducive to maximum visibility of the feature sought, is likely to repay its cost in additional information.

The B.L.M. came to several conclusions about low-sun-angle imagery for photointerpretation of Chacoan roads (Obenauf 1983). First, the time available after

Fig. 5.1. *Low-sun-angle photograph showing the east wall at Pueblo Alto. Compare with Fig. 5.2. The photographs were flown by the same contractor, from the same plane, two days apart. A–gravel pit; B–prehistoric wall trending approximately E–W; C–prehistoric road; D–prehistoric wall trending approximately N–S; E–prehistoric road; F–Chaco Culture National Historical Park boundary fence; G–historic road (photo courtesy of B.L.M.).*

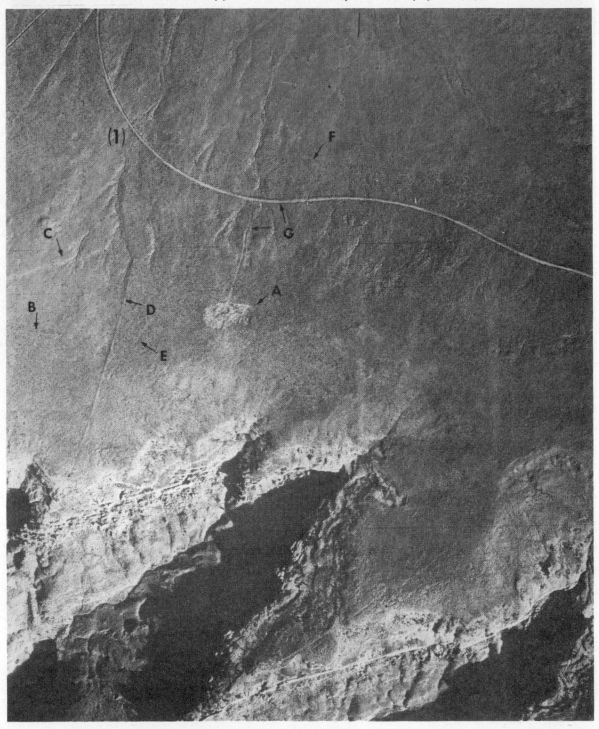

Fig. 5.2. Conventional aerial photograph. Compare with low-sun-angle aerial photo, Fig. 5.1, showing the same area (photo courtesy of B.L.M.).

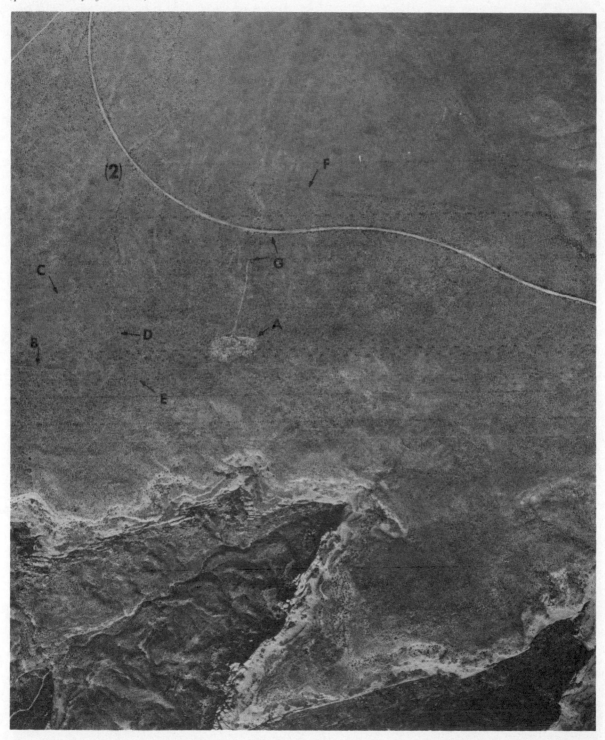

sunrise for lengthened shadows is about one hour, early morning being superior to late afternoon because of the lack of dust and haze. Second, roads are likely to be enhanced in the spring growing season, about two weeks after the first heavy rain of warmer weather. Next, the roads are most visible on low-sun-angle imagery at the same scales as on conventional imagery, about 1:20,000 to 1:30,000. Finally, the roads are difficult to see in broad daylight, even for an experienced photointerpreter. A pilot flying in the very early morning is unlikely to be able to find the roads. Oversized ground-control panels placed adjacent to the suspected location of the road, out of shadows, can greatly assist the pilot. Such panels should be placed periodically along the route, as well as at changes in angle or direction. The panels will later help to orientate the photointerpreter.

The later phase of the B.L.M. project (Nials, Stein, and Roney 1987) found aerial reconnaissance in fixed-wing aircraft to be one of the most useful means for locating previously unrecognized segments, as well as for evaluating photointerpreted segments. Helicopters were not used because of their higher cost. These flights were also made under low-sun-angle conditions. The oblique angle and moving perspective often permitted easier recognition of linear features. However, accurate mapping from oblique 35 mm slides is difficult and mapping in conjunction with conventional vertical imagery may be necessary.

The B.L.M. project concluded (Kincaid 1983; Nials, Stein, and Roney 1987:26) that ground observations of photointerpreted segments and those located during aerial reconnaissance is essential for verification. Archaeological indications such as road-associated sites, artifacts, and evidence of construction were considered to be bases for verification of Chacoan roads. Only roads formalized in this way are considered to be verifiable at this time.

Equipment

All of the prjects listed here (with the exception of Vivian's pilot project) used a mirror stereoscope mounted on a scanning track for photointerpretation of the prehistoric roads (Fig. 5.3). Three-power magnification of imagery at scales of around 1:20,000 to 1:30,000, with six-power magnification for closer inspection, has been most productive. Various types of portable stereoscopes have been used for field examination of photos; however, none has proved suitable for extended photointerpretation or roads. As is the case with most other types of photointerpretation, the expenditure for a mirror stereoscope, magnifying lenses, and scanning

track is more than justified by the ease of photointerpretation and information returned.

In the case of Chacoan roads, stereoscopic photointerpretation is not only more convenient, it is essential. Most of the roads exhibit a slight depression which is exaggerated two to three times by the stereoscope, making the roads much more visible. In addition, the three-dimensional image created by the stereoscope often makes it possible to discern a historical or geological explanation for a linearity.

For most of the projects discussed here, the photointerpreter marked linearities suspected to be Chacoan roads directly on the photographs in red with a pencil or china-marking crayon, one dot at each end of the linearity with a line along the side (Fig. 5.4). Various methods have been used to transfer the suspected roads to topographic maps. The early projects used the "eyeball" method to make the transfer. The resulting maps were used in conjunction with the original photos in the field and were adequate for ground-truthing the roads, even though they were sometimes inaccurate by as much as an eighth to a quarter of a mile.

As location of the roads in relation to other features such as sites or oil-well pads became more important, more accurate methods of plotting the roads were devised. The easiest of these utilizes an overhead projection device (in this case, a Map-O-Graph manufactured by the Art-O-Graph Co.) to enlarge the entire photo to the scale of the topographic map. Because of the small variations in scale inherent in aerial photography (Lyons and Avery 1977:16) the scale of a smaller area around each road segment was adjusted by lining up such landmarks as roads, mesa edges, and stock tanks.

Surprisingly, transfer using a Bausch and Lomb stereo-zoom transferscope proved to be less accurate

Fig. 5.3. Mirror stereoscope with magnifying lenses mounted on a scanning track.

Fig. 5.4. 1930s S.C.S. aerial photograph of the Peñasco Blanco to Ah-Shi-Sle-Pah Road, showing grease pencil markings made by the photointerpreter.

than transfer by overhead projector. With the overhead projector, the entire photo is projected onto the map, while the transferscope projects only a small portion of the photo at one time. In many parts of the San Juan Basin there are so few landmarks that accurate scale adjustments within such a small area are impossible.

Photogrammetric plotting using a stereoscopic plotter is the most accurate method of transferring the roads from the photos to maps. Accurate to within a few feet, photogrammetric mapping is often the least expensive way to map an area or large site. However, it is prohibitively expensive for the sole purpose of transferring roads.

Photointerpretation

There are thousands of short linear features visible on aerial photography of the San Juan Basin, most of which are not prehistoric roads. In order to narrow the search for Chacoan roadways, the first step in the photointerpretation process is to identify an area of interest using the mapped location of a previously known road as a starting point, or by defining by other criteria an area to be searched for roads. In general, roads tend to connect major sites. By beginning photointerpretation near outliers and following lineations outward, the problem is reduced to a more manageable size. This strategy is especially effective since Chacoan roads tend to be most distinct in the vicinities of outliers. For the photointerpretation upon which the B.L.M. project was based (Obenauf 1980; Kincaid 1983; Nials, Stein, and Roney 1987), the alignments of lineations within the vicinities of sites were followed to see if additional segments could be found.

In some cases, the entire distance between outliers was scanned for roads. Only rarely was a highly probable road segment located by this method if none was visible near the outliers themselves. However, field reconnaissance sometimes located evidence of a prehistoric road, even in areas where no roads were visible on the photos. This tactic worked best in areas where the route of a road was predictable on the basis of topographic constraints. Here photointerpretation was indispensable in defining possible routes for field check. Additionally, it may be possible to identify the route of a road through identification of road-related types of sites on the ground. Ideally, information from photointerpretation and field check can reinforce each other.

Besides roads connecting Chacoan sites, there are often short roads visible in the immediate vicinities of outliers and Chaco Canyon sites. Some of these roads have obvious destinations such as water sources; others

seem to go nowhere. If the vicinity of a site is defined as the area of interest for photointerpretation, the area is searched stereoscopically with an intensity that is impossible for the entire distance between outliers. All linearities are marked. However, field checking the results of this photointerpretation is usually unrewarding since most of the linearities are not visible on the ground, and often no destination is discernible for those that appear to be roads.

The problems of photointerpretation around outliers are multiplied in the Chaco Canyon area. There were literally hundreds of linear features in Chaco Culture National Historic Park mapped by the Park Service project. The field phase of this project was unable to locate most of the mapped linearities on the ground, although they sometimes found associated features which tended to indicate that the alignment was a road. There is a paradox in photointerpretation of site areas – of the many linear features visible, some are clearly prehistoric roads; of the rest, some are probably prehistoric features, others are not. Most of them cannot even be located during field check, much less verified as prehistoric roads, and we are left with a photo marked with linear features with no basis to assign meaning to them. Rather than an exact count of how many roads there are around an outlier, or how many of the linearities at Chaco Canyon are actually roads, it is probably more important to know that there are numerous short roads near Chacoan sites.

The factors affecting visibility of archaeological sites on aerial photographs are almost endless and the potential combinations of these factors are staggering. A previously unknown Roman villa in Great Britain, not visible for over thirty years during weekly flights, was suddenly visible for a short time following a drought, then disappeared again. Similarly, one Chacoan road, the Peñasco Blanco to Ah-Shi-Sle-Pah Canyon road, is highly visible for its entire distance. Across Ah-Shi-Sle-Pah Canyon there is no evidence of any of the available sets of imagery for its continuation. However, recently, as in the British case, a road was clearly visible during an overflight of the area. No matter how many sets of photos are examined for Chacoan roads, something new is always visible on the next set examined. Since most of the conventional imagery available (S.C.S., U.S.G.S., B.L.M.) was taken at times of year and day less than ideal for photointerpretation of Chacoan roads, the likelihood is high that more roads remain to be discovered, especially if more suitable imagery (such as low-sun-angle photography) can be obtained.

References

Kincaid, Chris (ed.)
1983 *Chaco Roads Project, Phase I: A Reappraisal of Prehistoric Roads in the San Juan Basin.* Bureau of Land Management, United States Department of the Interior, Santa Fe and Albuquerque

Lyons, Thomas R. and Thomas Eugene Avery
1977 *Remote Sensing: A Handbook for Archeologists and Cultural Resource Managers.* Cultural Resource Management Division, National Park Service, United States Department of the Interior, Washington, DC

Lyons, Thomas R. and Robert K. Hitchcock
1977 Remote Sensing Interpretation of an Anasazi Land Route System. In *Aerial Remote Sensing Techniques in Archeology*, edited by Thomas R. Lyons and Robert K. Hitchcock, pp. 111–34. Reports of the Chaco Center 2. National Park Service, Albuquerque

Nials, Fred, John Stein, and John Roney
1987 *Chacoan Roads in the Southern Periphery: Results of Phase II of the BLM Chaco Roads Project.* Bureau of Land Management, United States Department of the Interior, Santa Fe and Albuquerque

Obenauf, Margaret Senter
1980 The Chacoan Roadway System. M.A. thesis, University of New Mexico
1983 Evaluation of Aerial Photography. In Kincaid 1983: 4-1–4-21

6 Analysis of prehistoric roadways in Chaco Canyon using remotely sensed digital data

THOMAS L. SEVER
and DAVID W. WAGNER

Remote sensing has broad multidisciplinary applications to geology, geomorphology, biology, pedology, hydrology and climatology, as well as to anthropology ... The remote sensing perspective provides not only the synoptic overview otherwise unobtainable, but more importantly, a synergistic grasp of obscured physical and cultural phenomena.

(Lyons and Avery 1977:53)

Introduction

Prehistoric roadway systems have been located throughout the Americas; in the highlands of Peru, in the Yucatan peninsula of Mexico, at Casas Grandes in northern Chihuahua, and at Chaco Canyon in northwestern New Mexico.

Although they have a widespread distribution, the purposes for the American roadways remain shrouded in mystery, those at Chaco Canyon being no exception. Why were the Chaco roads designed with exacting linearity, which surmounted any topographic obstruction, built to a width of 20 feet or more, and constructed by people who did not even employ beasts of burden in their lives?

What is clear about the Chacoan roadway system is that the roads link Chaco Canyon with a number of similar cultural manifestations called "outliers," which surround the canyon and extend outward as far as 50–60 miles, and possibly much farther.

Delimiting the extent of this roadway system is one approach to understanding a complex, regionally based, prehistoric cultural phenomenon unprecedented in North America. Although much work in mapping the roadway system has been accomplished, much remains to be done.

Fig. 6.1. Chaco Canyon National Monument.

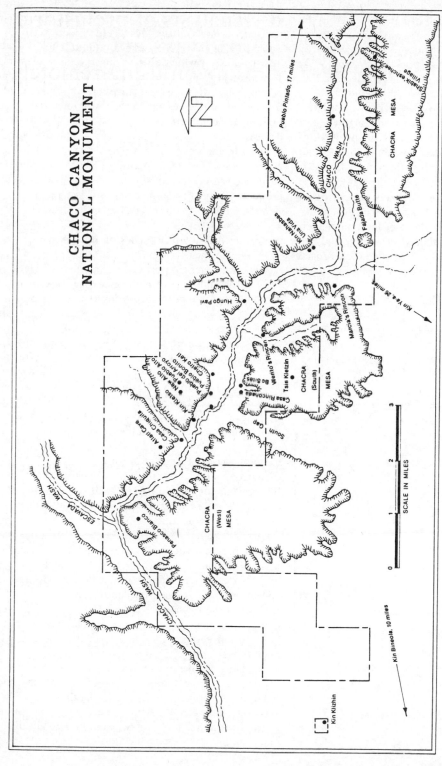

Physical aspects of Chaco Canyon

Chaco Canyon is an erosional formation located in the San Juan Basin in northwestern New Mexico (Figs. 6.1 and 6.2). The following description is drawn primarily from the work of Bryan (1954).

The canyon is bisected by the Chaco River, a 100-mile-long San Juan River tributary, of which only 15 to 20 miles is actually in the canyon. The river is an intermittent stream, and dry during most of the year; it begins at the altitude of 6,000 feet on the high plains north of Chacra Mesa. It flows northwest for almost 70 miles and turns due north where it flows into the San Juan.

The canyon lies in the southwestern portion of the great plateau area of the Four Corners, noted for its extensive flat surfaces with cliffs and canyon structures. The flat surfaces are resistant beds of horizontal sedimentary rocks as well as some lava outflows. The San Juan basin is the largest unit of the plateau and Chaco Canyon lies at the southern portion of the basin.

Fig. 6.2. Map of Chaco Canyon in the Four Corners region.

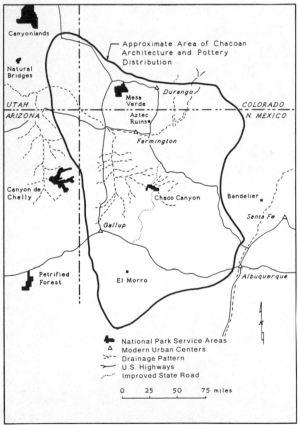

The characteristic rocks of Chaco are shale and sandstone, the canyon being cut into Cliff House Sandstone, the upper member of the Mesa Verde group.

Chaco Canyon receives a mean annual rainfall of 10 inches, much of which falls during the rainy season of July through August. Temperatures are those of a temperate region with mean average temperatures ranging from 47 to 60 degrees Fahrenheit, although daily fluctuations in temperatures may be as much as 40 to 50 degrees.

The canyon trends primarily east–west and is very asymmetrical. The main period of canyon cutting has been followed by cycles of alluviation and modern erosion is largely confined to alluvial deposits (see Fig. 6.3).

As Schalk and Lyons (1977:178) describe it,

> Chaco Canyon itself lies on an ecotone between the northeastern portion of the basin and the southwestern portion. Though vegetational distinctions between these two areas seem slight, the primary difference being the greater presence of juniper, pinyon, and big sagebrush in the northeast section, geological differences and resulting differences in soils are significant. The difference is basically one of deposits of terrestrial origin (sandstones to the northeast), and deposits of marine origin (the shales of the southwestern part of the basin). Chaco Canyon is an erosional feature which has eroded into the landscape at the contact zone between these two deposits.

Cultural aspects of Chaco Canyon

Chaco Canyon, during its cultural peak in the Classic Bonito Phase or Pueblo III (A.D. 1020–1220), stands as one of the most marvelous cultural achievements in prehistoric America north of the Valley of Mexico.

Chaco's human history goes back a long way. Although the canyon itself was not apparently occupied by Paleo-Indians, the surrounding plateau shows signs of Folsom hunters dating to 9000 B.C. Occupation appears to have been sparse until approximately 5500 B.C. when the Archaic or Desert Culture peoples were living in the area. These Archaic peoples were nomadic hunters and gatherers living on small game and wild plant foods.

The great change in southwestern culture occurred in the response to the domestication of maize which occurred in the American Southwest during the period 3400–1000 B.C. Between 1000 B.C. and A.D. 1, the culture called the Anasazi (a Navajo word meaning "the ancient ones") began to bloom in the San Juan Basin.

Fig. 6.3. Cross-section of Chaco Canyon (Hall 1977:1598): A, deposition of Fajada gravels; B, erosion and development of Fajada paleosol; C, erosion of paleosol; D, deposition of Gallo alluvium; E, erosion of valley fill; F, deposition of Chaco unit; G, erosion of post-Bonito channel system; H, deposition of post-Bonito alluvium; I, late nineteenth-century erosion of present arroyo and accumulation of Historic unit in arroyo channel; vertical scale in meters..

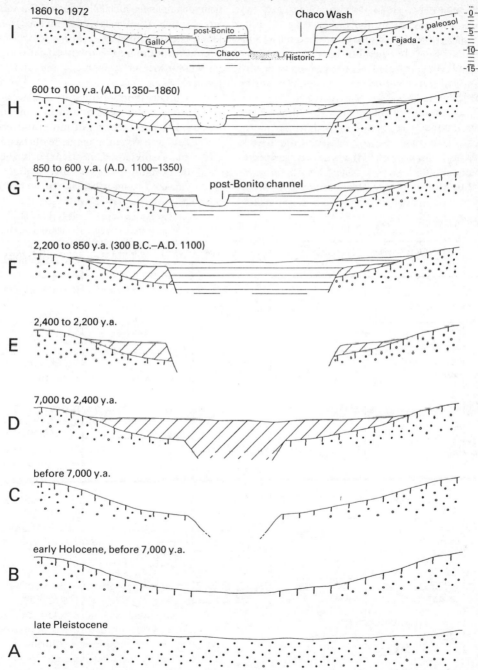

The Anasazi culture is marked by almost complete reliance upon corn, beans, and squash as an agricultural triad, and the beginnings of sedentary villages. Basketmaker III is the name given to the earliest Anasazi and marks the beginning phase of any chronological scheme proposed by archaeologists (see Fig. 6.4).

Chronologies vary between investigators and terminology can be rather confusing, but for this chapter, the terms Pueblo III or Classic Bonito will be used to refer to the apex of Chacoan culture (A.D. 1020–1220), during which time the roadways were constructed.

The distinguishing characteristics of the Classic Bonito are multi-storied buildings with pre-planned, symmetrical floor plans containing from 100 to 800 rooms. Additional characteristics are the kivas, or ceremonial chambers, the roadway system, and a construction technique known as core-veneer masonry.

Sharing a number of Classic characteristics such as the pre-planned multi-storied buildings, kivas, Classic ceramics, and the roadway association are a series of small villages located outside the boundaries of Chaco Canyon proper called outliers. The outliers are an important part of what Cordell (1984) refers to as a "system of regional integration," and are a key component in outlining the roadway network. As Obenauf (1980:789) writes,

> The discovery of the roadway network led to the discovery of more and more outliers; this in turn led to the discovery of more links in the roadway network. As the magnitude of the system of roads and outliers became clearer, it became obvious that events in Chaco Canyon could no longer be viewed as isolated from the rest of the San Juan

Fig. 6.4. Chaco Canyon chronology.

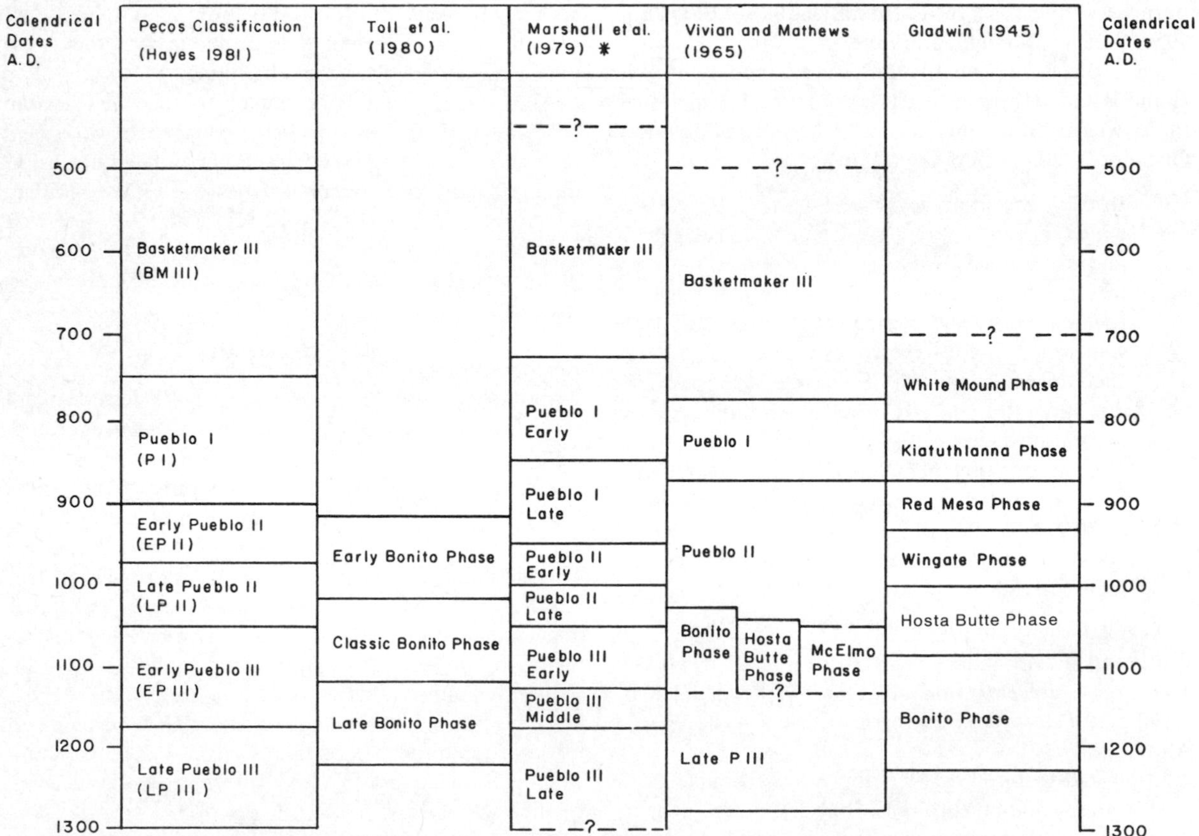

Calendrical Dates A.D.	Pecos Classification (Hayes 1981)	Toll et al. (1980)	Marshall et al. (1979) *	Vivian and Mathews (1965)	Gladwin (1945)	Calendrical Dates A.D.
			– – –?– – –			
500				– – – –?– – –		500
600	Basketmaker III (BM III)		Basketmaker III			600
				Basketmaker III		
700					– – – –?– – –	700
					White Mound Phase	
800	Pueblo I (P I)		Pueblo I Early	Pueblo I	Kiatuthlanna Phase	800
900	Early Pueblo II (EP II)		Pueblo I Late		Red Mesa Phase	900
		Early Bonito Phase	Pueblo II Early	Pueblo II	Wingate Phase	
1000	Late Pueblo II (LP II)		Pueblo II Late		Hosta Butte Phase	1000
1100	Early Pueblo III (EP III)	Classic Bonito Phase	Pueblo III Early	Bonito Phase / Hosta Butte Phase / McElmo Phase		1100
		Late Bonito Phase	Pueblo III Middle	– – –?– – –	Bonito Phase	
1200	Late Pueblo III (LP III)		Pueblo III Late	Late P III		1200
1300			– –?– –			1300

* Marshall et al. (1979) follow Vivian and Mathews in recognizing contemporary Bonito, Hosta Butte, and McElmo architectural phases, but with beginning and ending dates for the Bonito and Hosta Butte phases at ca. 950-1200.

Basin, that any explanation of culture change in Chaco Canyon itself must also account for the existence of the outlier system.

People originally felt that the outlying villages were merely the precursors of the towns. Kluckhohn was the first to believe them contemporaneous (Kluckhohn and Reiter 1939).

The outliers have been found as far as 50 miles away from the canyon (Fig. 6.5) and are often located in areas of potentially good agriculture. It is suspected that the outliers were support communities for the canyon proper but the true relationship between the canyon and the outliers is far from understood.

The roadway system

Although it is believed that the roadways may have functioned as trade routes, communication channels, travel routes, race courses, or well-engineered expressions of Anasazi cosmology, no one really knows the purpose of the roadway system (Wetherill 1948; Judd 1954; Sofaer, Marshall, and Sinclair 1986).

The roads were probably built during the Late Pueblo II and Pueblo III periods (Classic Bonito) at which time there was a large increase in Chacoan population. Obenauf (1980:4) offers the following description.

> Briefly, the roadways are engineered features which may be characterized by cleared roadbeds and borders of banked earth or, especially near major sites, masonry walls. Features such as rock-cut stairways, ramps, or "causeways" were sometimes constructed where roadways encountered some sort of obstacle. The roadways are quite straight and often go through or over natural obstacles rather than veer to avoid them. They may be up to 9 meters wide and seem to have been laid out on a preconceived route. When the roads change direction, they do so abruptly with a "dog-leg" turn rather than with a slow turn like modern roads in the area.

As mentioned, the primary roads are up to 20 feet in width and the secondary roads are up to 12 feet wide. The largest concentration of roads can be found converging at a stone wall on the north side of the Pueblo Alto.

Lister and Lister (1981) feel there is a probable east–west route running through Chaco Canyon proper, linking the main communities from Pueblo Pintado on the east to Peñasco Blanco on the west.

Roads also run from the canyon southward to such southern towns as Kin Bineola, Kin Klizhin, Tsin Kletzin and Kin Ya'a.

Currently, there are five different roadway systems known (Roney 1988, personal communication):

1) Great North Road – Pueblo Alto to Salmon Ruins (50 miles);
2) South Road – Chaco to Kin Ya'a and beyond (40 miles);
3) Ah-Shi-Sle-Pah Road – Peñasco Blanco to Ah-Shi-Sle-Pah Canyon and beyond (6 miles);
4) East Road – Chaco to Pueblo Pintado (10 miles);
5) Coyote Canyon Road – 15 miles.

Obenauf claims there are 100 miles of possible roads mapped within the monument and over 300 miles of possible roads mapped outside of the monument.

Concerning the relationship between the outliers and the roads, Obenauf (1980:iv) states, "Since possible roadways were discovered at almost all outliers which were in an environment where preservation of a road could reasonably be expected, it is probable that they were once present at most, if not all, outliers."

Although efforts have been made to trace the Chacoan roadway system from the canyon outward to outliers (Lyons and Ebert 1978) and from the outliers inward to the main canyon (Obenauf 1980), we are just beginning to consolidate these approaches with the detection methods employed by Sever (1983) to compile a comprehensive map of the Chacoan sphere of influence as indicated by the roadway system.

Remote sensing

Remote sensing is the science and art of detecting and recording objects or phenomena from a distance through devices that are sensitive to different bandwidths of the electromagnetic spectrum. In a sense, the eyes are remote sensors in as much as they allow man to gather information about his environment without physical contact. The technology of past centuries has produced instruments such as glasses, telescopes and camera lenses that have extended the range of human vision. These instruments allow man to gather information and subsequently better evaluate his surrounding world. Recent advances in remote-sensing technology now promise to make a quantum leap in man's technological capabilities, by allowing him to "see" information that his eyes, by themselves, cannot see.

All materials at temperatures above what is known as absolute zero (-273 C or 0 K) produce electromagnetic radiation in the form of waves. The electromagnetic

Fig. 6.5. Major Chacoan roads.

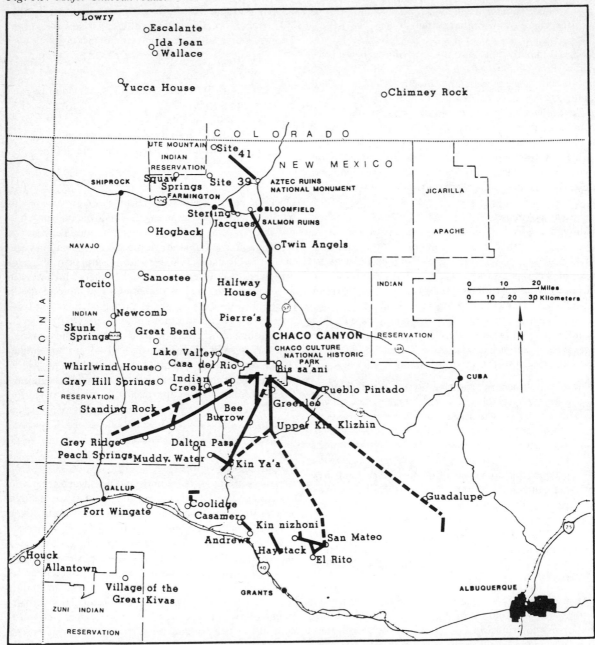

spectrum is a continuum of electric and magnetic wavelengths that extend from the short cosmic rays of high frequency at one end of the spectrum to long radio waves of low frequency at the other end. The limits of the electromagnetic spectrum are not known and may lie at infinity. Wavelength dimensions are used to bound regions within the spectrum although a discrete separation does not occur since the wavelengths themselves merge imperceptibly into each other. These regions are referred to as the ultraviolet, visible, near infrared, thermal infrared, microwave, etc. portions of the spectrum.

The detection, recording, and analysis of electromagnetic energy constitute the foundations of remote sensing. There is no single instrument which can detect emissions within the entire electromagnetic spectrum. The "visible" portion of the spectrum is extremely small since the human eye extends only from about 0.4 micrometers to approximately 0.77 micrometers (Fig. 6.6). In fact, if the known span of the electromagnetic spectrum was conceived of as analogous to the circumference of the earth, the human eye and conventional film would be able to see only that portion of it that is equal to the diameter of a pencil. In short, man is relatively blind to the universe around him.

Before the launch of the Landsat satellite in 1972, aerial photographs were the most familiar form of remote sensor data employed in most environmental studies. While cameras equipped with black-and-white or color film provide the greatest capability in terms of versatility or high resolution of detail, they nevertheless possess certain liabilities. For instance, they are limited to seeing only what the human eye can see. In addition they must operate in daylight, during clear weather, on days with minimal atmospheric haze, in order to produce an optimum product. Since cameras are not "real time" systems a certain time factor is involved for laboratory processing before the resultant images are available for analysis. This time gap can range from several hours to several weeks, as is the case for photographs made by cameras in space vehicles.

Color infrared (C.I.R.) film has improved man's visible range, by detecting longer wavelengths somewhat beyond the red end of the light spectrum. C.I.R. film was initially employed during World War II to differentiate objects that had been artificially camouflaged. While C.I.R. film can be successfully employed in studies dealing with vegetational differences, it is also subject to the limitations indigenous to conventional camera systems. Perhaps the major disadvantage for black-and-white as well as C.I.R. photography is the limited information that can be obtained when compared to modern remote-sensing detectors. While photographic systems are the most common types of sensor systems used in archaeological remote-sensing investigations to date, they cannot obtain information about the thermal characteristics (temperature and emissivity) of vegetation, soil, and water on the earth's surface. Non-photographic remote sensors, often referred to as scanner systems, are capable, however, of simultaneously collecting data in the visible, infrared, and thermal portions of the electromagnetic spectrum.

In a typical multispectral, optical-mechanical scanner system, the energy reflected and emitted from a small area of the earth's surface is "seen" by a scanning mirror and reflected through an optical system. This incoming reflected energy is spectrally dispersed through various detectors that are sensitive to various portions of the spectrum. The size of the resolution element, i.e., the instantaneous field of view (I.F.O.V.) of the scanner, is a result of scanner configuration and altitude of the aircraft or satellite platform. Resolution elements can vary dramatically. For instance, the Advanced Very High Resolution Radiometer (A.V.H.R.R.) satellite has a 1 km resolution while the M.O.M.S. airborne sensor is designed to produce a 1 foot resolution.

Fig. 6.6. Diagram of the electromagnetic spectrum.

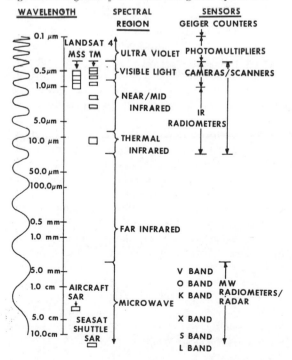

The energy received by the detector varies in signal strength as the resolution elements or pixels (picture elements) of the landscape vary in character. Each pixel is assigned a digital value between 0 and 255 by each detector. Thus, if a scanner system has twelve detectors, a resolution element on the ground will be "seen" twelve different ways. The output signals from the detectors are recorded on magnetic tape and can be played back later or displayed on an image display device as tones of dark or light depending on signal strength. The composite of all elements and scanlines for each detector renders an image similar to a photo. As a result, images can be produced that would normally be beyond the range of human visibility.

The human eye can discriminate only about twenty or thirty shades of gray under normal viewing situations. Under the same conditions it can discriminate a much larger number of color hues. Remote-sensing instruments can gather up to 256 shades of gray in numeric format for each channel of its detection array. In a twelve band scanner system, for instance, up to 3,060 pieces of gray-scale information are available. The same numerical data from a scanner system can be combined to produce millions of color hues of which the human eye can only separate a small proportion. In short, there is more information available than the investigator can "see"; what is more, by electronic manipulation of the data, the investigators extract information in a form that can be visualized.

Numerical data are essential for accurate quantitative analysis. Electronic manipulation of the data can increase or decrease emphasis, extract data selectively from the total, determine signature parameters and examine data characteristics normally not visible on the imagery. The combination of man and computer in an interactive system can lead to the solution of research problems that would otherwise be unattainable.

Technical background of the current study

In 1982 N.A.S.A. allocated discretionary funding to determine the potential utility of its advanced remote-sensing instrumentation for archaeological analysis. The application of N.A.S.A. technology had previously been well established in such disciplines as forestry, geography, geology, and agriculture. Previous attempts in archaeology had been limited to large-scale analysis because of the 80 m resolution of N.A.S.A.'s satellites. In addition the broad-based bandwidths of the sensors precluded any success in the detection of prehistoric features.

Chaco Canyon was selected as the first study area as a result of the efforts of the Chaco Canyon Remote Sensing Center (Lyons and Avery 1977). The vision of this center, in recognizing the potential of remote sensing, cannot be overlooked. The results of this center served as a baseline with which to compare the results of the N.A.S.A. project. Narrower bandwidths, greater resolution, and advances in computer statistical analyses which were developed through several years of N.A.S.A.'s fundamental research promised to improve upon the results of previous archaeological investigations.

If digital remote-sensing analysis was successful in Chaco Canyon, there would be a high success probability in transferring the techniques to other areas of the Southwest for archaeological survey. Also, the same techniques could possibly be used in other semi-arid lands such as North Africa and the Middle East. Continued research might eventually produce a comprehensive record and understanding of the nature of the prehistoric roadways and their relationship to the socioeconomic base of past culture. Finally, valuable remote-sensing information relative to archaeological phenomena could eventually be analyzed for potential global application to other arid environmental settings where much of the archaeological record is contained.

The investigation for Chaco Canyon was based on the need to examine the relationship between surface and subsurface archaeological features and bandwidth characteristics of remote-sensing instruments. Consequently the visible, near infrared, far infrared and broad thermal bands of the Thematic Mapper Simulator (T.M.S.) were compared to the narrow, precise thermal bandwidths of the Thermal Infrared Multispectral Scanner (T.I.M.S.).

Advantages of the T.M.S. and T.I.M.S. sensors are their multispectral characteristics and their use on an aircraft at various altitudes to acquire data with a spatial resolution commensurate with the size of archaeological features. These sensors were designed to permit acquisition of the 10 m and 5 m resolution necessary for the detection of archaeological sites, roadways, and associated features.

The digital data gathered by the T.M.S. and T.I.M.S. can be compared to that used to produce television transmissions, in that it breaks the picture into discrete light segments and then reassembles them onto a receiver screen. Since the data are composed of numerical values, they can be statistically manipulated to increase or decrease emphasis, extract data selectively from the total, determine spectral signature parameters of ground phenomena and examine data characteristics which are not normally visible.

Data analysis

Data were gathered from N.A.S.A.'s Learjet Model 23 aircraft. The T.M.S. data were collected in April 1982 while the T.I.M.S. data were gathered in August 1982 (Plates 1 and 2). Image enhancement techniques and statistical classifiers were applied to both sets of data for comparative analysis (Sever 1983).

T.I.M.S. data were found to be superior to T.M.S. data for the detection of archaeological features. T.I.M.S. data successfully located surface and subsurface phenomena such as prehistoric walls, buildings, agricultural fields and roadways. The research focused upon the detection of the Chacoan roadway system. Statistical filtering techniques were applied to the T.I.M.S. data to accentuate these lineaments since it was determined that a unique spectral signature does not exist for the roads, owing to the fact that they are composed of many soil variations and vegetations.

Several approaches to lineament enhancement, extraction or delineation are possible with digital processing (Moore 1983). Since conventional lineament interpretation analysis is subjective, the results depend upon the investigator and the purpose of the interpretation. One study (Podwysocki *et al.* 1975) showed that only 0.4 percent from a total of 785 lineaments were seen by four different expert investigators with significant differences in lengths, locations and densities.

Previously, a Chaco Canyon lineament map was produced using aerial photography (Lyons and Hitchcock 1977). This map was used as an aid for ground-truth investigations. Although most of the lineaments were found not to be roadways, the map nevertheless demonstrated the ability of remote sensing to reduce the area for investigative analysis significantly.

To improve the lineament enhancement technique, several high-pass and low-pass statistical spatial filters were developed to accentuate all lineaments in digital data (Sever 1983). Significantly, these techniques revealed linear and curvilinear patterns which were invisible in the raw T.I.M.S. imagery. As a result the Chacoan roads were detected in the T.I.M.S. imagery even though they were not visible in the simultaneously acquired color-infrared photography. The results of the investigation correlated with those of the Bureau of Land Management (Kincaid 1983).

Remote-sensing data from the thermal infrared region of the electromagnetic spectrum are particularly productive in arid regions. This is due in part to the contrast with humid regions, where vegetation covers most of the surface. In the thermal region, vegetation is spectrally colorless. This is because it is efficiently linked to the atmosphere and therefore maintains a nearly constant temperature. Prehistoric phenomena in humid regions may be detectable for only a few minutes in every 24-hour period. Arid regions offer a much more complex thermal system for study. While data are more difficult to analyze, the results are more fruitful for geological and archaeological applications.

The range of phenomena that can affect the thermal characteristics of sand, soil, and other geological materials is enormous. Examples include disturbances of soil texture (buried walls or old fields), changes in local, microscale relief (prehistoric roadways), and changes in soil moisture (sediment-filled irrigation trenches). Each of these phenomena can be explained in terms of its thermal-emissive parameters and can subsequently be detected in the imagery and mapped in a rapid, cost-effective manner.

Bands 1, 2, and 3 of the T.I.M.S. data were combined into a pseudo-true-color image. The color definition in this image reveals that individual thermal channels can be used singly or combined to obtain different results, depending upon the research objective. In this particular three-channel combination, the prehistoric roadways can be seen, as well as the major wall structures of the Pueblo Alto, Pueblo Bonito, Chetro Ketl and the prehistoric agricultural field near Chetro Ketl. In addition, the major wall structures of Pueblo Alto, a large trash midden, adjacent wall structures and prehistoric roadways converging at the north gate can be seen. Other anomalies were also detected, the nature of which will likewise be substantiated through future ground-truth reconnaissance. These phenomena are apparent in the image owing to the thermal inertial exchange with respect to the surrounding environment. These features dissipated heat through the night and then through midday their resultant cooler temperatures caused thermal inertia differences relative to their heated surroundings. As a result of this phenomenon, the D-shaped pueblos in Chaco Canyon can readily be detected in all thermal bands regardless of wall-structure height.

The daytime T.I.M.S. data revealed the existence of a prehistoric agricultural field southeast of Chetro Ketl. This field was first seen in a low-angle oblique photo taken by Charles A. Lindbergh in 1929. Photos taken since that time are inferior to those taken by Lindbergh. This is due to the increase in vegetation density that occurred after grazing in the canyon was stopped in 1946. In the T.I.M.S. imagery acquired at night, however, the exact perimeter of the field is delineated. The prehistoric roads, on the other hand, have reached thermal equilibrium in the 10:00 p.m. data and are not visible. This day/night comparison demonstrated the necessity for future research in understanding the thermal-emissive properties of archaeological features and their relationship in scheduling optimum times for data acquisition missions.

Future efforts

Owing to the success of the first T.I.M.S. analysis, N.A.S.A. agreed to continue its archaeological research in Chaco Canyon in 1988. The T.I.M.S. instrument was redesigned with better detectors and recording systems. Algorithms were also developed to correct for atmospheric variables which can severely affect the signal response. Consequently, current T.I.M.S. analysis promises to be 80–90 percent more effective than the original study. The objective of the research will be to extend the limits of the known roadway system as well as develop new technical methods for the detection of archaeological features. It is anticipated that these techniques will advance the state-of-the-art and be transferable to many other roadways studies in diverse environmental settings.

References

Bryan, Kirk
1954 *The Geology of Chaco Canyon, New Mexico, in Relation to the Life and Remains of the Prehistoric Peoples of Pueblo Bonito*. Smithsonian Miscellaneous Collections 122(7), Washington, DC

Cordell, Linda S.
1984 *Prehistory of the Southwest*. Academic Press, Orlando

Hall, Stephen A.
1977 Late Quaternary Sedimentation and Paleoecologic History of Chaco Canyon, New Mexico. *Geological Society of America Bulletin* 88:1,616–17

Judd, Neil M.
1954 *The Material Culture of Pueblo Bonito*. Smithsonian Miscellaneous Collections 124, Washington, DC

Kincaid, Chris (ed.)
1983 *Chaco Roads Project, Phase I. A Reappraisal of Prehistoric Roads in the San Juan Basin*. United States Department of the Interior, Bureau of Land Management, Albuquerque and Santa Fe

Kluckholn, Clyde, and Paul Reiter
1939 *Preliminary Report on the 1937 Excavations, Bc 50–51: Chaco Canyon, New Mexico, with Some Distributional Analyses*. The University of New Mexico Bulletin 345, Anthropological Series 3(2), Albuquerque

Lister, Robert H., and Florence C. Lister
1981 *Chaco Canyon*. University of New Mexico Press, Albuquerque

Lyons, T. R. (ed.)
1976 *Remote Sensing Experiments in Cultural Resource Studies: Non-Destructive Methods of Archeological Exploration, Survey, and Analysis*. Reports of the Chaco Center 1. National Park Service, Albuquerque

Lyons, T. R., and T. E. Avery
1977 *Remote Sensing: A Handbook for Archeologists and Cultural Resource Managers*. National Park Service, Washington, DC

Lyons, T. R., and James I. Ebert (eds.)
1978 *Remote Sensing and Non-Destructive Archeology*. National Park Service, Albuquerque

Lyons, T. R. and R. K. Hitchcock (eds.)
1977 *Aerial Remote Sensing Techniques in Archeology*. Reports of the Chaco Center 2, National Park Service and University of New Mexico, Albuquerque

Moore, G. K.
1983 Objective Procedure for Lineament Enhancement and Extraction. *Photogrammetric Engineering and Remote Sensing* 49(5):641–7

Obenauf, M.
1980 The Chacoan Roadway System. M.A. thesis, Albuquerque

Podwysocki, M. H., J. G. Moik, and W. D. Shoup.
1975 Quantification of Geologic Lineaments by Manual and Machine Processing Techniques. *Proceedings: N.A.S.A. Earth Resources Survey Symposium, Houston, Texas*, pp. 885–903

Powers, Robert P., William B. Gillespie, and Stephen H. Lekson
1983 *The Outlier Survey: A Regional View of Settlement in the San Juan Basin*. Reports of the Chaco Center 3, National Park Service and University of New Mexico, Albuquerque

Schalk, Randall F., and Thomas R. Lyons
1977 Ecological Applications of Landsat Imagery in Archeology: An Example from the San Juan Basin, New Mexico. In Lyons 1976

Sever, Thomas L.
1983 *Feasibility Study to Determine the Utility of Advanced Remote Sensing Technology in Archaeological Investigations*. Earth Resources Lab. Report 227. N.S.T.L. Mississippi

Sofaer, Anna, Michael Marshall, and Rolf M. Sinclair
1986 The Great North Road: A Cosmographic Expression of the Chaco Culture of New Mexico. *Proceedings of the Oxford II Conference of Archaeoastronomy*. Merida, Yucatan

Wetherill, Marietta
1948 Marietta Wetherill Tapes, Special Collections, Zimmerman Library, University of New Mexico, Albuquerque

7 Prehistoric footpaths in Costa Rica: transportation and communication in a tropical rainforest

PAYSON SHEETS and
THOMAS L. SEVER

Introduction

The objective of this chapter is to describe how erosional footpaths were formed and preserved in prehistoric Costa Rica, how they are detectable on remote-sensing imagery provided by N.A.S.A., and how they are being interpreted. These investigations are being conducted within the research design of the Proyecto Prehistórico Arenal, an archaeological–volcanological–botanical research project in Costa Rica sponsored by the U.S. National Science Foundation, the University of Colorado, National Aeronautics and Space Administration, and the National Geographic Society. We suggest that footpaths can be utilized as a window into a culture's religious, economic, political and social organization. As people travel along paths, for a variety of objectives including transportation, communication, and ritual, they leave behind them the record of their presence, in the form of erosional footpaths. This is an aspect of behavioral archaeology, the study of prehistoric features to understand networks of human activity and their underlying reasons for those activities.

The theoretical framework within which the Proyecto Prehistórico Arenal's research has been conducted in the mountains of northwestern Costa Rica is human ecology: the attempt to understand the dynamic inter-relationships among people, their cultures, the climate, and the biotic and physical environment. Aspects of culture of particular importance include political organization, economies and the use of productive and extractive resources, demography, and settlement patterns. The objectives and the early results of the Arenal Project are available in a special issue of the journal *Vinculos* (Sheets 1984), published by the National Museum in San José, Costa Rica.

Environment and ecology

The research design is regional, extending from the very moist, non-seasonal eastern end of the research area, over the continental divide at 700–1,000 m to the highly seasonal and much drier area on the Pacific side (Fig. 7.1). Archaeological sites are found throughout the area, although not in uniform densities or distributions.

The wettest area is around Arenal Volcano, with mean precipitation exceeding 6,000 mm. Soils are saturated year-round, and are quite acid, and solar radiation is restricted by the frequently heavy cloud cover. The combination of those factors effectively discourages seed-crop agriculture. The precipitation declines gradually toward the west, to about 2,500 mm at the western end of the lake and extending over the divide to the Tilaran area. The drier Pacific climate, with seasonal monsoon rains and lower precipitation totals, is at its extreme at the westernmost end of the research area, with only 1,300 mm of rain.

Tropical rainforests are known for being the most constant of terrestrial environments, with the greatest standing biomass and the highest species diversity (Richards 1973). It is significant that the forest of the Arenal area is one of the richest in flora and fauna of all Costa Rican rainforests (Tosi 1980). Some basic species counts give some idea of the tremendous present diversity: 500 plant species, 100 species of mammals, 25 species of fish, 150 species of amphibians or reptiles, and 400 species of birds. Forest cutting during the past few decades has impoverished the flora and fauna; prehistoric species totals would have been considerably higher. The edible wild biomass is both abundant and diverse.

Fig. 7.1. Location of Costa Rica, and map of the Arenal area, with Arenal Volcano on the right, and the enlarged Lake Arenal in the center. The continental divide angles across the lower left corner.

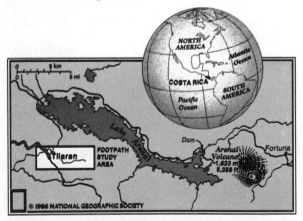

Explosive volcanic activity has affected the area repeatedly (Melson 1982, 1984) since the birth of Arenal Volcano about 4,000 years ago. There have been at least ten major explosive eruptions in prehistory that have deposited significant volumes of tephra downwind over the lake and Tilaran area, with a mean periodicity of about four centuries. Following each disaster, tephra weathering and soil formation occurred, along with plant and animal recolonization, and people eventually moved back into the area. The soils formed on volcanic ash tend to be fertile, with high amounts of organic matter, and pH readings range from 4.5 in the wetter areas to 6.6 in drier areas. However, ash-derived soils are low in phosphorus, potassium, zinc, and manganese, which discourages some cultigens. The pre-eruption soils are more typical of the tropics, with high clay content, large amounts of iron and aluminum oxides, low organic content, and moderate to low fertility.

Arenal's most recent eruption was in 1968, with an explosive phase that devastated many square kilometers of rainforest, some farms and ranches, and took some sixty human lives. The effusive phase, consisting of a sustained lava flow, has continued to the present, an unusually long duration for an eruption of Arenal, or of any Costa Rican volcano for that matter. Although the 1968–present eruption is significant, it is much smaller than the ten explosive eruptions of prehistory.

Brief culture history

Archaeological sites of all phases are shown in Fig. 7.2. Our earliest evidence of human occupation in the area is a complete Clovis point found on the Aguacate Formation (the weathered clay surface prior to Arenal's ash deposits) at site G-164. It was made from a locally available chalcedony. It indicates Paleo-Indian habitation of the area, probably dating to about 11,000 years ago. Their adaptation presumably was based on hunting and gathering of entirely wild species, probably with an emphasis on gathering vegetative sources of food. The predominant idea of Paleo-Indian populations adapting to drier and more open, grassy habitats in Central America is in need of rethinking, because of this find, the Turrialba site (Snarskis 1979), and the dearth of Paleo-Indian artifacts from the Santa Maria project in drier Pacific Panama.

Fortuna Phase (before 4000 B.C. to 2000 B.C.)

A few Archaic (Fortuna Phase) sites are known, which have yielded radiocarbon dates ranging from 4000 to about 2000 B.C. The principal means of creating acute stone cutting edges was an informal percussion core-flake industry. Established during this phase, it continued to the Spanish conquest, a striking case of stability over six millennia. Another significant, and wholly unexpected, index of adaptive continuity is the reliance on stone cooking technology throughout the Fortuna Phase and all later ceramic-bearing phases up to the Spanish conquest. Local stones were collected, and used for transferring heat from fires to liquid foods. It was surprising to see that the use of ceramics did not supplant the earlier technology; it was used in villages, and was particularly favored in cemeteries at considerable distances from villages during the Silencio Phase.

Tronadora Phase (2000–500 B.C.)

The earliest known sedentary occupation began about 2000 BC at the Tronadora Vieja site (G-163). Houses were constructed of pole and thatch, and were about 8 m in diameter. Ceramics of the Tronadora Phase were extremely well made and elaborately decorated by incision and painting. (Ceramic observations are taken from Hoopes 1984, and personal communications.) The most common shapes are large olla-tecomates. Similar pottery is found rather often in the Meseta Central and Atlantic drainage, but very rarely to the west of the Cordillera, in lowland Guanacaste. It appears that the earliest ceramic-producing Costa Rican societies were located in the moister tropical forests, and the adaptation to tropical dry forests lagged by a millennium or more. The closest similarities with ceramics outside of the country are with the Ocos pottery of Pacific Guatemala; if the dating of both is accurate, the direction of influence is from Costa Rica to Guatemala. In terms of culture area boundaries, the Cordillera would have to be placed with the Atlantic-Meseta area rather than with the lowlands to the west. (One might even question whether those lowlands were sufficiently settled to be considered a culture area at this time in the Early Formative.) Tronadora Phase ceramics began to be made in the Cordillera prior to the first eruption of Arenal Volcano, so it is not surprising that the earliest pottery did not use volcanic ash temper. However, for some reason the local inhabitants did not take advantage of the superior tempering properties of volcanic ash until centuries after it was first available, in the succeeding Arenal Phase.

Adequate watercraft were developed by this phase, as evidenced by the pottery found on the island (site G-166) in Lake Arenal. Similar pottery was found on Ometepe Island in Lake Nicaragua (Haberland, personal communication 1985). In addition to cooking with pottery, stone boiling continued from the Archaic. Burials during the phase apparently were within the village, in simple pits dug down into the clay soil, only occasionally accompanied by a pottery vessel offering.

The Archaic-to-Formative transition was remarkably

Fig. 7.2. Map of the Arenal–Tilaran area, with archaeological sites indicated by black dots. Map by Barbara Bolton.

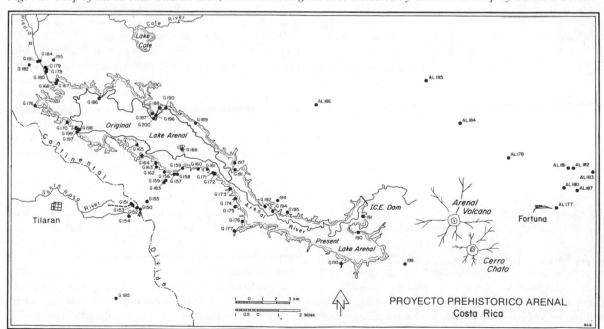

non-dramatic in this area. It is here defined as the emergence of sedentary village life and the making of pottery, with evidence of cultivated plants, but a number of other significant components of society were unaffected. Settlement patterns were not markedly altered, as it appears that many of the Tronadora Phase sites had Archaic occupations preceding them, and it is likely that Archaic peoples were at least semi-sedentary. The basic means of making cutting edges remained the same during both phases, as did the extensive use of stones for cooking. The nature of lithic raw materials used for both purposes remains the same, with only slight changes in the proportions of stone types.

Unexplained is how the transition occurred. Certainly there was no sudden, massive invasion of the area by ceramic-producing peoples. Rather, it appears that ceramics were adopted by largely self-sufficient tropical forest-adapted bands that were becoming more sedentary. They adopted a very complex, sophisticated ceramic industry from an unknown source.

Arenal Phase (500 B.C. to A.D. 500)

The Arenal Phase is the local expression of the zoned Bichrome horizon in Lower Central America (Lange 1984). Human population density had expanded to its prehistoric peak in the area, and cemeteries, located on prominent ridges close to villages, are marked by large quantities of round river rocks. Following the interment of the deceased and the filling of the burial pit, these rocks were violently smashed into place on top of the grave, often creating massive percussion fractures. Large numbers of whole vessels were also smashed on the surface of the rocks. During the earlier half of the phase, there are ceramic similarities with the extreme southern area of Costa Rica and into western Panama, but during the second half of the phase there are strongly affiliations with Greater Nicoya to the west. Even so, there are indications of continued connections with the Atlantic area throughout the phase. The number and the size of sites increase dramatically, to perhaps as much as ten times as many people in the Arenal as in the preceding Tronadora Phase.

Silencio Phase (A.D. 500–1200)

The Silencio Phase is marked by a population decline, by the advent of polychrome pottery, and by cemeteries on very prominent ridges at long distances from habitations. Ceramics are localized, but they show some affiliations with both the Atlantic and Greater Nicoya cultural areas. Some trade ceramics from Greater Nicoya were imported for funerary use, and were placed whole in Atlantic-style stone slab "cist" tombs. Some Atlantic-style gold pendants were also placed in the tombs.

The population decline is evidenced by a marked drop in the number of occupied sites, but the sizes of individual sites remain as large as they were during the Arenal Phase. Two large eruptions occurred during the phase, depositing what we call Geological Units 41 and 40. Two ash layers were also deposited along the Pacific coast at the Vidor site at roughly the same time (Lange 1978), but it is not known if they derived from Arenal or another source. Societies in both areas exhibited resilience, as recoveries were relatively rapid.

Tilaran Phase (A.D. 1200–1500)

The Tilaran Phase is notable for continued lowered population and a strong turn in cultural affiliation away from Greater Nicoya to the west, and toward the Atlantic area and southward. The overall population density was as low as during the Silencio Phase, but the distribution was different, with numerous small and widely dispersed villages rather than a few large sites. The ceramic change was dramatic, away from the elaborate polychromes of Greater Nicoya and a wholesale adoption of Atlantic-style decoration by appliqué, modeling, and other plastic techniques. The pottery is a dull, rough monochrome, with a strong domestic orientation.

Maize was domesticated and used from the Tronadora Phase throughout all phases to the Conquest; carbonized macrofossils have been found in remains of all phases. However, the analysis of stable carbon isotopes indicates that a maximum of only 12 percent of the diet could have been from maize. Specifically, the average C13 content of bone was − 19.6 per mil (Friedman and Gleason 1984). The interpretation that maize was utilized, but probably not as a staple, is also supported by the general lack of well-used utilitarian metates and manos. Domesticated beans were also found, along with a wide range of wild tropical-forest products. We conclude that local societies were able to maintain sedentary communities, without resorting to full-scale agriculture, by exploiting their very rich tropical-forest environment. The maintenance of relatively low populations at all times, compared with Mesoamerica and the Andes, contributed to the striking stability in adaptation, ceramic and lithic traditions, and society in Costa Rica. A measure of the effectiveness of their adaptation is the resilience with which they responded to eruptions of Arenal Volcano. Generally, they were able to reestablish themselves in the area with minimal changes following a major eruption and the natural recovery processes. Societies were predominantly egalitarian throughout the sequence. It is only during the Arenal and Silencio phases that they *may* have crossed the threshold into ranked society and established simple chiefdoms.

Remote sensing in the Arenal area

Before considering the data and interpretation, some background on the relationship of the project to the remote-sensing data and analysis provided by N.A.S.A. is necessary. Owing to the efforts of Sever, N.A.S.A. agreed in 1983 to assist two archaeological projects with remotely sensed data. The Coordinating Council of National Archaeological Societies and the N.S.F. were involved with selecting the two projects; the present Costa Rican project and the work on hominid evolution in East Africa by Glynn Isaac. His unfortunate death ended that research.

Under a three-year cooperative agreement, N.A.S.A. has provided two overflights for optical and digital remote sensing. Color and color-infrared aerial photography have been provided, L-band radar data have been obtained, and a laser profiler (L.I.D.A.R.) has been flown. In addition, various maps have been digitized, including topography, soils, landforms, and others.

Remote sensing is the science of data detection from a distance. By means of remote sensing an investigator can see information which may be imperceptible from ground level. At one time remote-sensing instruments were limited to photography, which is an optical and chemical process. In the last few years, however, advanced technology has produced an almost endless array of digital remote-sensing instruments which produce images electronically through computer analysis (Sever and Wiseman 1985). These instruments record millions of pieces of data per second across various parts of the electromagnetic spectrum, producing specific signals from earth objects. Generally the investigator is interested in only a minute portion of these spectral responses. Through advanced algorithms and computer analysis (Schwongerdt 1983) the object of interest can be extracted, viewed on an image display device, mapped and subsequently verified through on-site investigations.

Black-and-white photography provides the greatest versatility in terms of detail but only records about twenty-two perceptible shades of gray in the visible portion of the electromagnetic spectrum. Color-infrared film slightly improves the human visual range by detecting wavelengths beyond the red end of the spectrum. Both optical sources possess certain liabilities because they must operate in daylight, during clear weather, on days with minimal atmospheric haze. Digital sensors,

however, can view thousands of pieces of information simultaneously in the ultraviolet, visible, infrared, thermal infrared, and microwave portions of the spectrum. Radar instruments can penetrate through clouds, and because they are active sensors which produce their own energy, they can operate night or day. It is in the bandwidths beyond the range of human vision that information regarding surface and subsurface phenomena, such as soil composition, geological characteristics, and prehistoric activity, can be viewed for the first time. Consider, for example, a summer pasture. Subsurface prehistoric features, such as trenches and walls, could manifest themselves through differences in plant moisture, chlorophyll content, or temperature variation. To the human eye the entire pasture may appear as an undifferentiated green surface.

Clouds hinder the acquisition of data between the ultraviolet and thermal infrared portions of the spectrum. Unfortunately, Costa Rica, as with the tropics in general, has a heavy cloud cover during most months of the year. A N.A.S.A. aircraft acquired data during 1984 in the microwave portion of the spectrum by means of an L-band 1.225 GHz 24. 6-cm radar system. Radar systems, in addition to their capacity to penetrate clouds, are designed to detect linear and geometric patterns of surface phenomena in their reflected signals.

The radar system used in this study is a Synthetic Aperture Radar (S.A.R.) with multifrequency, multipolarization, and multilook-angle capabilities. Because longer wavelength radar waves can penetrate through the vegetation canopy, radar is a useful tool in studying complex targets. Past studies discussing the use of radar data were qualitative at best. Recently, however, new computer techniques for reducing speckle noise and for measuring the degree of separation have been developed (Wu and Sader 1987).

Topographic data were acquired using an Airborne Oceanographic Lidar (A.O.L.). Lidar (light detection and ranging) can be used to penetrate water to measure the morphology of coastal waters, detect oil forms, fluorescent dye tracers, water clarity, and organic pigments including chlorophyll. In this bathymetry mode a short laser pulse is transmitted to the water surface. Part of the pulse is reflected back to the aircraft while the other part continues to the bottom of the water and is reflected back. The time elapsed between the received impulses allows for a determination of water depth and subsurface topography.

The A.O.L. can also be used in forested environments to produce topographic information, as the instrument can function as a high laser altimeter. The tree canopy acts like the water surface, reflecting a portion of the energy to the aircraft, while the other part continues to the forest floor. Detailed topographic resolution can be attained to within centimeters because the instrument produces 400 pulses per second, striking the ground every 9 cm. The data can be computer processed to reveal tree height as well as elevation, slope, aspect, and slope length of ground features. The A.O.L. can even penetrate forest canopies that are 99.9 percent dense (Joyce 1983).

Both color and color-infrared aerial photography were acquired during the October 1984 and April 1985 N.A.S.A. overflights of the Arenal area. The primary activity of air photo interpretation involves making observations and measurements of image features. Air photo interpretation benefits from direct experience of the area by the interpreters. The following features of an image are measured during the process: tone, texture, density, shape, size, juxtaposition, pattern, drainage, and topography (with height in stereo images). Both N.A.S.A. flights in Costa Rica acquired air photos with 60 percent overlap to allow for stereo viewing.

While examining the color-infrared prints, Sever discovered a line leading westward from the G-150 site, a large Silencio Phase cemetery on the Continental Divide. His suggestion that it could be a road was met by weak verbal encouragement by Sheets. The latter harbored a deep skepticism about the linear feature having anything to do with prehistory. However, when Sheets noticed that the line made an obtuse angle bend around a repository of construction stone for the cemetery, divided in two, and headed down to a stream, he became suspicious that the feature might possibly be prehistoric. Then, when two lines were found to emerge on the other side, head straight up to a ridgetop, and then make an obtuse angle bend around the second building stone repository and continue westward, Sheets began seriously to consider them as possible prehistoric features. In April of 1985 we placed three shallow exploratory trenches in the features and successfully demonstrated that they had existed prior to the fall of the Unit 20 tephra, i.e., they were prior to 1400 A.D. They clearly were not historic or recent phenomena, and thus must have been prehistoric.

The basic research design used during 1985 and 1986 was to discover linear anomalies in the remote-sensing imagery, and then confirm or disconfirm them by excavation. In many cases, linear anomalies could be identified as contemporary features, such as roads, paths, powerlines, and fence lines. The most useful imagery so far has been the color-infrared photography obtained by the N.A.S.A. Convair 990 aircraft, which flew only 400

m above the terrain in October 1984. The color aerial photography and the conventional black-and-white photography have also been useful. Numerous linear features are discernible in the radar imagery, but this has yet to be systematically analyzed. The footpaths which are suspected and have been confirmed are indicated on Fig. 7.3.

In the computer analysis of digital radar data, the subjective analysis of the interpreter is replaced with mathematical algorithms which recognize statistical patterns in the data set. A median value filtering technique removes the speckled noise component from the data, allowing better separation between classes. Linear and curvilinear patterns within the Arenal area forest canopy have been mapped. In pastures, the features make sense and appear to be part of the pathway system. Verification of the radar-detected features has been complicated by two factors: 1. the radar is seeing phenomena invisible to the human eye, and 2. determining the location of the feature on the ground is hindered by the dense vegetation of the rainforest. The problem will be resolved in future fieldwork by use of the Global Positioning System (G.P.S.). The G.P.S. uses eighteen Navstar satellites in orbit around the earth. By using a G.P.S. ground-based instrument and pressing a button, the X, Y, and Z coordinates (latitude, longitude, and elevation) are displayed to within centimeters. In this way the features of interest can be located in spite of dense vegetation.

Footpath formation and preservation processes

Sufficient excavations have now been made of footpaths in various localities of their research area so that the various processes involved in their formation and preservation are reasonably well understood. The landscape is accretional, in that every few centuries there has been a large explosive eruption of Arenal Volcano which deposited an ash blanket around the volcano and downwind. In undisturbed, relatively low-lying areas, these are now visible as a series of lighter-colored ash layers, with darker soils formed on top of them. Fig. 7.4 illustrates the uniform, flat layers of volcanic ash with soils formed on top of each of them, and the eroded-away area of the footpath in the center. The photograph (Fig. 7.5) shows undisturbed and path-eroded stratigraphy, capped by the light-colored volcanic ash Unit 41 that marks the cessation of use. A footpath across a flat area leaves a negligible trace, but a slight degree of slope allows for erosion to take place. Initial use of the footpath results in minor compaction, which allows for channeling of runoff along the path. Of the 2,000 to 3,500 mm mean

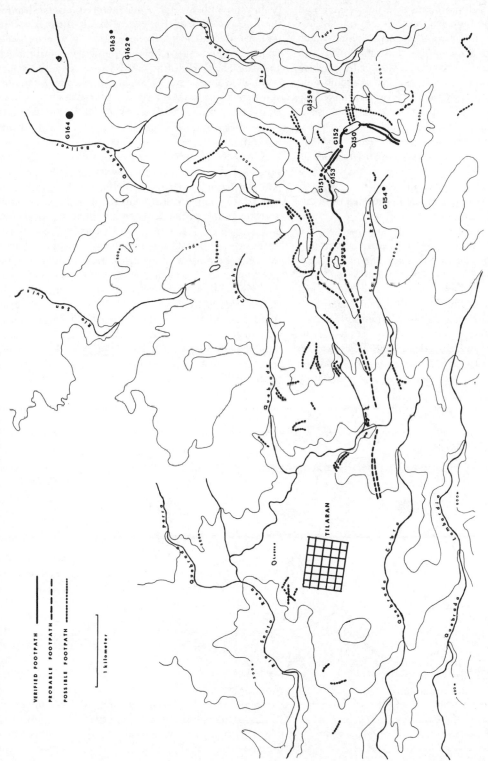

Fig. 7.3. Map of footpaths in the Silencio–Tilaran area. Map by M. Mueller.

annual precipitation in the Tilaran–Silencio area, about half is surplus beyond the evapotranspiration budget of the forest (i.e., is runoff), resulting in a high erosional potential. An approximate date for the initiation of path use is provided by noting the soil-ash layer from which erosion began. Similarly, an approximate ending date for the path is provided by the ash layer that uniformly blankets the abandoned path. Dating of path use is independently achieved by artifact analysis; some paths have sufficient ceramics or other artifacts that are chronologically diagnostic. However, many trenches do not result in sufficiently large or diagnostic collections. Another chronological indicator is the dating, by various means, of the sites at the end points or intermediate nodes of the paths.

The actual utilized path surface generally was only 30 to 70 cm wide. However, as the path itself would entrench, by erosion, down into underlying tephra-soil layers, the sides would become steeper, and thus provide a higher energy environment for microerosional processes. These processes would erode the banks back from the path, even though the banks themselves were not receiving any traffic. Thus, the path is a narrow entrenching U shape, but the sides are following along in an entrenching broad V shape. The stratum to which the path had eroded, of course, does not indicate the dating

or duration of use, but it is one factor that is indicative of the amount of use. Following abandonment, steeper parts of paths, and particularly their side banks, often underwent some further erosion and/or deposition. The surface was stabilized in virtually all cases by the next eruption in the sequence, which is preserved in the excavated trenches as an uneroded tephra blanket extending across the path. Thus, the volcanic stratigraphy is very useful in giving approximate beginning and ending dates for path use.

A number of variables are involved in the erosional process. Clearly, a greater amount of use will erode a path deeper, all other things being equal. And, by controlling for the relevant variables, there are cases where we can identify primary, secondary, and tertiary routes, and occasionally we can suggest explanations for these differences. Precipitation is a factor; areas with more than 6,000 mm of mean precipitation near the volcano erode much faster than areas near Canas with only 1,300 mm of precipitation. Slope is a major factor; as we trace the same path, we see a dramatic increase in erosion as paths descend from gently sloping pitches to land with 8–10 degrees slope or more. The matrix into which the path is incised is another factor; in general the ash-soil sequence is relatively uniform in density and thus in its potential for erosion, but there are some differences.

Fig. 7.4. Profile of Trench 22, 200 m south of the G-150 cemetery, on the way to the spring. Path use eroded the flat-lying tephra soils from the upper 50s down into Unit 61. The Unit 50 soil formed after path abandonment, and that was sealed by later tephra and soil units.

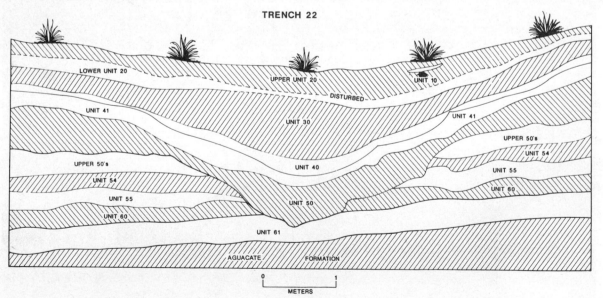

Unit 55 is the firmest of the tephra layers, being semi-consolidated. It is the most resistant to erosion, and paths are sometimes found eroding down to it and no farther. The underlying clay-laden soil on top of the Aguacate Formation probably is more resistant to erosion than most of the tephra-soil layers. And it appears in many cases that alternate routes were initiated when an older path had eroded down to the clay. Anyone who has tried to walk on that slippery, sticky tropical clay soil can readily understand the advantages of walking on a trail in the most porous volcanic ash matrix. Most of the trail alternatives discovered to date are parallel to the original trail, and located a few meters away. However, on steeper slopes (over 9 degrees) they often created a wide, looping alternative trail. In all cases

of these wide looping trails, the wide loops received less use than the primary trails heading more directly downslope. The wide loops are such distinctive features, in that they sacrifice distance for decreasing grade, in contrast with the more common paths routing straight up and down slopes. They may have been used for some unusual transportation circumstance, such as for someone carrying an unusually heavy load (a body, or a lot of laja?), or they could have been used by a more elderly or infirm traveler.

Some quantitative manipulations may be done with the variables involved with footpath use. The amount of erosion of a footpath is directly proportional to the amount of annual precipitation, to the amount of use at any time, to the total time that path is in use, and to the

Fig. 7.5. Photograph of Trench 22, showing the footpath eroded down into the tephra and soil units. Later ashfalls and soils bury the abandoned path.

slope. It is inversely proportional to the hardness of the materials through which it is eroding. For our purposes here, we disregard the minimal differences in resistance to erosion of most of the tephra layers and the soils developed out of them, other than to state that the Unit 55 tephra is semi-consolidated. The Unit 65 Aguacate Formation is the clay-laden pre-eruption soil, and thus it is more resistant to particulate erosion than the tephra layers. However, it need not be figured into these exercises at this point, because inhabitants generally shifted path location when the path eroded down to that sticky, slippery surface.

Therefore, Erosion = (Slope) × (Moisture) × (Use) × (Time). Erosion can be quantified as the area of tephra and soils eroded away, as seen in cross-section on the profiles. It is a figure in square meters. Slope can be measured in angle, in degree of slope, or in the number of meters drop in a hundred meters of horizontal distance. In order to minimize disparate measurement units, we are opting for the latter. Time of use is estimated duration of use in centuries, as indicated by the tephra layers emplaced at its time of initiation of use and at its termination. That allows us to solve the equation for Use, and we have

$$Use = \frac{Erosion}{(Time) \times (Slope) \times (Moisture)}.$$

The routing decisions for these paths were quite different from those used for routing of contemporary roads, of cattle paths, other animal paths, or other recent and historic linear features. Contemporary roads tend to minimize grade changes and sudden directional changes, and thus they contour around topographic features. They sacrifice distance for maintenance of similar elevation. In contrast, these prehistoric paths follow relatively straight lines as they travel across topographic changes rather than around them. This applies to the highs and the lows; hills have paths traveling over their tops rather than around their bottoms, and valleys have paths directly descending to their low points and directly ascending to the other sides rather than contouring around toward their headwaters. In one case, a short path from a village to a cemetery went right over the top of a small hill rather than around it. Also, whenever possible, a high route was preferable to a low route, even though both were of approximately equal distance. In this case, the explanation is probably drainage, as a path along a topographically higher route would be less moist than one along a low route.

Important considerations in investigating path or road systems are who is traveling along the route, and what they are transporting. We have some answers to these points. We do know that many live people and some dead people were moving along the paths, with the former carrying the latter for interment. The path into the cemetery from the village was frequented by people occasionally carrying relatives for burial. They also carried large quantities of laja, the flat-fracturing volcanic stone used in construction of tombs and retaining walls in the cemetery. Two laja repositories have been excavated (G-151 and G-152). Evidently, people would carry laja toward the cemetery for unspecified future use, but would not quite carry it all the way to the cemetery. They would carry laja most of the way to the cemetery, to the repositories, even though a particular construction was not immediately necessary, while they were visiting the cemetery for ritual purposes. The laja repositories were at least slightly organized internally, as people sorted and deposited stones using their typological distinctions. There was a tendency to separate flatter, larger slabs from smaller and more irregular slabs in both repositories, and G-152 had one section devoted to the elongated headstones, which were arranged in a line. The headstones are long and roughly cylindrical in shape, in contrast with the flat laja slabs, and they were used for marking the head end of the graves.

Footpath detection: in imagery and in the field

As noted above, the first detection of the footpaths was done on color-infrared low-elevation aerial photography, but we now know that they can be detected by using conventional aerial photography, particularly by enlarging a quarter of the standard 9 × 9 inch negative to about a meter square. On both color-infrared and conventional black-and-white aerial photographs, the paths often show up as positive crop marks, where the vegetation grows somewhat better because of a superior root matrix for growth. This is particularly true of pasture land, but it may be true of forested areas as well. The latter remains to be tested, and it will be tested during the 1987 research. Some of the paths can be seen and followed in the field, as linear depressions, particularly where they traverse slopes steeper than about 3 or 4 degrees. Their erosional effects are still visible, in spite of the smoothing effects of numerous volcanic ashfalls and other natural phenomena, over the hundreds of years after path abandonment. It is common for paths on slopes over 8 degrees to have incised themselves 1–2 m below the surface at that time, and in a few cases, they are even deeper. In spite of the narrowness of the path itself, the lateral erosional effects can extend 5 or more m to each side of the path itself.

It is possible that radar can detect footpaths, or the effects of footpaths on vegetation, but that has yet to be confirmed. The laser profiler (L.I.D.A.R.) can detect the paths as dips in the present terrain, as it traverses across a path that still leaves an erosional trace on the present landscape. However, it is sufficiently sensitive that it records a large number of dips in the terrain, and it would be difficult to turn this into a footpath discovery technique, because of the great number of places that would have to be investigated. It is limited in that it is recording topography as a linear slice, whereas the photographic and radar instruments are recording two-dimensional areas within which linear anomalies are readily apparent.

Comment, summary, and conclusions

Prehistoric footpaths have been detected as linear anomalies in a volcanically active tropical rainforest environment in northwestern Costa Rica. They have been detected most successfully, to date, in the color infrared and conventional black-and-white aerial photography, especially when each is blown up to an appropriate scale where features a few meters wide can be seen (Fig. 7.7; Plates 3 and 4). Radar shows considerable promise in detecting paths, even in forested areas. Paths have been confirmed by excavations; the volcanic ash layers from the ten large explosive eruptions of Arenal Volcano have assisted in dating path use and in determining the modes of path entrenchment and preservation after abandonment.

Methodologically, it is important to note that we have also developed the means to disconfirm linear anomalies as prehistoric features. For instance, at one location 1.4 km west of the G-150 graveyard, what appeared to be a dual parallel linear feature in the color-infrared photography virtually identical to other confirmed paths was located. Excavations, profiled in Fig. 7.6, indicated that the stronger depression on the left, and the weaker depression on the right, had been caused by activity that post-dates the fall of the Unit 20 pumice, and thus it must be historic. That the Unit 10 was also eroded away indicated that it was formed in the latter part of the historic period. Interviews with local landowners divulged the information that it was a small road that led from Tilaran to the earliest Finca El Silencio house, and was in use for a couple of decades from about 1930.

Archaeologists have probably spent less time looking for ancient paths, in imagery and on the ground, than they have spent looking for almost any other kind of feature. However, in spite of the obstacles presented by low population densities, a tropical moist environment, and frequent ash blankets being laid over the terrain, they have been detected and confirmed in the Arenal area of Costa Rica. Thus, the prospects of finding paths in other moist areas of the occupied New and Old Worlds appear sanguine. We suggest that available types of aerial photography, of a scale of 1:30,000 to perhaps 1:10,000, be examined for any linear features linking known sites. That will need to be followed by on-the-ground inspection and some excavations to determine

Fig. 7.6. Drawings of Trench 12, located 1.4 km west of the G-150 cemetery. This looked like a prehistoric path in the imagery, but turned out to be a historic road in use from 1930 to 1950. Note that the prehistoric units are flat-lying (Units 50 through 30), and the depressions were formed after the emplacement of Unit 20.

TRENCH 12

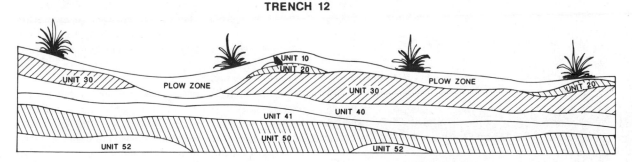

the processes leading to formation and to preservation, and means to separate prehistoric from modern and historic phenomena will need to be developed.

One of the unanswered questions of the project is how settlements were integrated during the Silencio Phase, a time when settlements were relatively large, but were widely separated. The footpaths provide an answer, or at least a partial answer. The integration appears to have been ritual. The multiple paths leading from the Silencio cemetery point in various directions toward villages that buried their dead in that cemetery. The heavily used paths which lead to the spring, as well as the voluminous occupational trash left in the cemetery, argue strongly for long-duration ceremonies in the cemetery, perhaps directed toward the ancestors and other spirits.

An unanticipated result of the footpath study was a direct contribution of data to help resolve one of the important issues facing the project, the degree of forest clearance in prehistoric times. Efforts have been made to interpret the pollen, phytolith, and carbonized plant macrofossil record to understand the natural and cultural vegetation (summaries in Sheets 1984). However, there are difficulties in interpreting these data sets, particularly when they are from samples taken from archaeological sites. The contribution made by the path

Fig. 7.7. Thermal Infrared Multispectral Scanner (T.I.M.S.) image showing the location of prehistoric footpaths in the dense forest canopy near the Silencio cemetery. Although there is circumstantial evidence to suggest that these features are prehistoric footpaths, they have been verified through excavation.

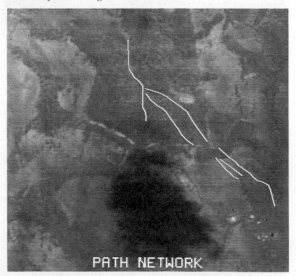

studies is based on the fact that the volcanic ash layers, particularly the Unit 55 tephra, will oxidize when exposed to significant solar radiation. Only one trench, out of twenty-four excavated so far, has encountered an oxidized tephra level. That was Trench 7, between the graveyard and the spring. In all other cases, the forest canopy was sufficiently closed to inhibit oxidation of the tephra layers exposed by path use and erosion, indicating a predominantly forested and uncut natural environment between sites. Within the village and the habitation sites, tephra layers are often oxidized, and sometimes intensely oxidized. The most oxidized area found to date is the lower area of the G-150 cemetery, which must have been devoid of vegetation and exposed to direct solar radiation for a significant period of time.

So, it appears that the G-150 Silencio cemetery was more than a place merely to bury the dead. There was extensive evidence of cooking in the cemetery, in pottery vessels but especially with cooking stones. Stone tools, particularly expedient stone tools, were manufactured, used, and discarded in the graveyard. Palynological evidence indicates some maize being grown near the graveyard. The forest was cut, particularly in the lower-status area. The footpaths leading in and out of the graveyard provide further evidence of extensive use of that graveyard. Judging by relative amounts of erosion, the traffic to and from the spring to the south of the cemetery was about three times the traffic along the main east–west path, indicating long stays in the graveyard, rather than rapid visits.

Footpath networks can provide a direct "window" on human transportation and communication in prehistory. Their discovery and interpretation in the Arenal area have been facilitated by the volcanic ash layers; efforts will be made over the next few years to modify the field and laboratory methodology to detect and confirm prehistoric footpaths outside of volcanically active areas, and in less moist climates.

Acknowledgments
We wish to acknowledge, with deep gratitude, the finacial support for this research provided by the U.S. National Science Foundation, N.A.S.A., the University of Colorado, and the National Geographic Society. John Hoopes and Brian McKee critiqued an earlier version of this paper; they should share none of the blame, but they should receive credit for any of the "better parts."

References

Friedman, I., and J. Gleason
1984 C13 Analysis of Bone Samples from Site G-150, El Silencio. *Vinculos* 10(1–2):113–14

Hoopes, J.
1984 A Preliminary Ceramic Sequence for the Cuenca de Arenal, Cordillera de Tilaran Region, Costa Rica. *Vinculos* 10(1–2):129–48

Joyce, A.
1983 Remote Sensing of Forest Dynamics in Tropical Regions. N.A.S.A. Office of Space Science and Applications. 20 May 1983

Lange, Frederick W.
1978 Coastal Settlement in Northwestern Costa Rica. In *Prehistoric Adaptations: The Economy of Maritime Middle America*, edited by Barbara L. Stark and Barbara Voorhies, pp. 101–20. Academic Press, New York
1984 The Greater Nicoya Archaeological Subarea. In *The Archaeology of Lower Central America*, edited by Fredrick W. Lange and Doris Z. Stone, pp. 165–94. University of New Mexico Press, Albuquerque

Melson, William G.
1982 *Alternation between Acidic and Basic Magmas of Arenal Volcano, Costa Rica*. Boletín de Volcanología, Heredia, Costa Rica
1984 Prehistoric Eruptions of Arenal Volcano, Costa Rica. *Vinculos* 10(1–2):35–55

Richards, Paul W.
1973 The Tropical Rainforest. *Scientific American* (Dec.):58–67

Schwongerdt, R.
1983 *Techniques for Image Processing and Classification in Remote Sensing*. Academic Press, London

Sever, T., and J. Wiseman
1985 *Conference on Remote Sensing: Potential for the Future*. N.A.S.A. Earth Resources Laboratory Report, N.S.T.L. Station MS

Sheets, P. (ed.)
1984 Archaeological Investigations in the Cordillera of Tilaran, Costa Rica, 1984. Special Issue of *Vinculos* 10(1–2), 14 Articles, 231 pp.

Snarskis, M.
1979 Turrialba: A Paleo-Indian Quarry and Workshop Site in Eastern Costa Rica. *American Antiquity* 44:125–38

Tosi, Joseph O.
1980 *Estudio Ecológico Integral de las Zonas de Afectación del Proyecto Arenal*. Centro Científica Tropical, San José, Costa Rica

Wu, S., and S. Sader
1987 *Multipolarization S.A.R. Data for Surface Feature Delineation and Forest Vegetation Characterization*. I.E.E.E. Transactions on Geoscience and Remote Sensing GE-25(1)

8 Cross-cutting relationships: the relative dating of ancient roads on the north coast of Peru

Introduction

The coast of Peru is ideal for road studies because the preservation of archaeological remains is excellent as a result of unusual climatic conditions which have produced one of the most arid climates in the world. Although annual rainfall averages less than 1 cm (O.N.E.R.N. 1973:43) the coast is not a wasteland because the fifty rivers flowing westward from the Andes to the Pacific Ocean support a high water table and irrigation systems. Vegetation is sparse outside the irrigated zones and is completely absent in many areas. Infrequently, probably no more than once or twice a century, a change in climatic conditions produces heavy rains and flooding as far south as the central coast of Peru. These rains devastate a region adapted to a dry climate. Major impacts on the archaeological remains have been confined to the rare floods, human activities and recurrent earthquakes.

Between 1976 and 1978, the author conducted a survey of ancient roads on the north coast of Peru which focused on the Moche Valley (Fig. 8.1). The valley was surveyed from the coast to a ravine 25 km inland. Along the coastal strip the survey began 15 km north of the modern irrigation zone in the Virú Valley, extended north through the Moche Valley and ended at the southern perimeter of the modern cultivation in the Chicama Valley. Over 150 roads and their associated sites were recorded in the course of this research and are reported in detail elsewhere (Beck 1979).

The Moche Valley is well known for its archaeological sites which have been studied by numerous researchers for many years. This research has demonstrated that the valley was a strong political center whose influence and dominance waxed and waned through time. The political importance of the region is reflected in the abundance of ancient roads built in the area.

Prior to the 1970s ancient roads (prehistoric and colonial) were rarely the focus of archaeological research in the Andean region. Strube Erdmann's (1963) and Regal's (1936) ethnohistorical research and von Hagen's (1975) publication on Inka roads were the only extensive documents devoted to this phenomenon. In general, most discussions of ancient roads attributed their construction to the Inka Empire or they were interpreted as ceremonial ways or astronomical markings (Ford 1949:33–4). Slowly evidence accumulated which indicated that the tendency to label all roads as products of the Inkas might be in error.

Two main reasons account for the emergence of this viewpoint. First, the great number of roads on the coast of Peru caused questioning that all of these roads could have been built and used by the Inkas. This suggested that many of the roads might be pre-Inka (Savoy

1970:49; Ubbeloehde-Doering 166:25; Willey 1953:361–70). Regal's extensive study of the Colonial documents produced two instances where the Indians told the Spanish that the Inkas remodeled existing roads in an area and that the Inkas did not originally construct them (1936:6–7). Second, it was repeatedly observed that ancient roads are directly associated with pre-Inka archaeological sites (Kosok 1965:93–4; Lumbreras 1974:162; Proulx 1973:84–92; Stothert-Stockman 1967).

Although this evidence indicated that pre-Inka roads probably did exist, the recurring problems were the inability to date these features and the reluctance of archaeologists to accept the existence of pre-Inka roadway systems. While working on canal systems in the Moche Valley, the author repeatedly encountered ancient roads which were thought to be undatable. By refining the methodology which was used to date the canals (developed by the Programa Riego Antiguo of the Field Museum of Natural History), it became possible relatively to date the construction and use of most of the Moche Valley roads.

Research methodology

Before research could begin, the problem of what constituted a road, and what did not, had to be resolved. Roads are planned alterations of the landscape which involve surveying, construction and usually maintenance in order for them to serve their purpose of facilitating and controlling the movement of people. Roads are distinguished from paths on this basis; size or length was not a consideration. A path is the result of wear and its course is geomorphic, following a route that is the easiest, more direct way between two points. A path usually does not climb bluffs in a straight line or cross deep depressions; it will avoid obstacles or repeatedly change its trajectory to minimize the difficulty of the terrain. A road, on the other hand, is a prepared zone of the landscape which may be more direct than a path because construction can overcome or minimize discontinuities on the land surface. To be considered a road, the feature had to show labor investment in the form of construction. In basic terms, a road is planned and built while a path is the result of wear.

Cursory analysis of the aerial photographs of the region demonstrated that a management plan for approaching the great number of roads in the Moche Valley area was required. So the study area was divided into twelve zones, based on geographical divisions, such as ravines, plains and intervalley areas (Fig. 8.2). Each zone was treated as a distinct unit for the fieldwork

Fig. 8.1. Map of Peru showing the location of the Moche valley.

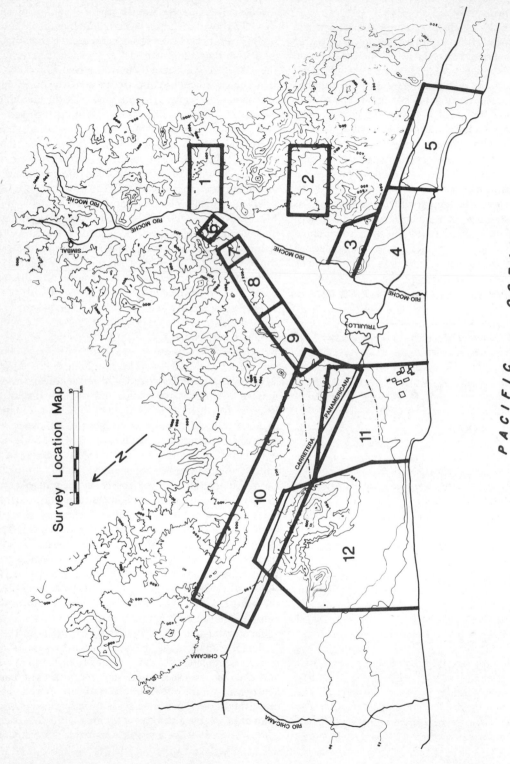

Fig. 8.2. Map of the survey zones.

phase of research and the following methodology was applied to each survey unit successively.

The initial stage of research consisted of analyzing the aerial photographs of the zone to locate archaeological features. Fortunately, two sets of aerial photographs (1942 and 1969) were available from the Peruvian Military. The 1942 flight provided much data on recently destroyed archaeological features. Many of the ancient roads are so distinct that current maps of Peru based on the air photos frequently show ancient roads as modern unpaved roads. Nevertheless, by air photo analysis alone it was possible to distinguish many unpaved modern roads from ancient roads. For example, often the modern roads cross dry riverbeds, whereas the ancient roads have been washed away by flooding and not repaired. Terrain was also a critical consideration. Modern wheeled vehicles cannot travel on extremely sandy surfaces, ascend steep gradients in a direct line or cross passes that are narrower than the vehicles themselves. Roads which were observed in these situations were marked as probably ancient. During this analysis the location of ancient structures, habitation sites, canals and walls was noted, since the repeated association of a road with archaeological remains is a strong indication of antiquity, and the relations between these remains and the roads would have to be understood.

Then a reconnaissance survey of the zone was conducted. Even if roads were not apparent on the photos, the entire area was surveyed. The survey was made on foot except in the intervalley areas where the distances were so great that walking the entire distance on each road was impossible. When a vehicle was needed, it was necessary to stop at frequent intervals to survey on foot and to record the roads and the associated archaeological features and sites.

During the road survey, extreme attention was paid to the natural configuration of the land. The man-made nature of road features is obvious to the observer if this person is aware of the variety of forms that a road may assume and how to recognize them. Any alteration of the landscape was carefully checked to determine if it reflected road construction.

Causeways and roadcuts are the most easily discerned indications of a road course because they can be seen for some distance and create a marked alteration of the natural configuration of the land. Road courses that were on sand often were lower than the surrounding terrain. This wear pattern is called troughing. The depressed surface is the result of grading and/or use. The Peruvian coast is constantly battered by winds. When a person or animal walks on dry sand they loosen it and frequently kick up the sand. The wind blows the lighter particles away and the heavier particles are redeposited on the surface. Eventually the surface of the road is demonstrably lower than the surrounding terrain. On the consolidated soil in the region, usually desert pavement, the wear patterns were different. There was a lightening of the road surface by wear, but more significant is the change in the landscape produced by clearing stones from the roadbed, similar to the method used to construct the Nazca lines. These roads were easily seen by their outlines.

After the completion of the reconnaissance survey, the third stage of research was instituted. This consisted of recording the roads and associated archaeological remains. The compass orientation and width of a road were checked repeatedly to determine changes in a road's trajectory and width. Notes were taken on the various construction features of a road, such as slope, size of roadcuts, ramps, walls, and curbs. The associated archaeological remains were mapped and described in detail.

After the fieldwork was completed, it was necessary to analyze the roads in each zone to determine, if possible, their age and/or relative construction sequence. Interpretation of the roads in relation to prehistoric and historic cultures and events hinged on the ability to date these features. A method which concentrated on the analysis of cross-cutting relationships was applied to the roads and produced good results. The basics of cross-cutting relationships and their application to roads and this project are presented below.

Cross-cutting relationships

In the latter part of the eighteenth century, James Hutton, the geologist who developed useful lithologic tools, clearly stated a principle that is usually referred to as the law of cross-cutting relationships (Mintz 1972:6–7). He stated that any body of rocks that cuts across the boundaries of other units of rocks must be younger than those it cuts. Hutton looked at the law of superposition and its statement that any layer of rocks overlying another layer is younger than the stratum beneath it. He then made the logical corollary of the law of superposition by explaining that any rocks which cut through existing strata must be younger than the material they cut through.

Archaeologists have used superposition as a basic interpretative tool in their work for years. But in some cases, they have applied the law only on a limited scale or ignored its utility. Everyone is familiar with cases where a pit is found to be intrusive into a midden, showing that the pit is younger than the midden; or one house wall foundation is discovered to cut through another foundation, demonstrating that the foundation that is cut through is the older of the two. When the law of cross-cutting relationships is applied to long linear archaeological features, such as roads, canals and long boundary walls, the actual implementation of the analysis is very complex and time consuming and requires that each case of a cross-cutting relationship be studied very carefully.

Roads can be conceptualized as man-made alterations of the landscape which can be relatively dated by the cross-cutting relationships with other archaeological features and geological events or features. Instead of layers of dirt overlying one another, these features overlap and cut one another as they cross the landscape. Taking Hutton's law of cross-cutting relationships and applying it to linear features required setting up a series of statements concerning the information available from each of the junctions of the features.

The basic rule is that each junction of two features establishes one as being older than the other, or the contemporaneity of the features. This does not provide absolute dates for the features but the relative dates of their construction. The reason roads are so useful for the application of cross-cutting relationships is because they cross great distances and the longer roads are, the greater the possibility of observing multiple junctions, creating greater opportunity for placing these features into a refined chronological framework. The critical aspect of working with these relationships is that the entire road must be surveyed to determine all junctions to obtain the maximum amount of information they provide about the time of construction and use. Besides the road itself, every feature which comes into contact with the road must be completely surveyed to understand its exact chronological placement. This approach has the potential to result in an archaeologist surveying every archaeological site in a given area. Beyond the time invested in the fieldwork, it may take days to organize and interpret the results of junction after junction and how they relate to each other. The hypothetical example presented below will show the amount of cultural data that can be retrieved by carefully monitoring all of the interrelationships.

Road A is crossed by Canal B. Canal B could have been constructed before or after the road or be contemporary with the road since canals can be crossed easily by small bridges and there is no evidence for one of these features preceding the other. A junction such as this does not provide chronological information. However, further along Road A, there is a solid wall (Wall C) crossing the road. Since the wall crosses and cuts off the road, the wall must have been constructed after the road. The next question is what is the relationship between the wall and the canal. By surveying along the wall, it is discovered that the canal cuts through the wall. Therefore, the construction sequence is road, wall and then canal. This information demonstrates that people were interested in using the area as a transportation route, so the road was constructed. Then a decision was made that the road should not be used past the wall and a wall was built across the road. Subsequently it was decided that the people needed to bring water through or to the area. So a canal was built which cut through the wall and road in order to achieve its purpose. Although the wall negated the utility of using the road past the wall in either direction, the canal cut would not necessarily negate the possible functions of the wall.

Utilizing this method the sequence of events is apparent, but when they occurred is unknown. There is no way to know whether or not the road, canal, and wall were constructed during the same year or over a thousand years. However, by utilizing additional data, it is often possible to refine the chronology and discuss construction events in terms of the cultures who built and used the roads.

In addition to analyzing the junctions of archaeological and geological features, direct evidence for age used in this road project consisted of analyzing the ceramics on the road courses and the road-associated sites. Surface ceramics were not collected but were studied in the field. Care was taken to determine whether the ceramics reflected disturbance of nearby sites during construction of the roads; if they were isolated occurrences and could indicate someone going cross-country; existed before the road was constructed; or were due to disturbance of nearby archaeological sites. The ceramic styles were considered important if they repeatedly occurred on the road courses and were not due to other causes. To ascertain the reason for the ceramics, the area outside the road course had to be surveyed for sherd scatters. In almost every case the sherds were confined to the road courses and a zone a meter or so wide adjacent to the roads where they had been thrown from the road itself.

Most of the archaeological sites in the Moche Valley are associated with roads. The wealth of archaeological information on the sites and the region aided the research by providing strong chronological control over the archaeological remains. Sites were considered road-associated when the site had direct access to the road, for example if the road ran through the site or to the site, or the site was alongside the road with a side of the road open for entry.

Every survey unit was studied in the manner just described. These units, like archaeological excavation pits, provided a relative sequence for each particular zone. In the same manner that the relations between different pits on an archaeological site can be determined after an analysis of the stratigraphy of each pit, the relations between the geographical zones were determined after the analysis of all of the units. This approach provided synchronic and diachronic data for the entire study area.

Analysis of one road network

The analysis of one survey zone in the Moche Valley is presented below as an example of actual data that can be recovered using cross-cutting relationships. The area was chosen because of the small number of roads and the great time span that they represent.

East of Cerro Campana

There are two routes between the Moche and Chicama valleys that do not cross rugged, mountainous terrain. One of the routes is east of Cerro Campana where the Pan-American Highway runs today, and the other route is west of Cerro Campana between the mountains and the ocean. The eastern route is the inland route and is the focus of this discussion. It is bordered on the west by Cerro Campana and on the east by the foothills of the Andes (Fig. 8.2, Zone 10). The land is crossed by a large dry riverbed which washes between two hills and then turns west and runs down to the ocean. Several other smaller, dry drainages cross the zone from east to west and eventually drop into the dry riverbed. Most of the land is covered by stabilized sand, cactus and zapote bushes. Stones and cobbles are common in the drainages and are present in small quantities in other areas. Near the hills the terrain is more rugged and uneven, leveling out near the course of the Pan-American Highway.

There are several major archaeological features in the eastern intervalley area (Fig. 8.3). The two dominant prehistoric constructions are the La Cumbre Canal and the La Cumbre Wall. The La Cumbre Canal was built by the Chimu to bring water from the Chicama river to the Moche Valley, where the canal joined the western extension of the Moche Valley canal system (Kus 1972). The La Cumbre Wall is a stone-faced, rubble-filled wall which has a height and width of over 2 m and, when built, it was a barrier which blocked the travel route east

Fig. 8.3. Map of survey zone 10, the intervalley area east of Cerro Campana.

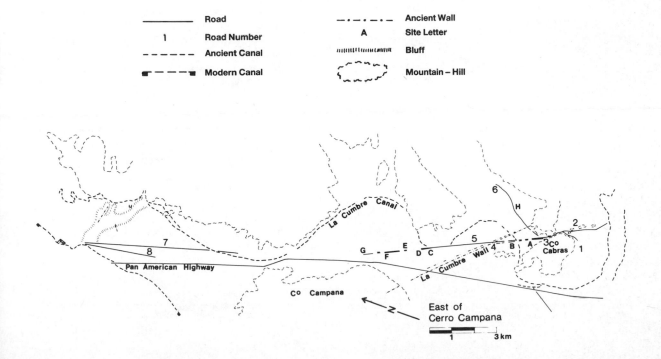

KEY – FIGURES 8.3 and 8.4

———————	Road	— · — · — · —	Ancient Wall
1	Road Number	A	Site Letter
— — — — —	Ancient Canal	⅏⅏⅏⅏⅏⅏⅏	Bluff
■— — — —■	Modern Canal	⌒⌒⌒	Mountain – Hill

of Cerro Campana. The wall begins on the lower northeastern slopes of Cerro Campana and ends in the pass between a small hill and Cerro Cabras. North of the La Cumbre Wall are remnants of an earlier unfinished wall.

There are eight roads in this zone (Fig. 8.3) which range in age from Cupisnique (1400–400 B.C.) into Colonial times. Roads 1 and 2 were the southeastern routes of several road courses (roads 3–6) which ran northwest of the Cerro Cabras pass, the major crossing into or out of the central and upper Moche Valley. Roads 3, 4, and 5 go north to the Chicama Valley. Road 6, however, heads northeast from the Cabras pass up a ravine towards the Andean highlands. Roads 7 and 8 are preserved in the northern half of this survey unit and extend south from the Chicama Valley.

In terms of chronology, the road sequence is complicated. Roads 1 and 2 are not associated with sites. On the sandy and rocky terrain, sherds were scarce and only a few Moche and Chimu sherds were observed on road 2. Road 1 probably never was a major route, but road 2 is critically located. Besides providing access to the central

and upper valley, it would have been the direct route to the large sites in the Early Horizon (Cupisnique), Early Intermediate Period (Gallinazo) and Middle Horizon (Moche V). Given the lack of alternative routes, this road or others built earlier in the same area would have been used for centuries. Today road 2 is preserved to its junction with the prehistoric maximum elevation canal for the valley.

Roads 3, 4, and 5 are parallel with each other and are numbered south to north (Fig. 8.4). These roads extend from the Cabras pass towards the Chicama valley. There are several relationships between these roads and other archaeological features and geological events. Road 3 is the earliest road preserved in the area and only about 1 km of its course survives. The south end of road 3 was damaged by flood water and completely washed away where it crossed a small drainage. Roads 4 and 5, which are upslope from road 3, are preserved across this drainage and these roads must have been built after road 3 was damaged and abandoned. It is interesting to note that the east side of road 5 in this area showed water erosion damage for a meter or so and the side had been

Fig. 8.4. Map of roads, sites, canal, and wall in the southern portion of the survey zone.

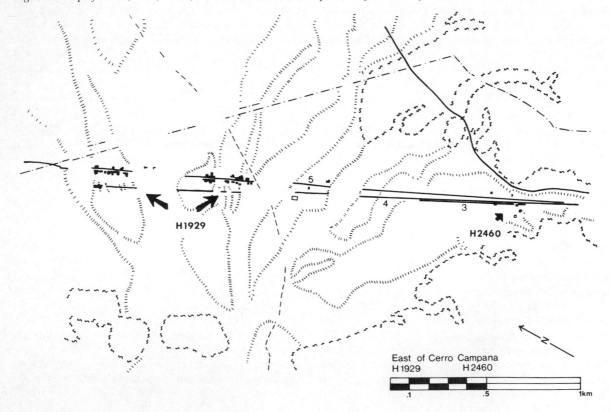

East of Cerro Campana
H1929   H2460

.1   .5   1km

rebuilt and reinforced by a stone facing. So flood damage after road 3's demise was controlled by maintenance.

Roads 4 and 5, although roughly parallel, were not built at the same time. All archaeological and geological evidence shows that road 4 was built before road 5. Near the southern end of road 4 there are at least ten small structures that are associated only with Chimu pottery (Fig. 8.3, Site A; Fig. 8.4, H2460). These structures are east and west of, but not on top of road 5. They are spread across roads 3 and 4, reflecting post-use construction.

About 1 km north of the Chimu sites, a rectangular stone structure is adjacent to road 4 on the south side (Fig. 8.3, Site B; Fig. 8.4, outlined structure south of road 4 at east end of H1929). George Bankes excavated this building and the data showed that the site was built in Cupisnique times and remodeled by Moche people with a Gallinazo occupation between the two events (1971:120). The interpretation of road 4 as being associated with this structure is reasonable, since other Cupisnique roads were found in the Moche Valley. Also, the sides of the roads are curbed or marked by very large boulders. Large boulders repeatedly occur along pre-Moche road courses and are probably a time-diagnostic construction technique. In contrast, road 5 has small stones forming the curb along its sides, a common Moche and Chimu method of marking road boundaries.

Nearby a large site consisting of agglutinated stone structures sits along both sides of road 5 for a distance of 1.2 km (Fig. 8.3, Site B; Fig. 8.4, H1929). Two of these structures were excavated by George Bankes and the major ceramic component was Moche III with a small number of Moche IV and Chimu sherds (Bankes 1971). The excavations demonstrated that this site and road 5 are contemporary, indicating that the road existed and probably was constructued in Moche III times. South of the main site are a few scattered structures, including llama corrals, that occupy the abandoned course of road 4. Some of the structures which are preserved in the northern sector of the Moche site sit in two small drainages that once carried enough water to destroy portions of road 4. The La Cumbre Wall is also preserved in these drainages. Since flood water would have had to flow across the land on which the wall and the Moche site stand, road 5, Site H1929, and the wall were built after the flood which washed away parts of road 4. The question arises as to why portions of the wall and the Moche site were not destroyed in subsequent floods. The drainages east and west of the preserved section of the wall and Moche site are slightly lower drainages, par-

ticularly the one to the west. Therefore, if water did flow down the riverbed, the channels on the higher zones would contain less water and the wall could divert the water into the wider and deeper drainages. Bankes excavated a section of the wall in this area and found mud backed up against the north side, supporting this reconstruction (1971:149).

In addition the ceramic evidence on the roads corroborates the geological and archaeological data. Only Moche and Chimu ceramics occurred on road 5. Roads 3 and 4 had Cupisnique, Gallinazo, Moche and Chimu ceramics. The presence of Moche and Chimu ceramics on roads 3 and 4 relates to the Moche and Chimu activity in the area. The absence of Cupisnique and Gallinazo ceramics on road 5 supports the road's date of construction in Moche times.

The relationships between the roads, the La Cumbre Canal and the La Cumbre Wall are also important. The La Cumbre Canal cuts across roads 4 and 5. Also, this canal cut through the edge of a Moche IV cemetery in the Chicama Valley, giving the canal a post-Moche IV date. Research by the Programa Riego Antiguo and Jim Kus dated this canal as a Chimu construction. The La Cumbre Wall, however, is difficult to date. Richard Keatinge excavated a small section of the wall and found a Moche IV sherd in the fill, indicating the wall is Moche IV or later (Bankes 1971:51). At the junction of the road and the wall, the wall is preserved and did cut across the roadbed of road 5, but foot traffic went over the wall repeatedly. Crossing over the wall probably became common in Chimu times. The Chimu site near the Cabras pass and the frequency of Chimu sherds on road 5 show that the Chimu were using this intervalley route frequently. All of the information indicates that road 5 and the Moche site were constructed before the wall, and that the wall is Moche IV or later.

Road 5 continues north of the wall. After 3 km the road and the La Cumbre Canal meet again (Fig. 8.3). The La Cumbre Canal was built on top of and in the bed of road 5 for a distance of 1.5 km. Road 5 was cut to a depth of 4 m through the small hills and it makes sense that the La Cumbre Canal would have utilized the existing route. Owing to the unevenness of the land the canal was aqueducted across depressions and gullies. In some places the road course is less than 1 m wide where the canal intruded upon the roadbed.

A rectangular stone structure with Chimu sherds sits west of the road and the canal (Fig. 8.3, Site C). Just after the separation of the road and the canal, two parallel prehistoric road courses are present. West of the roadbeds is a large, poorly preserved, undated multiroomed structure (Fig. 8.3, Site D). The parallel road-beds are probably the courses of roads 4 and 5, but it was not possible to determine which was road 4 and which was road 5; logic suggests that road 4 runs west of road 5.

The terrain to the north is very sandy and rough but relatively level. Preservation of the roads is sporadic but the parallel roads are preserved over half the distance to Chicama. The base of a small temporary shelter occurs on the east side of the roads almost midway between the two valleys (Fig. 8.3, Site E). At the midpoint, a two-room, rectangular stone structure was located west of the road; it contained Chimu pottery (Fig. 8.3, Site F). A short distance after Site F, only one of the roads could be traced and then the course became difficult to locate because of gravel quarry operations. Four temporary shelters were located on and to the west of the roadbed near the end of its preserved route (Fig. 8.3, Site G).

Roads 7 and 8 are located in the southeastern part of the Chicama Valley. In this area east of the Pan-American Highway sits the site of Quebrada del Oso, a Chimu rural administrative center consisting of a central compound and two attendant structures (Keatinge 1974:72–80). This site is west of the La Cumbre Canal, but the roads are over 1.5 km west of the site. Both roads are washed out in a dry riverbed at their northern end and should have converged as they continued. They head towards a mound that has not been systematically studied, but Moche sherds were on the surface of the site. Road 7 heads south towards the Moche Valley and is preserved south of the La Cumbre Canal. This road has a width of 84 m, but the wear on the road is confined to its eastern side. Road 8 veers more to the west and could have crossed into the Moche Valley along the same route as the Pan-American Highway. Ceramics on road 7 were Moche and Chimu; road 8 had Moche, Chimu, and Colonial wares.

Road 6 was not part of the Moche–Chicama inter-valley route. However, it also utilized the Cabras pass. Curving around the base of the hill north of Cabras, it crossed through the La Cumbre Wall and continued north up a ravine towards the highlands. Along the east side of the road is a three-sided, undated rectangular structure (Fig. 8.3, Site H). Since this road cuts through the La Cumbre Wall, it post-dates the construction of the wall. Chimu ceramics were frequent on the road, but one Moche sherd was found near the wall.

In summary, the eastern intervalley route provided an interior passage between the Moche and Chicama valleys. Roads 1 and 2 are related to the continual use of roads 3, 4, 5, and 6. The travel route on roads 3 and 4 was probably used in Cupisnique times, if not earlier. Road 4 was used by Gallinazo people and road 5 was used and constructed by Moche III people. Road 5 precedes the wall. The wall contained a Moche IV sherd and must have been built in Moche IV times or later. The La Cumbre Canal was constructed after roads 4 and 5, cuts a Moche IV cemetery, utilized the bed of road 5, and dates to Chimu times. The relationship between the wall and the canal cannot be determined because the junction of these two features has been washed away. Road 6 cuts through the wall and is probably Chimu. Road 5 was re-used in Chimu times, as is shown by the large quantity of Chimu sherds on the road and by the Chimu structures near the Cabras pass and along the road course midway to Chicama. The Chimu walked over the wall and they did not cut a hole through it.

Evidence of a flood between Cupisnique and Moche III is shown by the relationship between the La Cumbre Wall, the Moche site, and roads 4 and 5. Also, near the Cabras pass a small section on the east side of road 5 has been washed away. This event occurred after the construction of road 4 and may be related to an early Chimu flood identified by the Programa Riego Antiguo west of this area, at the north end of the Moche Valley. Roads 7 and 8 head towards a huaca that has a Moche component, but road 8 was also used in Colonial times. One of these roads, probably road 7, united with road 5.

This analysis, even as it is summarized here, is tedious and complex, but does contain much cultural information. The roads are direct evidence of where people traveled, when and under what conditions. In the case of Zone 10, the presence of a Cupisnique and a Moche site on the outskirts of the valley along road courses indicates early interest in monitoring and con-troling movement on the roads. The closing of the area by the construction of the La Cumbre Wall in late Moche or Chimu times shows an extreme move to stop the use of the area by travelers. This may have been in reaction to regional political instability or an attempt to channel all traffic by Chan Chan, the Chimu capital. The construction of the La Cumbre Canal and the re-use of the roads by the Chimu reflect great political change and the reinstatement of the area as an impor-tant route to the Chicama Valley. After all fourteen units were studied, it was possible to show the changes in the Moche Valley road networks through time and how the different cultures traveled to or cut themselves off from neighboring sites and geographical regions (Beck 1979:108–40).

Road construction techniques

Besides providing information on the transportation routes of the different cultures, the road survey produced interesting data on road construction techniques in the research zone. The construction of roads in the Moche Valley began as early as the Cupisnique culture, if not slightly earlier. Evidence of an earlier date consists of two undated roads that were cut off from use by a walled Cupisnique road. Therefore these roads must have been built before the walled road, but how much earlier is unknown. Initial Period potsherds were observed along one of these road courses, raising the possibility that road construction in the Moche Valley began in the Initial Period. No matter what the precise date of the first road in the area, road construction and/or use was practiced by all subsequent cultures which lived there and several roads included in the survey were active Colonial transportation routes. The roads cover a time span of at least 2,500 years. Surprisingly, road construction techniques were very similar for so many years and cultures.

Road types

Roads in the Moche Valley area take a variety of forms. The roads have one or several of the following five attributes or road elements.

1. Cleared. The surface of the road is systematically clearly of all stones or other debris, producing a strikingly uniform, clear strip of land for road transportation (Fig. 8.5).
2. Graded. The surface of the road is purposefully leveled or adjusted to minimize the angle of descents and ascents. Besides evening the land surface, grading included the construction of roadcuts and ramps (Fig. 8.6).
3. Curbed. The border elements which delineate the sides of the road are a line of stones or piles of stones which, in some instances, were built with the debris removed from the surface of the roads (Fig. 8.7).
4. Walled. The sides of the roads are marked by solid walls that range in height from approximately 30 cm to 2 m (Figs. 8.8 and 8.9).
5. Elevated. The road is on top of a man-made surface which is elevated above the natural surface of the land. Roads with this attribute are referred to as causeways (Fig. 8.10).

The common combinations of these attributes which were used to build the roads are: 1. cleared and graded roads; 2. cleared and curbed roads; 3. cleared, graded and curbed roads; 4. cleared, graded and walled roads; and 5. cleared, graded and elevated roads. Besides a road possessing several of these attributes, roads frequently change their appearance depending on the terrain. For example, one road was cleared, and graded for several kilometers; then it was cleared, graded, and walled for about one kilometer; then it changed to cleared, graded, and lined; and finally it was graded and elevated. There were no paved roads in the survey area. Whatever the road construction technique, law or custom would have required the traveler to remain within the roads' boundaries whether they be only cleared surfaces, curbs or walls.

The different attributes of the roads usually reflect different environments. All of the roadbeds had surfaces that were cleared of debris, such as rocks, to form a smooth walking surface. It varied whether or not broken pots and other cultural remains were systematically cleared off the roads and tossed along their sides. Grading was unnecessary where roads crossed uninterrupted, level terrain. However, minimizing descents and ascents seemed a constant engineering goal and grading varied from slightly leveling a roadbed to digging massive roadcuts through small hills, involving the removal of hundreds of cubic meters of dirt. If the cuts were adjacent to depressions or bluffs, the dirt was used to level the roadbed or to construct ramps which were sometimes stone-faced. Otherwise the dirt was thrown off to the side of the road, particularly on top of the roadcuts.

Cleared and graded roads occur in all situations but are most common on sand in relatively rock-free areas. Cleared and graded roads with side curbs are most frequent on hillsides or desert pavement and in or near the dry stream channels where the stones were readily available. If a road had to be cleared of rocks, piling the debris to make the curbs only required an organized rather than haphazard method of disposal. Occasionally stone curbs occur in an area where rocks are scarce, reflecting more labor investment than stone-curbed roads near rock sources.

Only five walled roads were recorded in the survey. The labor investment in a wall is great and entails considerable time and construction materials. Walls force people to enter and exit at very specific points. Some of the walled roads occur across irrigated fields, protecting the fields from people and animals, notably llama caravans. On one road, culverts were built at the base of the wall to permit the flow of water under the walls and across the roads. There are also situations where roads near canals are not walled and roads outside the irri-

Fig. 8.5. Road with cleared surface. Width: 6.25 m.

Fig. 8.6. Road with graded surface. Width: 17.1 m.

Fig. 8.7. Road with curbs. Width: 34.2 m.

Fig. 8.8. Road with low walls. Width: 9 m.

Fig. 8.9. Road with high walls. Width: 20.7 m.

Figure 8.10 Causeway. Width: 6.6 m.

gated zones are walled, providing physical barriers and control for other purposes.

Causeways were built of adobe and, sometimes, stones were used as fill and as a facing on the sides of the causeway. Causeways occurred in the irrigated areas and near the ocean.

The variations in the width of the roads, both on the same road and between roads, are surprising. Many roads maintained a precise width which never changed for their entire course while others varied 1 to 2 m in width; in the most extreme case, a variation of 58 m was recorded. Although uniform width on each road course appeared to be a goal, changes in width reflected variation in the terrain or the road passing by or through other archaeological remains, such as sites, walls, and irrigation fields. In general, most roads ranged between 6 and 12 m in width; however, widths between 18 and 63 m were not uncommon. The smallest width recorded on a road was 30 cm and was due to the terrain. It remained this narrow for only a short distance. The widest road was a Chicama–Moche intervalley road (road 7 in the example presented previously) that is over 6 km long and is 84 m wide. In terms of length, the shortest preserved road course was 30 m and the longest was 12.3 km.

The approaches to road technology by the several cultures who successively occupied the area varied little. Cleared and graded roads with stone curbs occurred in all cultures and road widths varied within all cultures. The only construction feature which may indicate age is the use of large boulders as curbs. This technique was confined to pre-Moche cultures. However, these people also used small stones to form curbs on some roads.

Roads with walls were built only by the Cupisnique and Chimu cultures. On the one Cupisnique walled road, the walls were stone-faced with rubble hearting. Of the four Chimu walled roads, three were stone-faced with rubble hearting and one had adobe hearting that was stone-faced and plastered. Obviously walls ensure that travelers will not leave a road course. Walls were used on two roads crossing irrigation fields. But the other roads were walled for other control purposes. It is interesting that in the 1,500 to 2,000 years that separate the Cupisnique and Chimu cultures, no other walled roads were built in the valley.

Causeways were found near the Chimu capital of Chan Chan in areas that were under cultivation. The elevation of the roads protected the roadbed from irrigation water and also made people very visible as they approached Chan Chan. Some of these causeways are still used today as roads for wheeled vehicles. Causeways

that were built or used by earlier cultures were not located by the survey.

Road engineering

Evidence for road engineering was scarce but present. In many cases, the proposed road course was marked by lines of stones, probably under the direction of road engineers. Then the roadbed was cut, leveled and curbed or walled. Archaeological data for this method of construction do exist. In some parts of the valley small sections of stone lines appear on the tops of roadcuts and at sporadic points along roads. More than likely these lines are remnants of the construction procedure and guided the road construction crews. One late Chimu-Inka road in the valley was abandoned when it was under construction. Lines of stones had been laid out for several kilometers over uneven terrain and up and down steep bluffs. But the road course was not cleared or graded and never used. Work ceased before the roadbed was made passable. In some cases, stone curbs along the sides of roads may be the remnants of construction activities. The road courses were built as straight as possible. When it was necessary to change direction distinct angles were made in the road course. However, roads did make curves when demanded by the terrain and obstacles.

Other construction information includes one road segment that was built for 200 m and abandoned; the road was then constructed several meters to the west. The situation suggests that a construction error was made and the road was built off course. Road 3 in the chronology examples presented previously may be another case of an engineering or labor crew making an error, as no other portions of the road could be found except for the one segment noted on the map. The misplacement of a road segment may indicate that several segments of a road were being built at the same time and one section was mislaid.

It is evident that road construction was an organized, coordinated effort which involved engineers determining the road course and construction crews building it. This procedure is documented ethnohistorically. Cieza de Leon stated that the king would send people to lay out the route of the road and then the local Indians would construct it. He says that part or all of the road could be built within a very short period of time or simultaneously (1967:137). Maintenance is shown by the excellent condition of many of the roads, but the system of maintenance is difficult to reconstruct archaeologically. Presumably, there was a system similar to the Inka methods where people, as part of their labor tax, kept the roads repaired and in good condition. The roads in the Moche Valley reflect a successful road building system which provided formalized travel routes for the areas' inhabitants for hundreds and hundreds of years.

Conclusions

The application of cross-cutting relationships combined with the analysis of time diagnostic artifacts and associated sites is a useful method for obtaining temporal control over road systems. Regions where extensive archaeological work has already been completed are ideal for this type of research. Strong chronological control of roads prevents many errors in interpretation. In the Moche Valley, if the types of roads existing at each culture's major site had been used as the only gauge for dating road types, the results would have been completely different and incorrect. For example, the Chimu roads at Chan Chan are all walled or elevated. However, in other parts of the valley, the Chimu built many roads with stone curbs.

The number of roads in the Moche Valley provided a unique opportunity to study roads in different contexts, but the abundance of roads seems uninterpretable to many. Yet, the roads do exist and modern views on roads should not be confused with prehistoric attitudes. It is important to remember that road construction in the area reflects over two thousand years of cultural events. Attempts to analyze and interpret road systems cannot concentrate only on the road courses themselves and produce meaningful results. The studies need to be integrated into research focusing on the region and include all associated sites and archaeological features. As a result, in many cases, road surveys are the most complete, integrative type of archaeological survey that can be conducted. Roads were built as part of functioning cultures and their analysis must relate to and reflect these cultural systems.

Acknowledgments

The author thanks the Instituto Nacional de Cultura in Peru for its assistance, and the Tinker Foundation and Lowie Museum of Anthropology for their financial support.

References

Bankes, George Henry Andrew
    1971 Some Aspects of the Moche Culture. Ph.D. dissertation, Institute of Archaeology, London
Beck, Colleen M.
    1979 Ancient Roads on the North Coast of Peru. Ph.D. dissertation, University of California at Berkeley. University Microfilms International, Ann Arbor

Cieza de Leon, Pedro de
    1967 *El Señorio de los Incas (Segunda parte de la Crónica del Perú) 1553.* Instituto de Estudios Peruanos, Lima
Ford, James Alfred
    1949 *Cultural Dating of Prehistoric Sites in the Viru Valley, Peru.* Anthropological Papers of the American Museum of Natural History 43, 1949–54, part 1, no. 2
Keatinge, Richard W.
    1974 Chimu Rural Adminstration Centers in the Moche Valley, Peru. *World Archaeology* 6(1):66–82
Kosok, Paul
    1965 *Life, Land and Water in Ancient Peru.* Long Island University Press, New York
Kus, James S.
    1972 Selected Aspects of Irrigated Agricultures in the Chimu Heartlands, Peru. Ph.D. dissertation, University of California at Los Angeles. University Microfilms International, Ann Arbor
Lumbreras, Luis Guillermo
    1974 *The Peoples and Cultures of Ancient Peru.* Translated by Betty J. Meggers. Smithsonian Institution Press, Washington, DC
Mintz, Leigh W.
    1972 *Historical Geology: The Science of a Dynamic Earth.* Charles E. Merrill Publishing Company, Columbus, OH
Oficina Nacional de Evaluación de Recursos Naturales (O.N.E.R.N.)
    1973 *Inventario, evaluación y uso racional de los recursos naturales de la costa; cuenca del Río Moche,* vol. I. O.N.E.R.N. Lima
Proulx, Donald Allen
    1973 *Archaeological Investigations in the Nepena Valley, Peru.* Research Report 13, Department of Anthropology, University of Massachusetts, Amherst
Regal, Alberto
    1936 *Los caminos del Inca en el antiguo Perú.* Sanmarti, Lima
Savoy, Gene
    1970 *Antisuyo; The Search for the Lost Cities of the Amazon.* Simon and Schuster, New York
Stothert-Stockman, Karen
    1967 *Pre-Colonial Highways of Bolivia. Part I: The La Paz–Yungas Route via Palca.* Academia Nacional de Ciencias de Bolivia 17, La Paz, Bolivia
Strube Erdmann, Leon
    1963 *Vialidad imperial de los Incas.* Instituto de Estudios Americanistas 33, Universidad Nacional de Córdoba, Córdoba

Ubbeloehde-Doering, Heinrich
  1966 *On the Royal Highways of the Inca.* Platt Publishing, Chur, Switzerland
von Hagen, Victor Wolfgang
  1975 *Highway of the Sun: A Search for the Royal Roads of the Incas.* First edition 1955. Platt Publishing, Chur, Switzerland
Willey, Gordon Randolph
  1953 *Prehistoric Settlement Patterns in the Viru Valley, Peru.* Smithsonian Institution, Bureau of American Ethnology, Bulletin 155, Washington, DC

9 Network analysis and the study of past regional organization

LARRY J. GORENFLO
and THOMAS L. BELL

Some introductory considerations: the importance of "spaces"

Despite an active interest in regional archaeology dating back to the 1930s (e.g., Strong 1935; Braidwood 1937), the analysis of regional archaeological data remains largely in its infancy. Of the several possible reasons for this lack of analytical development, perhaps the most likely concern the nature of the problems encountered. One major consideration is the types of sociocultural systems which archaeologists examine, systems which often do not lend themselves to analysis with models devised to study modern settings (Lewarch 1979; Evans and Gould 1982). Studying such systems generates a need to develop analytical tools more appropriate for the research settings of interest (Steponaitis 1978, 1981; Bell *et al.* 1988). Ultimately, however, the main source of difficulty in the regional study of archaeological data may well lie at the very foundation of this research – in the need to examine *space*, and how sociocultural systems use space.

Attracting little explicit attention in the human sciences outside of geography, the study of space can be extremely demanding. In the study of human behavior one may define several different types of space based upon different measures of *distance* (Watson 1955; Gatrell 1983; Gorenflo and Gale 1990). Bunge stresses this complexity in his distinction between the "raw" geographic distance which can be measured on a standard map, and the "real" distances such as travel time and cost which often represent the separation between places more accurately (Bunge 1966:52–60, 179–87; see also Gould 1985:200–7, 239–52). At an even more fundamental level, a distinction can be made between *continuous* and *discrete* space. Continuous space enables human movement from a given location in any direction to another location; this allows a straight-line connection between each pair of places in a particular area of interest (Fig. 9.1a). Discrete space, on the other hand, constrains movement to certain links or connections (Fig. 9.1b). For the majority of regional settings the most realistic perspective is the latter, where travel between places occurs along the system of roads and paths connecting them.

The primary importance of discrete space lies in how it influences patterns of human movement. This is particularly important in complex societies, where information and energy constantly flow among fixed settlements (Flannery 1972; Wright 1977, 1978). A more thorough understanding of the networks underlying such flows thus should provide additional insights to the nature of regional organization. One possible means of gaining such understanding is through examining the configuration of a transportation network itself. Another is through examining aspects of location where settlement interaction is based upon a network. A third approach involves the simulation of network configurations, to see how closely networks based upon carefully controled principles compare to empirically documented configurations. We discuss each of these broad approaches below, first in more abstract terms to provide brief, largely non-technical introductions, and then through a summary of select applications.

Methodological perspectives

Direct studies of network structure: graph theory
We begin our methodological discussion by focusing upon the study of networks themselves. Such examinations are usually conducted by representing a transportation network as a *graph*, and studying certain facets of its organization using *graph theory*. Graph theory forms part of a branch of mathematics called combinatorial topology. Introduced to regional science more

than three decades ago (Garrison 1960), it provides a means of assessing fundamental characteristics of network structure. Here we focus in particular upon the representation of a network as a graph, and upon evaluating particular aspects of its configuration. Numerous excellent introductions are available to supplement this brief overview, both on graph theory itself (Bondy and Murty 1976; Harary 1969) and on network analysis through the use of graph theoretic techniques (Haggett and Chorley 1969; Tinkler 1977; see also Tinkler 1979).

For present purposes a graph can be considered a diagram composed of separate points (usually called *vertices* or *nodes*) and various connections (*arcs* or *edges*) between them. In network analysis, graph theoretic conventions provide a formal means of representing a system of transportation connections. One means of conveying this information is through a schematic diagram (Fig. 9.2). Notice in this figure that the primary type of information contained in the graph is the *connectivity* between places; other information, such as the shape or length of the arcs, is not preserved. Another means of conveying the information contained in a graph is through the use of a table (Table 9.1). Such tables usually are called connectivity or adjacency matrices; they are constructed by placing a "1" in the cell corresponding to a vertex pair that is connected by a link, and a "0" elsewhere. This tabular representation contains essentially the same information as the diagram in Fig. 9.2. This correspondence is important, for it enables one to represent a graph in matrix form on a computer, and facilitates the examination of graphs with linear algebra.

Fig. 9.1. Potential movement between places in continuous (a) and discrete (b) space.

Table 9.1 *Connectivity matrix for the graph in Fig. 9.2b*

| | Nodes | | | | | | | | | | | | | |
	A	B	C	D	E	F	G	H	I	J	K	L	M	N
A	0	1	0	0	0	0	0	0	0	0	0	0	0	0
B	1	0	1	0	0	0	0	0	1	0	0	0	0	0
C	0	1	0	1	0	0	0	0	0	0	0	0	0	0
D	0	0	1	0	1	0	0	0	0	0	0	0	0	0
E	0	0	0	1	0	1	1	0	0	0	0	0	0	0
F	0	0	0	0	1	0	0	0	0	0	0	0	0	0
G	0	0	0	0	1	0	0	1	1	0	0	0	0	0
H	0	0	0	0	0	0	1	0	0	0	0	0	0	0
I	0	1	0	0	0	0	1	0	0	1	0	0	0	0
J	0	0	0	0	0	0	0	0	1	0	1	1	0	0
K	0	0	0	0	0	0	0	0	0	1	0	0	0	0
L	0	0	0	0	0	0	0	0	0	1	0	0	1	1
M	0	0	0	0	0	0	0	0	0	0	0	1	0	0
N	0	0	0	0	0	0	0	0	0	0	0	1	0	0

(Nodes)

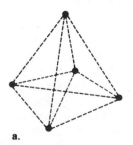

a.

b.

The graphs of present interest are *ordinary graphs*. Such graphs are defined by the following characteristics: they contain a finite number of nodes; each arc comprises a set of two nodes; each arc connects two different nodes; no more than one arc may join a particular pair of nodes; and no distinction is made for directionality, so that each arc allows two-way movement (Garrison 1960:127). Moreover, ordinary graphs are *planar*, defined by the presence of a vertex each time edges intersect. Certain measures of ordinary graphs are useful for the study of regional networks. These usually concern basic questions of *accessibility*, either focusing upon moving to and from a specific node (local accessibility), or upon moving around the network as a whole (global accessibility). A particular place with high local accessibility, for instance, may be desirable as a regional center since settlements administered by that settlement would be relatively accessible to it; a system with high global accessibility, on the other hand, might hinder

strong centralized authority as no single settlement would have an advantage in the interaction with others. In graphs such properties can be assessed with certain measures of connectivity or centrality. We summarize measures of these basic properties below; the format of presentation chosen is for the sake of brevity, and more elaborate treatments can be found in Kansky (1963), Lowe and Moryadas (1975:78–97), and Tinkler (1977). Variable definitions are consistent for all measures discussed.

1. *Nodality* (also called "degree," "local degree," and "valency"): A means of assessing the importance of a particular node by determining the number of arcs connected to it. For all individual nodes in a graph, nodality may be calculated via

$$\mathbf{r} = \mathbf{CI},$$

where $\mathbf{C}$ is the connectivity matrix for the graph, $\mathbf{r}$ is the degree vector of the graph, the ith entry representing the nodality of the ith node in matrix $\mathbf{C}$, and

    $\mathbf{I}$ is a column vector of 1's.

2. *König index*: A measure of the centrality of a particular node in terms of the *greatest* number of arcs which must be traversed from that node to any other in the network. The largest König index for a particular graph is called the *diameter* of the graph. The König index for a node i is defined as

$$K_i = \max a_{ij}$$

where a_{ij} is the number of arcs connecting nodes i and j, along the shortest path (fewest arcs) between them.

3. *Accessibility index*: A measure of how easily a particular node may be reached from any place in the network. For a node i, the accessibility index is calculated as

$$A_i = \sum_j a_{ij}.$$

4. *Multistep accessibility*: A measure of accessibility in terms of how many ways a node may be reached from another using a particular number of connecting edges. Multistep accessibility is calculated for all pairs of nodes in a graph through the use of *powered connectivity matrices* – that is, raising the original connectivity matrix to the power which represents the number of connecting edges one is interested in. For example, a powered connectivity matrix $\mathbf{C}^2$ would be calculated by multiplying $\mathbf{C} \times \mathbf{C}$; each entry c_{ij}^2 would represent the number of 2-edge paths linking nodes i and j.

Fig. 9.2. An example network (a) and its graph (b).

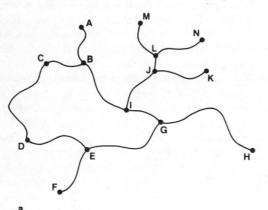

a.

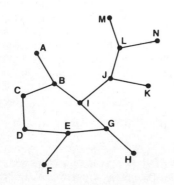

b.

5. *Mean nodality*: A global extension of simple nodality which provides a measure of accessibility for an entire graph in terms of average connectivity. Mean nodality is calculated as

$$\bar{r} = \sum_i r_i/n,$$

where r_i is the nodality of the ith vertex in the graph, and
n is the total number of nodes in the graph.

6. *Beta index*: A measure of global graph structure which represents the average number of edges available per node. The beta index is defined as

$$\beta = e/n,$$

where e is the total number of edges in the graph.

Beta index values fall within a range, from a minimum of 0.0 for disconnected graphs to a maximum of $(n - 1)/2$ for completely connected graps. An extension of this index, accounting for the problem of edges crossing regional boundaries (leaving the area of study), may be defined as

$$\beta' = e/(n + e_b),$$

where e_b is the number of edges crossing the boundary of interest.

7. *Gamma index*:   A measure of global connectivity which is based upon the ratio between the actual number of edges in a graph and the number of edges possible. The gamma index is calculated via

$$\gamma = e/[3\,(n - 2)].$$

Once again, values for this measure occur within a range – from 0.0 for completely disconnected graphs to 1.0 for completely connected graphs.

8. *Cyclomatic number*: A measure of global connectivity which focuses upon the number of independent *cycles* present in a graph. A cycle is a path beginning and ending at the same node, defined on at least three nodes. The cyclomatic number calculates the number of independent cycles which contain no smaller cycles within them, as

$$\mu = e - n + g,$$

where g is the number of separate components of the graph (that is, portions of a graph completely disconnected from one another).

9. *Alpha index*: A refinement of the cyclomatic number which is independent of the number of nodes involved. Based upon a ratio between the numbers of actual and total possible cycles in a graph, the alpha index is calculated as

$$\alpha = (e - n + g)/(2n - 5).$$

10. *Dispersion index* (also called the "Shimbel Index"): A global measure to assess *compactness*, representing the total number of arcs traversed between each pair of nodes, again using shortest connecting paths. The dispersion index is calculated via

$$D = \sum_i \sum_j a_{ij}.$$

As indicated by this brief summary, a variety of graph theoretic measures are available for the study of network configurations. Regional transportation networks usually are complex phenomena, however, and mapping such complexity onto single numbers or indices is not always extremely informative. This general limitation is complicated by the behavior of some of the above indices; for example, mean nodality can fail to distinguish between graphs whose configurations are very different, and the cyclomatic number can encounter similar difficulties by not accounting for graph size (cf. Tinkler 1977). Such shortcomings do not totally undermine the usefulness of graph theoretic measures for the study of network structure. But they do suggest that one employ these measures with care, and in conjunction with other means of interpreting regional organization.

Locational models

The term "locational model" refers to a broad range of different approaches to the study of settlements arranged in space. The locational models of interest in this paper are those generally defined within *operations research* (see Wagner 1975; Hillier and Lieberman 1980). Models from this area of inquiry already have been introduced to archaeology for evaluating the adaptive strategies of hunter-gatherers and simple horticulturalists (Reidhead 1976; Keene 1979, 1981). Such studies are often discussed under the heading of *linear programming* (Reidhead 1979), one of several computational approaches to solving problems of optimal system organization.

Operations research is instrumental in defining and solving a variety of problems with explicit locational emphases, such as the arrangement of facilities in a region to maximize their accessibility. These are most often referred to as *location-allocation* problems (Cooper 1963; Scott 1971). Networks can play two different roles in such research settings: as a possible locational constraint, perhaps requiring that facilities be located on the regional network; and as a means of measuring settlement interaction, to be incorporated into both the problem definition and the solution. There exist a wide variety of location-allocation models and a number of approaches to solving them (ReVelle *et al.* 1970; Törnqvist *et al.* 1971; Rushton *et al.* 1971; Hodgart 1978; Bell and Church 1986).

The two main components of a location-allocation model are an *objective function* and a *constraint set*. The former refers to a mathematical statement of the locational goal of a model. The latter, in turn, refers to the collection of requirements to be met in solving the objective. A main attraction of location-allocation models is the ability to formulate these two major model components to address specific locational questions. As a simple example, consider a region with several settlements, one of which is to function as a center for the storage and redistribution of food in times of shortage. Faced with such a situation, one basic goal might be to determine the best location for this center – with *best* defined unambiguously as minimizing the total redistribution costs incurred in meeting the needs of all settlements in the region. The total redistribution cost when the main site is placed at some location *i* can be defined as

$$\sum_j s_j c d_{ij},$$

where s_j is the amount of redistributed subsistence item required by settlement *j*,

c is the cost (perhaps in terms of energetic expenditure) of transporting one unit of redistributed item one unit of distance and

d_{ij} is the distance between center *i* and settlement *j*.

The above equation is our objective – the value to be *minimized* in selecting and optimal placement for the center. To define this problem further, we require that the objective be solved *subject to* the following constraint set:

$$s_j > 0, \text{ and}$$

$$\sum_j s_j \leq T,$$

where *T* is the total surplus stored at the center, and all other variables are defined as above.

In the present context, both of these constraints serve as clarifying assumptions necessary to define and solve the problem for a general case. The first disallows negative requirements at any settlement in the region: component settlements either will have no subsistence shortages, or will need redistributed food. This removes the possibility that more than one settlement can provide food for other settlements. The second ensures that the total redistribution requirements of the system will not exceed the amount stored at the center. This removes the need to consider how insufficient resources would be allocated, enabling one to focus upon the main locational problem at hand.

One can solve the above problem with or without information on the network used to transport the redistributed good throughout the region. As noted earlier, employing discrete space adds key knowledge to a regional system's operation; here it would be incorporated explicitly into the calculation of d_{ij}, the major *locational* component of the model. Thus considering an underlying network could greatly affect the accuracy of the solution, and ultimately our understanding of how well a particular system functioned. A solution to the model provides the optimal placement of the center for the objective of interest – a result which can be compared to the configuration documented to assess its locational efficiency in terms of the particular variables considered.

The simulation of network configurations

A third approach for the formal examination of past network configurations is *simulation*. In the present context, simulation refers to the imitation of one system by another organized to behave like it (Simon 1981:17). Today the imitating system often is a computer program. Simulation in general is a broad subject, by its very nature context-specific and best viewed as a way of approaching problems rather than a particular collection of methods and techniques. Because of this breadth, it is impossible to provide a conventional introduction to the topic, and probably the best way to acquire an appreciation for network simulation is to examine example studies – as can be found later in this essay.

One topic which deserves brief discussion here is the explanatory power of simulation. In the study of human behavior, the same *form* often can be generated by several different underlying *processes* (Olsson and Gale 1968; Olsson 1969). Many studies of network evolution examine empirical cases, and attempt to induce underlying causes or propose models of network development (e.g., Taaffe *et al.* 1963; Lachene 1965; Burghardt 1969). In such research, where one infers process from form, the distinction between these two concepts clearly has important implications. In the case of simulation studies, this importance persists – only now a researcher in essence begins by *proposing* underlying processes. As a result of the distinction between form and process, even when a simulated network is very similar to an observed configuration there is little ultimate justification for claiming discovery of the evolutionary processes which produced it. The crucial part of any simulation is a focus upon key variables interacting in a specific manner, and it is here that insights emerge (Doran 1970). Causality generally cannot be argued with certainty; but the controled, simulated results can be compared to the empirically observed case, and the performance of the latter interpreted in terms of how it compares with the former.

Example applications to the study of past systems

There have been surprisingly few applications of the above methods to the study of past regional systems. Those attempted have varied widely, both in the problems examined and in the techniques employed. In the following pages, we provide a sampling of previously conducted research on early networks, emphasizing studies of archaeological data as much as possible, but also citing studies of historic networks to provide example applications of certain analytical methods. We selected the cases discussed to highlight the types of insight possible through the use of different approaches to the study of networks and regional organization. In some instances, conclusions drawn from these studies support previous beliefs about the past organization of certain regions, while in others they challenge accepted views.

One of the first attempts to apply graph theory to a past regional network was a connectivity analysis of twelfth- to thirteenth-century medieval Russia (Pitts 1965). This study focused upon thirty-nine major settlements in this region, and the network of waterways linking settlements to one another (Fig. 9.3). The study attempted to assess the importance of various places by calculating the regional centrality of each based upon a graph of their connections (Fig. 9.4). The first measure employed was the multistep accessibility of each settlement in the region. The diameter of the graph was determined to be eight, requiring the calculation of a powered matrix of C^8 to connect the most distant places (Table 9.2). Adding across rows of the matrix provided a measure for the total connectivity of each place. This basic measure ranked Moscow, a settlement traditionally considered by historians as both the most accessible and most important in the region, fifth in terms of gross connectivity (with Kozelsk ranked as the most highly connected; Fig. 9.3). One shortcoming of using powered connectivity matrices in this manner is the possible incorporation of redundant paths between

places, producing misleading results. Thus, a complementary analysis of network centrality also was performed, calculating the shortest paths (in terms of numbers of connections traversed) from each settlement to all others. This measurement of topological distance increased the centrality of Moscow, ranking it second (behind Kolomna; Fig. 9.3), and provided an independent means of demonstrating the regional importance of this major center in medieval Russia. A similar study has been conducted with data on medieval settlement in Serbia, yielding comparable insights on the organization of yet another historically documented region (Carter 1969).

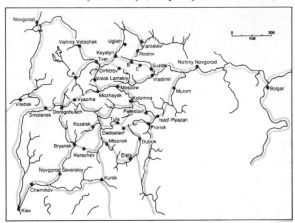

Fig. 9.3. *Major settlements and trade routes in twelfth- to thirteenth-century Muscovy (adapted from Pitts 1965).*

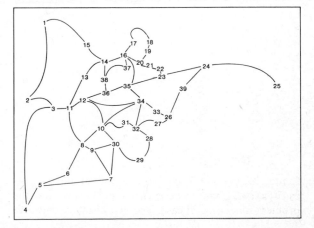

Fig. 9.4. *Graph of waterway connectivities linking thirty-nine settlements in twelfth- to thirteenth-century Muscovy (adapted from Pitts 1965).*

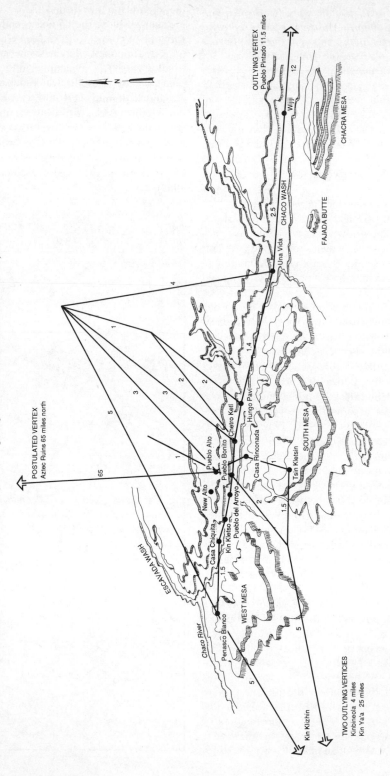

Fig. 9.5. Network of prehistoric roads in Chaco Canyon (adapted from Ebert and Hitchcock 1980).

Table 9.2 *Portion of* $\mathbf{C}^8$ *for thirty-nine settlements in twelfth- to thirteenth-century Muscovy. Values represent the numbers of 8-step paths between settlements, out and back for the same settlement (Pitts 1965:17)*

	Novgorod	Vitebsk	Smolensk	Kiev	Chernikov	
Novgorod	110	15	143	16	71	...
Vitebsk	15	155	21	167	27	...
Smolensk	143	21	580	32	418	...
Kiev	16	167	32	257	84	...
Chernikov	71	27	418	84	513	...
	⋮	⋮	⋮	⋮		

Another application of graph theory for the evaluation of regional organization can be found in a study of prehistoric roads in Chaco Canyon, New Mexico (Ebert and Hitchcock 1980). Through the use of remotely sensed imagery, researchers discovered approximately 200 miles of roads connecting settlements in this region during the peak Pueblo period of occupation. A few missing network sections, absent from the imagery due to sedimentation or erosion, were added to complete likely connections (Fig. 9.5). The resulting configuration then was examined with certain graph theoretic measures, including the β and β indices. The value of the former indicated a region which was poorly connected. These results were interpreted as indicating a *dendritic* regional system – that is, a system which promoted interaction between larger centers, the smaller settlements being incorporated and controled within the hinterlands of these centers. This interpretation suggests a strongly vertical system of administrative and economic control, a view which contrasts with most previous interpretations of the regional system in Pueblo period Chaco Canyon, providing new insights to the prehistory of this area.

The analysis of network configurations need not exclusively employ basic graph theoretic measures. One study which uses an alternative approach considers the main road system in Roman Britain (Dicks 1972; Fig. 9.6). This study employed a method which explores the *combinatorial ordering* of links in a network to rank various roads in terms of importance – with the importance of links often reflecting the regional roles played by

the settlements they connect. As a first step in conducting such a study, the complex, empirically documented network of connections in the system was decomposed into a simplified dendritic network centered upon London (Fig. 9.7). Then links in the system were ranked according to a topological ordering scheme originally developed to analyze drainage systems (Strahler 1952); this enabled the identification of routes of primary importance in the network, routes of secondary importance, and so on. The results of the study supported beliefs developed through historical research on the hierarchy of the Roman period road system. Routes considered important, notably the northern, midland, and western routes, all emerged as the highest-order paths in the network. This route-ordering approach also supported beliefs about the hierarchy of centers in the system – with the highest-order centers tending to be linked to London by higher order connections.

Fig. 9.6. *Major roads in Roman period Britain (adapted from Dicks 1972).*

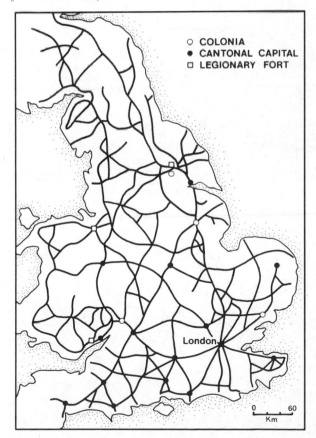

Example applications of locational models with a network basis also are rare in the study of past regional systems. The first such study examined Mississippian period settlement surrounding the regional center of Moundville in Alabama (Steponaitis 1978: Fig. 9.8). Here river connections between sites were considered, in addition to straight-line connections, to account for settlement interaction. The locational model employed was developed to examine tribute extraction in a chiefdom. The Moundville chiefdom was assumed to comprise a three-tiered settlement hierarchy, with minor centers and villages politically subordinate to the main capital of Moundville itself. The *centroid* model developed to locate the regional center optimally can be stated as

$$\text{Minimize } M_c = \sum_j t p_{cj} d_{cj}{}^2 + \sum_i T_i P_i D_i^2$$

where t is a proportional measure of annual, per capita tribute flowing to the capital from the villages in its immediate tribute area,

Fig. 9.7. Simplified dendritic network, centered upon London (adapted from Dicks 1972).

p_{cj} is the population of the jth village in the immediate tribute area of the capital,
d_{cj} is the distance from the jth village in the capital's tribute area to the capital,
T_i is a proportional measure of annual, per capita tribute flowing from the ith minor center to the capital,
P_i is the population of the ith minor center, and
D_i is the distance between the ith minor center and the capital.

The first main term of this model refers to the movement of tribute to the capital from the villages in its immediate hinterland. The second main term refers to tribute moving from all minor centers to the capital. A trade-off thus exists between the locational goals of placing the capital to extract tribute efficiently from the small villages surrounding it, and placing the capital to extract tribute efficiently from the minor centers in the region. In terms of the amount of tribute extracted, the latter almost certainly was pre-eminent; if one assumes this, it is possible to develop a ratio of spatial efficiency, defined as

$$E = \sum_i R_i^2 / \sum_i D_i^2,$$

where R_i is the distance from the ith minor center to the optimal location of the main center, and

Fig. 9.8. Mississippian period settlements in the Moundville region (adapted from Steponaitis 1978).

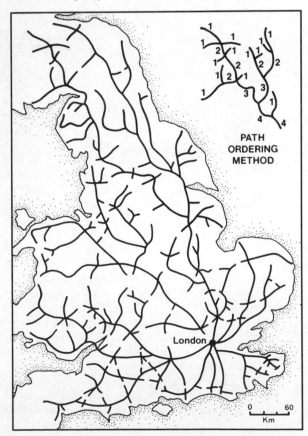

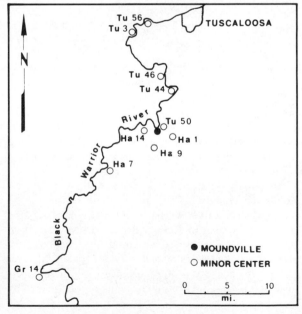

D_i is the distance from the ith minor center to the actual location of the main center.

A value of 1.0 for E suggests optimal location, whereas values less than 1.0 suggest suboptimality. Settlement data for the Moundville region enabled the application of the above model, and the calculation of Moundville's locational efficiency. When straight-line distances between minor centers and Moundville were employed, Moundville itself ranked as the second most efficiently located site in the system, behind site HA-14 (Fig. 9.8). When river distances were used, for those sites where such connections were likely, the location of Moundville ranked as the most efficient in the region.

Another locational model, called a *maximal covering model*, was employed to examine Late Horizon (Aztec) regional efficiency in the northeastern Basin of Mexico (Bell *et al.* 1988; Fig. 9.9). The problem here was to assess the arrangement of provincial centers in this region for the dual purposes of administration (processing information) and the extraction of surplus subsistence (processing energy). Settlement populations were used to indicate differing degrees of administrative demand; the amount of maize each site was capable of producing beyond the needs of its resident population, in turn, was used to indicate surplus energy availability. The actual interaction between settlements was based upon travel time estimates, to reflect in a more functional manner the separation between sites. A network for the region was developed based upon empirical tendencies gleaned from early Colonial period maps of the Basin of Mexico – such as direct connections between large sites, and a general avoidance of extremely abrupt topography. The model formulated for this study of location was defined as

$$\text{Maximize } z = w_1 \sum_{i \in I} \text{pop}_i z_i + w_2 \sum_{i \in I} \text{surp}_i y_i + w_3 \sum_{j \in J} v_j x_j$$

$$\text{subject to } \sum_{j \in N_i} x_j \geq y_i \quad \text{for all } i \in I,$$

$$\sum_{j \in N_i} x_j \geq z_i \quad \text{for all } i \in I,$$

$$\sum_{j \in J} x_j = p,$$

$$x_j = (0,1) \quad \text{for all } j \in J,$$

$$y_i = (0,1) \quad \text{for all } i \in I, \text{ and}$$

$$z_i = (\phi,1) \quad \text{for all } i \in I,$$

where I is the set of demand settlements,

     J is the set of administrative centers,

w_1, w_2, and w_3 are relative weightings for population, subsistence, and settlement type, respectively,

v_j is a measure of importance associated with particular settlement types ranging from 0.0 to 1.0,

$$x_j = \begin{cases} 1 \text{ if a center } j \text{ is located at site } j, \\ 0 \text{ otherwise,} \end{cases}$$

$$y_i = \begin{cases} 1 \text{ if a settlement } i \text{ is covered within } S_2, \\ 0 \text{ otherwise,} \end{cases}$$

$$z_i = \begin{cases} 1 \text{ if a settlement } i \text{ is covered within } S_1, \\ 0 \text{ otherwise,} \end{cases}$$

$$N_i = \{j \in J | d_{ij} \leq S_1\},$$

$$M_i = \{j \in J | d_{ij} \leq S_2\},$$

d_{ij} is the shortest distance (travel time) between settlements i and j,

S_1 is the travel time for administration, beyond which a settlement is "uncovered",

S_2 is the travel time for maize transport, beyond which a settlement is "uncovered",

pop_i is the population to be served at settlement i,

surp_i is the maize surplus available at settlement i, and

p is the number of centers to be located.

The first two weighting factors (w_1 and w_2) in this model determine the relative importance of the first and second terms of the objective, respectively signifying administration and subsistence surplus. The third weighting factor (w_3), in turn, represents the relative importance of selecting certain settlement types; this enables one to force the selection of documented center locations, for the purpose of comparing various configurations of centers generated by the model against the actual arrangement.

For each application of this model, coverage values were calculated as percentages of administrative and surplus subsistence totals. Results suggest that the documented arrangement of centers was suboptimal in all cases. For relatively large service distance values (enabling several centers to serve particular demand sites), the placement of fewer than the documented number of seven centers completely meets regional demands for information processing and energy extraction. For other, shorter service distances, centers can be arranged more efficiently than the documented pattern for the two stated coverage purposes. One possible interpretation of these results is that much of the adaptive pressure on Aztec settlement in the northeastern Basin of Mexico, as is generally assumed for this period of occupation, resulted from an inefficient regional organization where the above key variables were concerned.

Simulations of transportation networks most often deal with the processes underlying particular configurations – usually in historic contexts. One of the first attempts to simulate network evolution dealt with the rail network of early twentieth-century Sicily (Kansky 1963). This study ultimately is based upon a series of axiomatic primitives concerning the roles of complexity, shifting modes of transportation, and regional economic

Fig. 9.9. Late Horizon settlement in the northeastern Basin of Mexico (Bell et al. *1988).*

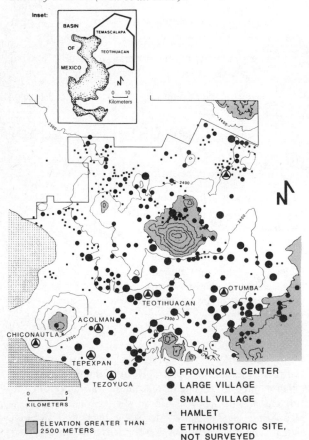

change in the evolution of a network – derived from examining several empirical examples (Kansky 1963:105–21, 125–6). The logical foundation embodied within these axioms, in conjunction with certain graph theoretic properties, was employed to produce the following model of network development:

$$T_s = (f(c_i) = g(\beta, V, N)$$

where T_s signifies transportation network structure,

   c_i is certain "regional characteristics,"

   β is the beta index,

   V is the total number of vertices, and

   N is the mean edge length.

In other words, the structure of a transportation system can be seen as a function of select regional traits (Kansky focused upon technological scale, size, relief, and shape), which in turn can be represented as a function of certain formal characteristics of its graph.

Kansky calculated the actual β, V, and N values from the documented Sicilian rail network, and estimated expected values through regression techniques. He then selected sixteen settlements in Sicily which, based upon population, absolute income, and relative income, should have been included on the 1908 network. Using the calculated values, the two largest of the sixteen settlements were connected; then links were added successively to the network, such that the next largest joined the closest center already on the network, until all settlements were included. Two subsequent adjustments were made. The first employed a "delta-wye" transformation to reduce the number of circuits in the simulated network, replacing ∇-shaped connections between three nodes with the Y-shaped connections more often found in real-world settings (Akers 1960). The second adjustment shifted some links based upon regional topography – again, incorporating real-world considerations. The resulting simulated network strongly resembled the documented network (Fig. 9.10), arguing for the influence of certain environmental characteristics, as well as economic and demographic considerations, on the development of rail transportation in the region.

A study of the nineteenth-century rail network in Maine approached the problem of network simulation in a different manner, generating a system of connections link-by-link from the main coastal city of Portland (Black 1971). The primary aim of this study was to examine the past growth of a network in terms of profit and revenue flow. However, owing to an absence of

Fig. 9.10. Documented (a) and simulated (b) rail networks in early twentieth-century Sicily (adapted from Kansky 1963).

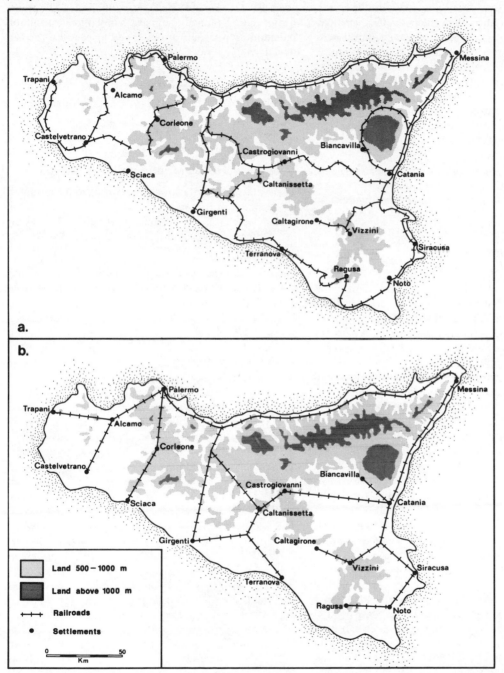

precise data on variables such as the volumes of specific commodities transported between certain towns – information necessary to develop a conventional link-location model – the study had to use surrogate measures of profit and revenue. Three of these surrogates were employed to develop the following model:

$$\Gamma_{ij(t+1)} = .0001\,[P_{j(t)}/d_{ij}] - .013 d_{ij} + .15 a_{hij} + .310,$$

where $\Gamma_{ij(t+1)}$ is a value calculated for each potential new link at time $(t + 1)$, and employed as a discriminant function,

$P_{j(t)}$ is the population of the jth potential node at time (t),

d_{ij} is the distance to the jth potential node, and

a_{hij} is the cosine of the angle formed by adding a new link i–j to the existing link h–i (to avoid backtracking).

In addition to the above model, the simulation employed two further considerations. First, a discriminant analysis using the above formula was performed on the documented regional rail network as it evolved from 1810 to 1910, to distinguish the 200 links built from the 1,185 not built; this produced a threshold value below which a link was not constructed. Second, a budget constraint was incorporated, measured as the number of track miles constructed for the specific period of interest (1840–51). The simulation then proceeded in an iterative manner. In each iteration, the value of Γij was calculated for all possible new links on the planar graph; the link with the highest value was selected, and its length subtracted from the budget. The simulation ended when either the total budget was exceeded or the value of Γ_{ij} fell below the threshold. The resulting network was quite similar to that documented, with 90 percent of the links correctly placed (Fig. 9.11). Such close agreement was cited in arguing for the importance of settlement location and profit in the evolution of this system.

Another simulation of rail network development focused upon Turkey between 1860 and 1964, employing an analytical framework which explored the influence of user location on network configuration (Kolars and Malin 1970). This simulation employed the proposition that transportation routes occur along lines defined by a *population accessibility surface* (Warntz 1966). Its development proceeded as follows. First, a population isopleth map of Turkey was constructed, with each isoline representing 100,000 people within 25 miles. The population peaks then were connected with ridge lines, pro-

viding a graphic summary of the information contained in the initial isopleth map – and in terms of population accessibility those links most desirable (Fig. 9.12). Ridge lines were arranged by calculating the interaction potential between all peaks, using a standard gravity model

$$I_{ij} = P_i P_j \,/\, d_{ij^2},$$

where I_{ij} is the estimated interaction between places i and j,

P_i and P_j are the populations of places i and j, respectively, and

d_{ij} is the distance between places i and j.

Then, starting with the lowest order peak and continuing in ascending order, each peak was connected with the peak to which it had the strongest attraction. The resulting configuration was adjusted via three procedures.

Fig. 9.11. Documented (a) and simulated (b) rail networks in mid-nineteenth-century Maine (adapted from Kolars and Malin 1970).

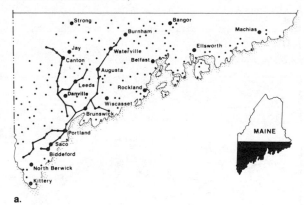

a.

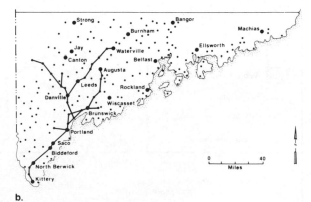

b.

First, redundancies in the form of similar routes connecting peaks in proximity to one another were removed by combining redundant links. Second, dead ends were removed by connecting each to its nearest neighbor peak. Finally, to convert the resulting network to a more realistic form, adjustments were made to reroute certain segments along intervening ridge crests between population peaks, natural passes, and coastal lowlands. The resulting simulated network correctly predicted 67.1 percent of the links empirically documented (Fig. 9.13), suggesting that the system had evolved in large part based on accessibility to the regional population distribution.

An attempt to simulate a prehistoric network again examined the Late Horizon occupation in the northeastern Basin of Mexico (Gorenflo 1989). Here attention focused upon behavioral considerations in the emergence of a network, as well as certain ecological ramifications of network configuration. The main variable dealt with was time, a measure both more sensitive than simple geographic separation for the purpose of representing proximity over the undulating topography of the Basin of Mexico, and documented as important in modern settings for judging separation between places

(Burnett 1978). Travel over land was assumed to be influenced by topographic slope, and walking velocity was estimated for each kilometer with a function developed by Waldo Tobler (personal communication) from data on marching over varying types of terrain:

$$v = 6e^{-3.5|s+.05|},$$

where v is walking velocity in km/hr,

s is the slope (vertical change/horizontal change) of the terrain, and

e is the base of natural logarithms.

Travel over water, in turn, was estimated as one third slower than walking velocity on level ground, based upon ethnohistorically documented evidence for travel by canoe in the central lake system of the basin (Alden 1979:175; see also Hassig 1985:64). As with the estimates for walking velocity, these calculations were made at 1 km intervals – producing a grid of 900 velocity estimates for the 30 × 30 km study area.

An optimal travel time network was simulated from these velocity data through the use of a computer

Fig. 9.12. Interaction ridges for late nineteenth-century Turkey, based on population isopleths (adapted from Kolars and Malin 1970).

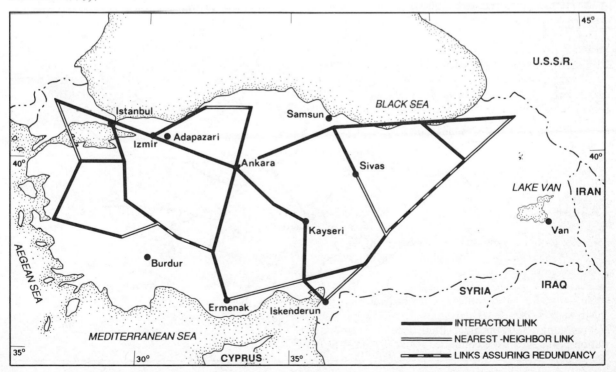

Fig. 9.13. Documented (a) and simulated (b) rail networks for Turkey, 1864–1960 (adapted from Kolars and Malin 1970).

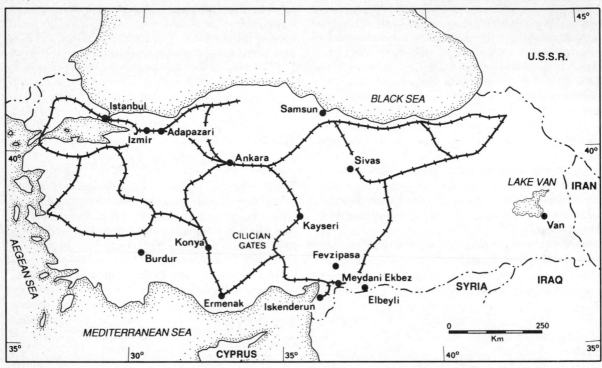

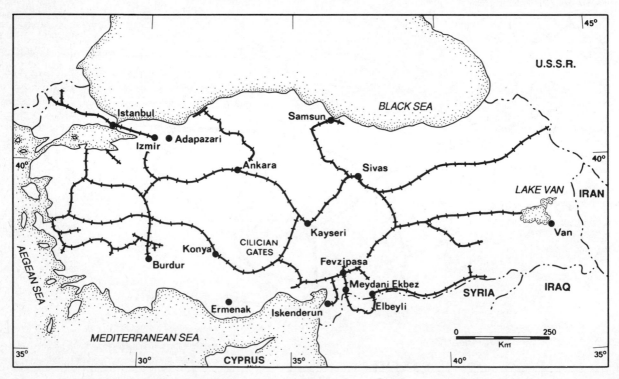

program called MINPATH. Written by Tobler and based upon the well-known shortest path algorithm of Dijkstra (1959), this program calculated and produced optimal travel time paths from the centrally located provincial center at Teotihuacan to the remaining 899 sample points in the region (Fig. 9.14). A detailed map of this region dating to A.D. 1580 (Paso y Troncoso 1905:208) provided some information on the transportation network of interest – with the tendency for most early Colonial roads in the basin to be based upon those of prehispanic times (Gibson 1964:361) arguing for the utility of such information. In the interest of avoiding potential problems with intervening destinations, only nodes with settlements directly connected with Teotihuacan were considered. The configuration resulting was quite similar to this early Colonial network for the same portion of the northeastern basin (Fig. 9.15). Moreover, these travel time efficient paths can be shown to be efficient energetically as well – enabling distance to be covered with relatively little energy expenditure.

Fig. 9.14. MINPATH results from connecting Teotihuacan with 899 other points in the Temascalapa–Teotihuacan region. Destinations comprise those ten Late Horizon settlements directly connected to Teotihuacan.

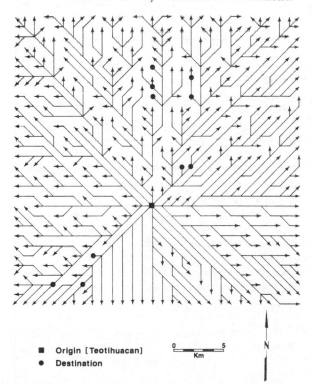

■ Origin [Teotihuacan]
● Destination

0   5
Km

N

Such energetic efficiency would have been an important advantage for this multisettlement system, and the extremely high population levels it supported.

Concluding remarks

This essay was prepared with three purposes in mind. The first was to introduce the concept of networks, both conceptually in terms of their importance to our understanding of regional systems, and in a more formal manner to provide a basis for the analysis of such systems. The second aim of the paper was methodological, designed to introduce select techniques for the analysis of networks and regional systems founded upon networks. The analytical tools chosen, notably graph theory, locational models, and simulation, were selected not because they are the only approaches available, but rather because they provide insights to aspects of regional organization of interest to anthropologists studying the past. Finally, the paper presented examples of previously conducted studies of networks and network-based location problems. All of these examples dealt with regional problems of the past, founded upon archaeological data, historical data, or some combination of the two.

Certain key research orientations should improve both the amount and quality of network analysis in archaeological settings. One is the acquisition of additional data. In general, the data required to conduct network analyses are either absent or available only for some of the links in a system. Thus the acquisition of additional information on the description of early net-

Figure 9.15. Documented (a) and simulated (b) networks for the Late Horizon/Early Colonial period in the Temascalapa–Teotihuacan region.

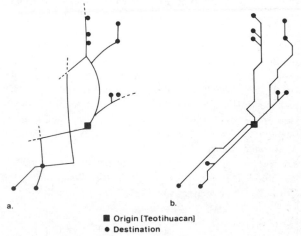

a.   b.

■ Origin [Teotihuacan]
● Destination

works should be a high priority for future research. Careful studies of ethnohistoric sources may provide a solution to this problem in some regions. The short-coming of such data, excluding maps themselves, is that in a very real sense they are *indirect*, requiring inferences from textual evidence to develop network configuration. Another possible means of acquiring information on past network configurations is with various remote-sensing techniques (Ebert 1984). Ancient roadways are a good example of ephemeral cultural features difficult to find on the ground, but often quite detectable through remote sensing (Ebert and Lyons 1983:1,264–5) – a claim supported in one of the studies cited above (Ebert and Hitchcock 1980).

A second research direction which we feel deserves increased attention is the development of models more appropriate for anthropological and archaeological problems. In two of the major analytical topics discussed above – locational models and network simulation – an emphasis upon specific model formulation is fundamental. The limited insights gained through the use of models originally developed to study modern industrial societies, or axiomatic models whose unrealistic assumptions greatly constrain their applicability, should come as no surprise. As archaeologists and regional scientists gain a greater understanding of sociocultural systems of the past, they gain an increased understanding of the variables and considerations which would have been important to the functioning of these systems. It is upon these key characteristics that attention must be focused if we hope to increase our knowledge of past regional organization in general, and past networks in particular.

The study of how people make use of space is a complex, demanding topic. Nevertheless, research in this area is essential to our understanding of regional systems at all levels of sociopolitical complexity, especially complex societies where settlements constantly interact with one another. The study of networks, of a discrete as opposed to continuous representation of space, provides a more realistic means of studying regional systems. The careful examination of past networks ultimately will provide increased understanding of past cultural adaptation at a regional level.

Acknowledgments

The figures accompanying this essay (excluding Figs. 9.9, 9.14 and 9.15) are thanks to the talents of Will Fontenez. Diane LaSauce assisted in editing the final draft.

References

Akers, S.B.
1960 The Use of Wye-Delta Transformation in Network Simplification. *Journal of Operations Research* 8:311–23

Alden, J.
1979 Reconstruction of Toltec Period Political Units in the Valley of Mexico. In *Transformations: Mathematical Approaches to Culture Change*, edited by C. Renfrew and K. Cooke, pp. 169–200. Academic Press, New York

Bell, T. L., and R. L. Church
1986 Location-Allocation Modeling in Archaeology. In *Spatial Analysis and Location-Allocation Modeling*, edited by A. Gosh and G. Rushton, pp. 76–100. Von Nostrand, Reinhold, and Co., New York

Bell, T. L., R. L. Church, and L. Gorenflo
1988 Late Horizon Regional Efficiency in the Northeastern Basin of Mexico: A Location-Allocation Perspective. *Journal of Anthropological Archaeology* 7:163–202

Black, W. R.
1971 An Iterative Model for Generating Transportation Networks. *Geographical Analysis* 3:283–8

Bondy, J. A., and U. S. R. Murty
1976 *Graph Theory with Applications*. Macmillan, London

Braidwood, R.
1937 *Mounds in the Plain of Antioch: An Archaeological Survey*. Oriental Institute Publication 48. Oriental Institute, University of Chicago

Bunge, W.
1966 *Theoretical Geography*. Second edition. Lund Studies in Geography, Series C. Gleerup, Lund

Burghardt, A.
1969 The Origin and Development of the Road Network of the Niagara Peninsula, Ontario, 1770–1851. *Annals of the Association of American Geographers* 59:417–40

Burnett, P.
1978 Time Cognition and Urban Travel Behavior. *Geografiska Annaler* (series B) 60:107–18

Carter, F. W.
1969 An Analysis of the Medieval Serbian Oecumene: A Theoretical Approach. *Geografiska Annaler* (series B) 51:39–52

Cooper, L.
1963 Location-Allocation Problems. *Operations Research* 11:331–43

Dicks, T. R. B.
1972 Network Analysis and Historical Geography. *Area* 4:4–9

Dijkstra, E. W.
1959 A Note on Two Problems in Connexion with Graphs. *Numerishe Mathematik* 1:269–71

Doran, J.
1970 Systems Theory, Computer Simulations and Archaeology. *World Archaeology* 1:289–98

Ebert, J. I.
1984 Remote Sensing Applications in Archaeology. In *Advances in Archaeological Method and Theory*, Vol. VII, edited by M. B. Schiffer, pp. 293–362. Academic Press, New York

Ebert, J. I., and R. K. Hitchcock
1980 Locational Modeling in the Analysis of the Prehistoric Roadway System at and around Chaco Canyon, New Mexico. In *Cultural Resource Remote Sensing*, edited by T. R. Lyons and F. J. Mathien, pp. 167–207. National Park Service, Washington, DC

Ebert, J. I., and T. R. Lyons (author-editors), *et al.*
1983 Archaeology, Anthropology, and Cultural Resource Management. In *Manual of Remote Sensing*, second edition, pp. 1,233–304. American Society of Photogrammetry, Falls Church, VA

Evans, S., and P. Gould
1982 Settlement Models in Archaeology. *Journal of Anthropological Archaeology* 1:275–304

Flannery, K. V.
1972 The Cultural Evolution of Civilizations. *Annual Review of Ecology and Systematics* 3:399–426

Garrison, W.
1960 Connectivity of the Interstate Highway System. *Papers of the Regional Science Association* 6:121–37

Gatrell, A. C.
1983 *Distance and Space: A Geographical Perspective*. Clarendon Press, Oxford

Gibson, C.
1964 *The Aztecs under Spanish Rule*. Stanford University Press, Stanford

Gorenflo, L.
1989 Regional Efficiency in Prehispanic Central Mexico: Insights from Geographical Studies of Archaeological Settlement Patterns. Ms on file, L.E.A.R.N., Inc., Port Townsend, WA

Gorenflo, L., and N. Gale
1989 Mapping Regional Settlement in Information Space. Submitted to *Journal of Anthropological Archaeology* 9:240–74

Gould, P.
1985 *The Geographer at Work*. Routledge and Kegan Paul, London

Haggett, P., and R. J. Chorley
1969 *Network Analysis in Geography*. Edward Arnold, London

Harary, F.
1969 *Graph Theory*. Addison-Wesley, Reading, MA

Hassig, R.
1985 *Trade, Tribute, and Transportation*. University of Oklahoma Press, Norman, OK

Hillier, F. S., and G. Lieberman
1980 *Introduction to Operations Research*. Third edition. Holden-Day, San Francisco

Hodgart, R. L.
1978 Optimizing Access to Public Services: A Review of Problems, Models and Methods of Locating Central Facilities. *Progress in Human Geography* 2:17–48

Kansky, K.
1963 *The Structure of Transportation Networks*. Research Paper No. 84. Department of Geography, University of Chicago

Keene, A. S.
1979 Economic Optimization Models and the Study of Hunter-Gatherer Subsistence-Settlement Systems. In *Transformations: Mathematical Approaches to Culture Change*, edited by C. Renfrew and K. Cooke, pp. 369–404. Academic Press, New York
1981 *Prehistoric Foraging in a Temperate Forest: A Linear Programming Model*. Academic Press, New York

Kolars, J. F., and H. J. Malin
1970 Population and Accessibility: An Analysis of Turkish Railroads. *The Geographical Review* 60:229–46

Lachene, R.
1965 Networks and the Location of Economic Activities. *Papers of the Regional Science Association* 14:183–96

Lewarch, D. E.
1979 Locational Models and the Study of Complex Societies: A Dilemma in Data Requirements and Research Design. *Western Canadian Journal of Anthropology* 8:75–88

Lowe, J. C., and S. Moryadas
1975 *The Geography of Movement*. Houghton Mifflin, Boston

Olsson, G.
1969 Inference Problems in Locational Analysis. In

Behavioral Problems in Geography: A Symposium, edited by K. Cox and R. G. Golledge, pp. 14–34. Department of Geography, Northwestern University, Evanston, IL

Olsson, G., and S. Gale
1968 Spatial Theory and Human Behavior. *Papers and Proceedings of the Regional Science Association* 21:229–42

Paso y Troncoso, F. del (ed.)
1905 *Papeles de Nueva España*. Segunda Serie, Geografía y Estadística, Vol. VI. Impresores de la Real Casa, Madrid

Pitts, F.
1965 A Graph-Theoretic Approach to Historical Geography. *The Professional Geographer* 17:15–20

Reidhead, V. A.
1976 Optimization and Food Procurement at the Prehistoric Leonard Haag Site, Southeastern Indiana: A Linear Programming Approach. Ph.D. dissertation, Indiana University. University Microfilms, Ann Arbor
1979 Linear Programming Models in Archaeology. *Annual Review of Anthropology* 8:543–78

ReVelle, C., D. Marks, and J. C. Liebman
1970 An Analysis of Private and Public Sector Location Models. *Management Science* 16:692–707

Rushton, G., M. F. Goodchild, and L. M. Ostresh
1971 *Computer Programs for Location/Allocation Problems*. Department of Geography, University of Iowa, Iowa City

Scott, A. J.
1971 *An Introduction to Spatial Allocation Analysis*. Resource Paper 9, Association of American Geographers Commission on College Geography. Association of American Geographers, Washington, DC

Simon, H. A.
1981 *The Sciences of the Artificial*. Second edition. M.I.T. Press, Cambridge, MA

Steponaitis, V. P.
1978 Location Theory and Complex Chiefdoms: A Mississippian Example. In *Mississippian Settlement Patterns*, edited by B. D. Smith, pp. 417–53. Academic Press, New York

1981 Settlement Hierarchies and Political Complexity in Non-Market Societies: The Formative Period in the Valley of Mexico. *American Anthropologist* 83:320–63

Strahler, A. N.
1952 Hypsometric Analysis of Erosional Topography. *Bulletin of the Geological Society of America* 63:1,117–42

Strong, W. D.
1935 *An Introduction to Nebraska Archaeology* Smithsonian Miscellaneous Collections Vol. 93, No. 10. Smithsonian Institution, Washington, DC

Taaffe, E. J., R. L. Morrill, and P. R. Gould
1963 Transportation Expansion in Underdeveloped Countries: A Comparative Analysis. *The Geographical Review* 53:503–29

Tinkler, K. J.
1977 *An Introduction to Graph Theoretical Methods in Geography*. Concepts and Techniques in Modern Geography 14. Geoabstracts, East Anglia
1979 Graph Theory. *Progress in Human Geography* 3:85–116

Törnqvist, G., S. Nordbeck, B. Rystedt, and P. Gould
1971 *Multiple Locational Analysis*. Lund Studies in Geography, Series C. Gleerup, Lund

Wagner, H. M.
1975 *Principles of Operations Research*. Second edition. Prentice-Hall, Englewood Cliffs, NJ

Warntz, W.
1966 The Topology of Socio-Economic Terrain and Spatial Flows. *Papers of the Regional Science Association* 17:47–61

Watson, J. W.
1955 Geography – A Discipline in Distance. *The Scottish Geographical Magazine* 71:1–13

Wright, H. T.
1977 Recent Research on the Origin of the State. *Annual Review of Anthropology* 6:379–92
1978 Toward an Explanation of the Origin of the State. In *Origins of the State: The Anthropology of Political Evolution*, edited by R. Cohen and E. R. Service, pp. 49–68. Institute for the Study of Human Issues, Philadelphia

10 Political, economic, and demographic implications of the Chaco road network

FRANCES JOAN MATHIEN

Introduction

The discovery of a well-developed prehistoric road network linking numerous areas in the Chaco Anasazi region of northwestern New Mexico (Figs. 10.1 and 10.2) contributed to the re-evaluation of archaeological interpretations of this cultural group. This extensive constructed and maintained roadway network is one variable that is used to determine the level of social complexity achieved in the semi-arid environment of the Colorado plateau. In this presentation, an attempt will be made to evaluate this variable as one that correlates with levels of social complexity among the Anasazi, as well as other culture groups; and the implications of the

Fig. 10.1. *Map indicating locations of Chaco Canyon and other areas in the Greater Southwest for which prehistoric roads and trails have been documented.*

Fig. 10.2. Map indicating locations of Chaco Canyon, the confirmed Chaco Anasazi road network and some Chaco structures which are part of the "Chaco Phenomenon."

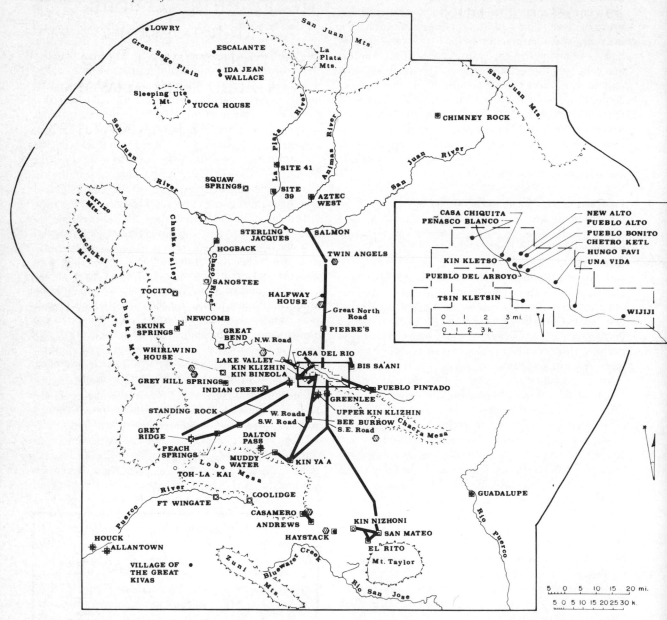

road network with regard to political, economic, and demographic factors will be discussed.

As in most studies, the work of many investigators provides the building blocks for future research. The discovery and interpretation of the Chaco road network had its beginnings in the early decades of this century and continues through the present. This study will refer only to those works that bear directly on the topics of concern. In addition to chapters in this volume by Obenauf, Sever, and Windes, Obenauf (1980a) and Vivian (1983b, 1983b) provide excellent historical documentation of the studies of Chaco roads and should be consulted by those wishing more in-depth information and references to specific studies.

Functions of the Chaco road network

One of the earliest suggestions for specific functions of Chaco roads, in addition to transport of goods and people, appeared in Judd (1954:350). It was proposed that the road segment on the south end of "The Gap" was part of a ceremonial highway. While he planned to elaborate on his knowledge of the road system, the only other reference to the roads by Judd (1964:141–2) suggests that a considerable amount of labor had been invested in the construction of stairs and roads between pueblos. However, the implications of this labor investment were not made explicit.

Vivian and Buettner (1973) realized that roads provided another category of evidence, in addition to water control, agricultural features and a number of architectural similarities, that demonstrated close interaction among the various sites in the canyon. These data suggested that town sites were not independent entities, but that there may have been some type of sociopolitical or economic integration among the sites in the canyon.

Survey of the roads by the National Park Service, and particularly the remote-sensing studies of the Chaco roads (Ebert and Hitchcock 1980; Lyons and Hitchcock 1977), as well as studies by Obenauf (1981b) who examined outlying areas, and the recent work carried out by the Bureau of Land Management (Kincaid 1983; Nials *et al.* 1987) leave no doubt that the road network covered hundreds of miles and linked numerous areas with Chaco-style structures throughout the San Juan Basin (Fig. 10.2) into a cultural system often referred to as "The Chaco Phenomenon" (Marshall *et al.* 1979; Powers *et al.* 1983). A number of studies used these data to make inferences about functions of the roads and the social organization of the Chaco Anasazi.

By 1973, the remote-sensing staff, building on the work of both Gordon and Gwinn Vivian, had examined a number of aerial photos of Chaco Canyon and ground checked many of the linearities observed. This provided Ebert and Hitchcock with sufficient information to idealize the road network. They adopted several geographical transport models to suggest implications of the system. Garrison's (1960) degree of connectivity was calculated to be 0.1645 (range 0–1); this figure suggested a fairly underdeveloped system with relatively low over-the-road costs and a high investment in facilities. This could mean that either high volumes of traffic or large amounts of goods were being transported over the roads. Kansky's (1963) beta-prime (1.58; range 0–12.17) and beta (5.21; range 0–infinity) values were also low. These too suggested the conclusion that "the Chaco region seems to tend toward the underdevelopment extreme of the continuum of economic integration" (Ebert and Hitchcock 1980:192).

The data were limited and there was, at that time, no way to know if all road segments were contemporaneous or even part of the same subsystem within the network. However, Ebert and Hitchcock were concerned with social implications since, at that time, ideas about the town–village dichotomy in the Chaco Canyon were being examined. Based on Johnson's (1970) observations on economic development, they suggested the Chaco system had poor utilization of space and a dendritic-like exchange system run by "unregulated and exploitive traders" who had monopolized exchange between high-level and lower-level centers. The Chaco roads connected mainly large centers and not smaller communities. The large pueblos in the Canyon were interpreted as probable bureaucratic centers, with the personnel located in them to manage labor. The roads were probably not laid out to gain political support but constructed by private entrepreneurs. Ebert and Hitchcock realized this was only a model based on the idealized road network and that it was limited to the Canyon area by the data available at the time. It needed to be tested against other archaeological data.

Lyons and Hitchcock (1977:130–1) pointed out that the well-engineered roads and their associated features would have required extensive labor in both construction and maintenance. The roads appeared to have been constructed *c.* A.D. 1000–1150 and the investigators reiterated that they "may have served to greatly facilitate redistribution of goods and/or services." They listed four specific functions:

1. the roads provided guidance and passage for the travel of groups and individuals;
2. the routes were used for the transport of goods and materials;

3. the roadways served to facilitate communication between widely separated population centers; and

4. the road system served as an integrative mechanism, the effectiveness of which remains to be demonstrated.

Morenon (1977) demonstrated that less energy was needed to walk on prehistoric roads in contrast to traversing the natural terrain. Ware and Gumerman (1977:164), upon excavating a gate 1 m wide through which roads passed just east of Pueblo Alto, remarked on the narrowness of the passage given that a number of roads from the north converged on this point; this suggested some type of traffic control. Numerous other investigators have reiterated these road functions (e.g., Hayes 1981:45; Lister and Lister 1981:146–7; Obenauf 1980b).

Recent research by Windes (1987a; this volume) demonstrates that there were multiple uses of roads, especially those in the central canyon area. Distribution of ceramic and chipped stone artifacts along road segments suggests some were probably used for transportation of imported items; some for local exchange; some as routes to water sources and some to terrace gardens. In key areas, certain paired room units are associated with traffic flow points and may have been the loci of storage facilities or traffic control. His comparison of other architectural features at the town sites of Pueblo Alto, Pueblo Bonito, and Chetro Ketl led to the conclusion that there were different administrative functions for these three sites and that the inhabitants of Pueblo Alto may have been responsible for control of people and goods passing to the north. However, they were probably subordinate to the inhabitants at the two larger pueblos. The lack of great kivas at Pueblo Alto, in contrast to the presence of several at Pueblo Bonito and Chetro Ketl, lends credence to this proposition, especially with regard to ceremonial matters. Windes' research on roads supports the concept of hierarchical social structure for the Chaco Anasazi discussed by Akins and Schelberg (1984), Grebinger (1973), Powers *et al.* (1983), Schelberg (1982), among others.

The Chaco political, social and demographic models

Recent work by the Bureau of Land Management reveals that there are now 640 km of documented Chaco roads (160 km within the Park proper and 480 km in the remainder of the San Juan Basin) (Kincaid 1983; Nials *et al.* 1987). In addition to the roads, there are a number of associated features that probably served functions similar to those found in other road/trail systems, e.g., stone circles, rock art, etc.

Road width, as recorded by a number of investigators, is variable. It ranges from 2.5 to 12.6 m, but the average is 9 m. Nials (1983) suggests several factors that account for this variability. Among these are proximity to sites; type of road; normal variations in construction, delineation, or utilization patterns; topographic position; secondary modification; and method of measurement. Differences in width of roads near sites is due not only to heavier traffic in some areas; the wider roads also exhibit more formalized construction through such features as berms, curbs, wall, etc. There is also some topographic variation; in areas with steep terrain, road widths narrow to less than 2 m (Nials 1983).

Nials makes a distinction between engineering and construction and notes there is evidence of both. There were a few surfaced roads reported in the Chaco literature, but surfacing was not felt to be a significant characteristic of Chaco roads. The few instances where paving is reported are not completely understood (Nials 1983). While this may not be the most sophisticated system in the New World, it required planning and labor management to some extent. This could suggest a need for some type of social complexity.

At present there are no estimates of the amount of labor needed to plan, construct, and maintain the Chaco road network. To gain some insight into the possible amount of labor involved and how this might affect social structure, reference is made to Lekson's (1984:257–60, 277–86) architectural studies. He used Ford's (1968) calculation that the modern ditch cleaning, a public activity at San Juan Pueblo, took 0.23 per cent of the work force's time. Applying this figure to the number of man hours estimated to build the number of walls constructed between A.D. 1095 and 1100 (the most intensive building period for Chaco-style structures), he suggested a population of 5,211 could have built the large pueblos in 0.23 per cent of their time. The figures are not absolute. For example, a small work force could have spent a larger percentage of time. Lekson admits that even a population in the Canyon as low as 2,000 could have constructed the large sites without excessive demands on their time. If one considers the population was also building/remodeling small houses, irrigation ditches, and roads all at about the same time, it is necessary perhaps to double the work force or the amount of time spent per man. This doubling of time still might not have strained the system.

The main point discussed by Lekson, however, is the need for a "highly formalized authority structure" or some degree of sociopolitical complexity to direct the labor efforts and maintain a schedule that would not conflict with other duties, such as agriculture. This coincides with Nials' (1983) need for planning and labor management.

The need for some form of authority to handle planning and labor management contrasts to some extent with the type of social organization attributed to both earlier and later inhabitants of the American Southwest (Fig. 10.1). The earliest road/trail system was described by Rogers (1939, 1966) who differentiated trails assigned to the Malpais/San Dieguito II culture (*c.* 9000 B.C.) from Yuman I–II trails (A.D. 800–1200) by the presence/absence of desert varnish on the trails and stone artifacts, and the location of trails in relation to modern water sources. Both Malpais and Yuman trails had associated features: trail shrines, sleeping circles, and stone configurations. From the descriptions and illustrations, some labor was involved to remove rocks from the trails and prepare sleeping circles; however, there were no major road-associated features (other than stone configurations) or large sites requiring great labor investment. Other surveys in Arizona (Breternitz 1957; Vivian 1965) and California (Davis 1961; Farmer 1935; Gates 1909; Johnson and Johnson 1957; Sample 1950; Wallace 1958) document trails a few feet deep, running in fairly straight lines, and associated with cairns, sleeping circles, rock art, shrines, and sherds. The time span ranged from A.D. 900 to the present (when dated by ceramics) or even earlier (as evidenced by desert varnish). Where figures were given, trails measured 0.15–0.3 m in width (Johnson and Johnson 1957).

Comparative data from more recent roads/trails among the Pueblo descendants of the Chaco Anasazi are much less detailed. It is difficult to discern exactly when a specific trail was used, but it is worth noting that most investigators have called the Chaco features "roads" and most of the later features "trails." Two width measurements were given: 0.5 m for the Jemez area (Fliedner 1975) and 4.72 m for Gran Quivira (Howard 1959). The latter is within the range of Chaco road measurements, but the Chaco average is 9 m; the narrower end of the Chaco range is usually found only where topographic features constrict road width.

In addition to the road at Gran Quivira, other pueblos in the Salinas province have road segments (Tom Carroll, Dwight Drager, and Jim Trott, personal communication, 1982). Segments have been noted at Quarai, Abo, Tenabo, and Pueblo Pardo. Jim Trott finds these are reminiscent of the Chaco roads, but they are narrower. Since there has been very little work outside the site areas, knowledge of the extent of this system is lacking. It does suggest that the fourteenth- to seventeenth-century Salinas area was interconnected. Spanish documents reveal Gran Quivira was the trading center for this group of Pueblo Indians who interacted with Plains Indians to the east.

Post-Chaco road features in the Chama/Gallina area include stairs cut into rock and the use of natural passes or breaks in cliffs (Douglas 1917). Trails in the Jemez Mountains had hand- and toe-holds and sometimes had stones placed along the valley sides for foundations (Fliedner 1975). A lack of information on walls and other formal features in most instances, however, does suggest a difference between these later trails and the earlier Chaco regional network, and one could expect some political, economic, and demographic differences between the Chaco Anasazi and their descendants.

Are there comparable differences in these variables? Data from survey and excavation in the San Juan Basin, while considerable, are not complete. Much of the information has been entered into the S.J.B.R.U.S. data bank of the National Park Service, and this information was used by Kneebone (1982) to estimate the population density during the time period when the formal road network was constructed and used. Using estimates of the number of rooms, etc., he projected a population of 64,000 for this, the most populous time period in the San Juan Basin.

For the Chaco Canyon area, several investigators have calculated populations for the Bonito phase (A.D. 1000–1150). Fisher (1934) used the amount of irrigable land available to predict as many as 10,000 people. Drager (1976) measured roofed-over floor space to conclude that not more than 6,000 people lived in the Canyon. Hayes (1981) arrived at 5,652 during the peak population, Windes (1987b) examined the number of firepits in town sites to suggest considerably fewer people. Thus there is a range from around 1,500 to 10,000 during the height of population density in Chaco Canyon.

For Contact Period data, Schroeder (1979) presents population estimates culled from the early Spanish records. These range from a total of 20,000 men to 130,000 to 248,000 people, the last being Espejo's exaggerated estimate. He considered Oñate's 16,000 to 60,000 as conservatively the lowest. By 1620 Benavides estimated 69,000 as a minimum of people in sixty-four pueblos, a figure not very different from that of Kneebone for the San Juan Basin.

Ethnographic data pertaining to individual groups or pueblos at the time of conquest also present quite a range: 2,600 Piro, possibly 10,000 Tompiro, 7,000 Southern Tiwa, 6,000 Tiwa, 6,000–30,000 Towa, possibly 10,000 Zuni, and 10,000 Hopi (Schroeder 1979). At this point, one begins to question whether the labor investments in roads are correlated with demographic factors in the earlier and later social systems because of the similarities in population estimates overall, yet differences in construction and features of roads found archaeologically.

Trying to make inferences about the economic and political systems and then comparing these with recent Puebloans is still more difficult. By the 1970's Vivian (1983b) realized Chaco was part of a large region owing in part to the architectural similarities among "outliers" in the San Juan Basin and/or the presence of roads. During the past decade, there has been a trend towards interpreting Chaco as some type of ranked or complex society, instead of a tribally organized society as found among historic Pueblo Indians. Several investigators began to discuss interaction among various populations in the Basin. After his study of the Great North Road, Morenon (1977) emphasized the role of the rural component in the development of a region.

A number of investigators were concerned with redistribution models. Judge *et al.* (1981) gave reasons why such a system could have developed in the Canyon and how it might have spread to outlying areas in the region through time. Others have concentrated on evaluating these proposals: Toll (1981) and Toll *et al.* (1980) concluded that ceramic goods came into the Canyon and possibly were redistributed from larger towns to smaller villages, but that there was a lack of ceramic evidence to support a regional redistribution system. Cameron's lithic analysis also demonstrates importation of non-local materials from the peripheries of the San Juan Basin, as well as a few sources slightly further away (Cameron 1982, 1984; Cameron and Sappington 1984). However, no lithic workshops were identified and no strong case for redistribution can be made from her data.

Several variations on geographic models, using the data on roads as one of the variables, have been applied. Allan and Broster (1978) felt the Chaco system fitted a central-place model. Others have utilized Carol Smith's regional models to suggest the type of system in operation. Winter (1980) concluded that Chaco fitted the dendritic central-place model, while Sebastian (1981) felt it could be subsumed under a solar central-place model. Schelberg (1982) combined an ecological-economic approach and concluded that the Chaco system represented a bounded hierarchy.

Schelberg examined the five correlates of a chiefdom listed in Peebles and Kus (1977).

1. The burial data gathered by Akins and Schelberg (1984) do support the concept of a ranked society. Paramount burials are found in Pueblo Bonito and there is evidence of differential burial patterns and grave goods among town and village burials.
2. There was a hierarchy of settlement types and sizes. At least three hierarchical levels could be identified when data on size and site, enclosed plaza areas, and presence of great kivas were evaluated.
3. Local subsistence efficiency could not be demonstrated. Schelberg felt probably no more than 4,000 people could have been supported using Canyon land; however, the margins of the Basin were more productive and food was probably imported.
4. There was organization of production activities as evidenced by the planning and labor force needed for the construction of towns, roads and the water-control system. In addition Mathien (1984) has presented evidence that indicates some jewelry craft shops.
5. There were societal buffering mechanisms. Many of the large rooms in the towns could have been used to hold food or other items; there was a mixed strategy for food exploitation as evidenced by non-domestic plants and faunal species. While there was no written calendar, there was a solar calendric marker.

Based on the fact that four of the five characteristics were fulfilled, Schelberg felt that Chaco was a complex chiefdom, but it was not partially commercialized as Winter and Sebastian's models would imply. The basic assumptions of a dendritic model were not met (e.g., urban center, export to international market, raw materials from the hinterland processed in the central place and returned as finished products, and commerce dominating politics). He felt there was some ceremonial control (but not political or economic control) exercised by Chaco over the rest of the Basin. Development was limited by the environment and resources of the San Juan Basin and Canyon which prevented the Anasazi from acquiring a resource that would allow them to buffer the stresses of a semi-arid ecosystem in the long run and therefore prevented continued development of social complexity. Rather when the limits of the ecological and social systems were stressed beyond endurance, the system reverted to an earlier, less complex form of chiefdom. Because semi-arid systems recover slowly and human interaction can have a severe degrading effect, the population decreased and eventually abandoned this area.

More recently, an analysis of political theory and models, as they pertain to the Chaco database, convinced Sebastian (1988:vii) that "the degree of investment in structure and elaboration, the evidence of settlement pattern hierarchy, and the level of formality, standardization, and planning apparent in the archaeological remains ... represent a society with institutionalized leadership."

In contrast, others still indicate the ethnohistoric model of a non-stratified society accounts for the Chaco manifestation. Ellis (1983) cogently expands on the cooperative social model rooted in both the literature and her own experience among living Pueblo Indians. She links all native authoritarian systems to the supernatural or ceremonial elements in the society. She stresses the cooperativeness of all members of the group in any and all priestly directed projects under the pain of punishment, yet notes that even priests were watched and did not live differently from the rest of the inhabitants of the pueblo. They did not inherit their positions, but were elected by the group. Ellis also offers a different interpretation of grave goods from Akins and Schelberg (1984) or Schelberg (1982). Individuals were buried with their personal possessions, if still owned and not given away prior to death. Often, however, their goods were placed on a shrine for the dead rather than buried with them. Goods may reflect a person's occupational talent (e.g., pottery making) or could also signify a gift from a talented relative. Thus she questions the interpretation of status burials based on the distribution of grave goods among the Chaco burials.

Roads as a variable indicating social complexity

The question that comes to mind then is what are the attributes of a road system that might correlate with a more complex society? Robertson (1983) examined New World prehistoric roads. He found that linearity was the most common feature of all road and trail systems. Shrines were used as markers along the route in several areas, and stone circles were present in several states. He noted width of roads was not consistent even within one culture. The only feature that seemed useful and one that varied considerably was the occurrence of paved surfaces. Roads documented among the Mexican, Mayan, and Peruvian systems differed in degree of surface preparation from those found in archaeologically less sophisticated areas.

Intermediate to states with paved road surfaces and societies with only trails are Chaco and the inhabitants of the Casas Grandes Valley of Chihuahua (Fig. 10.1) who also reached a level of social complexity that allowed them to plan, construct, and maintain somewhat more elaborate routes between probable central places and their outlying hinterlands. These were more labor-intensive investments than the trails of the rest of the Southwest and northern United States and suggest that these cultures differ from those societies and the state-level organizations. An attempt was made to compare these two areas based on information in the literature.

The Casas Grandes archaeological area encompasses 32,000 sq miles, 25,000 of which are in Chihuahua, an area similar in size to the 26,000 square miles in the San Juan Basin. There are three major river valleys within this zone that includes high mountains as well as dry sands within five different environmental zones (Di Peso 1974). There are no data on the population of the larger Casas Grandes zone. The central Casas Grandes area that was surveyed is a rectangle of some 11×13 miles; it had twenty-eight sites located along the river. This seems sparse but there is no discussion by Di Peso of an intensive survey. In contrast the 43 square miles of Chaco Canyon contained 2,220 sites ranging from Archaic through Navajo (Hayes 1981). Di Peso's population estimate for Casas Grandes and local hamlets was 4,700 between A.D. 1261 and 1340. He felt this period represented a highly sophisticated organization, but not an independent state (Di Peso 1974, Vol. IV:199–207).

The inhabitants of the Casas Grandes Valley also had a water-control system which included check dams coming down the sides of slopes, a drainage system that flowed under the floors of many of the houses in the city, walk-in wells, etc. This is more extensive than the canals and headgates of the Chaco Anasazi. Di Peso's data on turquoise and shell workshop areas at Casas Grandes are more extensive than those for the Chaco where (with one exception) there are usually only a handful to several hundred pieces of workshop debris (Mathien 1984). Yet the data on the road network suggest it was not as formalized as that of the Chaco Anasazi.

The Casas Grandes road network centers on top of Cerro de Montezuma where a road from the main site and several trails meet in a defensive site location. Di Peso's expedition traced two major routes and documented over 200 km of roads. None was paved. In areas where the trail is steep, steps were cut into rock. Wayhouses (single-room structures) were found along the "tracks" into the mountains. Sides of trails were sometimes banked. He felt this was a twelfth-century system and that it was an interlinking system encompassing a chain of settlements extending into Sonora (Di Peso, 1974, Vols. II and IV). Blackiston (1906) noted some sections of the major road at Cerro de Montezuma were 2.1–2.4 m wide. Bandelier (1892:654–9) noted the trail averaged only 1 m; only in one place where it wound up a steep slope did it appear to be 2.5 m wide; here it might have been part of a natural ledge. Loose rock, drift and boulders were removed from the trail.

Both Chaco and Casas Grandes areas are thought to be somewhat complex in their social organization, but with the data available, it is difficult to do much more than suggest they were chiefdoms of perhaps comparable size. The manufacture of copper bells at Casas Grandes and the large amounts of jewelry workshop material suggest higher investment in craft specialization. Water-control features in this area are also more labor intensive. Yet labor on roads does not seem to have been as intensive as in the Chaco area.

It may be that ecological and environmental factors played a role in both the construction and preservation of prehistoric road systems. Hulbert (1902) noted Indians in the eastern United States often had two or three routes between two points and that use depended on season and passability. With regard to preservation, Obenauf (1980b) noted how linearities disappear on aerial photographs when mountainous terrain is encountered. It is suggested, therefore, that studies of road systems, and inferences made from them, must be tempered by knowledge of environmental variables that could affect the amount of labor invested in their original construction, as well as rediscovery by archaeologists.

Indigenous versus external influence

This entire discussion has assumed that the Chaco phenomenon was the result of indigenous cultural development and not of major influence by more sophisticated neighbors to the south. There are several reasons for this assumption.

1. As noted above, the presence of trails has been documented in the Southwest as early as the Malpais/San Dieguito II culture. Many of the road-associated features, e.g., shrines and stone circles, were present earlier than the Chaco roads; these may or may not have had similar functions.

   Trails abound in other areas of North America. Mitchell (1933) described those found in colonial Connecticut, Wallace (1971) those in Pennsylvania, Hulbert (1902) those in New York and Pennsylvania; Myer (1928) those in Tennessee and surrounding southern states. In all instances, there were places to stop to rest and sleep, etc. Thus, the presence of roads in the Chaco area suggests that it is the formalization of trails c. A.D. 1050–1100 that is noteworthy, and not the existence of a trail network. If there was a major social change in the Chaco system at this time, this formalization may be the result of a change in the division of labor and the uses made of the labor force.

2. The characteristics of the formal Chaco road system are not "Mesoamerican" in style. The descriptions of the La Quemada system (Trombold 1975, 1976; Weigand 1978) and the Casas Grandes system are sufficiently different to preclude the conclusion that a person or group of people from one area was needed to show inhabitants of the Chaco how to construct their road network.

3. Recent studies by a number of investigators (e.g. Mathien 1981, McGuire 1980) discount the direct-influence concept. Instead, these authors suggest that there were numerous intervening culture groups that interacted with one another and through which both ideas and items of material culture were passed. The volume of Mesoamerican items and their distribution patterns does not support a long-distance-trade concept. The ecological analysis of Schelberg (1982) and the discussion of tenth-century developments by Judge *et al.* (1981) suggest reasons why there would be a social adaptation by the Chaco Anasazi that would be independent of any Mesoamerican influence. None of these authors denies that items appear in the Anasazi culture area that must have been imported from the south, but all agree that the mechanisms for their movement need not have been the result of a major Mesoamerican connection.

Conclusions

Increasing knowledge of the road network has been a major factor in the reshaping of archaeological theories regarding the social organization of the Chaco Anasazi. As the discovery of the number of roads increased so did the area attributed to the Chaco Phenomenon. Additional studies on architectural features of Chaco-style structures throughout the San Juan Basin and their associated ceramic artifacts suggest that this system may have been more complex and possibly hierarchically organized. Reconstruction of demographic, political, and economic aspects of social organization for the Chaco Anasazi and comparison of these social aspects with those documented for historic pueblo populations, as well as other pre-historic populations in the American Southwest, suggest that there was a differential investment of labor – a much larger input in the Chaco road system. However, the degree of social stratification that may have existed is questionable. Comparison with other road systems, specifically that at Casas Grandes, suggests that there were probably certain social and ecological considerations that influenced the degree of labor invested in a road network as opposed to other possible labor-intensive options.

When road data are analyzed as part of the entire data set for a system, they do add information that can be used for comparison with earlier and/or later cultural systems in the same area. The amount of labor invested and the extent of a formal network indicate the type of planning and harnessing of energy/labor needed to carry out the construction noted for the cultural system.

Acknowledgments

This paper was included in the symposium entitled "Pre-historic Transport Networks in the New World", 81st Annual Meeting of the American Anthropological Association, Washington, DC, December 4–7, 1982. This report is inventoried as Contribution No. 43 of the Chaco Center, National Park Service and University of New Mexico, for purposes of bibliographic control of research relating to Chaco Canyon.

References

Akins, Nancy J., and John D. Schelberg
  1984 Evidence for Organizational Complexity as seen from the Mortuary Practices at Chaco Canyon. In *Recent Research on Chaco Prehistory*, edited by W. J. Judge and J. D. Schelberg, pp. 89–102. Reports of the Chaco Center 8, Division of Cultural Research, National Park Service, Albuquerque
Allan, William C., and John B. Broster
  1978 *An Archaeological Application of the Christaller Model*. Paper presented at the 54th Annual Meeting of the Southwestern and Rocky Mountain Division of the American Association for the Advancement of Science, Albuquerque
Bandelier, Adolph F.
  1892 *Final Report of Investigations among the Indians of the Southwestern United States, Carried on Mainly in the Years from 1880 to 1885. Part II*. Papers of the Archaeological Institute of America, American Series IV
Blackiston, A. Hooten
  1906 Ruins of the Cerro de Montezuma. *American Anthropologist* 8(2):256–61
Breternitz, David A.
  1957 A Brief Archaeological Survey of the Lower Gila River. *The Kiva* 22(2–3):1–3
Cameron, Catherine M.
  1982 The Chipped Stone of Chaco Canyon. MS on file, Division of Cultural Research, National Park Service, Albuquerque
  1984 A Regional View of Chipped Stone Raw Material Use in Chaco Canyon. In *Recent Research on Chaco Prehistory*, edited by W. J. Judge and J. D. Schelberg, pp. 137–52. Reports of the Chaco Center 8, Division of Cultural Research, National Park Service, Albuquerque
Cameron, Catherine M., and Robert Lee Sappington
  1984 Obsidian Procurement at Chaco Canyon, A.D. 500–1200. In *Recent Research on Chaco Prehistory*, edited by W. J. Judge and J. D. Schelberg, pp. 153–72. Reports of the Chaco Center 8, Division of Cultural Research, National Park Service, Albuquerque
Davis, James T.
  1961 Trade Routes and Economic Exchange among the Indians of California. *Reports of the University of California Archaeological Survey* 54:1–73
Di Peso, Charles C.
  1974 *Casas Grandes: A Fallen Trading Center of the Gran Chichimeca*. Amerind Foundation/Northland Press, Dragoon and Flagstaff
Douglas, William B.
  1917 The Land of the Small House People. *El Palacio* 4(2):2–23
Drager, Dwight L.
  1976 Anasazi Population Estimates with the Aid of Data derived from Photogrammetric Maps. In *Remote Sensing Experiments in Cultural Resource Studies. Non-destructive Methods of Archeological Exploration, Survey and Analysis*, assembled by T. R. Lyons, pp. 157–72. Reports of the Chaco Center 1. Chaco Center, National Park Service and University of New Mexico, Albuquerque
Ebert, James I., and Robert K. Hitchcock
  1980 Locational Modelling in the Analysis of the Pre-historic Roadway System at and around Chaco Canyon, New Mexico. In *Cultural Resources Remote Sensing*, edited by T. R. Lyons and F. J. Mathien, pp. 169–207. Cultural Resources Management Division, National Park Service, Washington, DC

Ellis, Florence H.
1983 Foreword. In *The Architecture of Chetro Ketl* by Stephen H. Lekson and Peter J. McKenna. Reports of the Chaco Center Division of Cultural Research, National Park Service, Albuquerque

Farmer, Malcolm F.
1935 The Mojave Trade Route. *The Masterkey* 9(5):154–7

Fisher, Reginald G.
1934 *Some Geographical Factors that Influenced the Ancient Populations of the Chaco Canyon, New Mexico*. University of New Mexico Bulletin 244, Archaeologist Series 3(1)

Fliedner, Dietrick
1975 Pre-Spanish Pueblos in New Mexico. *Annals of the Association of American Geographers* 65(3):363–77

Ford, Richard I.
1968 An Ecological Analysis Involving the Population of San Juan Pueblo, New Mexico. Ph.D. dissertation, University of Michigan, Ann Arbor

Garrison, W. L.
1960 Connectivity of the Interstate Highway System. *Papers and Proceedings of the Regional Science Association* 6:121–37

Gates, P. G.
1909 Indian Stone Constructions near Salton Sea, California. *American Anthropologist* 11:322–3

Grebinger, Paul
1973 Prehistoric Social Organization in Chaco Canyon, New Mexico. *The Kiva* 39(1):3–23

Hayes, Alden C.
1981 A Survey of Chaco Canyon. In *Archeological Surveys of Chaco Canyon, New Mexico*, by A. C. Hayes, D. M. Brugge, and W. J. Judge, pp. 1–68. Publications in Archaeology 17A, Chaco Canyon Studies. National Park Service, Washington, DC

Howard, Richard
1959 Comments on the Indians' Water Supply at Gran Quivira National Monument. *El Palacio* 66:85–91

Hulbert, Archer B.
1902 *Historic Highways of America, Vol. II. Indian Thoroughfares*. The Arthur H. Clark Company, Cleveland

Johnson, E. A. J.
1970 *The Organization of Space in Developing Countries*. Harvard University Press, Cambridge, MA

Johnson, Francis J., and Patricia H. Johnson
1957 *An Indian Trail Complex of the Central Colorado Desert: A Preliminary Survey*. Papers on California Archaeology 48. Reports from the University of California Archaeological Survey 37

Judd, Neil M.
1954 *The Material Culture of Pueblo Bonito*. Smithsonian Miscellaneous Collections 124
1964 *The Architecture of Pueblo Bonito*. Smithsonian Miscellaneous Collections 147

Judge, W. James, H. Wolcott Toll, William B. Gillespie, and Stephen H. Lekson
1981 Tenth Century Developments in Chaco Canyon. In *Collected Papers in Honor of Erik Kellerman Reed*, edited by A. H. Schroeder, pp. 65–98. Papers of the Archaeological Society of New Mexico 6

Kansky, K. J.
1963 *Structure of Transportation Networks*. University of Chicago, Department of Geography, Research Paper 84

Kincaid, Chris (ed.)
1983 *Chaco Roads Project, Phase I. A Reappraisal of Prehistoric Roads in the San Juan Basin*. United States Department of the Interior, Bureau of Land Management, Albuquerque and Santa Fe

Kneebone, Ronald
1982 Population Estimates of the San Juan Basin. Paper for Anthropology 467, on file at the Division of Cultural Research, National Park Service, Albuquerque

Lekson, Stephen H.
1984 *Great Pueblo Architecture of Chaco Canyon, New Mexico*. Publications in Archeology 18B, Chaco Canyon Studies, National Park Service, Albuquerque

Lister, Robert H., and Florence C. Lister
1981 *Chaco Canyon: Archaeology and Archaeologists*. University of New Mexico Press, Albuquerque

Loose, Richard W.
1979 Research Design. In Marshall *et al.* 1979:355–62

Lyons, Thomas R., and Robert K. Hitchcock
1977 Remote Sensing Interpretation of an Anasazi Land Route System. In *Aerial Remote Sensing Techniques in Archeology*, edited by Thomas R. Lyons and Robert K. Hitchcock, pp. 111–34. Reports of the Chaco Center 2, National Park Service and University of New Mexico, Albuquerque

McGuire, Randall H.
1980 The Mesoamerican Connection in the Southwest. *The Kiva* 46(1–2):3–38

Marshall, Michael P., John R. Stein, Richard W. Loose and Judith Novotny
1979 *Anasazi Communities in the San Juan Basin*. Albuquerque Photo Lab, Albuquerque

Mathien, Frances Joan
1981 Economic Exchange Systems in the San Juan

Basin. Ph.D. dissertation, University of New Mexico, Albuquerque

1984 Social and Economic Implications of Jewelry Items of the Chaco Anasazi. In *Recent Research on Chaco Prehistory*, edited by W. J. Judge and J. D. Schelberg, pp. 173–86. Reports of the Chaco Center 8, Division of Cultural Research, National Park Service, Albuquerque

Mitchell, Isabel S.
1933 *Roads and Road Making in Colonial Connecticut.* Tercentenary Commission of the State of Connecticut, Committee on Historical Publications. Yale University Press, New Haven

Morenon, E. Pierre
1977 Letter to W. James Judge, on file at the Division of Cultural Research, National Park Service, Albuquerque

Myer, William C.
1928 Indian Trails of the Southeast. *Forty-Second Annual Report of the Bureau of American Ethnology.* Smithsonian Institution, Washington, DC, pp. 727–857

Nials, Fred L.
1983 Physical Characteristics of Chacoan Road. In Kincaid 1983:chapter 6

Nials, Fred, John Stein, and John Roney
1987 *Chacoan Roads in the Southern Periphery; Results of Phase II of the BLM Chaco Roads Project.* Bureau of Land Management Albuquerque District

Obenauf, Margaret S.
1980a A History of Research on the Chacoan Roadway System. In *Cultural Resources Remote Sensing*, edited by Thomas R. Lyons and Frances Joan Mathien, pp. 123–67. Cultural Resources Management, National Park Service, Washington, DC
1980b The Chacoan Roadway System. M.A. thesis, University of New Mexico, Albuquerque

Peebles, Christopher S., and Susan M. Kus
1977 Some Archaeological Correlates of a Ranked Society. *American Antiquity* 42:421–48

Powers, Robert P., William B. Gillespie, and Stephen H. Lekson
1983 *The Outlier Survey. A Regional View of Settlement in the San Juan Basin.* Reports of the Chaco Center 3, Division of Cultural Research, National Park Service, Albuquerque

Robertson, Ben P.
1983 Other New World Roads and Trails. In Kincaid 1983:chapter 2

Rogers, Malcolm J.
1939 *Early Lithic Industries of the Lower Basin of the* Colorado River and Adjacent Desert Areas. San Diego Museum Papers 3
1966 *Ancient Hunters of the Far West.* The Union-Tribune Publishing Co., San Diego

Sample, L. L.
1950 *Trade and Trails in Aboriginal California.* Reports of the University of California Survey 8, Department of Anthropology, University of California, Berkeley

Schelberg, John D.
1982 Economic and Social Development as an adaptation to a marginal environment in Chaco Canyon, New Mexico. Ph.D. dissertation, Northwestern University, Evanston

Schroeder, Albert H.
1979 Pueblos Abandoned in Historic Times. In *Handbook of North American Indians. Vol. IX, Southwest*, edited by A. Ortiz, pp. 236–54. Smithsonian Institution, Washington, DC

Sebastian, Lynne
1981 Final Project, Anthropology 457. MS on file, Division of Cultural Research, National Park Service, Albuquerque
1988 Leadership, Power, and Productive Potential: A Political Model of the Chaco System. Ph.D. dissertation, University of New Mexico, Albuquerque

Toll, H. Wolcott
1981 Ceramic Comparisons Concerning Redistribution in Chaco Canyon, New Mexico. In *Production and Distribution: A Ceramic Viewpoint*, edited by H. Howard and E. L. Morris, pp. 83–121. BAR International Series 120, Oxford

Toll, H. Wolcott, Thomas C. Windes, and Peter J. McKenna
1980 Late Ceramic Patterns in Chaco Canyon: The Pragmatics of Modeling Ceramic Exchange. *Society for American Archaeology Papers* 1:95–117

Trombold, Charles D.
1975 Prehispanic Site and Road Hierarchies in and around the Ruins of La Quemada, Zacatecas, Mexico. Paper presented at the 40th Annual Meeting of the Society for American Archaeology, Dallas
1976 Spatial Distribution, Functional Hierarchies and Patterns of Interaction in Prehistoric Communities around La Quemada, Zacatecas, Mexico. In *Archaeological Frontiers: Papers on New World Culture in Honor of J. Charles Kelley*, edited by R. B. Pickering, pp. 149–82. Southern Illinois University, Museum Studies 4, Carbondale

Vivian, R. Gwinn
1965 An Archaeological Survey of the Lower Gila River. *The Kiva* 30(4):95–146

1983a Discovery and Description: Chacoan Road Field Studies, 1963–1980. Appendix A in Kincaid 1983

1983b Identifying and Interpreting Chacoan Roads. An Historical Perspective. In Kincaid 1983:chapter 3

Vivian, R. Gwinn, and R. C. Buettner

1973 Pre-Columbian Roadways in the Chaco Canyon Region, New Mexico. Paper presented at the 38th Annual Meeting of the Society for American Archaeology, San Francisco

Wallace, Paul A. W.

1971 *Indian Paths of Pennsylvania*. The Pennsylvania Historical and Museum Commission, Harrisburg

Wallace, W. J.

1958 Archaeological Investigations in Death Valley National Monument, 1952–1957. *Reports of the University of California Archaeological Survey* 42:7–22

Ware, John A., and George J. Gumerman

1977 Remote Sensing Methodology and the Chaco Canyon Prehistoric Road System. In *Aerial Remote Sensing Techniques in Archeology*, edited by Thomas R. Lyons and Robert K. Hitchcock, pp. 135–68. Reports of the Chaco Center 2, National Park Service and University of New Mexico, Albuquerque

Weigand, Phil C.

1978 The Prehistory of the State of Zacatecas: An Interpretation. *Anthropology* 2(1):67–87, 103–17

Windes, Thomas C.

1987a The Pueblo Alto–Pueblo Bonito–Chetro Ketl Road Network. In *Investigations at the Pueblo Alto Complex, Chaco Canyon, New Mexico, 1975–1979. Vol. I. Summary of Tests and Excavations at the Pueblo Alto Community*, by T. C. Windes, pp. 95–140. Publications in Archeology 18F, Chaco Canyon Studies, National Park Service, Santa Fe

1987b Population Estimates. In *Investigations at the Pueblo Alto Complex, Chaco Canyon, New Mexico, 1975–1979. Vol. I. Summary of Tests and Excavations at the Pueblo Alto Community*, by T. C. Windes, pp. 383–406. Publications in Archeology 18F, Chaco Canyon Studies, National Park Service, Santa Fe

Winter, Joseph C.

1980 Human Adaptations in a Marginal Environment. In *Human Adaptations in a Marginal Environment: the UII Mitigation Project*, edited by J. L. Moore and J. C. Winter, pp. 483–520. Office of Contract Archaeology, University of New Mexico, Albuquerque

11 The prehistoric road network at Pueblo Alto, Chaco Canyon, New Mexico

THOMAS C. WINDES

Prehistoric roads have long been known in Chaco Canyon and throughout the San Juan Basin (Wetherill in Vivian 1948; Judd 1954) in northwestern New Mexico (Fig. 11.1). Those around Pueblo Alto and Chetro Ketl were first described in detail by Holsinger (1901). Both the Hopi (Waters 1963:42–3) and the Navajo (O'Bryan 1956:60–2) refer to them as "race tracks," and they have identified them on the ground in Chaco Canyon.

Recent research has focused closely on the Chacoan roads throughout the San Juan Basin and reveals that most, if not all, greathouses were connected to roads (Marshall *et al.* 1979; Obenauf 1980; Powers *et al.* 1983). There also have been numerous investigations of the Chacoan roads in and around Chaco (e.g. Brethauer 1978; Kincaid 1983; Lyons and Hitchcock 1977; Morenon 1975; Nials *et al.* 1987; Obenauf 1980; Vivian 1972, 1983b; Ware and Gumerman 1977). A number of major routes have been recognized radiating out from Chaco Canyon and eventually terminating at or near outlier communities in areas of high resource productivity and diversity. The commonly held regional perspective of the Chacoan roads attributes to them a major economic role in the redistribution of resources that are normally differentially distributed within the San Juan Basin (see Vivian 1983b for a summary, and Mathien, this volume).

Roads in Chaco are outstanding for their on-the-ground clarity, the density of cultural debris that litters the routes, and the many associated features. Chaco Canyon is one of the few areas where roads can be traced directly into sites. Every greathouse on the plateau or mesa (Fig. 11.2) bordering Chaco Canyon (Pueblo Alto, Pueblo Pintado, Peñasco Blanco, and Tsin Kletsin) reveals roads in direct association, while those in the

Fig. 11.1. Northwestern New Mexico showing Chaco Canyon and some of the major Chacoan outliers and communities.

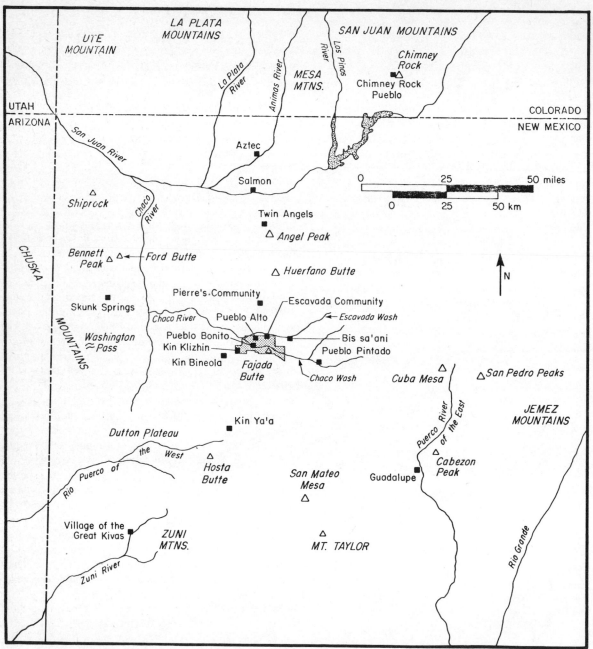

canyon bottom lack visible road associations because of sedimentation.

It is likely that roads fulfilled a multiplicity of uses, as Obenauf (1980) and Vivian (1983a) suggest, and that in some areas roads served local purposes unrelated to the regional economic system. In particular, the road complex in the bench and mesa-top area between Pueblo Alto, Pueblo Bonito, and Chetro Ketl (termed the central canyon area) has been of considerable interest to archaeologists. Most roads in this area converge on a single site, Pueblo Alto.

The number and proximity of roads around Pueblo Alto constituted a major factor in Pueblo Alto's ultimate selection for investigation between 1975 and 1979 (see Windes 1987a, 1987b). Because of previous road work (Ebert and Hitchcock 1980; Lyons and Hitchcock 1977; Vivian 1972; Ware and Gumerman 1977) and the interest in Pueblo Alto itself, little fieldwork on the associated road complex was started until after work at the site terminated. This section, then, clarifies the road network in the central canyon road area, examines it as a network for both local and regional perspectives, and discusses its ramifications at Pueblo Alto.

The Chaco Canyon road network

Two areas in Chaco Canyon are loci of prehistoric roads. One area (Fig. 11.3), around the large mesa-top greathouse, Peñasco Blanco, is the point of entry and departure of roads extending west and northwest from Chaco Canyon. Routes also lead east from the site toward the central canyon area and northeast toward the Escavada small-site community and Pueblo Alto. The other area is in the central-canyon road area (Fig. 11.4) and perhaps includes South Mesa on which Tsin Kletsin is located. Major arterials run north and south from this area, which is dominated by the greathouse giants of Pueblo Bonito and Chetro Ketl as well as numerous small houses. This area is often considered the center of the canyon occupation. East–west roads may also originate from here but at present cannot be identified in the canyon bottom. Most roads in these areas were mapped during the 1972 inventory survey and given Road Segment (RS) numbers.

In the central-canyon area, road segments abound, merging with at least two (RS 33 and RS 40) or more major routes (see Avery and Lyons 1981:Fig. 12). All terminate at or run close by Pueblo Alto (Fig. 11.5). Two

Figure 11.2 Important topographic features and greathouse sites in Chaco Canyon and its environs.

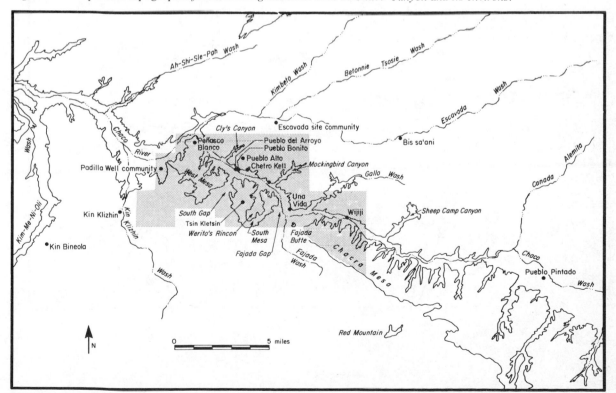

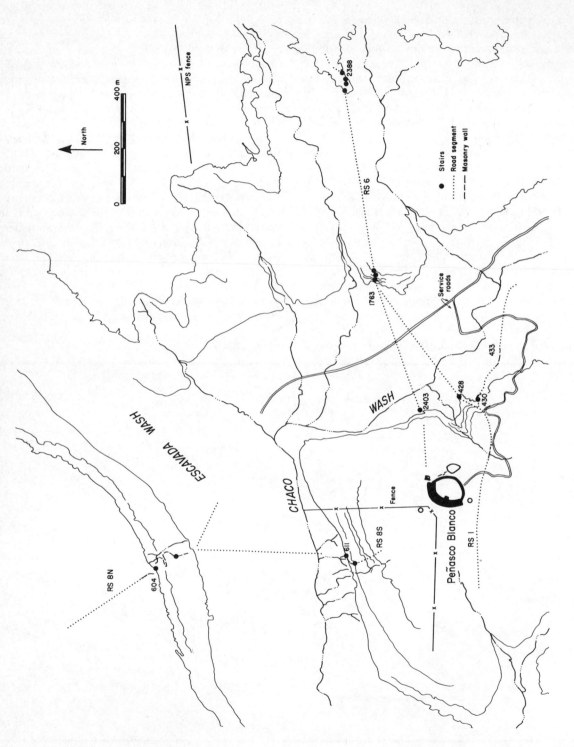

Fig. 11.3. The prehistoric road system in the vicinity of Peñasco Blanco at the west end of Chaco Canyon.

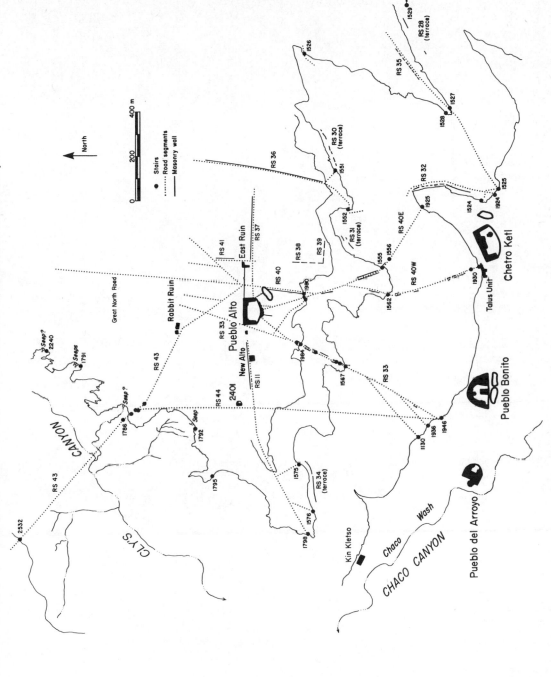

Fig. 11.4. The prehistoric road system in the vicinity of Pueblo Alto, Chetro Ketl, Pueblo Bonito, and Pueblo del Arroyo.

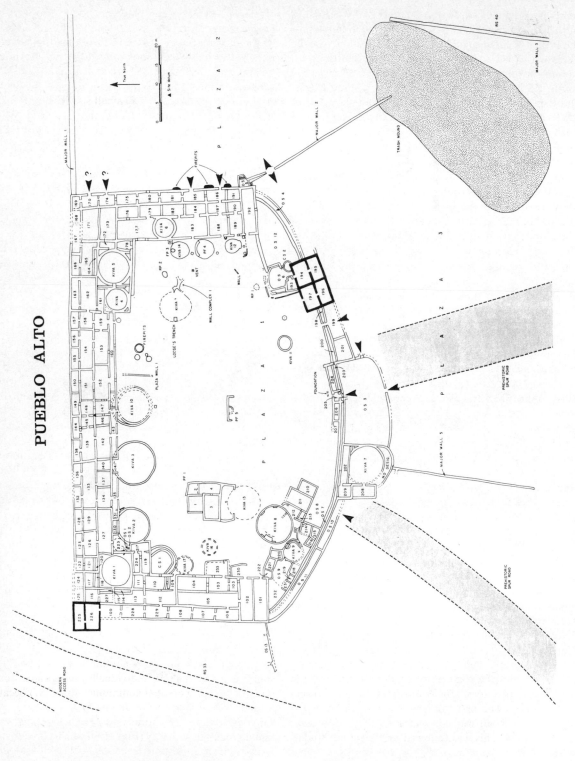

Fig. 11.5. *Roads passing by or entering Pueblo Alto.*

roads extend north–south past the East and West Wings of the site. The west one (RS 33) runs 270 m north past the Rabbit Ruin, a small Pueblo III ruin, and across the Escavada Wash to link with the Great North Road running north from the east side of Pueblo Alto. To the south, RS 33 crosses a number of benches and ledges, and then diverges to three ramps and stairs (see Vivian 1983b:Fig. A–6) that drop into the canyon just west of Pueblo Bonito. Its exact route from there is conjecture but is assumed to pass south by Pueblo del Arroyo and out through South Gap where a road is clearly visible on aerial imagery (Avery and Lyons 1981:Fig. 6).

At Pueblo Alto this route passes another road (RS 11) presumed to border the masonry wall that extends 210 m due west of Pueblo Alto past the north side of New Alto. The ultimate route of this road is unknown but it probably links several cut stairways descending the cliff southward to a gardening terrace (RS 34) and a cliff-ledge, rock-art site possibly related to astronomical sightings (William Gillespie, personal communication 1982). The terrace has been practically obliterated by the Civilian Conservation Corps road construction in the 1930s. Near the west end of RS 11, a cut in the crest of the topography suggests another road that crosses RS 11 at right angles. This cut is about 9.5 m wide and runs north past the only small house in the vicinity, 29SJ 2401, toward the Cly's Canyon seeps and RS 43. It also appears to run directly south to the Pueblo Bonito staircase.

On the east side of Pueblo Alto, a road (RS 40) passes north through an opening or gate 1 m wide in Major Wall 1 cleared by Prescott College in 1972 (Ware and Gumerman 1977) and then splits into five or more routes. This point is often referred to as the end (or starting point) of the Great North Road that eventually connects to the Salmon Ruin on the San Juan River (Obenauf 1980). The Great North Road and its three major associated communities have been extensively investigated. Salmon Ruin, the probable terminus of the road (Powers *et al.* 1983:97), was being excavated (Irwin-Williams 1972) at the time work commenced at Pueblo Alto. Along the same route, Twin Angels Pueblo in Kutz Canyon was partly excavated by Earl Morris in 1915 (Carlson 1966).

Further south, Pierre's, the first major community associated with the road north of Pueblo Alto, 15 km distant, was inventoried by Morenon (1977) and Powers *et al.* (1983). The first full-length investigation of the Great North Road was conducted by Pierre Morenon (1977) in 1974. This was followed up by caloric studies using a respirator to measure the potential functional efficiency of the roads (Morenon and Amick 1977). Later studies of the road were conducted by the Bureau of Land Management (Kincaid 1983), and it has been trenched a number of times by different institutions (Brethauer 1978; Nials 1983; Trott 1980).

Several routes angle to the northeast from the Pueblo Alto gate in the direction of a small-site Pueblo III (early A.D. 1100s) community along the Escavada Wash. Another (RS 43) goes northwest from the gate across RS 33 past the Rabbit Ruin and on to nearby Cly's Canyon and further to Peñasco Blanco.

Still on the east side of Pueblo Alto, yet another road (RS 37) runs due east from Pueblo Alto's east plaza (Plaza 2) past the East Ruin and on for another 430 m, bordered by a masonry wall or curbing, to terminate close to another curbed road, RS 36. Another (RS 35) runs southwest–northeast from the mesa edge and a series of stairs, just east of Chetro Ketl, and past the Poco site, a collection of unusual above-ground, low-wall, circular rooms connected by masonry walls (Drager and Lyons 1983), and on to sites along the Escavada Wash.

The Great North Road (an extension of RS 40) extends south through the gate across Plaza 2 at Pueblo Alto, past the Trash Mound (bordered by Major Wall 3), and down the first set of ledges to the bench below where it is paralleled by a long groove hammered into the bedrock (see also Judd 1964:Plate 40). Grooves such as this one have been associated with stick-racers at Laguna and Zuni (Parsons 1923:258–9, Fig. 20–2). The groove disappears at the point where the Great North Road (now RS 40) forks into two segments (RS 40E and 40W) that lead to ramps and stairways behind Chetro Ketl. An intermittent series of stairs, ramps, and wall segments allows a person to follow one segment (RS 40W) directly into the Talus Unit (see Lekson 1985; Morain *et al.* 1981:Fig. 8). Because of its connections, this route is known as the Alto–Talus Unit Road. The other fork (RS 40E) leads to masonry stairs or a ramp (Vivian 1983b:Fig. A–1) in the rincon behind Chetro Ketl.

RS 40E also continues around the bench top just east of Chetro Ketl, where it becomes RS 32, and then descends into Chaco Canyon by a series of closely spaced stairways and possible ramps. These ramps and stairs may be linked individually to specific roads (Gwinn Vivian, personal communication 1987) because a number of roads merge at this location. Across the canyon from this location is a spectacular and well-known rock-cut stairway (Fig. 11.6), which connects to a road running to Tsin Kletsin on top of South Mesa (route not shown on maps). The route is conspicuously devoid of cultural material, however, as the pueblo is of trash. The small site size, the isolation from habitation sites, and the proximity of several shrines and dams suggest that Tsin Kletzin may have provided specific non-secular duties related to hydrology, communications, and ritual.

Alignment of the two stairway sets suggests a continuous route that may stretch from Tsin Kletzin to Pueblo Alto. The setting of both sites on opposite mesa tops, and the association of stone animal figures (see below) with both, set the sites apart from the other canyon greathouses. The road to Tsin Kletzin is known to the Navajo as the "Zuni Trail" (Fransted and Werner 1974:75), a provocative reference to historic puebloan use. In fact, Chaco Canyon is considered by the Zuni as an ancestral site in Zuni migration legends, a place where prayer offerings are deposited (Ferguson 1981:Appendix 1).

RS 40 and RS 32 are particularly intriguing in that they may have once been marked at high points by stone animal figures set alongside the roads, perhaps as road markers or shrines. There may have been more than one such figure along the road to Pueblo Alto, aside from that mentioned by Holsinger (1901:68). "Shrines" marking the roads at Pueblo Alto and "across the wash" were anticipated and found by a Hopi informant

Fig. 11.6. The massive cut steps of 29SJ761 leading to the "Zuni Trail" road and Tsin Kletsin on top of South Mesa. The climber is the author.

(Waters 1963:43), but without carved figures in them. Mrs. Richard Wetherill, however, referred to another figure "northeast of Chetro Ketl," which is where RS 32 is located (Vivian 1948). Finally, another stone figure, very similar to the one purported to be from Pueblo Alto, was recovered in 1925 on the mesa top south of Pueblo Alto at Tsin Kletzin (Judd 1954:295, Fig. 80A). Despite confusion over location, it seems probable that carved-stone animal figures marked one or more of the roads in the central canyon complex.

Road-related features around Pueblo Alto

Masonry curbing (low masonry walls that often border one side of a road), ramps, and cut and masonry stairs are frequent road associations in the central canyon area. Many of these common features are described in detail by Vivian (1983b) and Pattison (1985, 1988) and need not be covered here. Work at Pueblo Alto has revealed another category of road-associated structures – paired-room units – that have not been recognized from previous work. The paired units common around Pueblo Alto may exist in the vicinity of other greathouses, although none has been recognized to date with the possible exception of the small L-shaped ruin on the northeastern side of Peñasco Blanco.

Four spatially distinct blocks of paired rooms at Pueblo Alto (Fig. 11.7) appear road related, although their exact function remains unknown. All were built with the long axis perpendicular to passing roads (e.g., Fig. 11.5). Each unit consists of two rooms joined along the long axis and, where a wall is standing, connected by a centrally placed door. Lengths of each room are identical but one room is always slightly larger (wider) than the other. Very few rooms and no room pairs in the primary Pueblo Alto roomblocks are similar in size to those of the paired units. In the group of eleven paired units there is little variation among the large rooms (629×324 cm; 20.4 m^2) or the small rooms (628×265 cm; 16.6 m^2) in mean dimensions and area, which suggests all were built from a standard plan.

The largest block, designated the East Ruin, consists of six paired units arranged in an "L" around a large Chacoan kiva. The East Ruin is 143 m due east of Pueblo Alto and connected to it by a massive masonry wall through which the Alto–Chetro Ketl/Great North Road passes. Each leg of the house contains three paired units situated at right-angles to RS 37 and 41. The East Ruin was built in the mid A.D. 1000s and occupied into the early A.D. 1100s (Windes 1987a).

Two short segments of wall, a single stone high, extend into the path of RS 37 from the southernmost paired unit. Another wall extends into RS 33 from the southwestern corner of Pueblo Alto. It would seem that the projection of these walls into the road would disrupt traffic patterns and, therefore, they may have served for traffic control. Similar projections into prehistoric roads have been noted at Kin Hocho'i and Ats'ee nitsaa in Manuelito Canyon and other greathouses in Arizona southwest of Chaco Canyon (Stein 1987).

A second block of paired rooms (Rooms 194–7) is located in the southern arc enclosing Pueblo Alto's interior plaza (see Fig. 11.5). Although at first glance the block appears part of the large array of rooms, the masonry style and wall abutments mark a former discrete unit of four rooms incorporated into later remodeling. The masonry suggests construction at about the mid A.D. 1000s. The block may have been built as an isolated unit, although the canter of the long axis of the set suggests that it was once part of an earlier enclosing arc.

Rooms 194–7 lie just east of an entry into the Pueblo Alto plaza from outside. Aerial photos plainly show a road angling northwest off the Alto–Chetro Ketl (RS 40) route and into Pueblo Alto at this point. When the spot was excavated, a door 68 cm wide was revealed in the north wall of Room 199 between two narrow structures (Rooms 198 and 200). The south wall of Room 199 was never verified, although a short segment extending from adjacent Room 201 seems to assure its presence. Construction of Room 199 may later have prevented through traffic. Nevertheless, the perfect alignment of the road and the passage into Plaza 1 suggests that the association of Rooms 194–7 is not fortuitous.

A third set of rooms appears in the northwestern corner of Pueblo Alto. This pair (Rooms 225 and 226) disturbs the otherwise symmetrical arrangement of the primary roomblock by jutting west beyond the adjacent rooms (Fig. 11.5). The pair matches other road-associated units except for an off-center door common to them. The main Alto–Bonito thoroughfare (RS 33) is a clearly defined swale that passes by the two rooms a meter or two away.

Fig. 11.7. Road-associated paired-room units at Pueblo Alto. Room numbers identify members of paired units.

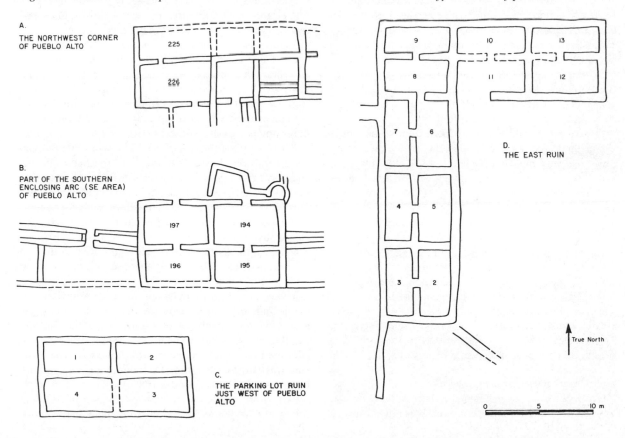

A.
THE NORTHWEST CORNER OF PUEBLO ALTO

B.
PART OF THE SOUTHERN ENCLOSING ARC (SE AREA) OF PUEBLO ALTO

C.
THE PARKING LOT RUIN JUST WEST OF PUEBLO ALTO

D.
THE EAST RUIN

True North

0   5   10 m

Finally, a fourth set of rooms, the Parking Lot Ruin, was found a short distance away from the West Wing Pueblo Alto rooms. The two contiguous pairs had been road-graded to the foundations, removing any traces of doors. The main Alto–Bonito thoroughfare (RS 33) passes by about 22 m to the east. Another road (RS 11) may pass close by the Parking Lot Ruin on the north side at the terminal end of a route coming west past New Alto. The position of New Alto and East Ruin equidistant from Pueblo Alto (to the east and west sides) and the respective association of similar walls and roads reveal symmetrical architectural pairings of road-related structures with Pueblo Alto.

Road entries at Pueblo Alto

There are several points at which roads pass through or terminate at gates or doors of the site (Fig. 11.5) aside from those mentioned above. A passage, 110 cm wide, extends through the enclosing arc west of the paired unit of Rooms 194–7. Another passage was found through the low wall of Other Structure 3 south of Room 205 that revealed surfaces compacted by foot traffic. The entry through the central point of the enclosing arc was apparently duplicated at Chetro Ketl where it is now marked by a distinct transverse depression across the unexcavated arc rooms. Jackson (1878:Plate 57) was the first to note this as a possible entry.

A second entry allows access through Other Structure 3. This enters the east side of OS 3 past Room 201 and is also blocked with masonry. It was about 52 cm wide but may have originally been as wide as 144 cm. Wall clearing and subsequent stabilization have altered the initial character of the entry, although there may have been a small masonry pillar on the south side of the entry.

Finally, a third road segment appears on aerial photos to form a dogleg northeast into the Pueblo Alto enclosing arc from the Alto–Bonito (RS 33) road. It is not known precisely where the road intersects the arc, because no breaks now occur in the expected entry area. Deep testing would be necessary in the much-remodeled arc to discover any entries that might exist. Rooms 208 and 209, nearby, may have been associated with this entry, although they are not at right angles to the suspected route and are dissimilar in other ways to the road-related units discussed above. Masonry veneer style suggests construction of the two rooms in the early A.D. 1000s, which predates the other room pairs.

Road function suggested by road termini

Transport of raw and finished materials must be considered a major road function. The quantities of ceramics (Toll 1981), chipped stones (Cameron 1984), and construction timbers (Dean and Warren 1983) imported into Chaco Canyon, for example, indicate a widespread network of exchange and movement of goods unlikely to have been transported off-road. Despite the emphasis on non-local movement of economic goods, there are probably a variety of other functions attributable to roads within the canyon. The fragility of the ecosystem in Chaco may have obliged the Anasazi to channel local traffic (via roads) in order to minimize environmental destruction (Schelberg 1982:108). Morenon and Amick (1977) emphasize the efficiency of the roads outside Chaco Canyon even for mere traveling. Examination of canyon road termini and road-associated artifacts suggests that some roads were used primarily for local activities.

Water procurement

RS 43 leaves Pueblo Alto from the north gate in Plaza 2 (as does the Great North Road) and runs northwest across RS 33 and past the nearby Rabbit Ruin. A number of stairways at the edge of nearby Cly's Canyon suggest multiple terminal points for this road (Fig. 11.4). The clearest route lies directly west of Rabbit Ruin and crosses the exposed undulating bedrock. It is marked by a small causeway, several series of small cut steps and piles of collapsed stone ramps or masonry steps, and terminates in a series of wide cut steps at 29SJ 1786 (Fig. 11.8). All the stairs descend near potential or active seeps. Some of these have been dug out historically and are continually active during even the driest years (i.e., they contain standing water).

RS 44, a spur route off of RS 33 between Pueblo Alto and Pueblo Bonito, leads to the seeps reached by RS 43 and may indicate that inhabitants at Pueblo Bonito and Pueblo del Arroyo were also drawn to these sources. The number of stairways associated with these major sources of water, the dominance of Pueblo II–early Pueblo III jars around the seeps and on the nearby cliffs, and the roads leading from Pueblo Alto and Pueblo Bonito toward this area make it likely that the route was one for water procurement.

Three of the four potential or active seeps have simple hand- and toe-hold steps descending nearby and these must have been solely for access to water. Unusual care was taken, however, to cut steps across the slightest bedrock rises along the route to the stairs at 29SJ 1786, perhaps to lessen the danger of stumbling with water-laden jars. Although there is a potential source of water nearby, the construction of this route beyond the best water sources, its higher labor investment than needed

Fig. 11.8. Route of Road Segment 43 as it crosses the slick rock from Pueblo Alto to Cly's Canyon on the route toward Peñasco Blanco.

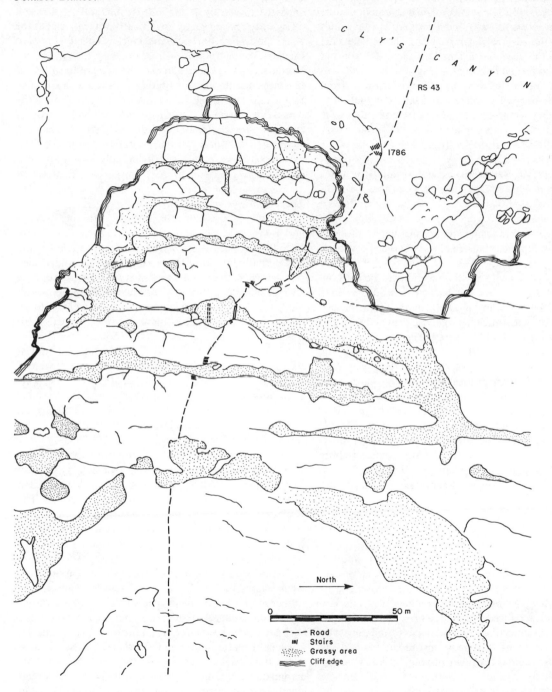

for stairs next to seeps, and the absence of ceramics make its function for water procurement alone questionable. It was suspected, then, that RS 43 served as a major route to the west across Cly's Canyon, but with spur routes leading to the several water sources. The main route, marked by the 29SJ 1786 stairs, led toward RS 6 and stairs leading to Peñasco Blanco (Fig. 11.3).

Another route (RS 8N) that led northwest from Peñasco Blanco to Ah-Shi-Sle-Pah Canyon passed a series of deep potholes, the Los Aguages tanks, that were used historically as a source of water (Kincaid *et al.* 1983:9–76–9–77; Stein 1983:8–10). The high ratio of jar fragments recovered from the Ah-Shi-Sle-Pah Road suggests that the Anasazi also had used the tanks for water (Kincaid *et al.* 1983:9–77; Windes 1987a:Table 5.4).

Terrace farming

Some road segments in the vicinity of Pueblo Alto are associated with areas that could have served as garden plots or terraces (Windes 1987a). At the base of the first cliff below Pueblo Alto are four sections of bench bordered by masonry walls and backed by alluvial sands (Vivian 1970:69; Vivian and Mathews 1965:13). These were incorrectly identified as road segments (RS 28, 30, 31, and 34) during the 1972 survey. The sites face southeast between 140° and 160° in a position favorable for morning summer sun and shady afternoons. They are located where the Cliffhouse formation shales stop downward movement of ground water through the thick overlying sandstone, which results in moisture accumulation that produces the seeps in Cly's Canyon. Similar topographic settings are favored by the Hopi for small "seepage" fields (Hack 1942:34). Each terrace is bordered by rock-cut stairways, some terminating at the terrace and others as part of more extensive, passing road routes.

Associated artifacts are less informative regarding use of the terraces. Most are ceramics, although a possible digging-tool (tchamahia) fragment that suggests agricultural activities was found on RS 31. It was expected that farming would require predominantly large jars with which to water plants and to carry produce, techniques that have historic analogues (Ladd 1979:Fig. 12). Two terraces produced a quantity of ceramics. One of these (RS 31) yielded the variety of types found in nearby greathouse middens, although it was dominated by whiteware jar sherds. The incidence of Chuskan culinary vessel fragments was low, however, as it was along the roads. Ceramics from RS 28 were also dominated by whiteware jars but with fewer culinary pieces present. This assemblage is similar to road refuse and closer to

expectations for terrace refuse. RS 28 ceramics revealed a mixture of types that suggest use of the terrace in the early A.D. 1000s through the early A.D. 1100s, although a few early ceramics may be indicative of activities in the A.D. 900s. The latter, perhaps, mark events unrelated to the terrace construction and use.

In summary, the location and exposure of these walled benches and their similarity to Hopi seepage fields make it possible that these features were an attempt by the Anasazi to maximize knowledge of the local hydrology to grow crops. On the other hand, recent work by Marshall and Sofaer (1988) suggests that these were elevated "stages" or platform complexes for outdoor ceremonies.

Local exchange routes

Two or more roads come together at the trio of stairways and ramps that descend the cliffs just east of Chetro Ketl. One (RS 32), discussed above, leads to Pueblo Alto and perhaps Jackson's Staircase (29SJ 1526). The other segment (RS 35) extends northeast and is bordered by a strip of masonry "curbing" on the mesa top as it heads for the Poco site (also connected to Pueblo Alto by another route) and the community of early A.D. 1100 houses along the Escavada Wash, northeast of Pueblo Alto. Roads leading beyond the Escavada community have not been found on aerial photographs (Obenauf 1983:Fig. 4–13). Because water and other resources seem to be absent along this route, RS 35 may have served to facilitate local exchange and procurement between the canyon residents (particularly Chetro Ketl's) and those of the Escavada community in a situation analogous to the ties connecting Chaco with Bis sa'ani, a Chacoan outlier community situated on the Escavada Wash to the east of Pueblo Alto (Breternitz *et al.* 1982). Alternatively, RS 35 may have facilitated traffic towards Tsin Kletzin from the Escavada area instead. Ceramic assemblages found along it are from the early A.D. 1100s, which indicates use contemporary with the communities it joins.

The proximity of Chetro Ketl to three or more stairways leading to RS 35 and RS 32 suggests considerable influence and traffic originating from Chetro Ketl. Of course, a number of roads also connect Pueblo Alto to the Escavada community, and others are suspected between the latter and Hungo Pavi and Peñasco Blanco. Thus, road ties between the canyon greathouses and the Escavada community suggest much interaction through the movement of people and goods, although the exact nature of the interaction must await further investigation. Different physical attributes may help to separate local and regional roads, but data on these were not utilized here.

Road function suggested by the material culture

Although the economic aspects of the Chacoan road system have at times been stressed (e.g., Ebert and Hitchcock 1980; Ebert and Lyons 1976:8–9), little effort has focused upon verifying this from road-associated artifacts. Previous collections have been made from the canyon roads, but only recently have such materials been analyzed and interpreted. It is known from these collections that ceramics comprise the major material recoverable from the Chacoan roads. Ceramics, therefore, are the primary artifact class with which to appraise road function and period of use.

Verification of ceramic association with roads

Morenon (1977) was the first to demonstrate that artifacts tended to concentrate along roads, although his samples were exceedingly small. Otherwise, there has been little work to verify that ceramics on roads actually related to road use. Anasazi ceramics in Chaco Canyon, in particular, seem to be found everywhere beyond house-site peripheries, even on Archaic sites (Hayes 1981:19). Pottery is abundant along the strips of bedrock bordering the canyon in the same areas where roads are readily apparent. To avoid the problem of monitoring ceramics unrelated to road use, scatters were examined just above road stairways, where breakage related to stair and road use was presumed to have occurred. In addition, three transects along strips of bench bedrock perpendicular to obvious on-the-ground roads (i.e., curbed segments in the vicinity of Pueblo Alto, Pueblo Bonito, and Chetro Ketl) were monitored to assess whether ceramics along the roads were derived from road use.

The results from the transects revealed that sherd density is associated with road proximity and is indicative of behavior related to road use and maintenance. Ceramics are sparse or absent well beyond the roads and increase in density as the road is approached. Highest densities are immediately peripheral to the roads, where sweepings are likely to have been deposited, and lower densities are found directly within the road (Fig. 11.9). These across-the-road samples were done in select areas of minimal topographical, geological, and environmental diversity, so that artifact densities should reflect cultural, not natural, processes. In these samples, however, there was no discernible temporal or typological change in the ceramic assemblages within the road and beyond, which suggests relatively short-term use of

the roads, primarily in the last half of the A.D. 1000s. It is thus unlikely that activities unrelated to road use would generate ceramics that followed the road alignments. Nials (1983) reports that bedrock detritus litters

Fig. 11.9. Sherd density variation along transects set perpendicular to visible prehistoric road alignments near Pueblo Alto. A–Across RS 40 as it approaches Pueblo Alto. B–Across RS 40 above the Talus Unit. C–Across RS 33 between Pueblo Bonito and Pueblo Alto.

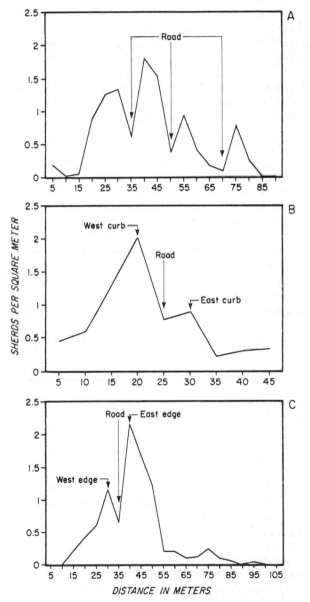

the road edges in a similar fashion, probably as a result of maintenance and sweeping activities.

Road function suggested by ceramics

At the onset of the road study, it was expected that cultural material, particularly sherds, would mirror house inventories. Preliminary work by Morenon (1977) suggested that this was the case for at least the Great North Road. Both local and non-local materials presumably were road transported, even if for a short distance, but ceramics made at a site would not need transport if they were consumed at the point of manufacture. Therefore, roads might yield higher ratios of trade (non-local) ceramics than would house sites. Although ceramics might be both imported and exported, Toll (1981) stressed the problems of producing local pottery. It is certain that many of the ceramics in Chaco Canyon during the A.D. 1000s and 1100s were imported, particularly Chuskan vessels that were made about 83 km to the west of Chaco Canyon and occur in large numbers at the canyon sites (Toll 1981, 1984; Toll *et al.* 1980).

In light of the importance of imported ceramics, it might be postulated that if road transport was primarily for importing goods, then higher ratios of imports would be found on the roads than in site assemblages. It also follows that roads would yield differential ratios of trade ceramics depending on the proximity of the road to the region of procurement. For instance, ceramics made in the San Juan River region to the north were expected to dominate assemblages or to be found in increased frequencies on roads leading into the canyon from the north as suggested by Morenon's (1977) work. Tusayan and Chuskan ceramics, produced in northeastern Arizona and northwestern New Mexico, were expected to be found in large numbers along the western Chacoan roads. Conversely, some pottery that may have been locally made (some Gallup, Chaco, and Chaco-McElmo black-on-whites) found on the Great North Road suggests export to Chacoan outliers (Morenon 1975:7), such as the Salmon Ruin (Franklin 1980).

Thus, it is rather surprising that Chuskan and other imported vessels rarely occurred along the roads examined in the central canyon area and in the vicinity of Peñasco Blanco. This discrepancy may be related to different modes of transportation that depend on vessel size and distance of travel. Some vessels may be hand carried and as a consequence more prone to breakage, while others may be restrained by packs and nested for long-range transportation as is practiced today in Yucatan (Thompson 1958:Fig. 28) and Guatemala (Reina and Hill 1978:Plate 382). Furthermore, some

vessel classes are likely to be road transported only to their destinations, while others may constantly be on the move outside the home.

Obtaining water in Chaco must have required considerable movement of water jars along the roads. These jars were probably hand carried or set on the head as in historic puebloan use (e.g., Garcia-Matson 1979:Fig. 8; Voth 1903:Plate 92). Ultimately, most would be broken in service during transport. All ceramic assemblages examined on the canyon roads for this study were overwhelmingly dominated by whiteware jar sherds, although this alone does not demonstrate that breakage was the result of hauling water. More convincingly, the few whiteware jar rims observed (61) along the roads revealed a preponderance of ollas, or water-storage jars (75 percent), along with small numbers of pitchers (13 percent) and canteens (11 percent). Culinary jar fragments, normally comprising half of the sherd assemblages from excavated house sites, were far below normal proportions with a single exception noted below, although massive numbers of the Chuskan variety must have been carried to the canyon greathouses along the roads. On the roads, culinary ceramics rarely comprised 20 percent of the total and often were half that.

In summary, most canyon ceramic breakage along roads was related to jar transport, particularly whiteware storage jars. Water would be a major requirement for inhabitants for drinking, mortar preparation, and pot agriculture, particularly at the mesa-top pueblos where water was located at some distance. Foodstuffs may also have been carried in large jars.

Lithic debitage on roads

Other goods undoubtedly moved along the roads but there is little physical evidence for them. These are likely to have been perishable items or items minimally prone to accidental breakage and discard. Chipped stone debris is second to ceramics in frequency along the roads but almost always is limited to a very few pieces. Often, chipped stone was absent on the roads. The exception occurred along RS 35 between Chetro Ketl and the Escavada community. A transect along this route yielded a high density of chipped stone (5.2 per m^2; n = 179) from several sources, including 7 percent Washington Pass chert from the Chuska Mountains about 83 km to the west. This chert is numerically abundant in the nearby Chetro Ketl, Pueblo Bonito, and Pueblo Alto trash mounds and may derive from ritual activities (Toll and McKenna 1987:154–5). The road debitage does not result from primary core reduction or tool manufacture, and thus, other sources of behavior (including ritual) must be considered. Other materials were so few in number that little can be said of them regarding road-use behavior.

Dating the roads
Dating the roads generally relies on association with house sites and, ultimately, ceramics. The long occupation evident at many sites and the relative scarcity of road-related materials outside the canyon, however, have hampered chronological assessment of the Chacoan roads. Fortunately, Chaco Canyon affords the best potential for using site association and road materials because of the extent of excavation in road-related greathouses and the preservation of materials along roads.

Road-associated ceramics are apt to suffer from factors typical of surface surveys. Beyond Chaco Canyon, roads are commonly buried along with the artifacts. Among the many exposed patches of bedrock on the benches above Chaco, however, detritus often traps cultural material including that along the roads. Exposure, unfortunately, increases the effects of sand blasting and other detrimental effects on the ceramics, leaving most without paint and slip. Animal and human traffic have also reduced the size and number of the ceramics.

Even with these hazards, tabulations of ceramics collected during R. Gwinn Vivian's 1970–1 investigations and the 1972 Chaco Center site inventory, and the non-collection counts made by the author in 1981–3 are remarkably consistent despite the different collection techniques. All ceramics from each project were re-sorted by the author to reduce variability of the typological assignments.

Seriation of road ceramics[1]
Recent efforts to date roads have relied on assigning dates to ceramic types present on roads (Kincaid *et al.* 1983). The sources for assigning dates in some cases were derived from work (i.e., Breternitz 1966) that had not been revised in decades. With the exception of the Peñasco Blanco area, the canyon road ceramics sampled appear to be a homogeneous lot, not biased by long-term deposition. A new multidimensional scaling program, KYST-2A (Kruskal *et al.* 1978), offers an objective, replicable seriation of taxonomic pottery assemblages and is useful for the present problem of dating road ceramics (see Windes 1987a:240–69).

In this study, control was provided by the inclusion of twenty-eight tree-ring-dated Cibolan ceramic assemblages from the San Juan Basin merged with the fourteen

road and road-related ceramic assemblages. The overall sample contained about 12,000 decorated sherds. The results (Fig. 11.10) suggest that refuse on the canyon road segments dates from between about A.D. 1050 and 1140. In all program runs (see Kruskal and Wish 1978; Windes 1987a, for the program explanation), the earliest positioning (at about A.D. 1050) was from RS 32, the rimrock road just east of Chetro Ketl, although a few late sherds suggest its continued use into the early A.D. 1100s. The remainder derive from the late A.D. 1000–early A.D. 1100s. The Alto–Talus Unit–Chetro Ketl roads, the area around the Alto–Cly's Canyon road, those from the stairs north of Peñasco Blanco (RS 8S), and the road east to the Escavada Wash from Peñasco Blanco fall into the span between A.D. 1050 and 1100. Ceramic-type ratios of painted sherds from these are much like those of the large canyon greathouse trash mounds, although culinary discard differs.

Recent work by the Bureau of Land Management (Kincaid *et al.* 1983) has suggested that roads south of Chaco Canyon are much earlier (i.e., A.D. 900s), although John Stein (personal communication 1983) believes that this inference is false and that the South Road reflects an A.D. 1000s use. The only road examined outside of Chaco during this study was a segment (RS 50) of the South Road that led southwest from Kin Ya'a (a Chacoan outlier near Crownpoint, New Mexico) onto the nearby mesas. In all KYST plots, this road clearly associates with the A.D. 1050–1100 span, supporting Stein's contention. The road assemblage is virtually identical to the painted ceramic assemblages associated with the main Kin Ya'a trash mounds and presumed to be contemporary with the late A.D. 1000s tree-ring dates from the site (see Windes 1982). However, a 1988 reconnaisance of the east end of Chaco Canyon revealed sites occupied in the A.D. 900s and early A.D. 1000s bordering the roads leading to Pueblo Pintado. Thus, some roads may have begun use earlier than the seriation results obtained above.

Early A.D. 1100s use is suggested by seriation for the Alto–Bonito segments, the Chetro Ketl–Escavada community road (RS 35), the Escavada Wash/Ah-Shi-Sle-Pah Road (RS 8N) north of Peñasco Blanco, and RS 1 extending east up Chaco Canyon from Peñasco Blanco. The roads leading north out of Pueblo Alto are also post-A.D. 1100 (Kincaid *et al.* 1983; Morenon 1975) and ceramically are a continuum of the Alto–Bonito road. Other roads in the canyon yielded few or no ceramics, partly because of aeolian deposits. Interestingly, the road to Tsin Kletsin crosses terrain identical to that around Pueblo Alto but yielded almost no ceramics.

Ceramics were also absent along RS 7 between Pueblo Alto and Peñasco Blanco. This may suggest that use patterns differed between these bare roads and those roads littered with refuse.

To summarize, seriation suggests that formal Chacoan roads first appeared in the central canyon during the mid A.D. 1000s, coincidental with other signs of the emerging Classic Bonito phase. Their use appeared to be relatively short-lived with little evidence of extensive use beyond about A.D. 1140 or so. At Pueblo Alto, Kin Ya'a, and Peñasco Blanco, road refuse indicates that use along some segments was relatively brief and may have lasted only between about A.D. 1050 and 1100. The roads leading east to Pueblo Pintado were not analyzed, however, and they may have been built earlier. In addition, ceramics at two terraces (RS 28 and 310) reflect

early A.D. 1100s activities with some possibility of earlier use for another.

Conclusions

Aside from other site functions (see Windes 1987a), Pueblo Alto's connection with the prehistoric roads that converge on it and the visibility of the roads from Pueblo Alto as they approach from far across the landscape were important. Not fortuitously did the rise of Pueblo Alto and the prehistoric roads coincide with a period of drought between A.D. 1030 and 1048. To what extent long-range planning influenced the construction of Pueblo Alto is unknown, but it seems certain that Pueblo Alto was an important first stage in establishing the formal Chacoan network to the northern periphery of the San Juan Basin.

Fig. 11.10. Multidimensional scaling plot showing the temporal associations of prehistoric roads and a terrace (RS31) with tree-ring and radiocarbon dated ceramic samples, using the KYST-2A program in five-dimensional space. The 2 by 1 dimension is shown, with a stress factor of .13. Site numbers are identified in parentheses (see Windes 1987a: Table 8.16).

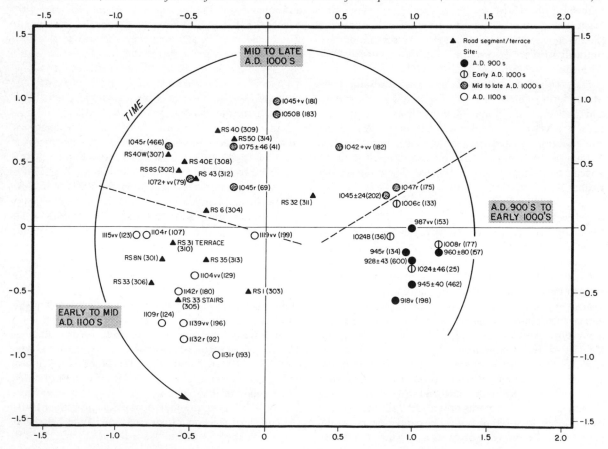

Roads around Pueblo Alto enter directly into the greathouse or pass-by structures (paired-room units) associated with Pueblo Alto. All road traffic going north from Pueblo Bonito, Pueblo del Arroyo, Chetro Ketl, and Talus Unit 1 would have borne inspection by the inhabitants of Alto. The road link to the west would have allowed goods and people to bypass Pueblo Bonito and Chetro Ketl and to be brought directly into Pueblo Alto past Peñasco Blanco. This link lessens the perceived dominance, because of size, of Chetro Ketl and Pueblo Bonito over Pueblo Alto. In addition, the conspicuous road links between Pueblo Alto and Chetro Ketl suggest political and economic ties, which ceramics and site construction place in the last half of the A.D. 1000s. Thus, Pueblo Alto's perceived role for controling access in and out of Chaco Canyon seems justified by the juxtaposition of the roads there.

If the size of the road-related structures is indicative of their importance or amount of use, then initial emphasis was on the routes passing east of Pueblo Alto. The East Ruin dwarfs the west side Parking Lot Ruin by having three times as many paired-room units. This suggests that the flow of traffic and goods to and from the Escavada communities was more important or more frequent than that passing by the west side of Pueblo Alto from Pueblo Bonito and Pueblo del Arroyo in the A.D. 1000s. By A.D. 1100, however, the East Ruin and Major Wall 3, bordering Road Segment 40 that led to Chetro Ketl, were apparently dismantled, which suggests a cessation in traffic and importance along the Alto–Escavada community route and with Chetro Ketl. In the early A.D. 1100s, however, continued or new ties appear to have developed between Pueblo Alto and Pueblo Bonito, and Chetro Ketl and the Escavada community. Shifts in road use and artifact discard parallel other lines of evidence documenting changes in the Chacoan social and political organization at about A.D. 1100 (i.e., Lekson 1984; Toll *et al.* 1980; Toll and McKenna 1987; Windes 1987a).

Nevertheless, not all roads appear to be regionally important. Roads leading to vital subsistence resources nearby may also have been necessary. Some that interconnect canyon greathouses or sources for water and areas of potential agricultural use could have served only local functions. Although we found no massed materials stored at Pueblo Alto, the several paired-room units and the exterior rooms along the Pueblo Alto wings appeared associated with roads (i.e., exterior doors open directly onto them) and thus the rooms are likely candidates for the storage of both local and regional transported road goods. The attendant houses around Pueblo Alto all sit astride roads that appear non-regional in context. It is suggested that these (New Alto, Parking Lot Ruin, East Ruin, and Rabbit Ruin) served specific needs associated with use of the roads, although no physical evidence for entries into them has been produced, suggesting that their relationship to the roads could have been fortuitous. Lekson (Lekson and Judge 1978; Lekson 1984:269) believes that the greathouses built in the early A.D. 1100s, such as New Alto, were primarily storage facilities. If all the associated houses were primarily for storage, then a case for their being road related could be strengthened.

Finally, roads would have ameliorated part of the problem of resource depletion, environmental stress, and population pressures by allowing rapid transportation of goods into Chaco and rapid dispersion of people out of it. In addition, if Chaco became an important ritual center (e.g., Breternitz 1982; Judge 1989), then the roads would have facilitated widespread participation in the ceremonies. Roads may not have been necessary to effect these changes, but they did allow greater flexibility and speed for the events to happen. Because of the lack of a local, small-house community, Pueblo Alto can be seen as important in a regional system that was linked to it by the many prehistoric roads.

Notes

1 Tabulations of road ceramics and other pertinent data may be found in Windes (1987a, 1987b).

References

Avery, Thomas Eugene, and Thomas R. Lyons
  1981 *Remote Sensing: Aerial and Terrestrial Photography for Archaeologists*. A Handbook for Archaeologists and Cultural Resource Managers, Supplement 7. Cultural Resources Management Division, National Park Service, Washington, DC
Breternitz, Cory Dale
  1982 An Evolutionary Model of Anasazi Cultural Development in the Central San Juan Basin. In Breternitz *et al.*, vol. III: 1,241–9
Breternitz, Cory Dale, David E. Doyel, and Michael P. Marshall, ed.
  1982 *Bis sa'ani: A Late Bonito Phase Community on Escavada Wash, Northwest New Mexico*, 3 vols. Navajo Nation Papers in Anthropology 14, Window Rock, AZ
Breternitz, David A.
  1966 *An Appraisal of Tree-Ring Dated Pottery in the Southwest*. Anthropological Papers of the University of Arizona 10. Tucson, AZ

Brethauer, Douglas P.
1978 *Archaeological Investigations in the Chaco Canyon Vicinity, New Mexico*. New Mexico State University, Department of Sociology and Anthropology, Cultural Resources Management Division Report 270. Las Cruces, NM

Cameron, Catherine M.
1984 A Regional View of Chipped Stone Raw Material Use in Chaco Canyon. In *Recent Research on Chaco Prehistory*, edited by W. James Judge and John D. Schelberg, pp. 137–52. Reports of the Chaco Center 8, Division of Cultural Research, National Park Service, Albuquerque

Carlson, Roy L.
1966 Twin Angels Pueblo. *American Antiquity* 31:676–82.

Dean, Jeffrey S., and Richard L. Warren
1983 Dendrochronology. In *The Architecture and Dendrochronology of Chetro Ketl, Chaco Canyon, New Mexico*, edited by Stephen Lekson, pp. 105–240. Reports of the Chaco Center 6, Division of Cultural Research, National Park Service, Albuquerque

Drager, Dwight L., and Thomas R. Lyons
1983 A Field Test of Remote Sensing in Archeology. MS on file, Division of Cultural Research, National Park Service, Albuquerque

Ebert, James I., and Robert K. Hitchcock
1980 Locational Modeling in the Analysis of the Prehistoric Roadway System at and around Chaco Canyon, New Mexico. In *Cultural Resources Remote Sensing*, edited by Thomas R. Lyons and Frances Joan Mathien, pp. 169–207. National Park Service, Washington, DC

Ebert, James I., and Thomas R. Lyons
1976 The Role of Remote Sensing in a Regional Archeological Research Design: A Case Study. In *Remote Sensing Experiments in Cultural Resources Studies*, assembled by Thomas R. Lyons, pp. 5–9. Reports of the Chaco Center 1, National Park Service, Albuquerque

Ferguson, T. J.
1981 Rebuttal Report of Plantiff Zuni Indian Tribe. MS on file, Zuni Archaeological Program, Pueblo of Zuni, NM

Franklin, Hayward H.
1980 Salmon Ruin Ceramics Laboratory Report. Investigations at the Salmon Site: The Structure of Chacoan Society in the Northern Southwest 2(5), edited by Cynthia Irwin-Williams and Phillip H. Shelley. MS on file, Eastern New Mexico University, Portales, NM

Fransted, Dennis, and Oswald Werner
1974 The Ethnogeography of the Chaco Canyon Area Navajo. MS on file, Chaco Center, National Park Service, Albuquerque

Garcia-Matson, Velma
1979 Acoma Pueblo. In *Handbook of North American Indians* Vol. IX, edited by Alfonso Ortiz, pp. 450–66. Smithsonian Institution, Washington, DC

Hack, John T.
1942 *The Changing Physical Environment of the Hopi Indians of Arizona*. Papers of the Peabody Museum of American Archaeology and Ethnology, Harvard University 35(1). Cambridge, MA

Hayes, Alden C.
1981 A Survey of Chaco Canyon Archeology. In *Archeological Survey of Chaco Canyon, New Mexico*, by Alden C. Hayes, David M. Brugge, and W. James Judge, pp. 1–68. Publications in Archeology 18A, Chaco Canyon Studies, National Park Service, Albuquerque

Holsinger, J.
1901 Report on Pre-historic Ruins of Chaco Canyon, NM. General Land Office Letter "P," National Archives, Washington, DC

Irwin-Williams, Cynthia
1972 *The Structure of Chacoan Society in the Northern Southwest: Investigations at the Salmon Site, 1972*. Eastern New Mexico University Contributions in Anthropology 4(3). Portales and Bloomfield, NM

Jackson, William H.
1878 Report on the Ancient Ruins Examined in 1875 and 1877. In *Tenth Annual Report of the United States Geological and Geographical Survey of the Territories Embracing Colorado and Parts of Adjacent Territories, Being a Report of the Progress of the Explorations for the Year 1876* by F. V. Hayden, pp. 411–50. Government Printing Press, Washington, DC

Judd, Neil M.
1954 *The Material Culture of Pueblo Bonito*. Smithsonian Miscellaneous Collections 124, Washington, DC
1964 *The Architecture of Pueblo Bonito*. Smithsonian Miscellaneous Collections 147(1), Washington, DC

Judge, W. James
1989 Chaco-San Juan Basin. In *Dynamics of Southwestern Prehistory*, edited by Linda S. Cordell and George Gumerman, pp. 209–61. Smithsonian Institution Press, Washington, DC
1983 *Chaco Roads Project, Phase I: A Reappraisal of Prehistoric Roads in the San Juan Basin*. United States Department of the Interior, Bureau of Land Management, Albuquerque and Santa Fe

N

1 Location of prehistoric roads in Chaco Canyon (in white) on the North Mesa. The roads are converging on Pueblo Alto. They were detected and mapped using the Thermal Infrared Multispectral Scanner (T.I.M.S.).

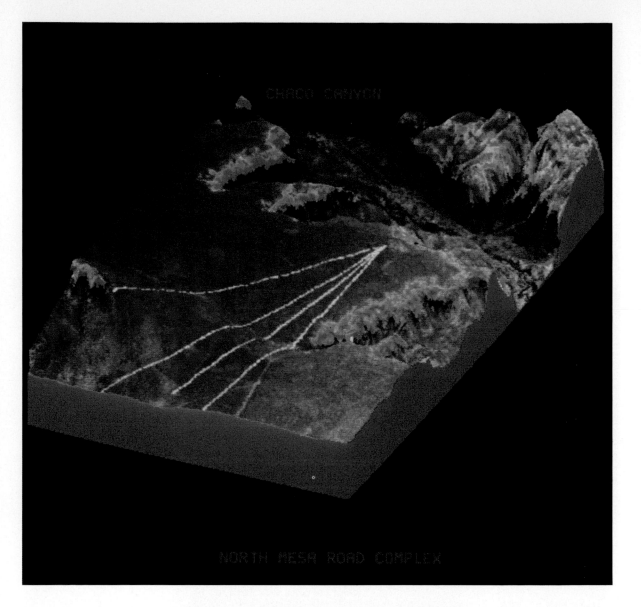

CHACO CANYON

NORTH MESA ROAD COMPLEX

2 Prehistoric roads in Chaco Canyon overlayed onto topographic data. Analysis of the data indicates that the prehistoric roads are maintaining their linearity despite topographic obstacles. Modern roads in the area avoid topographic obstacles, resulting in meandering patterns upon the landscape.

SE

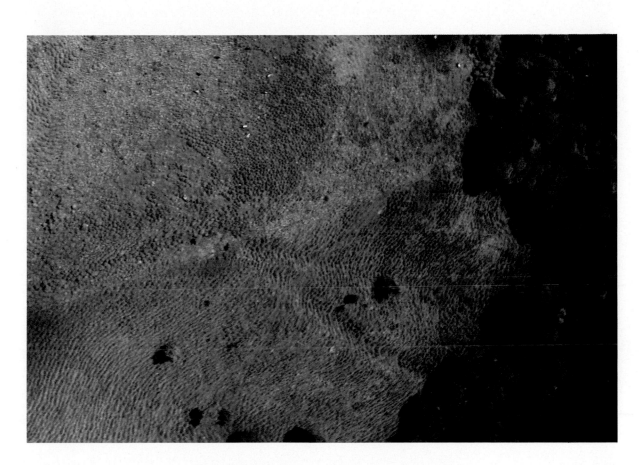

3 Color Infrared (C.I.R.) Photograph showing the
juncture of two prehistoric footpaths below the Silencio
Cemetery near Lake Arenal. Analysis of prehistoric
footpaths in Costa Rica indicated that C.I.R. photography was the optimum remotely sensed medium
for locating footpaths in grassland areas.

S

N

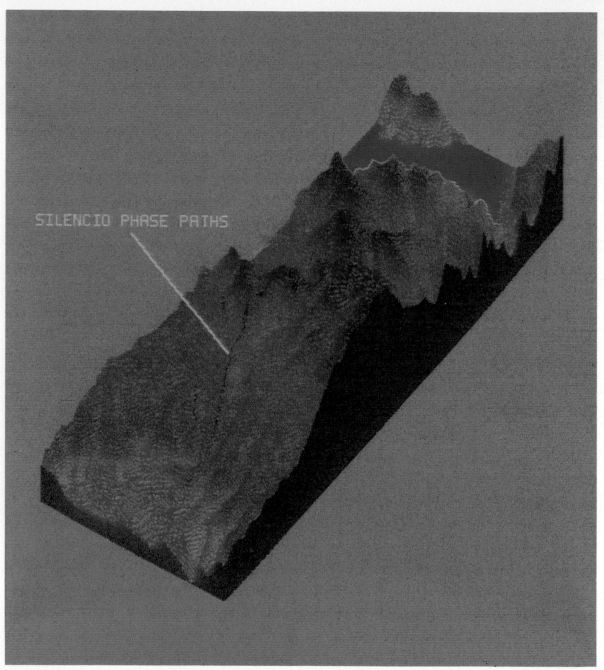

SILENCIO PHASE PATHS

4 Example of a footpath overlayed onto topographic data. This image illustrates that the paths are maintaining a relatively straight direction across the mountainous forest landscape.

Kincaid, Chris, John R. Stein, and Daisy F. Levine
1983 Road Verification Summary. In Kincaid 1983, chapter 9

Kruskal, Joseph B., and Myron Wish
1978 *Multidimensional Scaling*. Quantitative Applications in the Social Sciences 11. Sage University Paper, Beverly Hills and London

Kruskal, Joseph B., Forrest W. Young, and Judith B. Seery
1978 How to Use KYST-2A, a Very Flexible Program to Do Multidimensional Scaling and Unfolding. MS on file, Bell Laboratories, Murray Hill, NJ

Ladd, Edmund J.
1979 Zuni Economy. In *Handbook of North American Indians* Vol. VIII, edited by Alfonso Ortiz, pp. 492–8. Smithsonian Institution, Washington, DC

Lekson, Stephen H.
1984 *Great Pueblo Architecture of Chaco Canyon, New Mexico*. Publications in Archeology 18B, Chaco Canyon Studies. National Park Service, Albuquerque
1985 The Architecture of Talus Unit, Chaco Canyon, New Mexico. In *Prehistory and History in the Southwest: Collected Papers in Honor of Alden C. Hayes*, edited by Nancy Fox, pp. 43–59. Papers of the Archaeological Society of New Mexico 11, Santa Fe

Lekson, Stephen, and W. James Judge
1978 Architecture of the Bonito Phase of Chaco Canyon, New Mexico. Paper presented at the 77th Annual Meeting of the American Anthropological Association, Los Angeles

Lyons, Thomas R., and Robert K. Hitchcock
1977 Remote Sensing Interpretation of an Anasazi Land Route System. In *Aerial Remote Sensing Techniques in Archeology*, edited by Thomas R. Lyons and Robert K. Hitchcock, pp. 111–34. Reports of the Chaco Center 2, National Park Service, Albuquerque

Marshall, Michael P., and Anna Sofaer
1988 The Solstice Project – Archeological Investigations in the Chacoan Province. MS in possession of authors, Albuquerque and Washington, DC

Marshall, Michael P., John R. Stein, Richard W. Loose, and Judith E. Novotny
1979 *Anasazi Communities of the San Juan Basin*. Public Service Company, Albuquerque, and the Historic Preservation Bureau, Santa Fe

Morain, Stanley A., Thomas K. Budge, and Amelia Komarek
1981 An Airborne Spectral Analysis of Settlement Sites in Chaco Canyon. In *Remote Sensing; Multispectral Analyses of Cultural Resources: Chaco Canyon and Bandelier National Monument*, edited by Thomas R. Lyons, pp. 1–37. Remote Sensing: A Handbook for Archeologists and Cultural Resource Managers, Supplement 5. Cultural Resources Management, National Park Service, Washington, DC

Morenon, Pierre Ernest
1975 Chacoan Roads and Adaptation: How a Prehistoric Population Can Define and Control Its Social and Natural Environment. Paper presented at the 40th Annual Meeting of the Society for American Archaeology, Dallas
1977 A View of the Chacoan Phenomena from the "Backwoods": A Speculative Essay. MS on file, Division of Cultural Research, National Park Service, Albuquerque

Morenon, Pierre E., and Ben Amick
1977 Summary of Energy Study Results in Chaco Canyon National Monument. Fort Burgwin Research Center, Southern Methodist University. MS on file, Division of Cultural Research, National Park Service, Albuquerque

Nials, Fred L.
1983 Physical Characteristics of Chacoan Roads. In Kincaid 1983, chapter 6

Nials, Fred, John Stein, and John Roney
1987 *Chacoan Roads in the Southern Periphery: Results of Phase II of the BLM Chaco Roads Project*. Cultural Resources Series 1, United States Department of the Interior, Bureau of Land Management, Albuquerque

Obenauf, Margaret Senter
1980 The Chacoan Roadway System. M.A. thesis, University of New Mexico, Albuquerque
1983 Evaluation of Aerial Photography. In Kincaid 1983, chapter 4

O'Bryan, Aileen
1956 *The Díné: Origin Myths of the Navaho Indians*. Smithsonian Institution, Bureau of American Ethnology, Bulletin 163, Washington, DC

Parsons, Elsie Clews
1923 *Laguna Genealogies*. Anthropological Papers of the American Museum of Natural History 19, Part 5

Pattison, Natalie
1985 Rock Stairways of Chaco Canyon, New Mexico. In *Prehistory and History in the Southwest: Collected Papers in Honor of Alden C. Hayes*, edited by Nancy Fox, pp. 61–72. The Archaeological Society of New Mexico 11, Santa Fe
1988 Inventory of Stairways and Trails in Chaco Culture National Historical Park. MS on file, Branch of Cultural Research, National Park Service, Santa Fe

Powers, Robert P., William B. Gillespie, and Stephen H. Lekson
1983 *The Outlier Survey: A Regional View of Settlement of the San Juan Basin*. Reports of the Chaco Center 3, National Park Service, Albuquerque

Reina, Ruben E., and Robert M. Hill, II
1978 *The Traditional Pottery of Guatemala*. The Texas Pan American Series. University of Texas Press, Austin

Schelberg, John Daniel
1982 Economic and Social Development as an Adaptation to a Marginal Environment in Chaco Canyon, New Mexico. Ph.D. dissertation, Northwestern University, Evanston, IL

Stein, John R.
1983 Road Corridor Descriptions. In *Chaco Roads Project, Phase I: A Reappraisal of Prehistoric Roads in the San Juan Basin*, edited by Chris Kincaid, chapter 8. United States Department of the Interior, Bureau of Land Management, Albuquerque and Santa Fe
1987 Architecture and Landscape. In *An Archaeological Reconnaissance of West-Central New Mexico: The Anasazi Monuments Project* by Andrew P. Fowler, John R. Stein, and Roger Anyon, pp. 71–103. Submitted to the Historic Preservation Division, Office of Cultural Affairs, State of New Mexico, Santa Fe

Thompson, Raymond H.
1958 *Modern Yucatecan Maya Pottery Making*. Memoirs of the Society for American Archaeology 15

Toll, H. Wolcott
1981 Ceramic Comparisons Concerning Redistribution in Chaco Canyon, New Mexico. In *Production and Distribution: A Ceramic Viewpoint*, edited by Hilary Howard and Elaine L. Morris, pp. 83–121. British Archaeological Reports International Series 120, Oxford
1984 Trends in Ceramic Import and Distribution in Chaco Canyon. In *Recent Research on Chaco Prehistory*, edited by W. James Judge and John D. Schelberg, pp. 115–35. Reports of the Chaco Center 8, Division of Cultural Research, National Park Service, Albuquerque

Toll, H. Wolcott, and Peter J. McKenna
1987 The Ceramography of Pueblo Alto. In *Investigations at the Pueblo Alto Complex, Chaco Canyon, New Mexico: Tests and Excavations 1975–1979. Vol. III: Artifactual and Biological Analyses*, edited by Francis Joan Mathien and Thomas C. Windes, pp. 19–230. Publications in Archeology 18F, Chaco Canyon Studies, Branch of Cultural Research, National Park Service, Santa Fe

Toll, H. Wolcott, Thomas C. Windes, and Peter J. McKenna
1980 Late Ceramic Patterns in Chaco Canyon: The Pragmatics of Modelling Ceramic Exchange. In *Models and Methods in Regional Exchange*, edited by Robert E. Fry, pp. 95–117. SAA Papers 1

Trott, Joseph J.
1980 A Test Excavation Across a Prehistoric Anasazi Roadway Segment North of Pueblo Alto, Chaco Canyon National Monument. MS on file, Division of Cultural Research, National Park Service, Albuquerque

Vivian, R. Gordon
1948 Memorandum for Superintendent McNeil, Chaco Canyon. Interview with Mrs. Richard Wetherill. Chaco Center Archive 657. On file, Division of Cultural Research, National Park Service, Albuquerque

Vivian, Gordon, and Tom W. Mathews
1965 *Kin Kletso, a Pueblo III Community in Chaco Canyon, New Mexico*. Southwestern Monuments Association, Technical Series 6(1), Globe, AZ

Vivian, R. Gwinn
1970 An Inquiry into Prehistoric Social Organization in Chaco Canyon, New Mexico. In *Reconstructing Prehistoric Pueblo Societies*, edited by William A. Longacre, pp. 59–83. School of American Research, Santa Fe
1972 Prehistoric Water Conservation in Chaco Canyon. Final technical letter report for the National Science Foundation grant GS 3100. MS on file, Division of Cultural Research, National Park Service, Albuquerque
1983a Identifying and Interpreting Chacoan Roads: An Historical Perspective. In Kincaid 1983, chapter 3
1983b Discovery and Description: Chacoan Road Field Studies, 1963–1980. In Kincaid 1983, Appendix A

Voth, H. R.
1903 *The Oraibi Summer Snake Ceremony*. Field Museum of Natural History, Anthropological Series 3(4)

Ware, John A., and George J. Gumerman
1977 Remote Sensing Methodology and the Chaco Canyon Prehistoric Road System. In *Aerial Remote Sensing Techniques in Archeology*, edited by Thomas R. Lyons and Robert K. Hitchcock, pp. 135–67. Reports of the Chaco Center 2, National Park Service, Albuquerque

Waters, Frank
1963 *The Book of the Hopi*. Viking Press, New York

Windes, Thomas C.

1982 Lessons from the Chacoan Survey: The Pattern of Chacoan Trash Disposal. *New Mexico Archeological Council Newsletter* 4(5–6):5–14

1987a *Investigations at the Pueblo Alto Complex, Chaco Canyon, New Mexico: Tests and Excavations 1975–1979. Vol. I: Summary of Tests and Excavations at the Pueblo Alto Community.* Publications in Archeology 18F, Chaco Canyon Studies. Branch of Cultural Research, National Park Service, Santa Fe

1987b *Investigations at the Pueblo Alto Complex, Chaco Canyon, New Mexico: Tests and Excavations 1975–1979. Vol. II: Architecture and Stratigraphy,* Parts 1 and 2. Publications in Archeology 18F, Chaco Canyon Studies. Branch of Cultural Research, National Park Service, Santa Fe

12 The Sonoran connection: road and trail networks in the protohistoric period

CARROLL L. RILEY
and JONI L. MANSON

During the protohistoric period – particularly during the fifteenth and sixteenth centuries – Sonora was a vital link in the routes used for trade and other kinds of contact between Mesoamerica and the upper Southwest. The role of the Sonoran area in this transportation and communications network was obscured for a very long time by a lack of archaeological work in Sonora and by models of southwestern prehistory that stressed the "cultural sink" aspect of the region between the high cultures of Mesoamerica and the Southwest.

It is becoming increasingly clear that the paradigms of southwestern autonomy, so strongly held by archaeologists in the early part of the twentieth century, must be drastically modified in favor of models that recognize the considerable amount of contact which existed among the various cultures of the Greater Southwest. With this contact came a network of roads and trails that linked the Sonoran area both with the upper Southwest and with Mesoamerica. Unfortunately, very little physical evidence remains of the actual roadways used in Sonora during protohistoric times. Therefore, we must rely on other evidence. This includes archaeological and documentary indications of long-distance trade in both raw materials and luxury goods, and the archaeological remains and historical accounts of large urban centers and cultural sophistication in Sonora. From these various lines of evidence we can say a great deal about the exchange network in late prehistoric and early Spanish times. There are, however, many gaps in our data and there is much work for archaeologists, cultural geographers, and historians of the future.

In order to understand the situation in Sonora during protohistoric times, it is necessary to review the archaeological and archival studies that are now beginning to fix the Sonoran region in a firmer southwestern context. Little was known about Sonora before the pioneering studies of Carl O. Sauer and Donald D. Brand in the late 1920s and early 1930s. At that time the best known Sonoran aboriginal culture was that of Trincheras, named after the large terraced hillsides scattered throughout parts of northwest Sonora but with a very important concentration in the vicinity of Trincheras, a town near the Magdalena river.

In 1931 Sauer and Brand, as a result of a survey of northern Sonora, pointed out that the Trincheras area seemed to lie principally west of the Sonora river. Various summary statements (Amsden 1928; Brand 1935, 1944; Noguera 1958; Johnson 1963; Pailes 1972; Sauer 1932, 1934, 1935) gave the state of knowledge of the Sonora and upper Yaqui river regions as of the early 1970s. Since that time information has expanded greatly: see the work of Pailes (1976, 1978, 1980), Pailes and Reff (1985), Reff (1981, 1982), Braniff (1978, 1985), Doolittle (1979, 1980, 1981, 1984a, 1984b, 1988), and Riley (1976b, 1979, 1985, 1986, 1987, 1988).

The term "Serrana Province" has been applied by Riley in a number of publications to protohistoric northern and central Sonora, a time when the region had a considerable development of culture, including the appearance of what Riley calls "statelets." Previously, northern Sonora had been occupied by peoples using simple agricultural techniques, incised pottery, and crude above-ground stone structures, as well as pithouses. The Rio Sonora culture – probably a congeries of related cultures – extended throughout much of eastern Sonora from about the international border on the north to the Sinaloan border on the south (Pailes 1972:371–6). Dating for the Rio Sonora culture is not very secure but Pailes (*ibid.*:339), working in southern Sonora, suggests that the Rio Sonora culture in that area may appear at least as early as the eighth or ninth century A.D. This culture is in some degree related to the Viejo horizon at Casas Grandes, the great northwestern Chihuahua site, which was strongly Mesoamerican in its later Medio period. The Viejo period at Casas Grandes is dated by Di Peso (1974, Vol. I:100) to *c.* A.D. 700–1060 and the Medio to A.D. 1060–1340 (*ibid.*, Vol. II:289). The Rio Sonora incised ware, widespread from northern Sonora to northern Sinaloa, is very similar to Convento and Casas Grandes incised wares found at the site of Casas Grandes (Pailes 1978:139). There incised ceramics related generically to the Alma wares of the Mogollon. At Casas Grandes they probably began in the Pilon phase of the Viejo period, but Casas Grandes incised (derived from Convento incised) is

found throughout the Medio period (Di Peso, Rinaldo, and Fenner 1974, Vol. VI:48–54, 135–9).

Recent archaeological work in the Sonora valley indicates a somewhat Viejo-like occupation with pithouse structures (or more correctly "houses-in-pits," see Doolittle 1984b:17, 1988:27–9) dating from at least around A.D. 1000. In some cases, settlements seem to have been occupied as late as the mid-sixteenth century (Reff 1982). In later phases, both at the large site of San Jose, north of Babiacora (SON K:4:24:OU) and at the site of La Mora (SON K:4:72:OU), public structures appear, made of parallel platforms connected by end walls to form interior courts. These are quite large, the one at San Jose having interior dimensions of 46×24 m (Pailes 1978:140; 1980:26). Such features may have been ballcourts. Very large rectangular compounds are found at site SON K:4:16:OU, south of Las Delicious, and SON K:4:127:OU, across the Sonora river from Huepac. These unroofed structures, each about 30×18 m, were probably public buildings of some sort, perhaps temples (see Doolittle 1988:62–3; Pailes 1984:321; Riley 1987:96, 361). About this same time – though not too firmly dated – there also appear contiguous rectangular domestic structures with stone embedded foundations (Pailes 1978:140). An intermediate phase of pithouses has yielded a date of A.D. 1300 and there is some evidence by superposition that the surface structures overlay these pithouses. The rectangular houses and the large ceremonial structures seem to be late, appearing around and after A.D. 1300. At about this same time, a wide range of Chihuahua polychrome wares appeared in the Sonora river valley. Reff (1982; see also Pailes and Reff 1985) pointed out that in the period A.D. 1100–1350 the Sonora valley sites were receiving large amounts of trade goods, including copper, shell, and the entire range of Casas Grandes polychromes. Doolittle (1984b; 1988), however, doubts any extensive Casas Grandes influence on the Sonoran statelets. In a study of settlement patterns in the Sonora river valley over a period of several centuries, Doolittle has come to the conclusion that the Sonora statelets rose coevally with Casas Grandes and that any trade or migration from the latter would have had relatively little effect on the development of the statelets (1984b:22–3; 1988:59). In terms of contact with western Sonora, the San Miguel valley seems to have been the frontier between the Sonoran statelets and polities that fall under the rubric Trincheras (Braniff 1978:74–81).

The sociopolitical and economic picture of the late fourteenth and fifteenth centuries is still not well understood. Riley (1980:47–8) has suggested that the breakup of Casas Grandes was somehow related to the collapse of Classic Salado-Hohokam and this may also be true of the last phase of the Mimbres. As pointed out by Ravesloot (1984), a great deal depends on final resolution of the dating sequence for Casas Grandes. Indeed, Lekson (1984:59), in a review of Casas Grandes dates, suggests that the Paquimé phase of Casas Grandes may have ended around A.D. 1400, and the final Diablo phase sometime in the early A.D. 1400s. More recent work by Dean and Ravesloot (1988) also suggests a later terminus for the Medio and Tardio horizons at Casas Grandes. This actually would fit the scenario of Riley (1980:47–8) somewhat better than would a 1340 end date for the Medio period.

Whatever the sequence of events at Casas Grandes and in the Classic Hohokam, it seems clear enough that

> beginning about A.D. 1300 there was vigorous reworking of Mesoamerican traits already in the upper Southwest, as is evidenced by the Mexican flavor of Pueblo IV. The expansion of Pueblo Indian trade eastward which began in earnest around A.D. 1400 ... probably actually predates the opening of the camino real from western Mesoamerica (perhaps from the Tarascan area) up the west coast of Mexico to the Southwest. By Spanish contact times ... the network of contacts was completely interlocked throughout the Southwest and beyond (*ibid.:* 48).

The fifteenth century was, in fact, a period not only of reorganization but of expansion on the part of a number of southwestern societies. In some ways the Serrana country of northern Sonora was the most vital part of an expanding and vigorous Southwest. This was the period in which the Sonoran statelets seem to have had their major evolution; indeed, at the time of first Spanish contact they may have been still expanding.

By the late fourteenth or early fifteenth century the Sonoran statelets of Corazones, Señora, Batuco, Guaraspi, Cumupa, Sahuaripa, and Oera (see Fig. 12.1) were interacting with one another and with the Uparo (Seri) of the coast, the Yaquimi, or Yaqui, northernmost of the Cahitan groups, and others. At just about this time the Mesoamerican trails, probably already established in Nayarit and Sinaloa, reached the statelets. Originally these routes had gone inland through southern Sonora and Casas Grandes but now they radiated into the central and northern Sonoran area. The routes went on northward and westward, eventually linking up with other trails that crossed the Southwest from west to east – from the Pacific Ocean and the Gulf of California to the Little Colorado, the Rio Grande, and the Pecos river regions (Riley and Manson 1983:350–4).

In this paper we are concerned with the network as it spread through Sonora. Let us first give a brief summary of the cultural situation of the Sonoran statelets as they existed on the eve of the sweeping Spanish incursions into the Sonoran area which began in the year 1533 and continued with increasing intensity for two and a half centuries. By the eighteenth century any discussion of Sonoran statelets and aboriginal trade routes from Mesoamerica to the Southwest is quite academic. What we know of the culture of the statelets during the proto-historic period has been described by Riley (1987). In this paper, we will give only a short synopsis of the archaeological and historical record.

In the sixteenth century the area contained two major language groups, Opata and Pima. Riley suggested a number of years ago that the Pimans were indigenous

Fig. 12.1. Possible location of the Sonoran statelets, c. A.D. 1500.

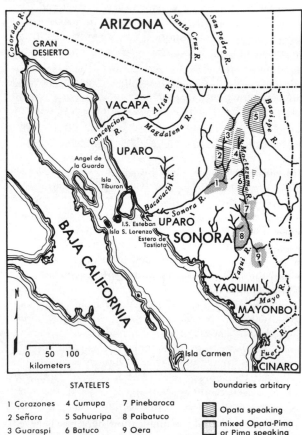

STATELETS			boundaries arbitary
1 Corazones	4 Cumupa	7 Pinebaroca	Opata speaking
2 Señora	5 Sahuaripa	8 Paibatuco	mixed Opata-Pima
3 Guaraspi	6 Batuco	9 Oera	or Pima speaking

people who, after perhaps A.D. 1300, were partly overrun by more sophisticated Opata speakers coming from the east. There is, however, archaeological evidence that the statelets developed in place from as early as A.D. 1000 (Doolittle 1988:59–61), and it may be that the Opata–Pima frontier that the Spaniards saw in the sixteenth century had been stable for some centuries (for a discussion of these matters, see Doolittle 1988:4; Riley 1987:47–51, 68–76). At any rate, as of around A.D. 1500, the Opata and related Eudeve seem to have controlled the middle and upper reaches of the Sonora, Moctezuma and Bavispe rivers, while Piman-speaking statelet-building groups held the Ures basin, and parts of the middle Yaqui valley. Most of the Lower Pima speakers in what is now Sonora were actually outside the polity of the statelets, living in rancheria settlements on the Altar-Magdalena, the San Miguel, the Bacavachi, the Sirupa-Tutuaca, and parts of the lower Sonora and Yaqui rivers. The Jova of the Aros region were probably also rancheria peoples, outside the statelet area (Riley 1987:50; Sauer 1934:50). For a further discussion of the Opata-Eudeve-Jova and the Lower Pima speakers, see Pennington 1979, 1980, 1981.

At the time of first Spanish contact, there were relatively dense populations with urban centers of several hundred to a thousand or more houses. The towns were laid out with streets and irrigation canals. There were both stone and puddled adobe structures, some of the latter of two or more stories (Doolittle 1988:26). Light jacal construction also appears and may have represented summer houses. Large towns were located at the center of what the Spaniards generally called "provinces" or "kingdoms" – Riley's "statelets" – each of which had an overall ruler. Statelets usually controlled river valleys or a section of valleys. The only statelet for which we have an indication of size is Señora, which was 600 leagues square (*c.* 10,520 km²) with a population of 20,000 (Cuevas 1924:148). Archaeologically, the capital of the statelet of Señora has been tentatively identified by Doolittle (personal communication) as the University of Oklahoma survey site (SON K:4:85:OU) east of San Felipe (about midway between Huepac and Aconchi) on the east side of the Sonora river. This is the "Sonora" of Nentvig (1971: map facing p. 64; 1980:10). The roughly rectangular site extends north and south (parallel to the river) on a flat mesa for approximately 300 m, the east and west measurement being 100 to 150 m. A photograph of part of the site appears as Plate 5 in Riley 1987:54.

Doolittle (personal communication) currently believes that the Spanish-named town of Corazones may have been in the Puerta del Sol area at the southwest entrance to the Ures gorge. This location was also favored by Sauer (1932:17). It is possible that the site of San Jose, just north of Babiacora and partially excavated by Pailes and associates, was Las Casas' Agastan, which Las Casas describes as "six leagues further on in the valley ... another town larger than Corazones" (Riley 1976a:20). Puerta del Sol is roughly six leagues from San Jose, and the latter is certainly a large site, covering some 25 ha (Pailes 1980:29; Reff 1981:101–2).

Locations for the various statelets (using the names given to them in sixteenth-century Spanish accounts) have been suggested by Riley (1987:72, map 6; see also Fig. 12.1, this volume). These identifications were based on documentary evidence, later mentions in the Spanish accounts, and, whenever possible, archaeological research. The extremely tentative nature of these sociopolitical units cannot be overstressed.

Population estimates of the statelets are crude at best. Sauer (1935:5) suggested that the Opateria in the sixteenth century had a population of 1.5 persons per km², or about 60,000 inhabitants. This was based on 1920 population-density statistics which indicated a population of 1.7 persons per km² in the same area. People of the Ures and Nuri areas practiced irrigation agriculture and possessed the same sophistication in the sixteenth century as the Opata but were probably Piman-speaking. These groups would have added about 5,000–7,000 people to the population of the Serrana. Using the available sixteenth-century demographic information, Riley (1987:57) suggests perhaps as many as 90,000 in the total Serrana region. Certain other estimates fall into the same range, see, for example, Doolittle 1984a:296.

The statelet organization had clearly broken down by the time the Spaniards reinvaded the northern Sonoran area after 1620. By that time population had declined and the natives had returned to rancheria-style living. This was at least in part attributable to disease, though the disruption of the great trans-southwestern exchange network may also have been a factor (Riley 1987:96, 325).

The Sonoran statelets depended on irrigation agriculture, and the towns were surrounded by extensive irrigated fields. Double cropping, and possibly even triple cropping, was practiced (see Riley 1987:59–68 for a detailed discussion of food resources). The trade in foodstuffs, mentioned by a number of the Spanish explorers, very probably reflects this rich agricultural situation.

Warfare was extremely common. The statelets fought each other but they were also able to unite against the Spaniards with war parties that could number in the thousands (Cuevas 1924:168). There were fortress sites and signal systems, one of which flashed news of the battle of Sahuaripa several hundred kilometers – to Cinaro on the Fuerte river – in two days (*ibid.*:171–2). These pyro-signal sites in the Sonora valley have been identified archaeologically (Doolittle 1988:32–3). The various statelets also formed federations. In the 1560s, when Ibarra went through the area, there were two major confederacies, a northern group led by Señora and a southern one, perhaps controlled by Oera. The buffer state of Batuco seems to have been hostile to both (Riley 1988:141).

We know very little about native religion, but both Las Casas (Riley 1976:20–1) and Castañena (Hammond and Rey 1940:250) mention temples, Las Casas calling them tall structures of stone and mud. Hearts of various animals were sacrificed to the gods (Cabeza de Vaca 1555:fol.xlvi; Riley 1976a:20–1), and the dried bodies of past rulers were leaned against the walls of the temple. According to Riley (1987:95):

> The keeping of desiccated bodies of leaders … may have been an outgrowth of seated burials found in the Casas Grandes Medio period. As late as 1624 Father Francisco Olindaño reported a shrine among the Aivinos of the Yaqui drainage. An "indio principal" of that group had been killed by lightning some years before. He was seated in his tomb, and the Indians brought offerings which included "white beads, with which they adorn themselves, sea shells, blankets, colored feathers, and other things which they value."

While our material on religion is scanty, there is even less information on political organization. About all that one can say is that the few indications of political ceremonies and the hundreds of richly dressed retainers who met the Spanish party at Oera and at Señora (Cuevas 1924:145–6, 148) imply a high level of political control.

Although the actual political organization of the statelets is unknown, the descriptions, especially the indications of differential wealth, suggest that it was something more than the egalitarian tribal society found in the upper Southwest. Lacking clear evidence, the authors have avoided such semantically loaded terms as "chiefdom" or "primitive state" since such terms, as currently used by anthropologists, imply specific types of sociopolitical and economic organization. Our feeling is that the Sonoran statelets had some sort of ranked society, perhaps influenced by, though not necessarily modeled after, that of Casas Grandes.

The economic life of the statelets was heavily orienta-

ted towards trade, as one would expect considering the geographic position of the Serrana *vis-à-vis* the trade routes from Mesoamerica to the upper Southwest. We have fair descriptions in the literature and a growing archaeological indication of what was traded and some ideas of the intensity of the trade, but almost nothing of the mechanisms of trade. Was there, for example, a barrio of foreign traders in the various towns, a sort of *pochteca*? We cannot rule out the possibility, but from the evidence now available it would seem that trade was largely in local hands. In the upper Southwest, for example at Pecos and Cibola, what Riley (1978:54) called an "entrepreneurial redistribution" system existed in which privately organized groups within the pueblo conducted trading operations. Trade parties were led by particular experts, perhaps members of the Bow Priesthood. The entire pueblo doubtless benefited by this trade through the crossties of kinship, but the pueblos themselves were probably not redistributive in the political sense. Whether the leaders of the Sonoran statelets had political control over the lucrative trade that passed through their territory – as Di Peso (1974, Vol. II:293) believed was the case at Casas Grandes – is not clear. Whatever the specific situation, we suspect that trade in Sonora was somewhat more centrally organized than was the case among the Pueblo Indians.

Trade northward into the upper Southwest involved a number of things, including parrot and macaw feathers and the actual birds, coral, shell, and metal ornaments. After about 1530 even materials made of iron entered the network (Riley 1976b, Vol. II:40). Traveling southward from the upper southwest to and through the Sonoran statelets were turquoise, dressed hides, such semi-precious stones as jasper, garnet, and peridot, cotton, pottery, and perhaps salt, powdered minerals, foodstuffs, and slaves (Riley 1976b:40–1; 1987:76–88; Weigand 1976:3–5). Cotton originated in the statelets themselves, and Pailes (1980:36) sees some archaeological evidence of a cotton-processing industry. Other locally produced materials were woven pita or agave fiber, foodstuffs, and slaves. It is clear from Obregón's observations (Cuevas 1924:146–7) that slaving was an important industry; slaves were imprisoned in stocks and kept for sale. They were traded for cotton mantas, feathers, foodstuffs, and especially for salt (*ibid.*). Since the north seems too egalitarian to have had a slave economy, one would assume that most trade in slaves was internal or went southward. Where slaves originated is another question. Considering the warlike nature of the Sonoran statelets, it seems likely that many slaves came from within the area itself, captured in one of the many wars. There, is of course, the possibility that Pueblo groups to the north found local war captives a profitable commodity to contribute to the Sonoran trade but we have no documentation for this. In fact, we have no real idea how the Serrana people *used* slaves other than in trade.

Certain trade goods were specifically bound for the upper Southwest. The statement of Cabeza de Vaca (155:fol.xlv) that the Serrana Indians at Corazones traded parrot plumes and feathers northward to the Pueblo area can be matched against the wealth of evidence of macaws and parrots, including illustrations on pottery and kiva walls as well as the actual bird bones found in protohistoric Pueblo sites (Riley 1987:82, 196–7, 212, 237, 248, 275, 277). Cabeza de Vaca (1555:fol.xlv) also noted the southward trade of turquoise. Pailes (1980:35) has documented the trade in turquoise from the Cerrillos and Azure areas of New Mexico into the Babiacora-Aconchi region of Sonora, and Riley (1976b:5–7) has given examples of turquoise spreading on south to the edges of Mesoamerica.

What then of actual routes? In Fig. 12.1 we have given the hypothetical locations of the statelets, with Marcos' settlement of Vacapa provisionally located in the Altar-Magdalena valley, taken from Riley (1987:72, map 6). The second map (Fig. 12.2) illustrates the road network that interlinked all major areas of Sonora. In preparing Fig.12.2 we took into account Jesuit and Franciscan mission trails, which in all probability followed the original tracks between native towns and statelets, just as the missions themselves were usually sited on or near older settlements.

There are, however, many gaps in the actual evidence. First, as we have already pointed out, the earliest missions in northern and central Sonora (1620–50) came during a time when the native population had already sharply declined, the towns of the sixteenth century seem to have been deserted, and the remnant groups of Indians lived in rancheria-type settlements. Second, although we have a series of adequate maps of the missions beginning in the seventeenth century, there is very little indication of actual routes on these maps, whether drawn by missionaries, soldiers or government officials, or by miners or other "civilians." This lack of roads, at least as indicated on the maps, is somewhat puzzling. Of course, the trails often followed river valleys and such routes may have seemed obvious to the mapmakers. But, maps aside, the mission fathers, in their extensive writings, normally left no very clear explanation of their travel routes. There are exceptions; Fathers Eusebio Kino and Juan Nentvig, for example,

do give us a fair amount of map information. It is also possible to utilize the later journeys of men like Adolph F. Bandelier and Carl Lumholtz in their exploratory trips through the Serrana. These trips are particularly valuable to us because Bandelier and other nineteenth-century explorers were specifically looking for ancient routes.

We can start a study of routes by considering the earliest Spanish expeditions into the Serrana. The first organized European penetration of this region (following the more or less accidental journey of Cabeza de Vaca and his three companions) was that of Marcos de Niza in 1539. There has been a great swirl of controversy over Marcos' route northward from western Mexico to Cibola-Zuni. We follow Riley (1971, 1987; see also Undreiner 1947) in our belief that Marcos generally remained west of the mountains as he traveled up the west coast of Mexico. He forded the Mayo and Yaqui rivers in their lower courses and was probably no more than 50 to 75 km inland when he crossed the Sonora river. This route – easy in the sense that there are no mountain barriers and, in northern Sinaloa and in Sonora, only broken vegetation or desert monte – led Marcos directly to the large irrigated Piman settlements in the Magdalena and Altar valleys. This also set his feet firmly on a major exchange route from western New Mexico (Cibola) to the Gulf of California. Indeed, Marcos documents a flood of trade goods – turquoise, bison hides, and probably pottery coming west and south over this route. At some point Marcos intercepted another major route – this one going southward into the Sonora valley, probably with major branching trails to the Moctezuma and the upper Yaqui valleys. For a detailed discussion of Marcos' exploration of these routes, see Riley 1987:119–22. The trunk route down the Sonora valley can be traced fairly accurately, in part because of the exigencies of the terrain. It is described in some detail in the various Coronado documents (Hammond and Rey 1940:164–7, 207–9, 250–2, 268–70, 284–5, 296–8) and in the Obregón account two decades later (Cuevas 1924:147–52, 155, 159–74). The major route ran from Cinaro, on the lower Fuerte river. The most detailed plotting of the southern part of this route has been made by Charles C. Di Peso (1974, Vol. III:819–20; Di Peso, Rinaldo and Fenner 1974, Vol. IV:104–6) who believed that it ran from the Fuerte up the Arroyo de Alamos to the Mayo river and then up the Cedros valley and overland to the Nuri-Chico. Di Peso located the southernmost statelet of Oera in the Nuri-Chico, as did Riley (1976b, 1987), and we accept this identification. From Nuri-Chico we believe that the trail

Fig. 12.2. Trade routes in Sonora, c. A.D. 1500.

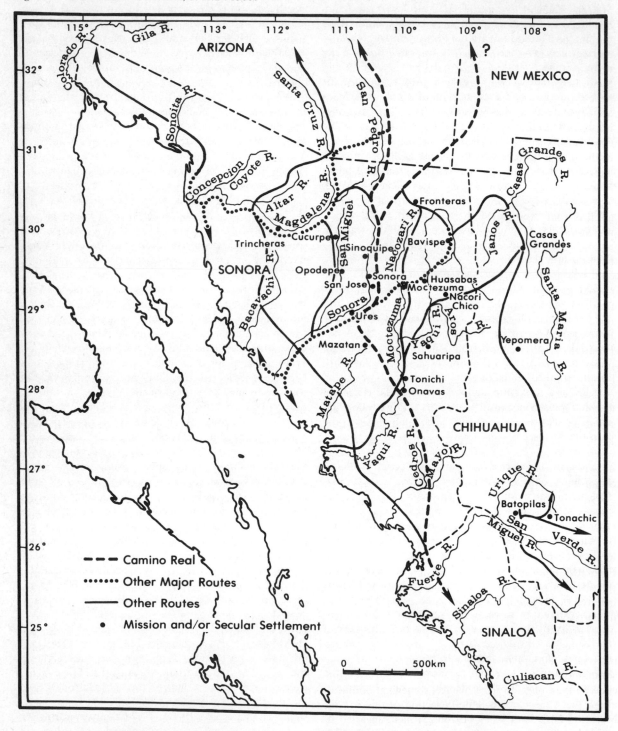

ran northward probably as far as Onavas or Tonichi, but at some point swung off to the west and skirted the headwaters of the Matape drainage, perhaps following the line of the old road that goes up through Mazatan and on to El Alamo and Ures. From Ures the trail led through the Ures gorge into the valley of the middle Sonora river – sixteenth-century Señora – and what we believe was the heart of the Sonoran statelets, the middle Sonora and Moctezuma river areas. The road continued northward, following the valleys of the Sonora river. One branch then went northward through modern Bacanuchi and on to the upper San Pedro drainage where it met with the Gulf of California route followed by Marcos.

A second branch swung northeastward, intercepting another route that ran through the Moctezuma valley northward to what is now the Douglas-Agua Prieta region on the present-day international border. From both the San Pedro route and the one going north and east through the Animas valley, the trails went on to Cibola. Still another trail branched off the Sonora river trunk route somewhere in the upper Sonora drainage. It ran "to Bacoachi across the Sierra de los Ajos into the Fronteras Basin" (Sauer 1932:46). This route crossed the Fronteras basin west to east, and continued into the upper Bavispe basin and eastward across Pulpit Pass into the Casas Grandes valley.

There were cross-linking trails. One was used by the Coronado party, while at Corazones in 1540, to commune with the coastal people (Hammond and Rey 1940:164–5). This route extended down the Sonora river where, probably in the vicinity of Hermosillo, it linked up with the lowland route from Sinaloa and southern Sonora to Vacapa in the Magdalena-Altar region.

It also seems likely that a trail ran from the middle Sonora valley to the Magdalena via the San Miguel. Ives (1936:89) has suggested that the route of Melchior Díaz in 1540 from the new Spanish settlement at San Geronimo de los Corazones in the Sonora valley to the lower Colorado followed a trail from Ures up the San Miguel river and then across to the Magdalena drainage. Ives believed that the trail ran down the Magdalena to about modern Altar and then overland, north and west to the upper Coyote drainage. According to this reconstruction, Diaz then followed the line of the modern international boundary to the Sonoita arroyo, continuing south and west to the Gulf of California and on up the coast to the Colorado river. We feel somewhat doubtful about the Altar–Coyote–Sonoita section of this trip of Melchior Díaz, and Riley (1976b:25) has suggested a more logical route down the Gila river.

At any rate, the fact that a trail ran from the Sonora to the Magdalena seems well established. In mission times there was contact up the San Miguel to the mission of Cucurpe and on to the Magdalena and the Magdalena-Altar missions. A road also seems to have connected the Banamichi-Sinoquipe region of the Sonora with Cucurpe. In fact, during the seventeenth century, much of this region was incorporated into the San Francisco Javier rectorship, which had seven dependent missions. According to Nentvig (1980:95–8), these included Cuquiarichi, 2 leagues from the presidio of Fronteras; Arizpe; Banamichi, 11 leagues south of Arizpe and 5 leagues south of Sinoquipe; Aconchi, 7 leagues south of Banamichi and four leagues north of Babiacora; Ures, Opodepe; and Cucurpe. Nentvig failed to provide specific information of the roads in this area except to note that the road from Bavispe to Cuquiarichi was "extremely bad" (*ibid.*:95). It seems likely that in the protohistoric period there was also direct communication between the Sonora river statelets and the rich Piman settlements on the Magdalena, and, further, that at least some contact between Sonora and the lower Colorado river peoples was made by traveling down the coast and then up the Concepcion-Magdalena-Altar systems. Such raw materials as *Glycymeris* shells, which were traded in the Serrana, came from the northern part of the Gulf of California and Marcos described intense commercial activity from Vacapa eastward.

Routes across the mountains from the Sonora to the Moctezuma and from the latter drainage to the Bavispe are somewhat less obvious. Indeed, Di Peso firmly believed that the major north–south route, the Camino Real, continued from the Oera up the Yaqui river. Recent archaeological information makes this unlikely and here we accept the Sonora river identification for Señora and Corazones. However, even today east and west movement in Sonora is anything but simple. This was also true in mission times, as indicated by Nentvig's descriptions of the region around Oposura. He states that the mission of Huasabas was located 17 leagues east of Oposura, and the village of Tonibabi was 12 leagues west of Huasabas, "through mountains full of ravines and canyons" (Nentvig 1980:86). The route from Tonibabi to Huasabas was a "twisting road … called [a] culebrilla. We must follow it because it affords a less difficult passage, but in so doing, instead of seven or eight leagues from Tonibabi to Huasabas we actually travel twelve. *But this applies to all Sonoran roads* [italics ours]" (*ibid.*:88).

One possible east–west route was that used in Bandelier's time (Lange and Riley 1970:474–5) which cut across the Sierra de Bacachi over "miserable trails" with "dizzy slopes" (*ibid.*:248), from Babiacora almost directly eastward to Oposura, near present-day Mocte-zuma. The trail through the Sierra de Granados was rough, but superior to the segment between Babiacora and Oposura. From Granados, the trail to Bacadeuchi was plainly visible – "the trail winds around and up slopes, very rocky, often cragged, covered with the usual thorny shrubs and succulent plants" (*ibid.*:256). Bandelier traveled from Granados to Huachinera, then followed the Arroyo de Tesorobabi to the Taqui, and proceeded on to Baserac. The trail ran through the river bottom from Baserac to Bavispe. From the latter town the road angled north and east, passing north of the Sierra de Baserac and the Sierra de San Pedro, eventu-ally reaching the Janos river and the flat grassy plain that leads southward to Casas Grandes or northward into the Jornada region. The road from Bavispe to Janos was 26 leagues, or about 110 km, in length. Bandelier continued on to Casas Grandes. At the Cerro de Moctezuma, he came upon an old trail. It was:

> only visible in parts, and where it is yet on the level loma, marks a broad trail, well trodden out, about a meter wide at most, and it seems as if this trail had been made by picking out the stones and rocks, and piling them up on the side ...
>
> It is singular that the trail nowhere shows any artificial filling, only cutting or rather grooving out. This trail widens out to apparently two to three meters, but in fact, it is never wider than one meter, the greater apparent width being due to washing. (*ibid.*:318–19)

The plan of the cerro showed that "roads of trails branch off across it" (*ibid.*:321).

Another later nineteenth-century explorer, who traveled through Sonora and Chihuahua noting aspects of his route, was Carl Lumholtz. Around Nacori (some 65 km from Granados), he noted "the frequent occur-rence of old trails across the hills, some quite plainly traceable for three or four hundred yards" (Lumholtz 1973, Vol. I:23). Near Casas Grandes, Lumholtz recorded the presence of a watch tower on a mountain to the southwest of the ruins:

> Well-defined tracks lead up to it from all direct-ions, especially from the east and west. On the western side three such trails were noticed ... The western side of the ridge is in some places quite precipitous, but there is a fairly good track running along its entire extent to the top. Some-

times the road is protected with stones and in other places even with walls, on the outer side. (*ibid.*:Vol. I,90).

From Casas Grandes, Lumholtz continued south-ward, through the grasslands of Chuhuichupa to Guay-nopa, and into the plain of Yepomera. He journeyed southward to the Barranca de Cobre, crossing the bar-ranca where it was some 1,000 m deep. "The track we followed was fairly good, but led along several danger-ous precipices ... [Then] following the windings of the well-laid out road we descended into the cañon ..." (*ibid.*, Vol. I:179).

Lumholtz eventually reached Batopilas. Here there were old and famous silver mines which were discovered in the seventeenth century. From Batopilas a fairly good track led south to Guachochic, a few miles from the pueblo of Tonachic. Lumholtz noted that "in missionary times [Tonachic] appears to have been of some import-ance, to judge from the church" (*ibid.*, Vol. I:229). In addition, "there was no difficulty in finding one's way from Guachochic to Norogachic. At one point I noticed an Indian trail leading up a ridge apparently consisting of volcanic tuff. To facilitate the ascent, steps, now worn and old, had been cut for a distance of a couple of hundred feet" (*ibid.*: Vol. I, 202).

Lumholtz made his way to Guadalupe y Calvo, and went on to Baborigame. At this town, he "was told that native travelling merchants from southern Mexico, called Aztecs and Otomies, pass through Baborigame every five years, to sell their goods" (*ibid.*, Vol. I:430).

Lumholtz's travels in Chihuahua take us a bit outside the Serrana province as it was known in the fifteenth and sixteenth centuries. His comments are interesting, however, because until at least the mid-fourteenth century Casas Grandes was the great hub of northwest Mexico and it seems likely that some of the routes to Casas Grandes were taken over by the Sonoran statelets. As Di Peso has pointed out, a series of shell routes ran from Casas Grandes to the Gulf of California, cutting across portions of the Serrana. In part following Tower (1945:43) and Brand (1973:100), Di Peso suggested two routes that could have brought shell to Casas Grandes. One ran up the Altar valley, then across to the Bavispe river and on to Casas Grandes, probably by one of the routes discussed above, perhaps the one taken by Bande-lier. A second shell route ran up the Yaqui valley, then up the Bavispe and cross-country to Nacori Chico. From the latter area the trail climbed into the high Tres Rios region and on north and eastward to Casas Grandes (Di Peso 1974, Vol. I:205).

There is also considerable evidence for trade routes from Casas Grandes running eastward and southward. A major one seems to have hugged the eastern flank of the Sierra Madre, extending into southern Chihuahua and Durango where the Casas Grandes peoples interacted with those of the Chalchihuites culture (Di Peso 1974, Vol. III:624). J. Charles Kelley (personal communication, see also Kelley 1986) has identified the site of Cañon de Molino in the Guatimape valley northwest of the modern city of Durango, as a western terminus for trade goods coming across the Topia gateway from the Culiacan region of the Mexican west coast. Kelley has also traced routes running northward, east of the main sierra from southern Durango state. He now believes that a major route for settlement and/or trade extended up the San Juan/Balleza drainage of the upper Conchos river, and over a low divide into the basin of the Laguno de los Mexicanos. The trail continued northward over essentially open country to the upper Papigochic drainage. Casas Grandes material begins at Timosachic in the upper Santa Maria valley, just over a minor divide from the Papigochic.

This and other natural roadways were followed in post-Casas Grandes times by Spaniards who, in a matter of a half century, pushed their western frontier from the Lake Chapala region to southern Chihuahua, with expeditions going northward into New Mexico. It was almost certainly along these routes that the native traveling merchants of Lumholtz's time, the "Aztecs and Otomies," and the Tarascans came with their backpacks of trade goods (Lumholz 1973, Vol. I:430; Vol. II, 368–9).

Although the collapse of Casas Grandes came before the full flowering of the Sonoran statelets it is reasonable to assume, as we stated above, that the earlier Casas Grandes-orientated trails were adapted to centers in northern Sonora itself. The trails served two major purposes for the active and expanding Serrana polities: they allowed the circulation of goods (and perhaps services) within the region, and connected the Sonoran mountain and valley settlements with the riches of the Pacific Ocean. The demand for shell, so much in evidence at Casas Grandes, was, in fact, widespread throughout the Greater Southwest, and can be traced back to Archaic times. There was another very important commodity, however, that the highland people needed and which generally was lacking in the Sierra Madre. This was salt, and clearly this staple was much in demand from early times; the demand increased, of course, as population rose after about A.D. 1000. Obregón, in the sixteenth century, indicated the eagerness with which the Serrana

groups traded for salt (Cuevas 1924:146). The salt trails were of such importance that they were still in use in the latter part of the eighteenth century (Caxa 1772). As we have already mentioned, other internal trade in the Serrana seems to have involved cotton articles, slaves, and foodstuffs. One commodity, much valued and fought over, according to Obregón, was alum (probably aluminium sulfate) which was traded in the form of small loaves and may have been used as a condiment. The alum sources were controled by Batuco, a buffer state between the northern and southern confederacies of statelets (Riley 1988;140, 143).

Beginning in the early fifteenth century – possibly at the end of the fourteenth – the Sonoran trail network took on another much broader function. At about that time the Serrana became linked both with western Mesoamerica to the south and with the upper Southwest to the north. It is very likely that this phenomenon was part of some more extensive rearranging of intergroup contacts that was going on in the Greater Southwest and in Mesoamerica. Whatever the case, after the early fifteenth century, the Serrana peoples became middlemen for a vigorous and expanding trade that linked Mesoamerica to the far reaches of the Southwest. The flow consisted mainly of luxury goods; the materials and their routes have been described above. This period, lasting for a century and a half, saw the apogee of the Sonoran statelets. Spanish contact, however, marked the beginning of the end. Even if European disease and Spanish military and religious expansionism had not overwhelmed them, the statelets might well have collapsed at this time. The destruction of the Indian societies and rich markets at either end of the Camino Real undermined not only the economic foundation of the statelets, but much of their cultural raison d'être as well. The old road and trail networks that served the Serrana peoples so well in their trading activities during the protohistoric period were now adapted to the imperialist needs of the Spaniards.

References

Amsden, Monroe
  1928 *Archaeological Reconnaissance in Sonora*. Southwest Museum Papers 1, Southwest Museum, Los Angeles
Brand, Donald D.
  1935 The Distribution of Pottery Types in Northwest Mexico. *American Anthropologist* 37:287–305
  1944 Archaeological Relations between Northern Mexico and the Southwest. In *El Norte de México y el sur de Estados Unidos. Tercera reunión de mesa*

redonda sobre problemas antropológicos de México y Centro América, pp. 199–203. Sociedad Mexicana de Antropología, Mexico

1973 Aboriginal Trade Routes for Sea Shells in the Southwest. In *The Classic Southwest,* edited by B. C. Hedrick, J. C. Kelley, and C. L. Riley, pp. 92–101. Southern Illinois University Press, Carbondale and Edwardsville

Braniff Cornejo, Beatriz

1978 Preliminary Interpretations Regarding the Role of the San Miguel River, Sonora, Mexico. In *Across the Chichimec Sea,* edited by C. L. Riley and B. C. Hedrick, pp. 67–82. Southern Illinois University Press, Carbondale and Edwardsville

1985 La Frontera protohistórica Pima-Opata en Sonora, México. Proposiciones arqueológicas preliminares. Ph.D. dissertation, Universidad Nacional Autónoma de México

Cabeza de Vaca, Alvar Núñez

1555 *La relación y comentarios.* Valladolid

Caxa, J. A.

1772 Carta al Virrey, ii de Diciembre. *Ramo de Provincias Internas* 81. Archivo General de la Nación, Mexico

Cuevas, Mariano

1924 *Historia de los descubrimientos antiguos y modernos de la Nueva España, escrita por el conquistador Baltasar de Obregón, año de 1584.* Departamento Editorial de la Sría. de Educación Pública, Mexico

Dean, Jeffrey S., and John C. Ravesloot

1988 The Chronology of Cultural Interaction in the Gran Chichimeca. Paper given at the Seminar Culture and Contact: Charles C. Di Peso's Gran Chichimeca. Amerind Foundation, Dragoon, Arizona, 2–7 October 1988

Di Peso, Charles C.

1974 *Casas Grandes: A Fallen Trading Center of the Gran Chichimeca,* Vols. I–III. Amerind Foundation Publication 9 and Northland Press, Dragoon and Flagstaff

Di Peso, Charles C., John B. Rinaldo, and Gloria J. Fenner

1974 *Casas Grandes: A Fallen Trading Center of the Gran Chichimeca,* Vols. IV and VI. Amerind Foundation Publication 9 and Northland Press, Dragoon and Flagstaff

Doolittle, William E.

1979 La población serrana de Sonora en tiempos prehispánicos: La evidencia de los asentamientos antiguos. *Memoria, IV Simposio de Historia de Sonora,* Instituto de Investigaciones Históricas, Hermosillo, Mexico, pp. 1–16

1980 Aboriginal Agricultural Development in the Valley of Sonora, Mexico. *Geographical Review* 70:328–42

1981 Obsidian Hydration Dating in Eastern Sonora, Mexico. In *Obsidian Dates III,* edited by C. W. Meighan and G. S. Russell, pp. 155–60. Institute of Archaeology, University of California, Los Angeles

1984a Cabeza de Vaca's Land of Maize: An Assessment of its Agriculture. *Journal of Historical Geography* 10:246–62

1984b Settlements and the Development of "statelets" in Sonora, Mexico. *Journal of Field Archaeology* 11:13–24

1988 *Pre-Hispanic Occupance in the Valley of Sonora, Mexico.* Anthropological Papers of the University of Arizona 48, Tucson

Hammond, George P., and Agapito Rey (eds.)

1940 Narratives of the Coronado Expedition, 1540–1542. *Coronado Cuarto Centennial Publications, 1540–1940.* University of New Mexico Press, Albuquerque

Ives, Ronald L.

1936 Melchior Díaz – the Forgotten Explorer. Notes and Comments. *Hispanic American Historical Review* 16:86–90

Johnson, Alfred E.

1963 The Trincheras Culture of Northern Sonora. *American Antiquity* 29:174–86

Kelley, J. Charles

1986 The Mobile Merchants of Molino. In *Ripples in the Chichimec Sea,* edited by F. J. Mathien and R. H. McGuire, pp. 81–104. Southern Illinois University Press, Carbondale and Edwardsville

Lange, Charles H., and Carroll L. Riley, eds.

1970 *The Southwestern Journals of Adolph F. Bandelier: 1883–1884.* University of New Mexico Press, Albuquerque

Lekson, Steven H.

1984 Dating Casas Grandes. *The Kiva* 50:55–60

Lumholtz, Carl

1973 *Unknown Mexico.* 2 vols. Rio Grande Press, Glorieta, New Mexico. Originally published in 1902

Nentvig, Juan

1971 *Descripción geográfica de Sonora.* Edición preparada por Germán Viveros, segunda serie, número 1. Publicaciones del Archivo General de la Nación, Mexico

1980 *Rudo Ensayo. A Description of Sonora and Arizona in 1764.* Translated, clarified, and annotated by A. F. Pradeau and R. R. Rasmussen. University of Arizona Press, Tucson

Noguera, E.
1958 *Reconocimiento arqueológico en Sonora*. Instituto de Antropología e Historia, Informe 10, Mexico

Pailes, Richard A.
1972 An Archaeological Reconnaissance of Southern Sonora and Reconsideration of the Rio Sonora Culture. Ph.D. dissertation, Southern Illinois University, Carbondale
1976 Relaciones culturales prehistóricas en el noreste de Sonora. In *Sonora: Antropología del desierto*, edited by B. Braniff and R. Felger, pp. 213–28. Colección Científica 27. Instituto Nacional de Antropología e Historia, Mexico
1978 The Rio Sonora Culture in Prehistoric Trade Systems. In *Across the Chichimec Sea*, edited by C. L. Riley and B. C. Hedrick, pp. 134–43. Southern Illinois University Press, Carbondale and Edwardsville
1980 The Upper Rio Sonora Valley in Prehistoric Trade. In *New Frontiers in the Archaeology and Ethnohistory of the Greater Southwest*, edited by C. L. Riley and B. C. Hedrick, pp. 20–39. Transactions of the Illinois State Academy of Science 72.
1984 Agricultural Development and Trade in the Rio Sonora Valley. In *Prehistoric Agricultural Strategies in the Southwest*, edited by S. K. Fish and P. R. Fish, pp. 309–25. Arizona State University Anthropological Research Papers, Tempe

Pailes, Richard A., and Daniel T. Reff
1985 Colonial Exchange Systems and the Decline of Paquime. In *The Archaeology of West and Northwest Mesoamerica*, edited by M. S. Foster and P. C. Weigand, pp. 353–63. Westview Press, Boulder

Pennington, Campbell W.
1979 *The Pima Bajo of Central Sonora, Mexico, Vol. II: Vocabulario en la lengua névome*, edited by C. W. Pennington. University of Utah Press, Salt Lake City
1980 *The Pima Bajo of Central Sonora, Mexico, Vol. I: The Material Culture*. University of Utah Press, Salt Lake City
1981 *Arte y vocabulario de la lengua dohema, heve, o eudeva* ... Universidad Nacional Autónoma de México. Instituto de Investigaciones Filológicas, Mexico

Ravesloot, John C., Jr.
1984 Social Differentiation at Casas Grandes, Chihuahua, Mexico. An Archaeological Analysis of Mortuary Practices. Ph.D. dissertation, Southern Illinois University, Carbondale

Reff, Daniel T.
1981 The Location of Corazones and Señora: Archaeological Evidence from the Rio Sonora Valley, Mexico. In *The Protohistoric Period in the North American Southwest*, edited by D. R. Wilcox and W. B. Masse, pp. 94–111. Arizona State University Anthropological Research Papers 24, Tempe
1982 Protohistoric Exchange Networks in Sonora, Mexico. Paper presented at the 81st annual meeting of the American Anthropological Association, Washington, DC

Riley, Carroll L.
1971 Early Spanish–Indian Communication in the Greater Southwest. *New Mexico Historical Review* 46: 285–314
1976a Las Casas and the Golden Cities. *Ethnohistory* 23: 19–30
1976b *Sixteenth Century Trade in the Greater Southwest*. Mesoamerican Studies 10, Research Records of the University Museum. Southern Illinois University, Carbondale
1978 Pecos and Trade. In *Across the Chichimec Sea*, edited by C. L. Riley and B. C. Hedrick, pp. 53–64. Southern Illinois University Press, Carbondale and Edwardsville
1979 Casas Grandes and the Sonoran Statelets. Paper presented to the Chicago Anthropological Society, 1979
1980 Mesoamerica and the Hohokam: A View from the Sixteenth Century. In *Current Issues in Hohokam Prehistory: Proceedings of a Symposium*, edited by D. Doyel and F. Plog, pp. 41–8. Arizona State University Anthropological Research Papers 23, Tempe
1985 Spanish Contact and the Collapse of the Sonoran Statelets. In *The Archaeology of West and Northwest Mesoamerica*, edited by M. S. Foster and P. C. Weigand, pp. 419–30. Westview Press, Boulder
1986 An Overview of the Greater Southwest in the Protohistoric Period. In *Ripples in the Chichimec Sea*, edited by F. J. Mathien and R. H. McGuire, pp. 45–54. Southern Illinois University Press, Carbondale and Edwardsville
1987 *The Frontier People*. University of New Mexico Press, Albuquerque
1988 Warfare in the Protohistoric Southwest: An Overview. *Cultures in Conflict*. Proceedings of the 20th Annual Chacmool Conference, 1987, pp. 138–44. Calgary

Riley, Carroll L., and Joni L. Manson
1983 The Cíbola–Riguex Route: Continuity and Change in the Southwest. *New Mexico Historical Review* 58:347–67

Sauer, Carl O.
1932 The Road to Cibola. *Ibero-Americana* 3
1934 The Distribution of Aboriginal Tribes and Languages in Northwestern Mexico. *Ibero-Americana* 5
1935 Aboriginal Population of Northwestern Mexico. *Ibero-Americana* 10
Sauer, Carl O., and Donald D. Brand
1931 Prehistoric Settlements of Sonora, with Special Reference to Cerros de Trincheras. *University of California Publications in Geography* 5:67–148. University of California Press, Berkeley

Tower, Donald B.
1945 *The Use of Marine Mollusca and their Value in Reconstructing Prehistoric Trade Routes in American Southwest.* Papers of the Excavators' Club 2(3), Cambridge, MA
Undreiner, George J.
1947 Fray Marcos and his Journey to Cíbola. *The Americas* 3: 415–86
Weigand, Phil C.
1976 Rio Grande Glaze Sherds in Western Mexico. *Pottery Southwest* 4:3–5

13 Causeways in the context of strategic planning in the La Quemada region, Zacatecas, Mexico

CHARLES D. TROMBOLD

Introduction: the northern Mesoamerican frontier

The northern limit of the Mesoamerican *oikoumene* at the onset of Spanish conquest was rather sharply defined both culturally and environmentally. It extended from the mouth of the Sinaloa river in the far northwest, eastward to the Western Sierra Madre mountain range. From the highlands of northeastern Jalisco and southern Zacatecas the boundary extended eastward along the middle Lerma river valley, then northward again along the Moctezuma river in southern Queretaro to the Tamuin and Tamesi drainages in eastern San Luis Potosi. From there it arched northeast to encompass the Gulf coast lowlands as far north as the Soto La Marina river in Tamaulipas (Armillas 1964a:291). This perimeter generally coincided with the limits of agricultural productivity. The area north of this boundary was known for its chronically unpredictable rainfall cycles and inability to sustain the minimum requirements for complex stratified societies that depended on large aggregated sedentary populations.

Until about the beginning of the twentieth century it was generally assumed that this boundary had remained fairly constant throughout most of Mesoamerican development. The few notable exceptions located north of it, such as La Quemada, fit well into Aztec migration myths and were not given undue attention. The concept that prevailed for several centuries after the conquest was that cultures north of the historic Aztec–Tarascan borders were wholly barbarous or weak imitations of central Mexican civilization.

However, as a result of increased archaeological attention over the last thirty years, it became apparent that the historic frontier was a late and transitory development. Research, particularly in the areas north and northwest of this border, has shown that during the Early through Middle Classic period (*c.* A.D. 1 to 500) the agricultural frontier was continually extended further northward and that a generalized Mesoamerican presence had succeeded in spawning several very vigorous cultural traditions. Despite recent studies, however, it still cannot be determined with certainty to what degree this was due to an actual movement of colonists from the Central Highlands or to progressive acculturation of peripheral groups.

J. Charles Kelley (1974) proposed a scenario of cultural drift that may account for a combination of these factors. He suggested that by "budding off" of lineage groups, small numbers of farmers on the northern peripheries took with them a portion of their basic Mesoamerican heritage. These Mesoamerican cultural traits were then recombined with others such as Chichimec traits in such a way that the next wave of colonization carried with it modified or mixed variations of the basic Mesoamerican pattern. Adding to this "soft diffusion" was "hard diffusion" ostensibly carried by direct Mesoamerican penetration in the form of organized trade endeavors from the south. Significantly, this period of early colonization or acculturation of north-central Mexico coincided with the decline of the Chupicuaro tradition and the rise of great city-states such as Teotihuacan in the Central Highlands. While I doubt that Teotihuacan or any other single major center in Central Mexico played a direct part in controling developments on the northern frontier, almost certainly secondary or tertiary effects emanating from that area played a major role.

Whatever the means, by about A.D. 850 most of the frontier had reached its greatest northern limits. It included much of present-day Zacatecas, Jalisco, Nayarit, Guanajuato, and Aguascalientes as well as the southern portions of San Luis Potosi and Durango. Several factors were probably constantly at play in this advance. One of these may have been optimum climatic conditions between about A.D. 100 and 600. Another was probably population pressure, both in terms of gross population increases in the south and competition between agriculturalists for the most favorable land along major north–south river drainages (i.e., Rio Lajas, Santiago, Bolaños, Juchipila, Chapalangana). Giving impetus to this advance may also have been exploitation of mineral wealth and establishment of trade networks with the Greater Southwest (Weigand *et al.*, 1977; Weigand 1978). Having penetrated these new areas, refinements in maguey (*Agave* spp.) and nopal (*Opuntia* spp.) processing were important for maintaining the subsistence stability of these people. This perhaps more than many other factors may have permitted the successful colonization of the north (Parsons and Parsons 1990). It undoubtedly was of major importance in the La Quemada region as reflected by the high proportion of specialized lithic tools (see Spence 1971:36; Trombold 1985a:254–65) suited for this purpose.

While the factors that limited earlier Mesoamerican expansion were probably similar to those that formed the boundary during later Postclassic times, the buffer zones were evidently much wider and more flexible. During periods of favorable environmental conditions this would have enabled greater penetration of marginal lands despite their present reputation for chronically unpredictable rainfall cycles. Ultimately even here there was a threshold beyond which aggregated sedentary populations could not cross without unacceptable cultural loss. Thus populations could continue to grow and occupy more lands within the buffer zones, but as a group they could not cross it permanently.

This situation may have lasted for several hundred years. Then around A.D. 800/900 the advances that had characterized northward expansion during Early and Middle Classic times became reversed (Nalda 1976). The reasons for this are not clear, yet the possibility of long-term desiccation would have to rank high. Armillas (1969) suggested that severe climatic deterioration initially dislodged the northern peripheral agriculturalists. As this continued, populations residing behind the receding frontier would have to contend not only with lower agricultural productivity, but with an influx of refugees as well as barbarian depredations. Thus by a snowball effect even areas that were not directly affected climatically would share a similar fate.

Although almost certainly associated with intense warfare, this abandonment may have been somewhat more gradual than the sudden apocalypse envisioned by Armillas. Kelley's extensive work in western Zacatecas, for example, lends some support for at least a localized abandonment in that region. Although he cautiously suggests *c.* A.D. 850 for the termination date of the ceremonial center of Alta Vista, Kelley (1985) notes that the remnant population was not suddenly displaced southward, but colonized the Rio Guadiana area to the north beginning with the Calichal phase (*c.* A.D. 850–950). Nevertheless, the buffer zone as a whole suffered a drastic population decline and loss of key cultural traits. Within less than about 200 years agriculturalists in much of Zacatecas, San Luis Potosi, Aguascalientes, Guanajuato, and portions of Queretaro had either adapted to a semi-nomadic existence or

Fig. 13.1. Major stream drainages of central northwestern Mexico (map by Michael J. Simpson).

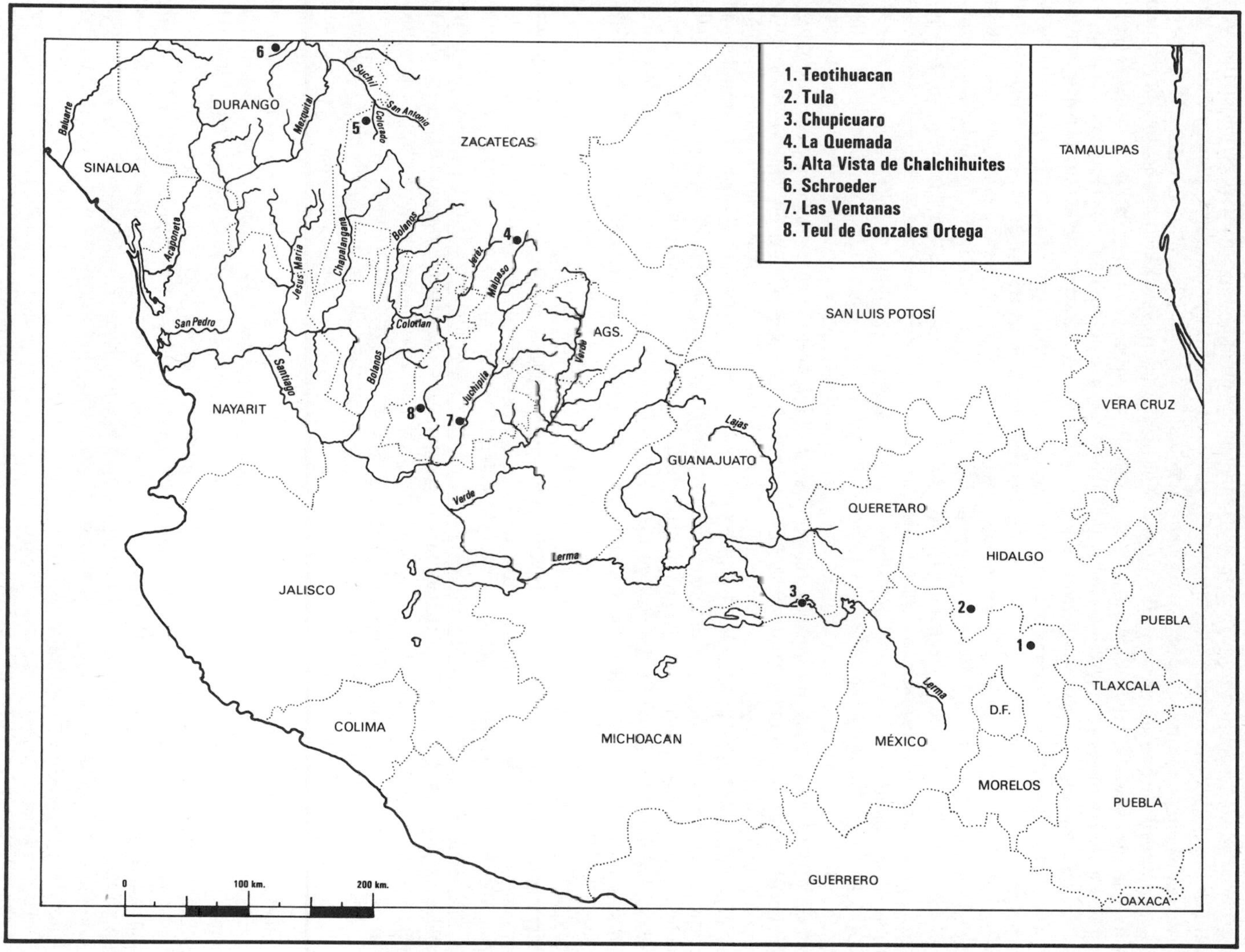

1. Teotihuacan
2. Tula
3. Chupicuaro
4. La Quemada
5. Alta Vista de Chalchihuites
6. Schroeder
7. Las Ventanas
8. Teul de Gonzales Ortega

had been displaced by a radically different cultural tradition.

The La Quemada region

One region on the northern frontier that witnessed early colonization and subsequent abandonment was occupied by the extravagantly fortified ceremonial center of La Quemada. This and the densely populated region surrounding it were situated directly on the buffer zone. Because of its position and the fact that it represents one of the largest sites north of Teotihuacan, it is of key importance in understanding the processes shaping the northern frontier. Presently neither the extent of its influence nor the range of its trade relations are known. Judging from its magnitude and lack of comparable centers for hundreds of kilometers around, its impact was probably considerable.

The focus of La Quemada occupation was on the middle Malpaso valley in south-central Zacatecas. Despite its extreme northwest position relative to other Mesoamerican high cultures, the site was not an isolated phenomenon. It almost certainly represents an integral part of the greater Chalchihuites cultural tradition.[1] While there is evidence of previous occupation of the valley, i.e., a local Canutillo substrate possibly dating from *c.* A.D. 300 to about A.D. 600, the major La Quemada occupation seems to have been initiated by outside forces that reached florescence here between *c.* A.D. 600 and 800. These influences, manifested primarily in subtle changes in intrasite layout, increased population and construction activity, and a few different ceramic types, appeared suddenly and fully developed (Trombold 1990).

The citadel

The ruins of the citadel cover the entire south face and summit of an elongated twin-peaked mountain rising steeply from the Malpaso valley (Fig. 13.2). The summits afford particularly good strategic vantages, giving an unrestricted view for considerable distances up and down the valley. While the north and south ends of the mountain lack the precipitous inclines of the sides, they nevertheless maintain a steep gradient. Protecting the north and northeast portions of the mountain where defense would have been weakest, a massive stone masonry wall 4 m high by 4 m wide was constructed to a length of somewhat over 800 m. Within the citadel, particularly on the south face, a series of constructed terraces provided level places for monumental-scale architecture. On these terraces are found elaborate orthogonal sunken plaza complexes surrounded by large palace-like structures, pyramids, and room compounds.

The site was built on multiple levels interconnected by wide staircases. The lowest level was located at the extreme southern portion of the mountain where the incline begins. It consists of a raised elongated platform measuring somewhat over 200 m in length associated with a large square-based tiered pyramid. This platform possibly served as a first line of defense since its original height was probably at least 2 m. It is near this pyramid and platform that the largest causeways in the valley converge on the citadel from various hinterland settlements. Much of this area is now covered by dense vegetation and rubble, yet several of the major causeways are still plainly visible.

The second level, higher up the incline, is the first level of the inner fortifications. This was connected to the first level outer defenses by a wide (35 m) causeway and stairway flanked by two guarding pyramids. That and another wide inset staircase near the Votive Pyramid on the east side were the citadel's main entrances. This level is located where the physical restraints of the incline are least, thus enabling the builders to construct larger structures with somewhat more freedom for overall design. Some of these include the Hall of Columns with an adjoining plaza complex, and a large I-shaped ballcourt (Fig. 13.2, center right) with other smaller sunken plaza complexes orientated to it.

The third level is generally more isolated, being confined by steep taluded masonry walls that served not only to support the artificial terraces higher up, but also provided formidable defenses. The main access to this level from the former was by means of a steep staircase located west of the Votive Pyramid and low stairs strategically placed at the crux of two protruding platforms. Structures on this level include room clusters and another large square plaza complex with evidence of contiguous rooms surrounding it.

The next level was even more inaccessible, being linked to the former by a single steep staircase on the south side. This level likewise contains a large elaborate plaza complex, but differs from the former in that it is surrounded by large single structures instead of multiple contiguous rooms. The relative inaccessibility of this level possibly restricted public participation in any activities carried out here, as well as access to those responsible for them. This level and the one above it extended along the south and west side of the mountain where topography permitted.

The highest and most inaccessible group of structures in relation to the main body of the citadel is on the northern summit (Fig. 13.3). This is connected to the

Fig. 13.2. Aerial view of the south face of La Quemada.

former by a low causeway 6.2 m wide that gradually ascends the crest of a narrow ridge to where the northern summit expands and becomes more level. Several smaller spur roads can be seen on aerial photos leading directly down to defensive positions from both sides of this main artery. The structures that formed the northern precinct seem to have been established for religious and/or elite activities. It is also clear that this precinct performed a military function since it is closely associated with the massive wall mentioned previously. Leading to a small ballcourt on a nearby lower level to the northeast is a stepped causeway measuring 10.5 m wide and 70 m long.

Flanking its upper entrance were two skull-shaped boulders, one of which has since been dislodged.

Most of the citadel's immediate population resided on the east, south, and west sides of the mountain, and in a few nucleated settlements not far to the east. That there may also have been a substantial non-elite resident population residing within the citadel is shown by the presence of common utilitarian ceramics and lithic debris far up the east side of the mountain, even in relatively inaccessible places. Some of this, however, may have been due to a later ephemeral reoccupation (possibly Chichimec) after the citadel had fallen.

Fig. 13.3. Upper northern precinct of La Quemada. Note the axial alignment formed by causeway, plaza stairs, central altar and large building. Stepped causeway connects the upper precinct to a nearby ballcourt and other structures at lower elevation. Contour intervals are approximate.

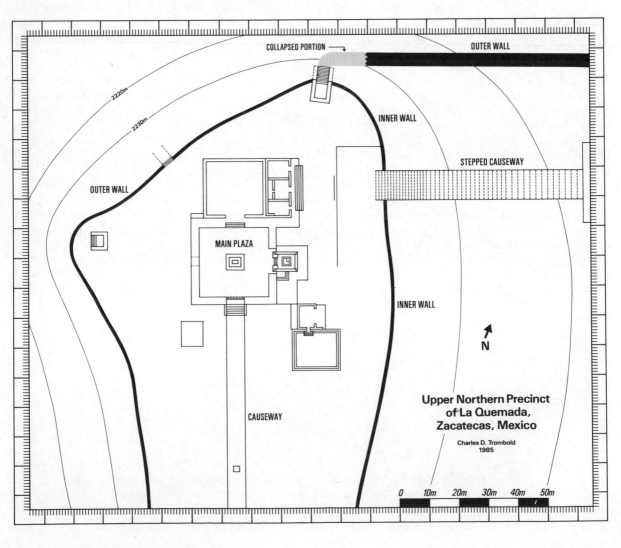

To summarize, architectural layout within the citadel is characterized by a conscious effort to accommodate the rectangular symmetry of the plaza complex to the constraints of topography. This had several results. First, on the lower level where the physical constraints were least, larger structures could be built to accommodate a greater number of people and activities. Access to higher elevations was severely restricted whereby vertical movement was possible only by means of a few steep stairways that effectively segregated certain plaza groups and activities that took place there. Horizontal access on the upper levels was facilitated by construction of avenues, some of which had low protecting walls facing the precipices. In general, horizontal access was far easier than vertical access and reflects a well-developed sense of strategic planning and construction skill.

The La Quemada hinterland

Unlike the modern population which is aggregated into a few towns and hamlets, the prehispanic settlement pattern was dispersed into numerous small sites occupying a variety of physiographic situations (Fig. 13.4). This reflects a certain adaptive efficiency given the constraints of their environment and technology. This pattern, where close proximity to streams and floodplains with optimum water table seems imperative, may indicate that unpredictable or insufficient rainfall cycles were prevalent. Most of these sites are small, ranging in size from 0.25 to 0.5 ha. The larger sites, though far fewer in number, range from about 2 to 5 ha. Most habitation sites are found on alluvial terraces overlooking the floodplains of major streams and their tributaries; some are found on high hills or mesas commanding good vantage and defensive positions. Many are located near streams on the gently sloping grasslands with seemingly few defensive considerations at all.

Internal settlement layout appears as consistent throughout the surrounding region as it was in the citadel. Almost invariably sites, regardless of size, were composed of one or more orthogonal sunken court complexes consisting of long rectangular masonry platforms orientated to the cardinal directions. On top of the platforms and facing the plazas were either one single structure or, most often, several contiguously arranged structures (Fig. 13.5). Typically these had low masonry foundations that supported plastered wattle and daub walls (Trombold 1986). Often a small square shrine or altar was located near the center of the plaza. Larger sites retained this basic design, but usually consisted of accretions of three or more plaza groups. In addition, some sites had special architectural features such as structures with round or square masonry colonnades. Since the plaza complex represents the basic architectural unit of sites throughout the entire area, it is likely that it reflected a fundamental social unit as well.

There is only one type of site recognized so far that does not conform to this pattern. This is the *nido*. Typically these are located on lower escarpments, buttes, or other elevated positions with good vantage in all directions, yet are usually not visible from lower elevations. They are round to oval in shape and rarely exceed 6 m in diameter. Their rims are never elevated more than about 75 cm above ground level and seem to be made hastily of low piles of non-coursed masonry. Nidos may have had a minor defensive or communication function and are frequently in association with roads or causeways.

Three site aggregates in the La Quemada hinterland have been distinguished which correspond with the three major stream drainages of the immediate region. The first of these lies in the vicinity of La Quemada near the Malpaso river (termed the Rio La Partida in this locality) and covers an area of approximately 40 km². The second aggregate is clustered loosely around the second largest center in the region, Los Pilarillos, located 5 km southwest of La Quemada on the Arroyo Coyotes. This covers an area of about 50 km². The third intergrades with the La Quemada aggregate further south on the Malpaso river (termed the Rio Villanueva here) and covers an area of about 25 km². Habitation sites in each aggregate follow a roughly linear pattern near stream and tributary courses. While larger sites in the La Quemada and Villanueva aggregates are especially noted for their locations on natural terraces overlooking the floodplains, those of the Pilarillos aggregate are more dispersed on the flatter grasslands. Each aggregate, however, is in proximity to a major hillside agricultural terracing work that is invariably associated with a large defensive position on its summit. Linking each of these aggregates and terraced hillsides to the citadel is a network of slightly raised roads or causeways.

Formal routes in northern Mesoamerica

Ancient roads or causeways in northern Mesoamerica are not unique only to La Quemada, yet it is here that they are best known (see also Trombold 1985a:243–5). Before discussing the La Quemada routes in detail it is important to examine their occurrences and contexts in other areas of north central Mexico. In the Rio Lajas drainage (a northern tributary of the Lerma) and in the Bajio of Guanajuato, R. B. Brown (1985:226–31) identifies five sites with causeways dating to the Classic period.

Fig. 13.4. Distribution of sites and agricultural terraces in the immediate La Quemada region. Location of the isolated pyramid complex in Fig. 13.8 is circled, far middle right (map by Michael J. Simpson).

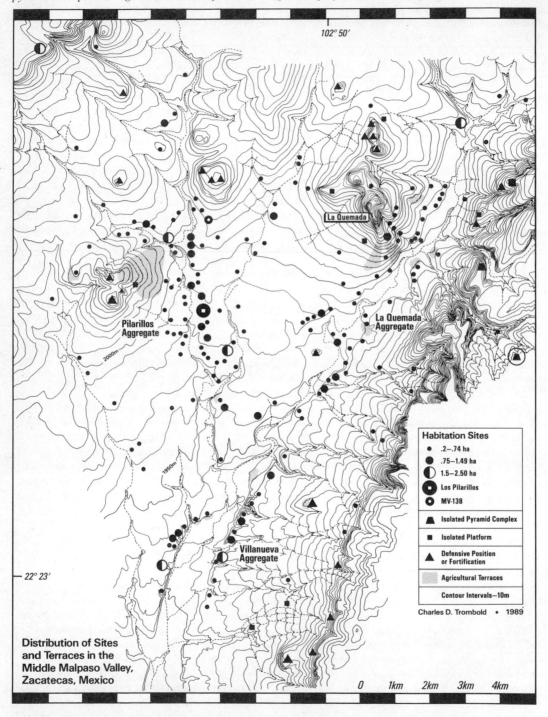

Habitation Sites

- • .2—.74 ha
- ● .75—1.49 ha
- ◐ 1.5—2.50 ha
- ⊡ Los Pilarillos
- ⊙ MV-138

- ▲ Isolated Pyramid Complex
- ■ Isolated Platform
- ▲ Defensive Position or Fortification
- ▦ Agricultural Terraces
- Contour Intervals—10m

Charles D. Trombold • 1989

Distribution of Sites and Terraces in the Middle Malpaso Valley, Zacatecas, Mexico

0   1km   2km   3km   4km

La Quemada

Pilarillos Aggregate

La Quemada Aggregate

Villanueva Aggregate

102° 50′

2000m

1950m

— 22° 23′

Fig. 13.5. Excavated portion of site MV–138 showing typical arrangement of structures around sunken plazas. The northern terminus of a causeway 2.4 m wide (S1-7 in lower middle), if extended directly southward 2.5 km, would connect with Pilarillos. Since there is no trace on aerial photos it may represent a short intrasite span connecting plaza groups. Excavated portion represents about two fifths of the entire site (diagram by Michael J. Simpson).

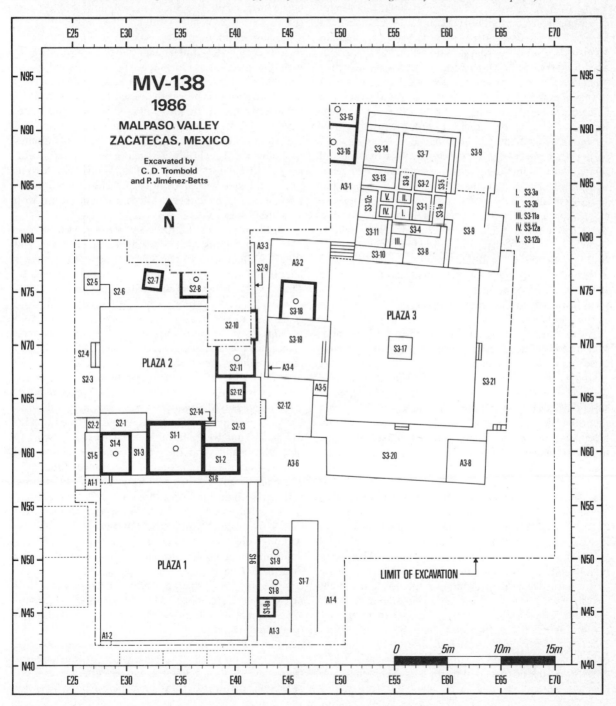

These include Cañada de Alfaro dating to Early Classic times, reported to have two roads (see also Zubrow and Willard 1974:24). Later Classic period sites with causeways include Graceros (see also Crespo 1976); Rancho Viejo with a causeway measuring 400 m in length extending from a series of plaza complexes; Cañada de la Virgen which is associated with a road 600 m long and 10 m wide extending from a pyramid/plaza compound; and the Cerro de la Mona/Morales site group which is associated with a causeway extending half way across the Rio Lajas valley to a series of ceremonial structures. In central Guanajuato the site of San Bartolo Aguacaliente is shown to be associated with a causeway over 225 m in length and about 8 m wide extending to a spring (Castañeda *et al.* 1988: Fig. 7). Many of these and related sites at this early date are especially significant because of their architectural similarity (*viz.* round and square columns, orthogonal sunken plaza complexes, stepped pyramids) to that of the La Quemada region and the Chalchihuites tradition in general. This suggests strong cultural currents contributing to the development of the Chalchihuites tradition from the Bajio, Rio Lajas and middle Lerma areas rather than directly from the Basin of Mexico. It may also underscore the north-central, rather than more western Mexican antecedents of the La Quemada region.

Approximately 140 km to the south of La Quemada, Weigand (1985a:173) notes the possibility of roadways existing in the immediate vicinity of the site of Las Ventanas (Fig. 13.1) on the basis of aerial photos. This was a large Caxcan stronghold/ceremonial center in southern Zacatecas. Although it was occupied during the Spanish conquest, its antiquity almost certainly extended well into the Classic period. Similarly the large fortified Caxcan center of Teul de Gonzales Ortega located in southwestern Zacatecas may also be associated with formal routes.[2] The significance of this is that the presence of formal routes (in addition to other traits) in the Caxcan area might further support the contention of Weigand (1985a:169) and others that the Caxcan were largely the cultural descendants of the Chalchihuites tradition. In this sense the La Quemada-Alta Vista regions might be seen as a proto-Caxcan hearth.

Formal routes are also found on the northern salient of the Chalchihuites culture (the Guadiana branch). Kelley (1971a:788), for example, mentions them in association with the Schroeder site in north-central Durango. Although chronology for the Guadiana branch is not yet firmly established on the basis of ^{14}C dates, the major occupation of the Schroeder site appears to date around A.D. 900–1100 (see Kelley

1985:283–4). In terms of the overall Chalchihuites sequence this is somewhat late. Almost certainly the practice of road building was well known beforehand in this region and thus would be predicted in earlier phase occupations of the Rio Suchil branch in western Zacatecas, i.e., the Alta Vista region.

An important boundary existed to the west of the regions occupied by the Chalchihuites tradition. Coeval with the major La Quemada and Rio Suchil occupations, the Teuchitlan tradition was dominant in the lake district of north-central Jalisco and had spread its influence further north into Nayarit and western Zacatecas (Weigand 1985b:60–91). Unlike the orthogonal structures and site layout typical of the Chalchihuites tradition, the Teuchitlan was characterized architecturally by circular structures and concentric site layout, often associated with shaft or crypt tombs. Significantly, no causeways have been found in association with Teuchitlan sites to date.

Formal routes in the Chaco Canyon region of New Mexico are discussed by Mathien (Chapter 10) and Windes (Chapter 11). The Chaco roads in particular have been frequently compared to those of La Quemada. There seem to be general similarities in terms of straightness, widths, connecting outlying sites, construction of stairways to overcome topographic obstacles and perhaps roadbed preparation in some cases. At first glance this might suggest direct contact between the two regions. There are problems here, however. The two were quite distinct culturally, chronologically and geographically, being separated by about 200 years and over 1,800 linear km. Most important is the apparent dissimilarity of road-articulated architecture (compare Fig. 11.5 to Fig. 13.3 and S1–7 in Fig. 13.5).[3] This and the scarcity of cultural debris on the La Quemada routes would suggest that the two networks functioned differently. There also seem to be important structural differences. Unlike the Chacoan roads, those at La Quemada rarely show evidence of linear depressions, and berms (linear ridges paralleling the road margins) are absent. Although direct contact between them thus appears very doubtful, a general Mesoamerican presence seems evident at Chaco based on (among other things) the comparatively widespread occurrence of earlier road networks in north-central Mexico. The macro-morphological similarities found in association with traditional Chaco architecture may indicate that the practice of road building was "grafted on" an already well-established cultural tradition. The mechanisms for this are far from clear, yet especially strong cultural waves were sweeping northward from somewhere in north-central

Mexico between *c*. A.D. 600 and 800. This could have been the result of political upheaval further south, realignment of exchange patterns, elite marriage alliances, religious ferment, conquest or any combination of these. Whatever it was, in Mexico it manifested itself suddenly and decisively – and primarily in certain aspects of architecture and intrasite layout. It may be more than just coincidence, then, that formal routes were constructed at La Quemada between *c*. A.D. 600 and 800; at Schroeder between *c*. A.D. 900 and 1100; and at Chaco between *c*. A.D. 1050 and 1140. At the very least, this may indicate the spread of mesoamerican symbolism to demonstrate elite power and legitimacy.

Formal routes in the La Quemada region
The historical accounts
Ever since the discovery of La Quemada by the first Spaniards around 1540, the causeways have provided a major topic of interest. Although Spanish chroniclers mentioned the citadel and speculated on its origin, it was not until Mexican independence in 1821 that any systematic studies were done. This was due in part to a new sense of nationalism and an influx of foreign mining engineers following the break-up of the Spanish monopoly on the rich silver mines near Zacatecas. The first detailed description of the causeways and ruins was by an English mining engineer, Captain G. F. Lyon, in 1826:

> A slightly raised and paved causeway of about twenty-five feet descends across the valley in the direction of the rising sun, and being continued on the opposite side of a stream which flows through it, can be traced up the mountain at two miles distance, until it terminates at the base of an emense stone ediface, which probably may also have been a pyramid (Lyon 1828:229)

and

> from the summit of the rock we could distinctly trace three straight and very extensive causeways diverging from that over which we first passed. The most remarkable of these runs S.W. for two miles, is forty-six feet in width, and crossing the grand causeway is continued to the foot of the cliff, immediately beneath the cave which I have just described. Its more distant extreme is terminated by a high and long artificial mound, immediately beyond the river towards the Hacienda of La Quemada. We could trace the second S.S.W. to a small rancho named Coyotes, almost four miles distant. And the third ran S.W. by S. still further,

ceasing, as the country-people informed us, at some mountain six miles distant. All of these roads had been slightly raised, were paved with rough stones still visible in many places above the grass, and were perfectly straight. (ibid.:239–40)

The most important and long-lasting contribution, however, came from a state antiquities act in 1831 requested by Governor D. Francisco García of Zacatecas. This act provided for the conservation of ancient buildings, excavations, maps and sketches of the ruins, and the eventual construction of a state museum. After ratification in 1831, the act was implemented in the same year with the commission of C. de Berghes and his associate, Joseph Burkart, both German mining engineers, to draw the first detailed map of the citadel and the surrounding region. The map completed by Berghes two years later is now one of the most important single sources of information for the archaeology of the area. It depicted most of the prehispanic causeways, many of the larger sites, and the location of several large terracing works.[4] Apparently two versions were drawn. The original[5] covered a smaller geographical area than the second, but gave greater detailed information on present land use, land ownership, and archaeological features. The second map, reproduced in Fig. 13.6, covered a wider area and was mostly restricted to archaeological and physiographic data. Both maps were important because they depicted major sites, causeways, and terraces in detailed relationship to recognizable topographical and modern cultural landscape features such as colonial roads and hamlets. About the same time Carlos Nebel (1839) visited the site and later published two drawings as well as the first detailed map of the citadel (Fig. 13.7). Burkart (1836) also published a map of the citadel and some of the causeways, but this was far less detailed than that of Berghes or Nebel. He did leave a verbal description, however, and this formed the basis of much of Seler's (1908) later account. In describing the causeways Burkart wrote:

> There are only two roadways leading down [from the lower east side of the citadel], ending in still recognizable roads which go far beyond Edificios. One of these roads disappears before crossing the stream, the other, however, crosses the stream and can be seen continuing at the other side of the stream. It leads up the hill which borders on the valley to where a large heap of stones is an indication that there was once a pyramid. The roadway ends on Cerro Cuisilla. These roads are straight like a line, 13 to 14 [Rhenish] feet wide

Fig. 13.6. Map by C. de Berghes showing the location of major sites, terraces and roads as they may have existed in 1833. This map was also published in France by E. Guillemin Tarayre, in 1869.

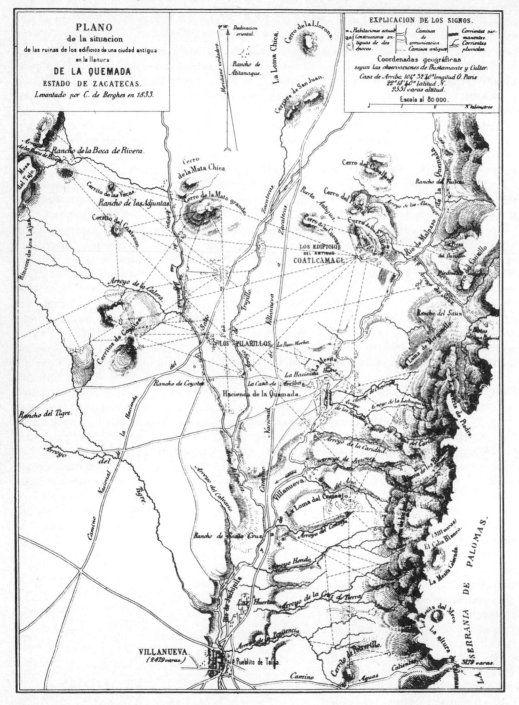

and paved. A third road seems to lead to the hamlet of La Quemada. It, however, is less visible than the other ones. Almost west of the main building [the Hall of Columns] a number of roads originate from a circle-like place and some of these roadways can be seen a long way until they disappear in the plain. The most important of them heads in a southwestern direction for almost a league and in the opposite direction until it reaches a mountain. A second one goes westward and toward the east to the main building. These roads rise only a little bit above the plains and are paved with raw stones so that it appears as if the now totally dry plain might once have been swampy ... (1836:103, my translation).

One other mention might be made of descriptions from this period. Rivera (1843) described a causeway network extending from the citadel to the San Juan hills, 2.5 km to the northwest. This extension was completely omitted by Berghes with the result that more recent studies tended to underestimate the importance of the valley north of the citadel.

Modern studies in the La Quemada region

From the period of the early 1830s until 1963 the La Quemada causeways were not a specific research objective. Although they were mentioned by various visitors, it was not until Pedro Armillas' (1963) investigations that an attempt was made at systematic survey. In addition to tracing several major causeways in the valley, Armillas excavated a portion of the road mentioned by Lyon and Burkart leading south. Over fifty sites were also located in the valley, some of them directly associated with these causeways.

In 1974 I renewed the work started by Armillas a decade earlier. My goals at that time were to identify and describe all the prehispanic cultural landscape features in the region, including those mapped by Berghes 141 years earlier. The ecological and geomorphological settings of these features were recorded, and cultural material was collected from the surface of most sites. This survey resulted in the discovery of 226 sites, 3 major and 16 minor terracing works and the location of considerable numbers of features not depicted by Berghes (see Fig. 13.4).

Three methods were constantly employed in defining the archaeological landscape: intensive 100 percent ground survey, use of aerial photos, and reference to the Berghes maps. Survey strategy consisted of several trained individuals walking abreast in 15 to 20 m continuous swaths within units defined by enclosed fields or other boundaries. This insured that all surveyed areas would be methodically covered and that no visible feature or unusual landscape configuration would escape detection. Boundary strips between fields were especially noted because narrow causeways may have provided areas that later became convenient repositories for rocks removed during plowing. Larger areas with dense vegetation, uneven terrain and few enclosures presented more of a problem, especially in areas between the Malpaso river and the eastern escarpments. Other large areas with little vegetation and fewer enclosures were more successfully surveyed on horseback using the same general procedures.

Two sets of black-and-white aerial photos were used. One set consisted of large 50×50 cm print sheets on a scale of 1:12,500 that accompanied the survey crew. The other consisted of smaller stereo pairs on a scale of 1:25,000. The former were used to denote the location of a particular feature with its identification number while the latter were used to assist survey strategy. When a site was located it was given an identification number and surface collected for cultural material. Its area was measured in the field and the perimeter was marked on aerial photos. The latter could often show if a site was in direct association with a causeway alignment or only in proximity.

The Berghes map proved to be highly valuable because of its minute detail and surprising accuracy. Photocopies had previously been made and were used constantly in conjunction with modern topographic maps and aerial photos. Thus by comparing stream morphology, the location of Spanish colonial roads and fences, and topographic features, it was possible not only to replot, but reinterpret Berghes' observations on modern maps.

The three techniques needed to be used together to obtain optimum results because each had serious shortcomings. Aerial photos were generally best for areas that had been plowed or consisted of virgin grasslands. In previously plowed areas, traces of causeways often appeared as thin dark lines. Likewise in some undisturbed areas suspicious linear vegetation markings indicated the possible presence of a causeway. Usually, however, intact causeways were not readily visible with aerial photos unless their location was known beforehand. This was especially true in areas heavily strewn with surface rocks. Conversely the presence of causeways or terraces in plowed areas was not visible to ground surveys, even though they stood out clearly on aerial photos. This was also the case in a few undisturbed

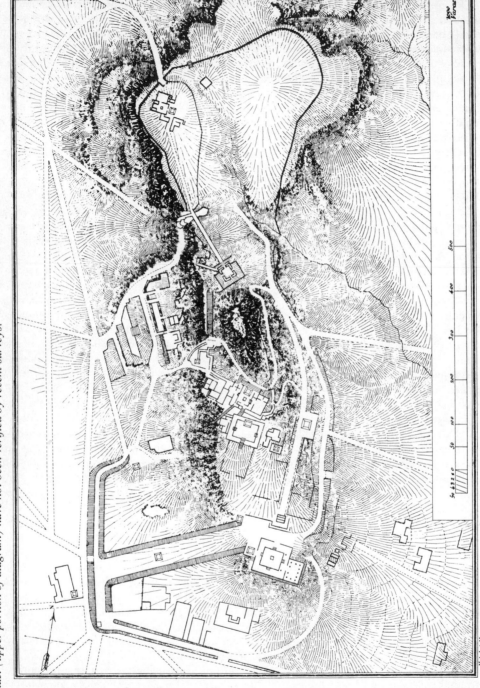

Fig. 13.7. *The first detailed map of La Quemada, published by Nebel in 1839. Locations of roads shown on the west side of the citadel (upper portion of diagram) have not been verified by recent surveys.*

areas – some short segments were visible on aerial photos, but almost impossible to find on the ground. In a situation like this, as in portions of the area north of the citadel not mapped by Berghes, ground survey aided only by aerial photos had to be used exclusively.

Aside from the causeways Berghes missed, such as on the far north side of the citadel and some in the Villanueva aggregate, he may have invented several. This may have been true for at least one major "site" he depicted in the Pilarillos aggregate shown as a connecting point for ten causeways. Another problem was that Berghes' map contained an error in its baseline calculations. However, by redrawing the baseline on modern topographic maps, correction could be achieved by triangulation and distance-ratio compensation.

Ground survey likewise had its complications. The region has been under Hispanic occupation for the last 400 years resulting in an accumulation of linear features. Some of these include Colonial-era roads and irrigation systems, fallen stone fences, cattle trails, and boundary strips between plowed fields where discarded stones were placed or paths developed. Possibly most devastating has been the change of emphasis from cattle raising to agriculture over the last fifty years. Heavy machine plowing is now taking its toll, especially in marginal lands that had successfully resisted the horse-drawn plow until recently. Adding to the problem of recognition is that some of the causeways may have provided either foundations or a convenient source of building material for large stone boundary fences. Nature itself has destroyed many. Occasionally all that remains of a causeway is a linear concentration of rubble that may show an intact portion. These would be easy enough to trace if it were not for natural rubble from centuries of sheet erosion that usually litters the ground as well.

General attributes of the routes

There may have been at least two styles of route construction. The first and best known is the paved causeway. Here two low parallel retaining walls of slab stones were built to the desired height and width similar to the transverse profile shown by Folan in Fig. 18.3. The elevation of narrower causeways (2 to 3 m wide) was probably never more than about four masonry courses high. The widest causeways (12–14 m) were seldom more than six masonry courses high and were usually not elevated more than about 50 cm above ground level. The area between the two walls was then filled with rock and rubble. This design seems to be a particular adaptation of the rubble core technique used extensively except that here it was the fill and not the wall that assumed import-

ance. The span was then capped with flat stones and perhaps topped with clay. Since some stairs and buildings within the citadel were finished with lime plaster, it may be that a few causeways in the immediate vicinity of the citadel were also plastered. No evidence for this has been found, however. Except for the very largest, most seem to have been built without camber to facilitate rainfall runoff.

The second style is only speculative since no excavations have been done for verification. It may consist of a straight route of uniform width without border elements or stone paving with little more than packed earth and minimal roadbed preparation. Evidence for this is derived mainly from undisturbed areas some kilometers south of the citadel where several routes can be seen clearly on aerial photos, yet border elements and linear elevation are completely lacking. Some of the longer routes, such as between the citadel and the Pilarillos aggregate, may have incorporated both styles.

Causeway width does not seem to vary significantly along any given segment. There are some exceptions to this such as the causeway mentioned by Lyon and Burkart leading to the "Pyramid of the Moon." This widens to approximately 20 m from an average width of about 8 m as it approaches that complex. In general causeways 7 to 10 m in width connect site aggregates to La Quemada. The most densely populated portion of the Pilarillos aggregate, for example, was connected to the citadel by two major causeways, each of which terminates near a major habitation site. It is only within 2 km of the citadel that the widest causeways are found. One leading up from the south (excavated by Armillas) measures slightly over 14 m wide while another from the east is 12 m wide.

Types of architectural structures directly associated with the routes are also important. At present this is difficult to determine accurately with regard to hinterland sites because of poor surface preservation and general lack of excavation data. There are other ways of obtaining a glimpse, however. One is by looking at certain causeway-associated structures on the citadel where architectural detail is relatively unobscured. One well-preserved causeway and associated building complex is represented in the upper northern ceremonial precinct. Here a causeway 4 m wide leads directly to a plaza compound (Fig. 13.3) from a distance of about 275 m. Although in later periods the stairs were blocked off and the compound wall heightened, the abutment of the causeway to the plaza follows a symmetrically planned pattern where an axis is formed by the causeway, stairs, altar, and a major structure on the opposite side of the plaza. This general layout also seems to be similar for most hinterland habitation sites. The original Berghes map shows this arrangement on many sites and while his depictions may be stylized in some cases, my own observations tend to confirm that causeway termini are most often associated with staired platforms and sunken courts such as the arrangement shown in Fig. 13.3.

There are also some unusual exceptions to this pattern. At two locations (MV-296 in the northern Pilarillos aggregate and MV-223 in the Villanueva aggregate) the routes develop into low ramps (*c.* 50–60 cm high) as they enter the site, whereupon they terminate abruptly. These are quite conspicuous, being noticeable from the elongated concentration of small boulders and other rocks that served as fill and foundation support. The ramps are usually the same width as the route, but their length rarely extends more than about 10 m along the same projected alignment.

Other features occasionally found in direct association with the causeways are small square altars. When present, these were placed in the center of the route and their size seems to have been determined by causeway

Fig. 13.8. Isolated pyramid complex (circled in Fig. 13.4) located on the crest of a high elongated mesa forming the boundary between the Malpaso valley and another valley to the east. This complex may have served as a signal relay between La Quemada and a major fortification in the eastern valley. No causeways were readily apparent linking this site to others, despite indications on the Berghes map (diagram by Michael J. Simpson).

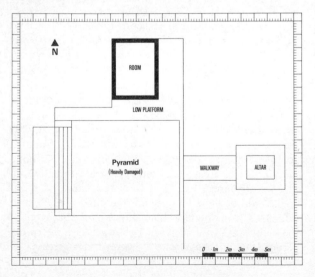

width. At times their base barely measures more than 1 m². These are usually only found in proximity to major architectural complexes as in Fig. 13.3 and probably performed a ceremonial function. However, others may have been considerably more isolated (see Trombold 1985a:246, Fig. 10.2). Other structures such as small square platforms are occasionally found at route junctions even when no immediate habitation is evident. Within some sites, however, narrow causeways of short extension (5 to 10 m) may be terminated by an altar as seen in Fig. 13.8. This arrangement occurs far less frequently and has only been found within sites, usually in close proximity to other architecture.

The regional network

An attempt is made to describe highlights of the causeway network in terms of location, termination points, and various features it connected. To facilitate this, the discussion focuses primarily on the area immediately surrounding the citadel. It should be noted, however, that there is reason to suspect that various routes may have extended somewhat beyond the core region shown in Fig. 13.9. This is based on inspection of aerial photos covering areas to the north and west, and informants who assert that a portion of the network may extend at least as far as the Hacienda de Encarnacion, 26 km to the southwest.

Northern extensions

The area most recently surveyed but least understood is north of the citadel. There are two well-defined entrances in the walls of the far northern precinct. From the wider of these, located at a lower elevation to the northeast (not shown on Fig. 13.3), a causeway extends toward the northwest approximately 0.5 km, then angles sharply to the west where it terminates on a large, low masonry platform. The other (Fig. 13.3) enters the upper northern precinct by means of a narrow inset staircase and descends the mountain directly where it seems to curve to the south to link structures on the lower west side of the citadel. Both of these are barely visible on aerial photos and although Berghes noted them in 1833, only remnants of the former are visible on the ground. North of the former there appears to be a hiatus extending as far as a group of steep hills (Cerro del Caballero on Fig. 13.6). In this area, however, several roads can be distinguished. One extends northwest toward the San Juan hills. This is only visible on aerial photos. Another that is ground-visible continues northward to a small platform. Leading from this road are spurs that terminate at elevated positions on the Cerro de Caballero. The

Fig. 13.9. Sites, terraces and causeways in the immediate La Quemada region (map by Michael J. Simpson).

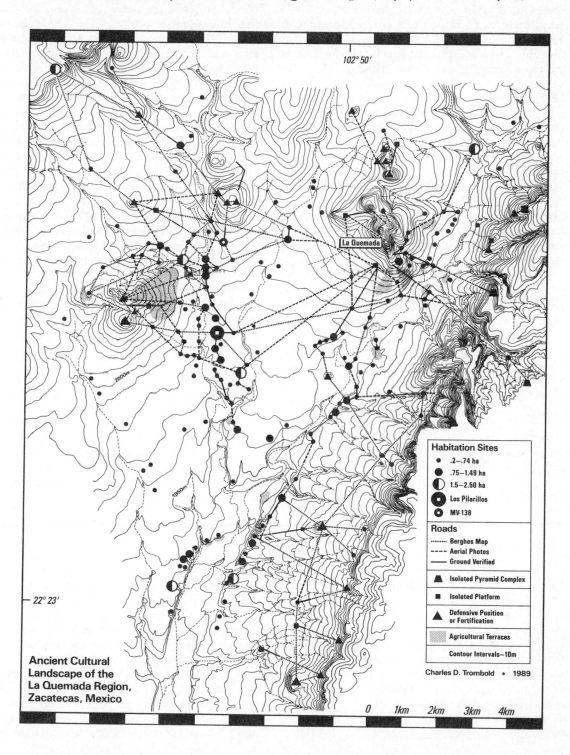

presence of causeways in this northern sector is significant in that all of them lead to defensive positions on elevated terrain. These positions are far removed from any permanent habitation sites,[6] suggesting that the causeways or roads were related exclusively to military and not civilian activities in this area.

Eastern extensions

Aside from those mentioned previously in the northern sector, there are at least ten other causeways that connected sites and other defensive positions directly to the citadel. In addition to these there are at least three others that lead to strictly defensive zones within or near the citadel. Of the former, the first is a well-constructed route slightly over 5 m wide located on the lower east side of the citadel. On aerial photos this leads to the northeast, perhaps up to 4 km, and links several habitation sites before becoming obscured. Another measures nearly 7 m in width with a height of about 30 cm. It extends eastward to a low, wide platform and stairway overlooking a steep escarpment, then descends to the stream below. Continuing up the steep slope on the opposite side it leads to a large defensively situated pyramid complex (the "Pyramid of the Moon"). This and the afore-mentioned causeway converge on the east side of the citadel together and enter by means of a wide inset stairway in the wall east of the Votive Pyramid. Berghes, who had very accurately plotted the location of so many other obscure causeways, made several mistakes in showing the location of these which are quite distinct. Another causeway in the eastern sector is massive, measuring 12 m in width and approximately 40 cm in height. The upper terminus for this is a square plaza complex just northeast of the Hall of Columns. It passes through a large agricultural terracing work directly to the stream below and, according to Berghes, leads eventually to the isolated pyramid complex shown in Fig. 13.8.

Southern extensions

Converging on the citadel from the south and southwest are several other major causeways. These are the longest and widest in the valley, some being uninterrupted by a site for up to 4 km. One in this group, excavated by Armillas, measures slightly over 14 m wide and is about 2.5 km long. This was the causeway previously described by Lyon as terminated "by a high and long artificial mound." It is unique in that approximately 150 m south of its articulation with the lower portion of the citadel, evidence of a small square structure is visible in the center of the causeway. Its foundation differs from altars

encountered occasionally and from a modern perspective it might resemble a toll station or small guardhouse. This causeway leads directly to a large habitation site, but does not end there. Rather, the width narrows to about 4 m and it connects several smaller habitation sites. Berghes' map shows it ending on a steep slope (La Mezita in Fig. 13.6) near the modern hamlet of La Quemada. Almost certainly he was correct, but nothing is visible now, even on aerial photos.

The second causeway of this group leads to the southwest and is approximately 5 km long and not less than 7 m wide.[7] Unlike the former, this leads directly to a small habitation site even though a large site (Potrero Nuevo, MV-110) is in very close proximity. This causeway is readily visible from the summit of the citadel and on aerial photos, but is not well defined on the ground in terms of linear elevation or concentrated rubble. This may indicate that not all routes received the same quality of workmanship, or it could reflect a different construction style mentioned previously.

Western extensions

The third causeway of this group is similar in many respects to the one just mentioned. Its length is about 5 km and it also shows very poor preservation despite prominent visibility from an elevated vantage. It is peculiar in certain respects, however. Within proximity of the citadel and extending southwest a few hundred meters it is closely associated with a shallow linear concavity. It is doubtful, though possible, that this depression represents the roadbed. Rather, it appears that the causeway was located above and immediately parallel to it on the downslope side of the terrain. This could represent a channel to direct runoff rainfall into agricultural lands between the La Quemada and Pilarillos site aggregates. From the air the alignment is visible 1.5 km from the citadel until the soil markings stop abruptly. This hiatus is about 0.75 km long, but resumes later on the same projected alignment. Traces continue for another kilometer until they become associated with a number of intersecting linear features (Fig. 13.10). These may represent a small irrigation system since they are located in proximity to a small stream and near an area that contained dense prehispanic population. Significantly neither this causeway nor the one previously mentioned terminate directly on nearby large sites.

Berghes shows four other causeways extending west from the citadel. These are not visible on aerial photos, making ground verification impossible at present. At least one of these may be spurious. However, Berghes depicts a causeway in this group extending 8 km west to a small steep mesa (Cerro de Quatezon on Fig. 13.6). The 1974 survey verified the presence of a small segment of this and an associated low platform at a junction approximately 1 km east of that mesa. Its eastward projected alignment would place it precisely in the location shown on the 1833 map.

Another is shown to extend from the citadel to a defensive position on the eastern slope of the Cerro de la Mata Grande. No trace of this has been found in proximity to the citadel either, although portions may be vaguely seen on aerial photos closer to the base of that hill. A nearly intact segment not shown by Berghes was found extending toward Cerro de la Mata Chica from the northern base of the former. This measured approximately 4 m in width but stopped abruptly well before reaching that destination. It appeared that construction had ceased on this span or that it had continued with a different, more perishable style of architecture.

The final causeway depicted by Berghes extending from the citadel is relatively short. Unlike the routes that extend to the Pilarillos aggregate from the lower southwest portion of the citadel, this extends northwest from a square sunken plaza complex situated on the saddle between the north and south summits and terminates on the low masonry platform mentioned previously.

Considerable numbers of settlements within site aggregates were connected as well. However, the precise locations of many of these cannot be determined until more sophisticated methods of detection are used. Curiously settlement size does not appear highly significant in terms of connectivity. The large site of Los Pilarillos, for example, is shown by Berghes to be connected by six causeways.[8] However, Berghes also shows some sites a fraction of the size of Los Pilarillos connected by an equal number of routes. Similarly, in the Pilarillos aggregate several well-defined routes connect small sites without deviating from their alignment to link nearby large sites. Temporal variation is not a likely explanation for this. Ceramic types were found in similar percentages on most of these sites which suggest that they were largely contemporaneous. Rather, the answer may lie in the functional content of settlements directly associated with the causeways. Whatever these road-related functions were, they seem not to have been predicated on a certain gross population threshold residing in any one given settlement.

In general there are two underlying similarities of the causeways. They link strictly defensive positions and they also ultimately link subregions of greatest habitation density to these positions. The Pilarillos aggregate,

Fig. 13.10. Aerial photograph of causeway traces (a) between La Quemada and a site near Pilarillos, and intersecting linear features (b), possibly irrigation canals. The site of Los Pilarillos is located toward the lower left.

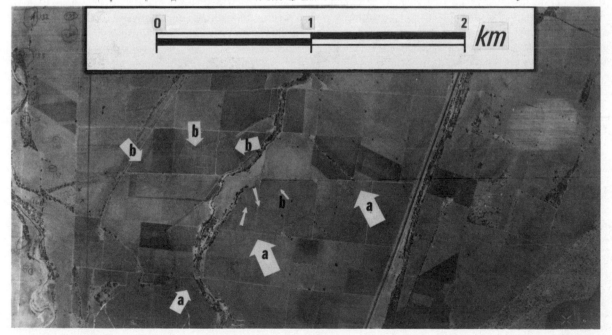

for example, is well connected not only with the citadel, but with major defensive works atop the terraced hills immediately to the west. The pattern is repeated in the Villanueva site aggregate. Here many habitation sites are connected to each other by causeways, yet ultimately these lead to elevated defensive positions on the eastern escarpment as well as major fortifications crowning a terraced hillside. There are other causeways, not shown by Berghes, that link strictly defensive positions with one another. These seem to be unrelated to any habitational zone.

Discussion

It seems clear that one of the primary functions of the causeways was military. The avenues facilitating horizontal access across the upper levels of the citadel give us the first clue. Other evidence includes: 1. the causeways north of the citadel and Cerro de la Mata Grande that lead into areas without substantial habitation; 2. the general lack of cultural material found in direct association with the routes outside site perimeters; 3. the fact that hilltop fortifications were often termini; and 4. that largest habitation sites were not necessarily connected directly to the citadel or each other.

Causeway width as well as location may also yield insights as to their use. Although Hyslop (Chapter 4) reminds us of the risk of ascribing too much reliance on road width as a reflection of traffic volume, in this case it would be unwise to discount it completely. The widest and most well-constructed causeways lie within 2.5 km of the citadel. The widths of these range between 14.3 and 12 m. In the Pilarillos aggregate at least three of the major causeways leading to the fortifications atop the terraced Cerritos de Coyotes range from 4 to 8 m wide. Causeways in the Villanueva aggregate and peripheries of the Pilarillos aggregate are generally narrower and range between 2.4 to 4.6 m wide with the average being somewhat over 3 m. Nevertheless, the pattern is consistent throughout: in no case would the causeway widths or labor invested in their planning and construction justify what would almost certainly have been a low volume of regular foot traffic.

There are several ways of viewing the causeways in a military context. First, there is the possibility that the routes were for rapid movement of troops from one trouble spot to another. The first person to propose this for La Quemada was Agustin Rivera (1875:11). He suggested that a level and straight roadbed would facilitate an army traveling from one destination to another and that low defensive walls would offer some protection to a warrior's unshielded side. At present, however,

there is no evidence of walls on any causeways aside from a few avenues near precipices within the citadel.

Causeway width in relation to military use is made clear in the context of Ross Hassig's observations (Chapter 3). If we assume that actual usage defined minimum width and that roads were primarily for the movement of troops in this region, then according to Hassig's estimates most of the causeways leading to isolated defensive positions could accommodate three to four persons abreast with an unknown number, though perhaps no more than six, to a column. This would give a unit strength of approximately eighteen individuals. The wider causeways (12 to 14 m) could accommodate a proportionately greater number, say twelve abreast and twenty-five to a column – or a unit strength of 300 persons. Thus the causeways would be well suited to expedite reinforcement of already established defensive positions and fortifications, as well as to facilitate movement of large masses of warriors to break sieges on the citadel. They would probably have had limited effectiveness, however, to bring large masses of troops to encounter a mobile enemy more than about 2 km from the citadel unless certain other strongholds were permanently garrisoned as well.

There are two other ways of viewing the causeways militarily. The first is not so much in terms of an external enemy as to insure the subjugation of a resident population. In the event of civil unrest, warriors could easily pour out of these strongholds to subdue any internal uprising. The second might be as a civil defense device to facilitate rapid evacuation of outlying settlements to safety in times of strife. As noted previously, most of the major fortifications were linked to population aggregates by causeways ranging from 8 to 14 m wide. Thus most of these causeways were wide enough to facilitate mass evacuation from the populated areas to the more secure strongholds. Although these differences in use would not be distinguishable in the archaeological record, it is evident that they could not be employed for the same purpose simultaneously.

Certainly there are other ways of interpreting the causeways. One might be for religious purposes, i.e., processions or connecting shrines within the region (see Bancroft 1882:591). Throughout Mesoamerica altars, pyramids, and other structures possibly associated with purely religious functions were often constructed on elevated or prominent terrain. Thus it is possible that what we perceive here as fortifications were actually shrines. This is doubtful in light of research to date, however. Evidence throughout the region points overwhelmingly to major or at least endemic strife. This is based mostly on the presence of numerous isolated strategic outposts or lookout points, major hilltop fortifications, defensively situated habitation sites and, ultimately, the citadel. The causeways, then, can be seen as a conscious effort to reduce travel time and natural impediments to and from strongholds. In this sense they can be interpreted as an integrated extension of the citadel's defenses throughout the valley. Although the network and the amount of labor expended in its construction demonstrate centralized planning and an extensive power base to implement decisions, it may reflect an acute sense of urgency as well.

As previously noted, some may have been associated with hydraulic works in ways that are not yet understood. Undoubtedly they also performed symbolic functions. Two of the more obvious would be to symbolize the authority and legitimacy of the polity. If that polity was benign to its resident population, the causeways could have represented security and stability. If the polity was antagonistic, however, they may have been a constant reminder that retribution would be swift in the event of civil disorder. Almost certainly they were also associated with ritual activities as seen by the location of small altars found occasionally near prominent architectural complexes. Likewise, as Hirth (Chapter 17) mentions about the elite at Xochicalco, those at La Quemada also seem never to have missed an opportunity to impress others with their importance. This is amply seen in the embellishment of various entrances to the citadel and the axial symmetry created by the placement of stairs, altars, and major structures.

Conclusion

We see that the La Quemada region was only one of several in north central Mexico possessing regional causeway networks. It is now becoming clear that these are not isolated curiosities, but distinct cultural attributes. They are not casual occurrences, carried as easy mental baggage such as ceramic designs or flaking techniques on projectile points. Rather they represent the tip of a cultural iceberg in that behind their presence lies extensive planning, engineering, mobilization of labor and monumental-scale construction. Most important, there was a well-defined and socially sanctioned purpose to justify all this.

As attributes they have both time depth and close association with certain other architectural traits. On this basis they could be primarily associated with the Chalchihuites cultural tradition or at least a Bajio–Rio Lerma/Lajas hearth. There, as at La Quemada, is a clear association between orthogonal settlement pattern con-

sisting of plaza compounds with sunken courts, stepped pyramids, columned structures, and causeways. This constellation of traits at an early date is significant because it may point to a culture from which the Chalchihuites tradition later crystalized. The Bajio/Rio Lajas areas also received and undoubtedly retained earlier Preclassic influences from the Chupicuaro tradition. Quite possibly this area witnessed an amalgam of some Chupicuaro traits with those more directly related to Central Mexico. If this area did provide a population that expanded north, it may have resulted in a chain of local cultures with only relatively minor regional distinctions that served as a conduit for the flow of goods and information between the Mesa Central and Durango along the eastern flank of the Sierra Madre Occidental, and possibly much farther.

There may also be a warning in the La Quemada study. This is that just because the causeways connected hinterland settlements, they should not be construed to mean that the region was *ipso facto* well integrated socially or economically. The causeway network seems to have been created to serve specific needs. There are few natural impediments to common foot traffic in the valley, at least none that would have required the use of causeways for everyday travel. As such the causeways cannot be used as the basis of economic or social models until the settlements they connected are more thoroughly examined.

If the causeways were primarily for military purposes, i.e. facilitating movement of troops, then what does this reflect of military organization,[9] tactics and logistics? Although ethnohistorical data frequently document various battles, it is extremely vague on the mode of aboriginal troop movement from one place to another. The military function of roads is also mentioned by Gorenstein and Pollard (Chapter 14) in the Tarascan area. One can only surmise that tightly organized warrior groups traveled, perhaps phalanx-style, to and from selected places of battle. We know that from the aboriginal perspective there were clear-cut military objectives but the organizational procedures to accomplish these are far less understood. The study of Mesoamerican warfare, particularly in terms of strategy and logistics, might prove quite fruitful at some later date.

Acknowledgments

Research in the La Quemada region from 1974 to the present has been made possible primarily by the National Science Foundation (grants GS-43184 and BNS-8419064) and the Wenner Gren Foundation (grant

4926). The following have also been of crucial importance to these studies: the Department of Anthropology, Washington University; Director de Monumentos Prehispánicos, Ing. Joaquín García-Barcena; Sr. Federico M. Sescosse of Zacatecas; Robert L. Huff; Michael J. Simpson, and the good people of the State of Zacatecas. Also appreciated were the comments and suggestions given by Jeffrey Parsons regarding certain aspects of this paper.

Notes

1. The term "Chalchihuites Culture" was first coined by J. Alden Mason (Mason 1971) as a result of his 1935 field studies in Durango and Zacatecas. He conceptualized a more or less homogeneous culture ranging from the region of Alta Vista near the present-day town of Chalchihuites in western Zacatecas to the region of Zape in northwestern Durango. He also included the La Quemada region in this culture (p. 132). On the basis of more recent studies the Kelleys restrict their use of this term to the area between Alta Vista and Zape, excluding the La Quemada region. They see the Chalchihuites culture consisting of two branches: the Rio Suchil which is coeval with the major La Quemada occupation and located in general proximity to the modern town of Chalchihuites, Zacatecas, and the later northern salient in Durango termed the Guadiana branch. This restrictive view of the Chalchihuites culture was probably justified at the time inasmuch as little was known of the La Quemada region until recently.

In light of field investigations in the La Quemada region (1974 to 1986), a few more differences and similarities have become clearer. As the Kelleys (1971a:175) claim, the major differences lie in decorated ceramics, i.e., Michilia, Mercado, and Suchil in the Alta Vista region, counterbalanced by Villanueva, Coyotes, and Atitanac types in the La Quemada region (see Trombold 1985a:250–5). Chronologically underlying these, however, is a more homogeneous Canutillo component represented throughout western Zacatecas and the La Quemada region. The ceramic differences noted above are possibly the result of local influences emanating from the Chapalangana and/or Bolaños basins. Despite these differences there is an underlying cultural unity or tradition shared by both the Alta Vista and La Quemada regions. Shared traits include architectural details (i.e., special hearths, stepped pyramids, use of columns in construction, slab-masonry constructions, sunken plazas), internal settlement layout, lithics (see Spense

1971; Trombold 1985a:254–7), jewelry and other artifacts (see also Lister and Howard 1958 and Hers 1989:24–35).

Regardless of this we would still be faced with determining the southern limits of La Quemada's sphere of influence. This may be quite difficult since the tradition is possibly composed of a chain of closely related subcultures extending southeastward into Guanajuato or beyond, punctuated primarily by variations in decorated ceramics yet still retaining close similarities in architectural features and site layout. Deciding on criteria for distinguishing subcultures within this tradition should clearly be one focus of future research.

2. This is based on inspection of aerial photos in 1985, courtesy of Peter Jiménez.

3. This can only be a very tentative comparison since both Mexican examples are taken from intrasite locations.

4. See Kelley's (1971b:xv–xvi) annotation regarding the Berghes map.

5. A copy of this is published in Noguera 1970. The original is presently in the possession of Sr. Federico M. Sescosse, Centro Regional de Zacatecas (I.N.A.H.), Mexico.

6. There are habitation sites as well as a petroglyph site near and on Cerro Colorin, 9.5 km north of the citadel.

7. This was measured from aerial photos and estimated using several measurements in the field. The problem is that border elements are not visible despite the slight difference in soil color.

8. Some of these may be spurious on the Berghes map since, unlike some others nearby, these cannot be seen on aerial photos nor is there any trace on the ground.

9. Weigand (1975) presents an interesting Huichol myth that may indicate a military organization not unlike that found at the time of Spanish conquest in central Mexico.

References

Armillas, Pedro
n.d. La Quemada, Excavaciones Diciembre 1951–Enero 1952. MS on file, Southern Illinois University Museum, Carbondale
1963 *Investigaciónes Arqueológicas en el Estado de Zacatecas. Boletín del INAH* 14. Mexico
1964a Northern Mesoamerica. In *Prehistoric Man in the New World*, edited by Jesse D. Jennings and E. Norbeck, pp. 291–329. University of Chicago Press, Chicago

1964b Condiciones Ambientes y Movimientos de Pueblos en la Frontera Septentrional de Mesoamérica. In *Homenaje a Fernando Marquéz-Miranda*, pp. 62–82. Publicaciones del Seminario de Estudios Americanistas y Seminario de Antropología Americana, Universidades de Madrid y Sevilla
1969 The Arid Frontier of Mexican Civilization. In *Transactions of the New York Academy of Sciences*, Series 2, 31(6):697–704. New York Academy of Sciences, New York

Bancroft, Hubert H.
1882 *The Native Races of the Pacific States of North America*. Vol. IV, pp. 578–92. A. L. Bancroft, San Francisco

Berghes, C. de
1833 Plano Geométrico y Topográfico de las Tierras de la Hda. de La Quemada (map)

Braniff, Beatriz
1961 Exploraciones Arqueológicas en el Tunal Grande. *Boletín del INAH* 5:6–8. Mexico
1965 Estudios Arqueológicas en el Río de la Laja, Guanajuato. *Boletín del INAH* 19:12–13. Mexico
1974 Oscilación de la frontera septentrional mesoamericana. In *The Archaeology of West Mexico*, edited by Betty Bell, pp. 40–50. Sociedad de Estudios Avanzados del Occidente de México, Ajijic

Brown, R. B.
1985 A Synopsis of the Archaeology of the Central Portion of the Northern Frontier of Mesoamerica. In *The Archaeology of West and Northwest Mesoamerica*, edited by Michael S. Foster and Phil C. Weigand, pp. 219–35. Westview Press, Boulder

Burkart, Joseph
1836 *Aufenthalt und Reisen in Mexico*, Vol. II, pp. 97–106. E. Schweinerbart's Verlagshandlungen, Stuttgart

Castañeda, Carlos, *et al.*
1988 Interpretación de la Historia del Asentamiento en Guanajuato. In *Primera Reunión sobre las Sociedades Prehispánicas en el Centro Occidente de México. Memoria*, edited by Rosa Brambilla and Ana María Crespo, pp. 321–56. Centro Regional de Querétaro (INAH), Mexico

Crespo, Ana Marie
1976 Villa de Reyes, San Luís Potosí. In *Colección Científica-Arqueología* 42. Departamento de Monumentos Prehispánicos, Instituto Nacional de Antropología e Historia, Mexico

Davies, Nigel
1977 *The Toltecs*. University of Oklahoma Press, Norman

Guillemin Tarayre, Edmond
1869 L'Exploration minéralogique des régions mexicaines, deuxième partie; *Notes archéologiques et ethnographiques; vestiges laissées par les migrations américaines dans le nord du Mexique*. Vol. III, pp. 341–470. Ministère de l'Instruction Publique *Archives de la Commission Scientifique du Mexique*. Imprimerie Impériale, Paris

Hedrick, B., J. C. Kelley and C. Riley (eds.)
1971 *The North Mexican Frontier*. Southern Illinois University Press, Carbondale

Hers, Marie-Areti
1989 *Los Toltecas en Tierras Chichimecas*. Instituto de Investigaciones Estéticas. Cuadernos de Historia del Arte 35. Universidad Nacional de México, Mexico

Kelley, J. Charles
1971a Archaeology of the Northern Frontier: Zacatecas and Durango. In *Handbook of Middle American Indians*, Vol. XI, edited by G. Ekholm and I. Bernal, pp. 768–801. University of Texas Press, Austin
1971b The C. de Berghes Map of 1833. In *The North Mexican Frontier*, edited by B. Hedrick *et al.* pp. xv–xvi. Southern Illinois University Press, Carbondale
1974 Speculations on the Culture History of Northwestern Mesoamerica. In *The Archaeology of West Mexico*, edited by B. Bell, pp. 19–39. Sociedad de Estudios Avanzados del Occidente de Mexico, Ajijic, Mexico
1985 The Chronology of the Chalchihuites Culture. In *The Archaeology of West and Northwest Mesoamerica*, edited by Michael S. Foster and Phil C. Weigand, pp. 269–287. Westview Press, Boulder

Kelley, J. Charles and Ellen Abbott Kelley
1971 *An Introduction to the Ceramics of the Chalchihuites Culture of Zacatecas and Durango, Mexico. Part I: The Decorated Wares. Mesoamerican Studies* 5. Southern Illinois University Museum, Carbondale

Lister, Robert and Agnes Howard
1958 The Chalchihuites Culture of Northwest Mexico. *American Antiquity* 21(2):122–9

Lyon, Capt. G. F.
1828 *Journal of a Residence and Tour in the Republic of Mexico*, Vol. I, pp. 225–43. J. Murray, London

Mason, J. Alden
1971 Late Archaeological Sites in Durango, Mexico, from Chalchihuites to Zape. In *The North Mexican Frontier*, edited by B. C. Hedrick, J. C. Kelley and C. L. Riley, pp. 130–43. Southern Illinois University Press, Carbondale

Nalda, Enrique
1976 Proposiciones para un Estudio del Proceso de Contracción de Mesoamérica. *XIV Mesa Redonda (Tegucigalpa)*. *Sociedad Mexicana de Antropología*, Vol. I, pp. 51–60. Mexico

Nebel, Carlos
1839 *Viaje Pintoresco y Arqueológico sobre la República Mexicana, 1829–1834*. Paris.

Noguera, Eduardo
1970 *La Quemada, Chalchihuites*. Guia Oficial del INAH (second edition). Mexico

Parsons, Jeffrey R. and Mary H. Parsons
1990 *Maguey Utilization in Highland Central Mexico: An Archaeological Ethnography*. Anthropological Papers, Museum of Anthropology, University of Michigan No. 82, Ann Arbor

Rivera, Agustin
1875 *Viaje a las Ruinas de Chicomoztoc (Llamadas Vulgarmente de La Quemada) Hecho en 1874*. Typografía de José Martin, San Juan de los Lagos.

Rivera, Pedro
1843 Ruinas de La Quemada en el Departamento de Zacatecas. *El Museo Mexicano*, Vol. I, pp. 184–8. Mexico (reprinted from 1831)

Seler, Eduard
1908 Die Ruinen von La Quemada im Statte Zacatecas. In *Gesammelte Abhandlungen zur Amerikanischen Sprach und Alterthumskunde*, Vol. III, pp. 545–59. Behrend, Berlin

Spense, Michael
1971 *Some Lithic Assemblages of Western Zacatecas and Durango. Mesoamerican Studies* 8. Southern Illinois University Museum, Carbondale

Trombold, Charles D.
1985a A Summary of the Archaeology in the La Quemada Region. In *The Archaeology of West and Northwest Mesoamerica*, edited by Michael S. Foster and Phil C. Weigand, pp. 237–67. Westview Press, Boulder
1985b Conceptual Innovations in Settlement Pattern Methodology on the Northern Mesoamerican Frontier. In *Contributions to the Archaeology and Ethnohistory of Greater Mesoamerica*, edited by William J. Folan, pp. 205–39. Southern Illinois University Press, Carbondale
1986 Field Notes, MV-138. MS on file with author
1990 A Reconsideration of Chronology for the La Quemada Portion of the Northern Mesoamerican Frontier. *American Antiquity*, Vol. 55(2):308–24

Weigand, Phil C.
1975 Possible References to La Quemada in Huichol Mythology. *Ethnohistory* 22(2):15–20
1978 La Prehistoria del Estado de Zacatecas: una interpretación. In *Zacatecas, anuario de historia*, edited by Cuahtemoc Esparza Sanchez, Vol. I, pp. 203–48. Departamento de Investigaciones Históricas. Universidad Autónoma de Zacatecas, Zacatecas
1985a Considerations on the Archaeology and Ethnohistory of the Mexicaneros, Tequales, Coras, Huicholes, and Caxcans of Nayarit, Jalisco and Zacatecas. In *Contributions to the Archaeology and Ethnohistory of Greater Mesoamerica*, edited by William J. Folan, pp. 126–87. Southern Illinois University Press, Carbondale
1985b Evidence for Complex Societies during the Western Mesoamerican Classic Period. In *The Archaeology of West and Northwest Mesoamerica*, edited by Michael S. Foster and Phil C. Weigand, pp. 47–91. Westview Press, Boulder

Weigand, Phil, G. Harbottle, and E. Sayre
1977 Turquoise Sources and Source Analysis: Mesoamerica and the Southwestern U.S.A. In *Exchange Systems in Prehistory*, edited by T. K. Earle and J. E. Erickson, pp. 15–34. Academic Press, New York

Zubrow, Ezra B. W. and A. R. Willard (eds.)
1974 *Models and Innovations: Archaeological and Regional Approaches to Guanajuato, Mexico*. Department of Anthropology, Leland Stanford Junior University, Palo Alto

14 Xanhari: Protohistoric Tarascan routes

SHIRLEY GORENSTEIN
and HELEN PERLSTEIN
POLLARD

The Tarascan polity, contemporary with the Aztec, is important to Mesoamericanists and prehistorians because it provides scholars with an example of choices that led to a distinctive complex society. That society was characterized by its administrative nature. It was not only highly organized but also highly centralized. Tzintzuntzan was the capital city of this state, but more than that, it was the focal center of Tarascan life and history. This study of Tarascan routes shows the importance of that city in determining the form and function of its transport network, within its heartland, within its territory, and beyond its frontiers.

The Tarascans controled a territory of some 75,000 km^2 in west central Mexico. The north was bordered by the Lerma River, the south by the Balsas-Tepalcatepec river basin. The western frontier was in flux, but the eastern frontier had been well fixed by a series of fortifications that faced a no man's land shared with the Aztecs (Fig. 14.1).

The heartland of the territory was the Lake Patzcuaro Basin. Some 929 km^2, it was characterized by the large lake that covered about 16 percent of the basin area. The lake was surrounded by a narrow lakeshore zone, which, at the time of the Protohistoric, was surrounded by an area of continuously increasing elevation from 2,050 m at the lakeshore to 3,200 m at the basin periphery. The basin landscape, then, can be described as dominated by the lake and as marked by a largely broken topography.

By the time of the Spanish Conquest, the Tarascans had established a polity characterized by strong administration, that is, by the management and control of most aspects of society. The capital of that polity was Tzintzuntzan and the basin was its core. In a recent study of the basin, Gorenstein and Pollard (1983) looked at the relationships within the basin as the source for the establishment of the larger polity. The history of the basin showed the development of those patterns and processes that led to the ability to incorporate, manage, and control land and populations within a single administrative system.

The settlement study of the basin, by focusing on the function of settlements and their relationships to each other, revealed those patterns and processes. By the Protohistoric period (AD 1450–1520), there were ninety-one settlements in the basin. The Tarascan capital, Tzintzuntzan (X01), was in the basin and was a primate center. There were eight secondary centers on the next hierarchical level, namely Eronguariquaro (X25), Pechataro (X24), Urichu (X23), Pareo (X16), Pacandan-Xaraquaro (X42–X50), Itziparamucu (X41), Uayameo (X33), and Patzcuaro (Fig. 14.2).

Tzintzuntzan was one of three market centers for the settlements in the basin. Of the other two, one, Pareo, was in the basin; the other, Asajo, was just outside its northeast periphery (Fig. 14.3). There were eight relig-

ious centers within the basin. Besides Tzintzuntzan, there were Itzicuaro in the northeast, Sipixo and Ihuatzio in the central basin, Ahterio and Patzcuaro in the south, and the islands of Pacandan and Xaraquaro (Fig. 14.4).

This study of Tarascan routes began with ethnohistorical and archaeological data on roads, paths, and canoe routes, the latter marked by landings. In this study the most valuable ethnohistorical information came from Relación de Michoacán (see Gorenstein and Pollard 1983 for a discussion of this source).

The Relación referred to routes in the Protohistoric period. There was a road around the lake ("camino cabe la laguna") that linked lakeside settlements. Among the well-known parts of the route are those between Tzintzuntzan (X01) and Patzcuaro (X12), between Urichu (X23) and Eronguariquaro (X25), and between Ahterio (X11) and Haramutaro (X19) (Relación de Michoacán 1980:68, 70, 191). Lakeside settlements were also linked by canoe. Indeed, this was a common means of transport, especially to convey information and in warfare (see, for example, 1980:152, 156). Routes (either roads or paths) came down from the hills and joined the circuit lake route. Itziparamucu (X41) is linked to Tzintzuntzan, Ahterio (X11) is linked to Patzcuaro (X12), and Pechataro (X24) is linked to Urichu (X23) (1980:61, 177–9, Plate 2 following p. 176, 191).

A series of maps drawn in the 1540s showing the Lake Patzcuaro Basin settlements as well as roads and paths (see Gorenstein and Pollard 1983 for reproductions of these maps and interpretations) have been used to infer paths from settlements in the higher elevations to those in the lakeshore zone. Fig. 14.5 is a reconstruction of the basin routes based on this information as well as additional information given below on external routes, that is, routes leading to settlements outside the basin.

The Tarascans refer to routes in the narrative of Tarascan history and everyday life transcribed in the Relación de Michoacán (1980). A number of references describe their role in warfare. For example, before battle, spies were sent out to look for trails leading to the settlement under attack. Special roads ("un camino real") were built for the basin division to advance to the staging area outside the settlement; other units went by trail ("por los herbazales") (1980:246, 248).

Sections of roads have been located in the field. They are cobbled beds about 3 m wide. However, no excavation was done that would have confirmed their Protohistoric date.

Transport routes within the Lake Patzcuaro Basin were the means by which persons, goods, and information

Fig. 14.1. Minimal limits of the Tarascan territory.

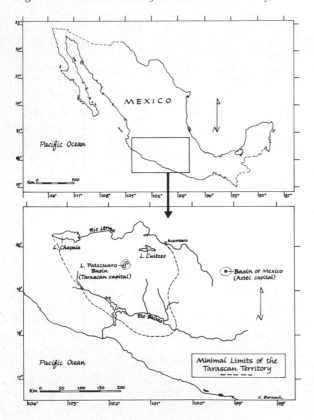

Fig. 14.2. Lake Patzcuaro Basin, administrative centers (drawing by Helen Pollard after CETENAL 1976).

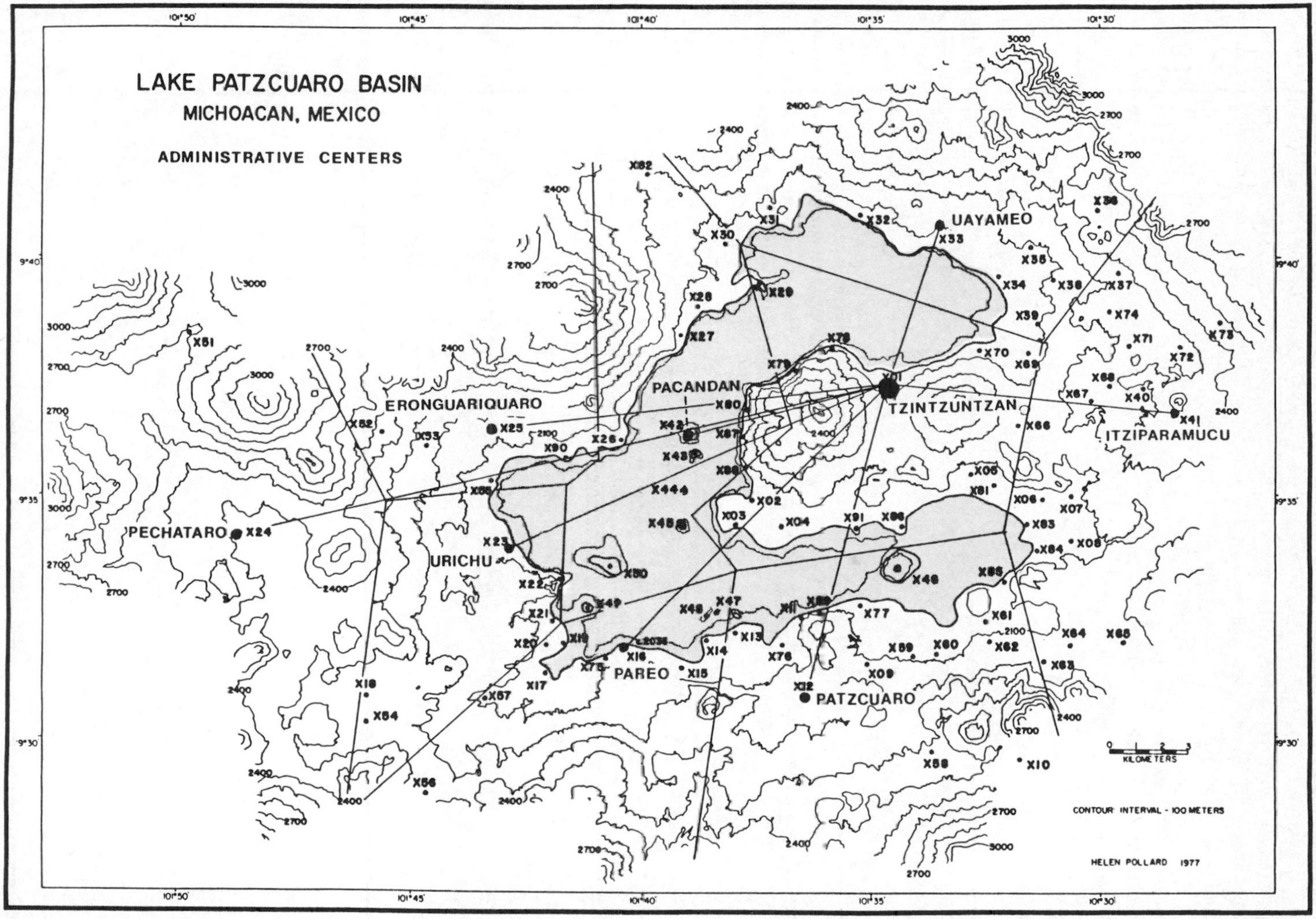

Fig. 14.3. Lake Patzcuaro Basin, market centers.

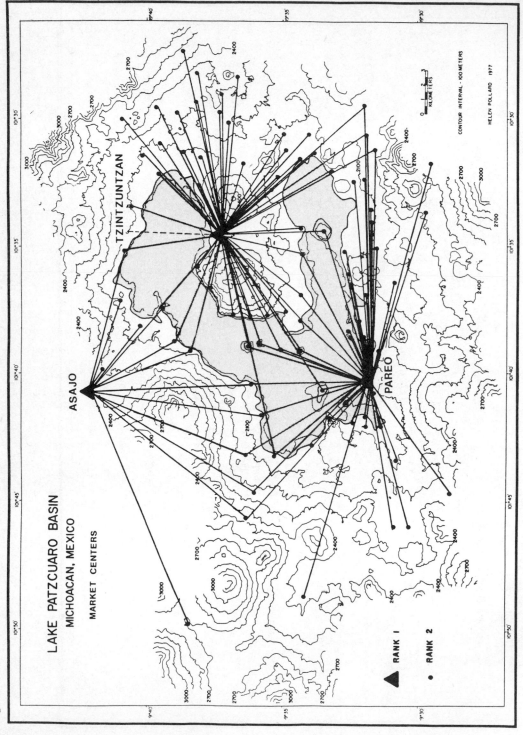

LAKE PATZCUARO BASIN
MICHOACAN, MEXICO

MARKET CENTERS

TZINTZUNTZAN

ASAJO

PAREO

▲ RANK I

● RANK 2

CONTOUR INTERVAL - 100 METERS

HELEN POLLARD 1977

KILOMETERS

Fig. 14.4. Lake Patzcuaro Basin, religious centers.

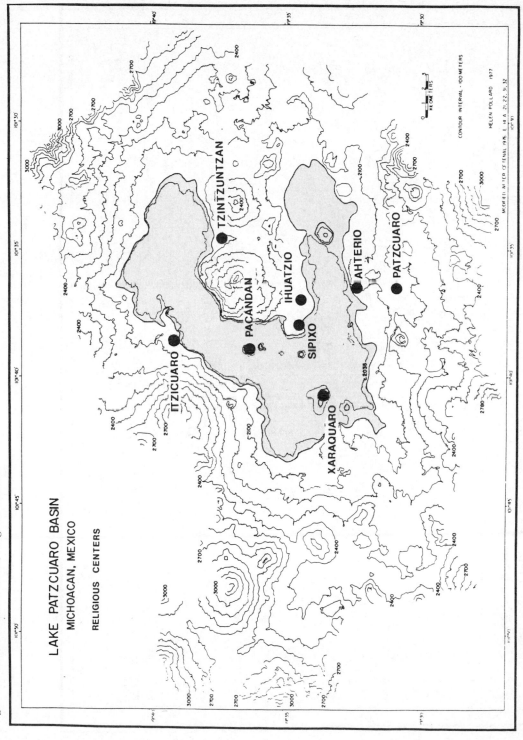

LAKE PATZCUARO BASIN
MICHOACAN, MEXICO

RELIGIOUS CENTERS

TZINTZUNTZAN

ITZICUARO

PACANDAN

IHUATZIO

SIPIXO

AHTERIO

PATZCUARO

XARAQUARO

CONTOUR INTERVAL · 100 METERS

HELEN POLLARD 1977

MODIFIED AFTER CETENAL L.14-A, 21, 22, 31, 32

KILOMETERS

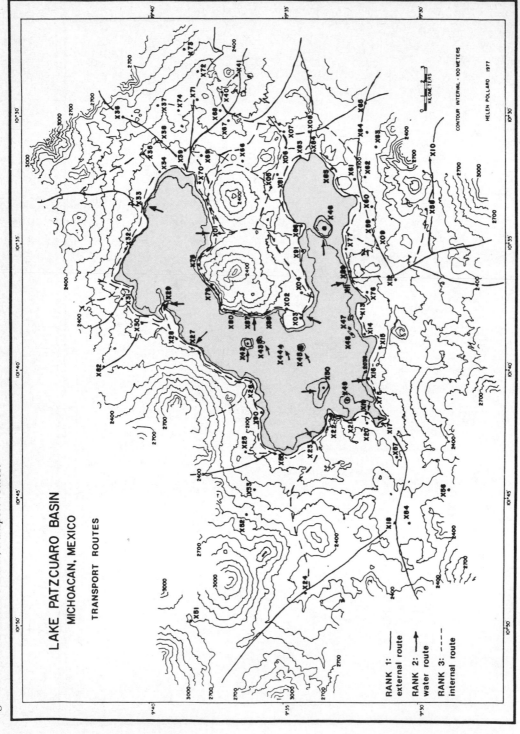

Fig. 14.5. Lake Patzcuaro Basin, transport routes.

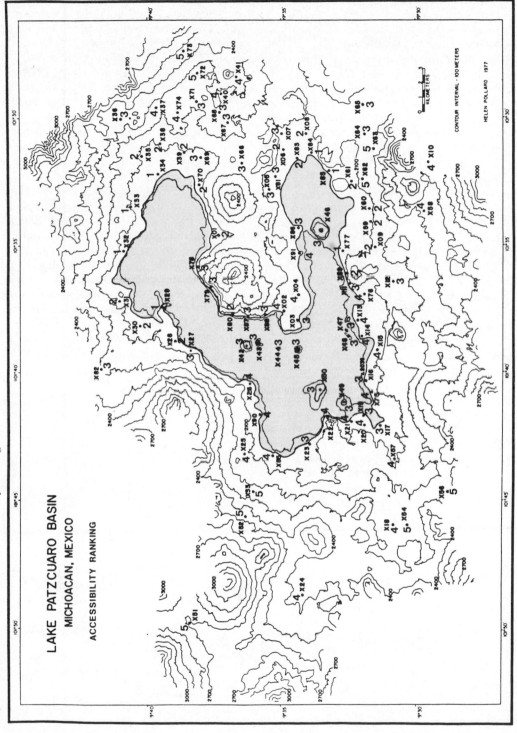

Fig. 14.6. Lake Patzcuaro Basin, accessibility ranking.

moved among settlements. As such, they are indicators of the relationships among settlements, particularly of the relative importance of the roles of settlements in the conveyance of persons, goods and information.

To analyze basin transport routes in relation to settlement role, accessibility was determined (Fig. 14.6). Accessibility is a measure of the relative ease by which persons, goods, and information move between any two points on the transport graph. (The analysis here deals primarily with the flow of people and information rather than bulk loading.) In other words, accessibility is the reachability of a settlement. The measure is done by recording the presence or absence of direct linkages between nodes (settlements). In the simplest measure of accessibility, the settlement with the greatest number of direct linkages to other settlements is the most accessible (see Taaffe and Gauthier 1973:119ff.). By forming a matrix of connections (or linkages) between all pairs of settlements, each settlement is scored on the number of such direct linkages. In a complex cultural system, however, it is more helpful for understanding the functioning of the system to analyze accessibility by including indirect linkages, that is, linkages between two settlements that involve passing through other settlements. This allows discrimination between the settlement located near the periphery of the system and one in the center, each having the identical number of direct linkages.

The standard approach to measuring accessibility is to use matrix multiplication whereby the matrix of direct linkages between settlements is used to compute a series of matrices reflecting the number of 2-step, 3-step ... x-step connections possible until all settlements have been interconnected at least once. This approach records all possible ways two nodes may be interconnected, and is, therefore, redundant. In this study, where there are large numbers of settlements that are well connected, the redundancy is great; attempts to use matrix multiplication resulted in numbers too large for meaningful results. An alternative approach was used. That approach was to record not the total number of paths between any two nodes, but only the most efficient paths. In principle, this approach is similar to shortest-path matrices (Taaffe and Gauthier 1973:133), but it is different in that the shortest path is not measured in distance but by number of linkages. Distance was considered less important than linkages, in this case, because the transport routes covered a relatively small area and differences in distances were not significant.

Thus, a series of matrices were constructed: the matrix of direct linkages, the matrix of 2-step linkages ... x-step

linkages, recording for each matrix the number of nodes each settlement could reach once if the most direct path was chosen. When all settlements could be reached once by all settlements, the procedure was halted. For each settlement a count was made of the number of linkages needed before all other settlements could be reached. This number, which varied from as few as five linkages to as many as twelve linkages, was called the accessibility score. The more accessible settlements have the lower scores, the less accessible settlements have the higher scores. Settlements not having any roads or paths were scored 0. Finally, settlements were ranked into five groups (Tables 14.1 and 14.2).

There are three factors that account for the ranking of settlements in the transport network: geomorphology, their Protohistoric functions, and their previous functions. Given the level of technology of the Protohistoric, it was not possible to wrest a settlement from its environmental constraints and make it as accessible as its functions might reasonably demand. The lakeshore zone was a level area, and a road around the lake would have been easy to construct and maintain. The circuit route was described as the short and easy way to move among the lakeshore communities. For example, it was considered shorter to go from Tzintzuntzan (X01) to Ihuatzio

Table 14.1. *Settlement accessibility and rank.*

Number of settlements	Score	Rank
7	7–8	1
17	9	2
34	10	3, includes islands, scoring 9
24	11–12	4
9	9	5

Table 14.2. *Settlements identified by rank.*

Rank 1:　X29 X32 X33 X34 X77 X84 X85

Rank 2:　X01 X06 X08 X09 X28 X30 X31 X35 X38 X39 X59 X60 X61 X70 X80 X83 X89

Rank 3:　X03 X05 X07 X11 X12 X16 X17 X19 X23 X27 X36 X42 X43 X44 X45 X46 X47 X48 X49 X50 X63 X64 X65 X66 X67 X68 X69 X71 X78 X79 X81 X82 X86 X87 X88

Rank 4:　X02 X04 X10 X13 X14 X15 X18 X20 X21 X22 X24 X25 X26 X37 X40 X41 X55 X57 X58 X74 X75 X76 X90 X91

Rank 5:　X51 X52 X53 X54 X56 X62 X63 X72 X73

(X02), a major religious center, by the lakeshore circuit route, a distance of 12 km, than to use an inland route, a distance of 8 km. Because of the topography and the circuit route, all the most accessible settlements (ranks 1 and 2) were within the lakeshore zone. Conversely, the upland settlements were the most inaccessible (ranks 4 and 5). Tzintzuntzan's accessibility (rank 2 when rank 1 would be expected) was affected by its location between two hills and the increase in elevation even within the environs of the settlement itself.

The evaluation of function is hindered somewhat because, of the seven rank 1 settlements, four are known ethnohistorically and three are not known. However, of the known rank 1 settlements, it can be said that none was a major market, and only one, Uayameo, held a comparatively high rank in the administrative network. None was a religious center and none was the base for an elite social class.

To look at function another way, the high-ranked markets, administrative centers, important religious centers and settlements with resident elite social classes were not, for the most part, highly ranked in the transport system. Of the two markets within the basin, only Tzintzuntzan was ranked 2; Pareo (X16) was ranked 3. An accessibility study cannot account for the increased efficiency of the use of canoes for bulk transport (see Hassig 1985). Thus, Tzintzuntzan and Pareo, because they are on the lakeshore, are more effective as marketing centers than their accessibility score would indicate.

Of the administrative centers, Tzintzuntzan ranked 2; Itziparamucu (X41) ranked 4, Patzcuaro (X12) ranked 3, Pareo (X16) ranked 3, Urichu (X23) ranked 3, Pechataro (X24) ranked 4, Eronguariquaro (X25) ranked 4, and Pacandan (X42) ranked 3. The only administrative center that was more accessible than Tzintzuntzan was Uayameo (X33).

Of the religious centers, Tzintzuntzan (X01) ranked 2, Sipixo (X03) ranked 3, Ihuatzio (X04) ranked 4, Ahterio (X11) ranked 3, Patzcuaro (X12) ranked 3, and the islands of Xaraquaro and Pacandan ranked 3. Of the settlements with a resident elite social class, Tzintzuntzan ranked 2 and all others, namely Itziparamucu, Ihuatzio, Patzcuaro, Pareo, Urichu, Pechataro, Eronguariquaro, and the islands of Pacandan and Xaraquaro, ranked below it at rank 3 or rank 4.

More accessible settlements had no major Protohistoric functions for the basin population with one exception, Uayameo. Previous function explains Uayameo's high Protohistoric rank. In the pre-Protohistoric period Uayameo was an important administrative center within the basin before the basin population was unified under

Tzintzuntzan (Relación de Michoacán 1980:30, 32–3, 301–2). In the Protohistoric, it became a rank 2 center under Tzintzuntzan's administrative organization.

Another rank 1 center, Yrapo, with no major function in the Protohistoric, appears to have been a religious center or possibly a center with local administrative role in the pre-Protohistoric (Relación de Michoacán 1980:33).

The transport system in the Lake Patzcuaro Basin was not designed to make markets accessible (although as noted above the two lakeshore markets were highly accessible for the purposes of bulk transport by canoe), or administrative centers accessible. It was a system that made a highly multifunctional center, Tzintzuntzan, accessible, although not most accessible. The reasons it was not most accessible had to do with the geomorphology of the basin and the history of settlement within the basin, a history in which other settlements had had local administrative power.

What we see in the Lake Patzcuaro Basin transport system is the optimization of Tzintzuntzan's functions, given environmental and historical constraints that could not have been or were not leavened by technology. Tzintzuntzan, as a primate center and the highest-ranked central place in the market and administrative networks and the most important religious and social elite settlement, is accessible enough to carry out its functions successfully. It could have become more accessible if road-building, a technology well known by the Tarascans, was put into the service of the basin transport system as it was apparently put into service in the territory (Relación de Michoacán 1980:248).

The examination of settlement location within the Lake Patzcuaro Basin, then, does not indicate that settlement sites were chosen for transport considerations. Protohistoric Tarascan settlement location was affected strongly by geomorphology and the history of settlement location and function in the pre-Protohistoric. The location of markets and administrative centers, particularly administrative centers, was chosen among already existing settlements in order to carry out those functions in relation to already existing smaller settlements on lower hierarchical levels.

The Tarascan territory

Transportation within the Tarascan territory was hindered by the mountainous terrain, including the southern escarpment of the Mesa Central and its drop into the Balsas depression, a descent of more than 2,000 m (Fig. 14.7).

Routes to two areas of the territory were plotted.

Fig. 14.7. The Protohistoric Tarascan territory.

THE PROTOHISTORIC TARASCAN TERRITORY

1 Tarindaro	10 Cheran
2 Comanchen	11 Aran
3 Zipiajo	12 Nahuatzen
4 Matujeo	13 Siuinan
5 Zinziro	14 Pechataro
7 Azajo	15 Erongaricuaro
7 Uayameo	16 Urechu
8 Itzipanamuco	17 Pareo
9 Cherani	18 Patzcuaro

0   Km   10

after DETENAL 1977-1981
[1] 3, [1] 4-1, [1] 4-12
[1] 3-6, [1] 4-4, [1] 4-10

H.P. Pollard

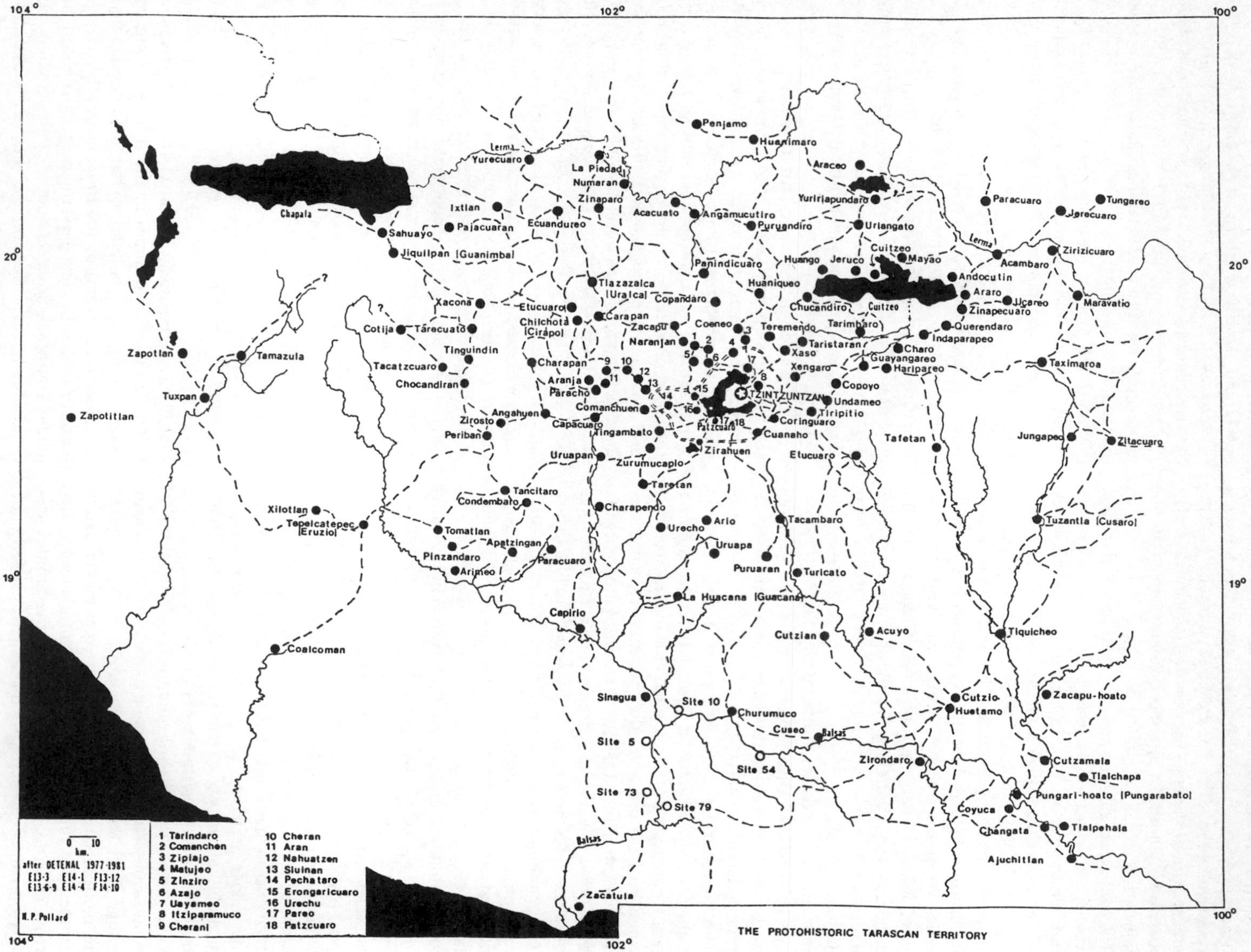

Those two areas were to the south and to the east. The first area is the Balsas Basin where there was a major mining enterprise. The second area was the eastern frontier, which was marked by fortifications facing, across a no man's land, a similar group of Aztec fortifications.

The routes that enabled these areas to function for the Tarascan polity were identified through a combination of air photo analysis (Cia. Mexicana Aerofoto series 1:50,000 and 1:20,000), map interpretation (CETENAL 1976–1979 50,000, Dirección General de Geografía del Territorio Nacional 1:250,000), field identification, and ethnohistorical information (Brand 1943; Feldman 1978; Paredes Martinez 1976; Pollard 1982; Relación de Celaya, Relación de Sirandaro y Guayameo 1945–46; Relación de Ichcateopan, ... de Acapetlaguaya, ... de Alahuiztlan, ... de Ostuma, ... de Tetela del Río 1905; Relación de Michoacán 1980; Relación de las Minas de Temazcaltepec, ... de las Minas de Sultepec 1906; Relaciones geográficas 1958; Warren 1968, 1977). Archaeological data came from Armillas 1942–44, Gonzalez Crespo 1979, and Lister 1940–41.

The procedure was first to identify Protohistoric settlements and Protohistoric mining and military enterprises from ethnohistorical and archaeological data. Second, Protohistoric routes identified in the ethnohistorical data were noted. Third, routes linking Protohistoric settlements with each other and with Protohistoric cultural features were identified in the field and/or through aerial photos. The assumption was that routes associated with Protohistoric settlements were Protohistoric. The attributes of these routes were then determined. The route attributes are: 1. along rivers; 2. through mountain passes; and 3. along level elevations. Finally, these native attributes were used to predict probable routes connecting already identified Protohistoric settlements and cultural features (Fig. 14.6).

The Tarascan mining enterprise in the Balsas Basin

Within the central and southern sectors of the Tarascan territory local market centers and important mining centers have been identified from ethnohistoric data (noted above) and placed on a map along with rank 2 and 3 administrative centers (Fig. 14.7).

Given these ethnohistorical data and the topography of the Tarascan territory, routes from the central Tarascan territory, the Lake Patzcuaro Basin, to the Balsas Basin were plotted, based on assumptions concerning native attributes (see Fig. 14.7). These assumptions were that narrow canyons were often avoided, that routes followed low ridges between arroyos, then dropped into the

wider canyons and river basins that flowed into the Balsas and Tepalcatepec rivers where they were constrained severely by the rugged topography while suiting the needs of the small number of settlements in the area. The resulting transport network is dendritic, with little branching, few interconnections, and, therefore, low redundancy.

Within the Balsas Basin routes were presumed to follow the tributaries of the Balsas, predominantly north–south, and paralleled the main channel of the Balsas for distances of 10–20 km. Several routes ended at the head of the tributary river basins and at the Balsas river itself, suggesting that canoe travel along these tributaries and the Balsas was a prominent part of the transport system. However, the settlements located on the north bank of the Balsas had to have been connected to the Lake Patzcuaro Basin by overland routes. Since settlement along the shores of the Balsas is linear, the transport network was plotted by considering the north–south routes to the Lake Patzcuaro Basin and the east–west flow of the river itself. Travel to the Pacific Ocean, specifically to the trading port of Zacatula, was accomplished either by land, south from Uruapan, or by a combination of land and the Balsas water routes.

The transport network within the southern portion of the Tarascan territory reflects the role this region played in the economic structure of the Tarascan polity. (The following discussion is based on primary sources referenced and interpretation offered in Pollard 1980, 1982.) Initial Tarascan expansion into this zone was to secure reliable sources of temperate and lowland products for the elite of the Lake Patzcuaro Basin. These products, including cotton, cotton cloth, tropical fruits, cacao, and feathers, were obtained through the operation of the tribute system, and by the mid-fourteenth century were flowing in a regularized pattern into the basin. As the population of the Lake Patzcuaro Basin expanded and high proportions of non-food-producing elite and artisans were concentrated in largely tribute-supported urban settlements, the tribute from the southern temperate and tropical zones shifted to include basic foodstuffs, especially maize.

By the mid-fifteenth century, the Tarascan government had developed the central Balsas as a primary source of copper, gold, and silver (for more detail, see Pollard 1987). Some mines in the tribute system continued to operate as before, but others experienced government intervention in staffing and in the setting of production levels. The government also opened new mines. The mines along the southeastern periphery, near Cutzamala, Pungari-hoato, and Ajuchitlan, and in the

Fig. 14.8. The Tarascan–Aztec frontier.

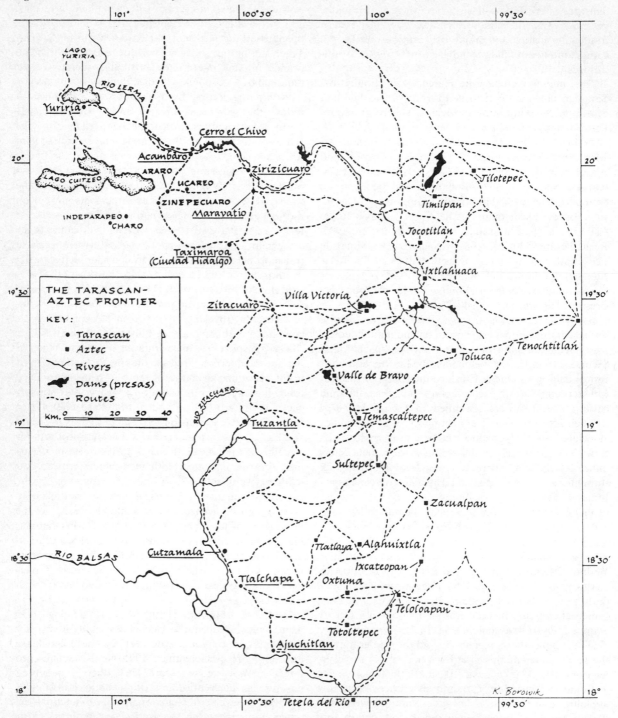

THE TARASCAN-
AZTEC FRONTIER
KEY:
- • Tarascan
- ■ Aztec
- ⋏ Rivers
- ⬟ Dams (presas)
- --- Routes
Km. 0   10   20   30   40

far west, were among those untouched by the changes. This may have been because they were: 1. located on politically unstable frontiers; 2. more than one day from a smelting center and more than five days from the capital at Tzintzuntzan; and 3. largely inhabited by non-Tarascan ethnic groups and speakers. Within the central Balsas, mining centers were expanded at Churumuco, Sinagua, Huetamo-Cutzio, Cutzian, and La Huacana. Smelting operations were focused at La Huacana, Cutzian, and Huetamo-Cutzio.

Analysis of the transport network in combination with a 1533 description of the government mining operation (Warren 1968) indicates that settlements for workers and local administrators were located away from the military frontiers along the northern margins of the Balsas Basin and within half a day's travel (10–15 km) from the mines. Smelting centers were located close to the mines because unprocessed ore was heavy and difficult to transport. Unprocessed ore was of considerable bulk, and one witness indicated that one ingot could be produced from the mining activity of one person per day. This activity would produce roughly half a celemin (Warren 1968:37) or 2.25 liters of ore (Brand 1951:132). Each ingot was approximately one hand wide (or one hand and two fingers) and one finger thick (Warren 1968:37). These measurements translate into dimensions of 18 cm long by 10 cm wide, or an ingot of about 180–270 cm^3. At 8.89 g/cm^3 (Hodgman 1960:2,117), an ingot weighed between 1.6 kg and 2.4 kg.

Thus, the location of smelting centers along the northern edge of the mining zone reflects not only the need for access to a sparsely inhabited zone with ample wood for the smelting process, but also the pull of the administrative capital at Tzintzuntzan and transport efficiency.

Processed ingots were transported for final manufacture on the backs of porters (called *tamenes* in Nahuatl). Each porter carried between twenty and thirty ingots (Warren 1968:47, 49) for a total weight of 32–72 kg. Sixteenth-century informants gave information (recorded in the Minas de Cobre) on how many days it took or how many leagues had to be walked to move copper from the smelting centers to Tzintzuntzan. In addition, days or leagues were given for some trips from one mining center to another.

On the basis of this information, a day's travel by copper-laden porters can be calculated as ranging between 21 and 43 km. The shorter distances were those crossing rough terrain between locations within the Balsas Basin. Along the major north–south quebradas nearly 30 km/day could have been covered. Thus, the

major smelting centers of La Huacana and Cutzian were within two days' journey of the capital. A third day's journey would put the traveler at the mining centers along the Balsas river. Four days would be needed to reach the mining and smelting zone of Huetamo-Cutzio. To move goods from the farthest southern frontier (marked by Cutzamala, Coyuca, Pungari-hoato, and the Ajuchitlan region), at least five or six days were needed. Similarly, at least five or six days were needed to transport smelted copper, silver, or gold from Tamazula, Tuxpan, Zapotlan, and even Coalcoman to the Tarascan capital at Tzintzuntzan.

Distance was clearly a constraint in the formation of efficient economic patterns in this zone. Although most basic resources were within two days' journey of the capital, many resources came from areas that were six days' journey away. The dispersion of settlement in the temperate and tropical zones of Michoacan in association with a weakly developed dendritic network suggests a region linked to the Lake Patzcuaro Basin by administrative ties rather than by market-system ties. A well-developed internal market system was not formed because of the lack of internal connectivity. Indeed, the essentially tributary, "colonial" relation between the Balsas Basin and the Lake Patzcuaro Basin was fostered by the absence of strongly developed marketing patterns. At the same time, this transport network had large sections with few or no major routes leading into the Lake Patzcuaro Basin. Settlements in the Balsas Basin show little Tarascan influence (e.g. sites 5, 10, 54, 73, 79 shown on Fig. 14.7, Gonzalez Crespo 1979). The relationship between the Lake Patzcuaro Basin and the Balsas Basin appears to have been circumscribed by the tributary system.

The Tarascan eastern frontier

The most active and best-known Tarascan frontier zone was that on the east (Fig. 14.8). Ten settlements with military functions can be identified as marking the limits of the eastern frontier. These were Yuriria, Acambaro, Zirizicuaro-Maravatio, Taximaroa, Zitacuaro, Tuzantla, Cutzamala, Chapultepec near Tlalchapa, and Ajuchitlan (Brand 1943; Hyslop 1976; Ponce 1968; Relación de Michoacán 1980; Relación de las Minas de Temazcaltepec 1906; Relación de Celaya, de Sirandaro y Guayameo 1945–46, Relaciones geográficas 1958; Torquemada 1723).

This Tarascan frontier zone faced a similar Aztec frontier zone of settlements with military functions that were counterparts of the Tarascan settlements to the west. These settlements were Jilotepec, Timilpan (Titlmilpa), Jocotitlan, Ixtlahuaca, Villa Victoria, Valle de Bravo, Temascaltepec, Sultepec, Zacualpan, Tlatlaya, Alahuistla, Ixcateopan, Oxtuma, Teloloapan, Totoltepec, and Tetela del Rio (Armillas 1942–44; Barlow 1949 [map based on the Matrícula de Tributos]; Durán 1967: II; Hyslop 1976; Relación de Ichcateopan, ... de Acapetlaguaya, ... de Alahuixtlan, ... de Oxtuma, ... de Tetela del Río, ... de Teloloapa, ... de Tutultepec 1905; Relación de Michoacán 1980; Relación de Minas de Temazcaltepec, ... de Minas de Sultepec 1906; Holt [1979] names Iztapa as a frontier garrison and Acapetlaguaya as a supplier town to Oztuma).

The two lines of military settlements were separated by as much as 90 km in the north and as little as 40 km in the south. This zone, intermediate between the two fortified lines, was occupied by a number of ethnic groups, probably the most important of whom were the Otomi (Carrasco 1950; Relación de Michoacán 1980:199, 239; for a fuller discussion of the Tarascan–Aztec frontier see Gorenstein 1985).

The relationship between the Tarascan and Aztec civilizations, as with all civilizations in close proximity, was both hostile and cooperative. During the Protohistoric period, there was not only military engagement between the two powers, but also frequent, if not constant, communication between them, requiring the permanent presence of Nahuatl–Tarascan language interpreters in Tzintzuntzan for the Cazonci's use (Codex Ramirez 1944:75; Durán 1967:II, 231–4; Lienzo de Jucutacato interpreted by Jiménez Moreno 1947:151–7 and León 1979:1–41; Relación de Michoacán 1980:70–2, 140–1, 213–14, 237–8, Lámina f39, ff. 272, 296–355 passim; Rea 1643:33; Tezozomoc 1944:289; Torquemada 1723:220).

Protohistoric routes along the Tarascan frontier zone and across the intermediate zone were reconstructed according to the method described above (Fig. 14.8). The following is a description of those routes, comparing their speed and ease of crossing as well as the role of the Tarascan military settlements as mustering points and Aztec military settlements as points of defense for Tenochtitlan, the Aztec capital, and Toluca, a major resource center.

A route in the north began at Yuriria and continued about 60 or 70 km to Acambaro. That portion of the route was along a stream bed, then cut through a pass between two hills and followed the Lerma river to Acambaro. At Acambaro the route branched; one branch led to the east and the other led south before turning to the east. If the first branch were chosen, then the Lerma river would have been followed, either by canoe or by foot. The route passed through Zirizicuaro after 35 km. At the

end of the 160 km water route, the traveler would have been about 10 km from Toluca and less than 50 km from Tenochtitlan.

If the second or southern route out of Acambaro were followed, then the traveler would have marched overland within the Tarascan territory, and after about 60 km would have arrived at the frontier settlement of Taximaroa. Taximaroa is commonly mentioned as a settlement of entry and departure to and from the territory. It is likely that several routes led to Taximaroa from Tzintzuntzan. The route from Taximaroa across the intermediate zone was reconstructed overland along level ground and crossing two rivers. With this route, the distance between Taximaroa and Tenochtitlan was 160 km.

A shorter linear distance between the Tarascan and Aztec frontiers was between Zitacuaro and Villa Victoria. This route followed an approximately level elevation of about 2,600 m and was very narrowly circumscribed. The traveler leaving Zitacuaro and seeking to cross the intermediate zone was directed through mountain passes. The fortification at Villa Victoria could have been bypassed easily, and Toluca could have been reached after a journey of 70 km. The most direct route to Tenochtitlan, the Zitacuaro–Tenochtitlan route, was 115 km. Another route from Zitacuaro to Tenochtitlan that avoided the fortifications at both Villa Victoria and Valle de Bravo went south and then east through mountain passes and was longer.

Another short distance of about 35 km between the two frontiers was from Tarascan Tuzantla to Aztec Temascaltepec. This distance was covered easily by the river route. From Temascaltepec to Toluca was another 40 km by land and to Tenochtitlan it was another 80 km. To avoid Temascaltepec, a difficult southern route from Tuzantla across the intermediate zone could be taken. Even taking advantage of the mountain passes, the traveler had to walk uphill from a low elevation of 500 m through steadily increasing elevations until the 2,000 m elevation was reached at the Aztec frontier. Two or three streams had to be crossed as well. By this route the distance between Tuzantla and Toluca was 80 km and between Tuzantla and Tenochtitlan was 125 km. Thus, avoiding the military defense at Temascaltepec not only added kilometers to the journey but also required crossing difficult terrain.

Water routes brought travelers from the three southernmost frontier settlements, Cutzamala, Tlalchapa, and Ajuchitlan, to Aztec territory. Within Aztec territory, these water routes gave way to land routes at Sultepec and Zacualpan. The journey from these points to Tenochtitlan was difficult once the routes took the traveler though different elevations to reach mountain passes.

An examination of the routes in the intermediate zone from the point of view of density, that is the kilometer length of road per km^2 of area (Haggett 1965:61–86), assuming all routes were actual, indicates that the intermediate zone had a high route density and therefore that the routes had specialized functions. These functions can be derived from the ethnohistoric literature. Indeed, the enumeration of specialized route functions in the documentary sources affirms the likelihood of many routes in the intermediate zone and the actuality of the reconstructed routes.

The most important cargo carried over these routes was information, and the Tarascan information carriers were members of the Tarascan administrative system. They were employed and supervised by a government official called *uaxanoti* and were continuously on duty in the palace where they waited at the ready to undertake an information-carrying or information-seeking mission. The former were news events and did not call for a response. For example, the Tarascans were informed of the succession of Aztec rulers and their conquests (Relación de Michoacán 1980:237–8). The second kind of information required an immediate decision by the Tarascan government. For example, in 1519–20 messengers moved continuously between Tzintzuntzan and Tenochtitlan negotiating the terms of a proposed alliance between the two powers (Relación de Michoacán 1980:296–355).

Wartime spies were also part of the government bureaucracy, but were in a different department and reported to their own supervisor. Their job was not only to report on troop movements during a war, but also to determine topographic features in order to draw the maps used in the strategic planning sessions and to lead tactical maneuvers (Relación de Michoacán 1980:228, 245–7).

Outside the civil service system were the Otomi who knew the routes in the intermediate zone, their homeland, as well as if not better than either the Tarascans or the Aztecs. The Otomi were used as spies by both the Tarascans and the Aztecs not only for this reason but also because they spoke both the Tarascan and Aztec languages and at least one of the languages of the ethnic groups in the intermediate zone in addition to their own (Relación de Michoacán 1980:296–9, 311–12).

In the transmission of information, the information carriers, both Aztec and Tarascan, did not usually travel directly from Tenochtitlan to Tzintzuntzan, rather they appear to have been required (probably a Tarascan requirement) to stop at a Tarascan frontier settlement and deliver their message or request to the frontier settlement administrator, who then relayed it to Tzintzuntzan. A response from Tzintzuntzan either invited the information carriers to continue to Tzintzuntzan or relayed a reply through the frontier administrator. Some information exchanges were accompanied by gift exchange. When the Aztecs asked the Tarascans to join them in a war against the newly arrived Spaniards, they brought turquoise, green feathers, preserved food, shields, belts, blankets, and mirrors. This particular cargo of gifts was carried by ten messengers. The Tarascans gave the Aztecs blankets, gourd dishes, deerskin jackets, and some smaller items to accompany their refusal to Tenochtitlan (Relación de Michoacán 1980:296–9, 307–16).

Although the intermediate zone routes were important as highways for information, they were also used in commerce. The frontier settlements transmitted to Tzintzuntzan products that by either type or quantity could not have originated at those settlements. These included armaments, metal objects, cotton cloth, clothing, silver, gold, jaguar and coyote skins, eagle feathers, tropical feathers, cacao, deer, chile peppers, and maize (Pollard 1982; see also Gorenstein and Pollard 1983:Appendix V). It may have been that the Aztec long-distance traders were bringing their products to these Tarascan frontier settlements where they were exchanged for products brought to these settlements by the Tarascan long-distance merchants. In this way, certain Tarascan frontier settlements served as official ports of trade. At least one of these, Taximaroa, was also responsible for military action.

The routes that existed across the Tarascan–Aztec intermediate zone appear to have been used for the transmission of information and the transport of cargo. Certain routes were efficient for quick travel. The Relación de Michoacán (1980:292–5, 311–12) records travel from Ucareo to Tzintzuntzan, a distance of 100 km, as taking three days during a slow journey, and from Tzintzuntzan to Taximaroa, a distance of 100 km, as taking one and a half days during a fast journey. The distance between the Tarascan frontier and Tenochtitlan was as short as 115 km. At the fast rate of 70 km a day, Tenochtitlan was within less than two days' journey from the Tarascan frontier. This means that information could have been transmitted between the capitals in four days. Those routes that went through areas of largely unchanging elevations and involved water travel were efficient for the transport of cargo. There is no information about the amount of time it took to transport cargo across the intermediate zone or from Tenochtitlan to either the frontier or Tzintzuntzan. Undoubtedly, this is because time was not as notable a matter in the transport of cargo as it was in the transmission of information.

Summary

This study of the routes of the Tarascan heartland, its southern mining region, and the eastern frontier zone reveals the importance of Tzintzuntzan as a focal center for the Tarascan state. In the heartland, the transport network facilitated Tzintzuntzan's functions as administrative center, market center, religious center, and as the residence of the highest elite class. Those multifunctions honed administrators' skills in organizing the Tarascan polity, first in the heartland and then in the territory. In the southern mining region the transport network was built not to serve a local market economy, but rather to serve tribute economy controled by Tzintzuntzan. Finally, from the vantage of the eastern frontier, the behavior of the polity as a whole can be seen. The routes across the intermediate zone link the Tarascan state with a foreign power for purposes of political interchange, warfare, and trade. The placement of frontier settlements at the places where those routes entered Tarascan territory provided a military bulwark to the territory and Tzintzuntzan and provided a commercial sentry-post to safeguard the tributary system to prevent an open-market system. The study of Tarascan routes, then, reveals a solar pattern in which the primary organizing functions were administrative as well as economic. That pattern is different from what is known in other parts of Mesoamerica.

Acknowledgments

The field work on the Tarascan eastern frontier by S. Gorenstein was funded by a grant from the Columbia University Council for Research in the Social Sciences and was conducted with the permission of the Instituto Nacional de Antropología e Historia and with the cooperative aid of Eduardo Matos M. and Emilio Bejarano. The first draft of Fig. 14.8 was drawn from maps at the scale of 1:500,000 and at 1:50,000 by Athan Kuliopulos who followed the third step of the procedure described above. We thank him for his innovativeness in devising techniques for transposing maps of different scales and for his meticulousness in conveying meaningful features. Corrections of this map were made and it was redrawn by Kathleen Borowik. Other maps were redrawn by Sylvie Brown. An earlier version of this paper was presented at the 1982 annual meeting of the American Anthropological Association.

References

Armillas, Pedro
1942–44 Oztuma, Gro., fortaleza de los mexicanos en la frontera de Michoacán. *Revista Mexicana de Estudios Antropológicos* 6(13):165–75
1948 Fortalezas mexicanos. *Cuadernos Mexicanos* 41(5):143–63

Barlow, Robert
1949 The Extent of the Empire of the Culhua Mexica. *Ibero-Americana* 28

Barrett, Elinore
1981 The King's Copper Mine: Inguarán in New Spain. *The Americas* 38:1–29

Brand, Donald
1943 An Historical Sketch of Geography and Anthropology in the Tarascan Region. Part I. *New Mexico Anthropologist* 6–7(2):37–108
1951 *Quiroga, a Mexican Municipio.* Smithsonian Institution, Institute of Social Anthropology 11, Washington, DC
1980 A Persistent Myth in the Ethnohistory of Western Mexico. *Tlalocan* 7:419–36

Carrasco, Pedro
1950 *Los otomies.* Universidad Nacional Autónoma de México. Instituto de Historia y Instituto Nacional de Antropología e Historia

C.E.T.E.N.A.L.
1976–79 Topographic Map Series, 1:50,000. Secretaría de Programación y Presupuesto. D.G.I.A.I., Mexico

Chadwick, Robert
1971 Archaeological Synthesis of Michoacan and Adjacent Regions. In *Handbook of Middle American Indians*, Vol. 11, edited by G. Ekholm and I. Bernal, pp. 657–93. University of Texas Press, Austin

Codex Ramirez
1944 Editorial Leyenda, Mexico

Compañía Mexicana Aerofoto
Aerial Photographs B Qro. and Z Mor. series 1:20,000

Dirección de Geografía y Meteorología
1:500,000 and 1:250,000. Secretaría de Agricultura y Ganadería

Durán, Diego
1964 *Historia de las Indias de Nueva España e islas de la tierra firme*, Vol. II. Editorial Porrua, Mexico

Feldman, Lawrence
1978 Timed Travels in Tarascan Territory: Friar Alonso Ponce in the Old Tarascan Domain. In *Mesoamerican Communication Routes and Cultural Contacts*, edited by T. Lee and C. Navarrete, pp. 141–4. Papers of the New World Archaeological Foundation

Gonzalez Crespo, N.
1979 Patrón de asentamientos prehispánicos en la parte central de bajo Balsas: un ensayo metodológico. INAH, Departamento de Prehistoria, Colección Científica 73

Gorenstein, S.
1985 *Acambaro: A Settlement on the Tarascan–Azetc Frontier*. Vanderbilt University Publications in Anthropology 32

Gorenstein, S., and H. P. Pollard
1983 *The Tarascan Civilization: A Late Prehispanic Cultural System*. Vanderbilt University Publications in Anthropology 28

Haggett, Peter
1965 *Locational Analysis in Human Geography*. Edward Arnold, London

Hassig, Ross
1985 *Trade, Tribute, and Transportation: The Sixteenth-Century Political Economy of the Valley of Mexico*. University of Oklahoma Press, Norman

Hodgman, C. D. (ed.)
1960 *Handbook of Chemistry and Physics*. Chemical Rubber Publications, Cleveland

Holt, Homer Barry
1979 Mexica–Aztec Warfare: A Developmental and Cultural Analysis. Ph.D. dissertation, University of Texas at Austin. University Microfilms, 7920135, Ann Arbor

Hyslop, J.
1976 The Frontier between Michoacan and the Culhua Mexica. In *The Tarascan–Aztec Frontier: The Acambaro Focus*, edited by S. Gorenstein, pp. 1–35. Department of Anthropology/Sociology, Rensselaer Polytechnic Institute, Troy, New York

Jiménez Moreno, Wigberto
1947 Historia antigua de la zona tarasca. In *El Occidente de México*. Sociedad Mexicana de Antropología, Mexico

León, Nicholás
1979 *Los tarascos* (first edn. 1903). Editorial Innovación, Mexico

Lister, Robert
1940–41 Cerro Oztuma, Gro. *El México Antiguo* 5:109–19

Paredes Martinez, Carlos
1976 El tributo indígena, en la región del Lago de Patzcuaro, siglo XVI. Unpublished Tesis de Licenciatura, Universidad Nacional Autónoma de México

Pollard, Helen Perlstein
1980 Central Places and Cities: A Consideration of the Protohistoric Tarascan State. *American Antiquity* 45:677–96

1982 Ecological Variation and Economic Exchange in the Tarascan State. *American Ethnologist* 9:250–68
1987 The Political Economy of Prehispanic Tarascan Metallurgy. *American Antiquity* 52(4):741–52

Ponce, Alonso
1968 *Relación breve y verdadera de algunas cosas de las muchas que sucedieron al padre Fray Alonso Ponce en las provincias de la Nueva España, siendo comisario general de aquellas partes (1586)*. Corresponsalia del Seminario de Cultura Mexicana, Guadalajara

Rea, Alonso de la
1643 *Crónica de la orden de nuestro seráfico padre San Francisco*. Provincia de San Pedro y San Pablo de Michoacán en la Nueva España. Mexico

Relación de Celaya, Relación de Sirandaro y Guayameo
1945–46 *Papeles de Nueva España*, Vol. VII, Supplement. Mexico

Relación de Ichcateopan, Relación de Acapetlaguaya, Relación de Alahuistlan, Relación de Ostuma, Relación de Tetela del Río, Relación de Teloloapa, Relación de Tutultepec
1905–6 *Papeles de Nueva España*, Vol. VII, edited by F. del Paso y Troncoso. Madrid

Relación de Michoacán
1956 *Relación de las ceremonias y ritos y población y gobierno de los indios de la provincia de Michoacán (1541)*. Reproducción facsímil del Ms ç UV 5 de El Escorial. Aguilar, Madrid
1980 Fimax Publicistas Editores, Morelia, Michoacan, Mexico

Relación de las Minas de Temazcaltepec, Relación de las Minas de Sultepec
1905–6 *Papeles de Nueva España*, Vol. VII, edited by F. del Paso y Troncoso. Madrid

Relaciones geográficas de la diocesis de Michoacán
1958 1579–1580. *Papeles de nueva españa*, Vol. I. Guadalajara

Taaffe, E and H. Gauthier
1973 *Geography of Transportation*. Prentice-Hall, Englewood Cliffs, NJ

Tezozomoc, Hernando Alvarado
1944 *Crónica mexicana (1598)*. Editorial Leyenda, Mexico

Torquemada, Juan
1723 *Primera parte de los veinte i un libros rituales i monarquía indiana*, Vol. I. Madrid

Warren, J. Benedict
1968 Minas de Cobre de Michoacán 1533. *Anales del Museo Michoacano* 6:35–52
1977 *La Conquista de Michoacán 1521–1530*. Fimax Publicistas, Morelia

15 The influence and legacy of Teotihuacan on regional routes and urban planning

THOMAS H. CHARLTON

Introduction

Teotihuacan, the setting for Mesoamerica's first urban civilization, has a recognized and well-described formal plan. The site is divided into quadrants by a single north–south axis, the "Street of the Dead," and an east–west axis consisting of two avenues, the East and West Avenues, which terminate in the center of the city at the Ciudadela and the Great Compound respectively. Included within the quadrants, to varying degrees, are enclosing walls and precincts, plaza complexes, barrios, apartment compounds, streets, and roads. Most buildings are orientated to the same north–south axis (Drewitt 1967; Millon 1970, 1973, 1981).

Teotihuacan's "influence" throughout Mesoamerica and beyond is usually identified through the presence of similarities in styles of sculpture, ceramic vessels, ceramic figurines, and architecture, through evidence of mineral resource exploitation, and through evidence of trade in obsidian and ceramics (see papers by Braniff 1972; Coe 1972; Corona Núñez 1972; Marquina 1972; Paddock 1972a,b; and Snow 1972 – Porter Weaver 1981:218–24 presents a recent summary of relevant data). Although the style of individual buildings is frequently cited as evidence for Teotihuacan's influence, the overall highly structured site plan of Teotihuacan does not seem to have traveled any distance with the structures.

In this paper I shall examine the evidence for the extension of roads from Teotihuacan to the other sites in the Teotihuacan valley and the degree to which Middle Horizon site plans in the Basin of Mexico and immediately adjacent areas incorporated components of Teotihuacan's plan. The extension of one of the city's main axes, the East Avenue, into a major road or route between Teotihuacan and Calpulalpan is one of the topics I shall examine. The other is the impact of the orderly intrasite plan of Teotihuacan on various types of sites in the several zones making up its immediate hinterland.

Teotihuacan street extensions

Sanders in describing the Teotihuacan period sites located during his Teotihuacan Valley Project suggested that the "suburbs and rural sites are oriented on the axes of urban avenues" (1965:121, Fig. 8). In support of this proposal he pointed to the apparent alignment of rural sites to the main axes of the city as defined by Millon. On the basis of Stage I settlement pattern data alone (Charlton 1984) he argued that sites located as far away as 2.3 km to the north of the Moon Pyramid, 4.5 km west of the Great Compound, 5.3 km south of the Ciudadela, and 11 km to the east of the Ciudadela were in essence aligned on the north–south and east–west axes of the city (Figs. 15.1 and 15.2). He did not imply that there was any evidence for the physical extension of the "Street of the Dead" and the East and West Avenues beyond the limits proposed by Millon. He merely suggested that if they

Fig. 15.1. The Basin of Mexico and adjacent areas with Middle Horizon sites and settlement zones noted (map after Lorenzo 1968:54, Fig. 1).

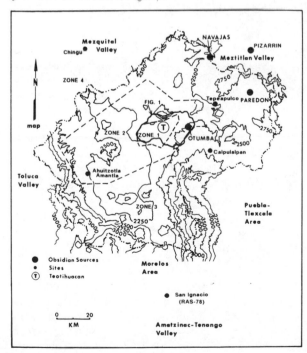

were projected beyond their physical limits numerous rural sites were aligned with them.

Some of the sites Sanders proposed as falling at the end of the projections of the north–south and east–west axes of the city mark the natural physiographic limitations of any potential physical extensions of Teotihuacan's north–south "Street of the Dead" and East and West Avenues. The "Street of the Dead" and the West Avenue are restricted by nearby hills and mountains, leaving only the East Avenue with the potential to extend any distance from the city.

The East Avenue

Millon (1973) and his colleagues (Millon, Drewitt, and Cowgill 1973: Map 1) trace the West and East Avenues approximately equal distances (about 2.5 km to N1W6 and N1E6 respectively) from the structures where they begin in the center of the city. In the case of the East Avenue, the orientation of structures on the map through N1E7 and N1E8 suggests an additional 1 km extension. According to Sanders (1965: Fig. 8) and Drewitt (1967:83) the East Avenue continued an additional 0.5 km to the edge of the Barranca Huixcoloco northeast of the Hacienda Metepec. Beyond this point the alignment of other Teotihuacan period sites (Sanders 1965: Fig. 8) and some linear marks on a 1959 1:25,000 composite aerial photograph of the region suggest a further extension of the East Avenue by some 7 km into the eastern piedmont of the Teotihuacan valley (Charlton 1972:57, 111, 1981; Drewitt 1967:84; Sanders 1965:121) (Fig. 15.2).

Drewitt (1967:84) has described the East Avenue within the city of Teotihuacan as being about 40 m in width. It is marked primarily as an open space between buildings aligned on both sides (Millon 1973: Fig. 31b). The occasional structures within the avenue have been interpreted as markers of the edge of the city at different times during its development (Millon 1973:43). Although construction of the southern extension of the "Street of the Dead" involved its being literally carved into the tepetate (Millon 1973:38) no such activity has been reported for the East Avenue. Nevertheless there remains the distinct possibility that the East Avenue extension, from the Barranca Huixcoloco to the eastern terminus at TC 87, TC 88, and TC 89 was marked by construction activity of some kind (Fig. 15.2).

During survey through this area in 1968 and 1969 I noted on the 1:25,000 composite aerial photograph (Vuelo No. 1476, Hoja No. 52, April, 1959, Cía Mexicana Aerofoto S.A.) the dark, linear marks previously mentioned. These align with the known location

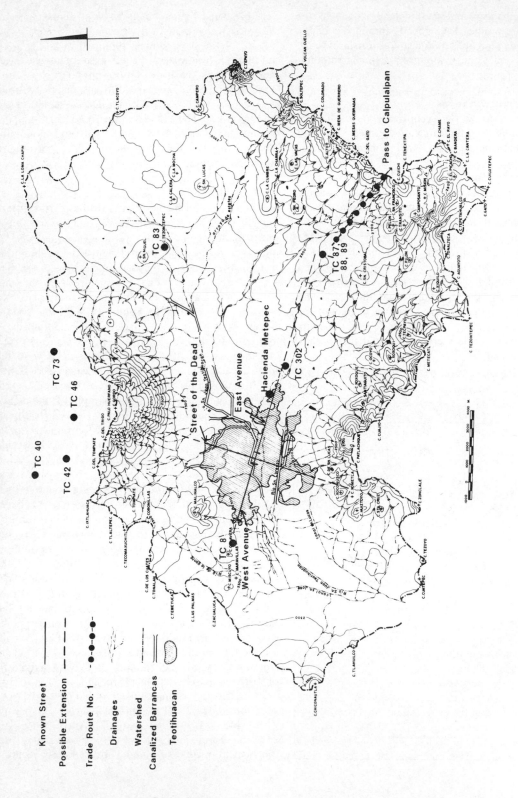

Fig. 15.2. The Teotihuacan valley with Middle Horizon sites and roads (base map after Lorenzo 1968:Fig. 2).

of the East Avenue within Teotihuacan and are about 40 m apart. The marks were not noticeable during survey, either as ditches or as variations in vegetation growth. I carried out excavations at the terminus of the marks in the TC 87, TC 88, TC 89 site complex (1972: 56–7, 74–80) and at TC 302, near their beginning in the Middle Valley alluvial plain (1972: 110–17). Neither during the excavations nor during the detailed mapping and survey which accompanied the excavations did I encounter any physical correlates to the marks. The marks, however, are still present on the most recent aerial photographs of the area (Hoja 36, 2808–S.A.R.H.–C.A. Valle de México–January, 1983, 1:25,000 Cía Mexicana Aero-foto) in the piedmont areas. In the Middle Valley alluvial plain they have been obscured through land leveling which was underway in 1968 (Fig. 15.2).

They mark, I believe, an extension of the East Avenue to the foothills of the eastern Teotihuacan valley where a topographically low and direct pass to Calpulalpan is located. This pass was utilized during the Teotihuacan period to bring, among other goods, various kinds of Thin Orange pottery to the Teotihuacan valley. It is tempting to look for the East Avenue of Teotihuacan to continue, if projected in a straight line, to Calpulalpan with only a slight deviation so that the low pass through the Sierra del Malpais could be used. However a straight line projection of the East Avenue to the southeast does not intersect with Calpulalpan (Las Colinas) but passes to the north by about 1 km. Perhaps the development of more precise topographic maps and aerial photographs would reduce this distance.

In a general sense the East Avenue does extend to Calpulalpan. In a strict sense, however, any prolongation of the East Avenue from Teotihuacan ends where Sanders suggested, at the complex of sites TC 87, TC 88, and TC 89 (Fig. 15.2). Beyond that point the routes are topographically expedient and not, apparently, subject to planning or layout on the basis of the city's orientation except in the most general sense. Undoubtedly movement of people and goods between Teotihuacan and Calpulalpan took place over the pass and along the East Avenue as I have discussed previously (Charlton 1970, 1978, 1987). However, the formal road system from Teotihuacan can only be tenuously traced even as far as TC 87, TC 88, and TC 89.

In a previous paper (Charlton 1987) I noted that the Thin Orange pottery in surface collections and excavations at sites along the possible extension of the East Avenue (from the city's edge near the Barranca Huixco-loco to its apparent terminus near TC 87, TC 88, and TC 89) does not occur in frequencies greater than those

encountered at other sites. In other words, although Thin Orange pottery was probably imported to Teoti-huacan over the pass from Calpulalpan and along the proposed prolongation of the East Avenue the sites located there did not have greater access to that pottery. However, in the sites surveyed between the projected eastern terminus of the East Avenue (at TC 87, TC 88, TC 89) and the eastern end of the pass near Calpulalpan (Charlton 1987) Thin Orange and Thick Orange ceramics occur in much higher frequencies than usually encountered on rural Teotihuacan valley sites. This probably means that sites in the hillslope and pass areas where no evidence of a formal roadway has been found were heavily involved in support and transport activities related to trade. Although the East Avenue may have been the formal entry into Teotihuacan from this direction those sites located along the proposed prolongation had no obvious functions directly related to trade activities.

Intrasite settlement patterns

In the previous section I have examined the evidence for the direct continuous extension of the main axes of Teotihuacan from the urban center into the rural areas of the Teotihuacan valley. I wish now to turn my attention to the evidence for the presence of Teotihuacan-like site plans in Middle Horizon sites of the Basin of Mexico and immediately adjacent areas. By intrasite settlement patterns I refer to the spatial relationships between structures within a site (Charlton 1965:6). The totality of the relationships form the site plan. The intrasite settlement pattern characteristics at Teotihuacan most frequently attributed to other sites include the five following items:

1. *Compact and nucleated* remains of structures and artifactual debris derived from tightly nucleated settlements.
2. *Apartment compounds*, described in detail by Millon (1981: 103–210) at Teotihuacan, appear to be the source of the compact and dense structural and artifactual remains at Middle Horizon sites in the basin and in areas immediately adjacent, where mounding has been preserved.
3. *A grid plan* organizes the apartment compounds within Teotihuacan (Millon 1973; Millon, Drewitt, and Cowgill 1973). Where preservation is satisfactory similar plans seem to serve as organizing principles in other sites.
4. *A ceremonial avenue*, the "Street of the Dead," forms a basic element of the grid plan at Teoti-

huacan in combination with pyramid/plaza complexes. Similar alignments have been reported for other sites although at a much reduced scale.

5. *The pyramid/plaza complex* is well described at Teotihuacan. It occurs in other sites either alone or in combination with linear arrangements of structures along ceremonial avenues.

Although Stage I settlement surveys have been carried out throughout most of this area, to the best of my knowledge, no site has been surveyed and mapped with an intensity and detail comparable to the research carried out by Millon and his colleagues at Teotihuacan. Similarly there have been many fewer excavations in rural Teotihuacan period sites. Of course we must keep in mind the obvious point that not all rural sites are suitable for such intensive surveys and excavations. The type of preservation needed is frequently absent owing to modifications brought about by post-Teotihuacan occupations from A.D. 750 to the present. Thus it will be difficult to make detailed comparisons between Teotihuacan and other sites given the variations in the data bases. Nevertheless I believe it will be useful to summarize what has been claimed about Teotihuacan's impact on intrasite settlement patterns. In addition I will evaluate the data on which these claims are based. Through such syntheses I should be able to outline the level to which Teotihuacan's influence extended within its immediate hinterland and suggest areas for further investigation.

Site plans: reflections of Teotihuacan

Within the Basin of Mexico Sanders *et al.* (1979:52–60, 108, Maps 14, 24) have defined a variety of site types for the Middle Horizon (Table 15.1). These sites occur in four settlement zones within the Basin of Mexico (Sanders *et al.* 1979:123–9; Sanders and Santley 1983:262–5) (Fig. 15.1). Zone 1 is located immediately around Teotihuacan. Zone 2 extends south, east, north and west around Zone 1 and reaches the western edge of the central part of the basin. Zone 3 is located in the south of the basin while Zone 4 is located in its northeastern portion. Zones 1 and 2 are the most heavily populated (Sanders *et al.* 1979:123–9, Maps 14, 24) during the Middle Horizon. I have attempted to list the extent to which components of Teotihuacan's plan have been described for Provincial Centers (2), Large Nucleated Villages (3) and Small Nucleated Villages (4) in Zones 2, 3, and 4 (Table 15.2) (Sanders *et al.* 1979:123–9; Sanders and Santley 1983:262–5).

Table 15.1. *Basin of Mexico site summary: Middle Horizon.*

	Site type	No.	Notes
1.	Supra Regional Center	1	(Teotihuacan)
2.	Provincial Centers	10	
3.	Large Villages	17	(15 Nucleated; 2 Dispersed)
4.	Small Villages	77	(55 Nucleated; 22 Dispersed)
5.	Hamlets	149	
6.	Small Isolated Ceremonial Precincts	9	
7.	Large Ceremonial Precincts	2	
8.	Indeterminate	4	
9.	Obsidian Quarry	1	(Otumba)
10.	Gravel Quarry	1	

A review of the data presented in Table 15.2 suggests that the Provincial Centers located within settlement Zone 2 have intrasite patterns with all five intrasite plan characteristics which occur at Teotihuacan. Large and Small Nucleated Villages in Zone 2 also possess those applicable Teotihuacan site plan characteristics. They are compact and nucleated with evidence for apartment compounds arranged according to a grid plan. Ceremonial avenues and pyramid/plaza complexes occur in varying degrees of elaboration. No Large Nucleated Villages have been reported for the Middle Horizon in the other two settlement zones. The Small Nucleated Villages in Zones 3 (2) and 4 (13) are represented by compact and nucleated concentrations of ceramic and structural debris lacking any good evidence for apartment compounds, grid plans, ceremonial avenues, and pyramid/plaza complexes.

Thus Teotihuacan's influence on intrasite patterns is greatest in Zone 2, and much reduced in Zones 3 and 4. This is evidenced by the great number of Dispersed Villages in Zone 3 and Hamlets in both Zones 3 and 4. Sanders *et al.* (1979) and Sanders and Santley (1983) argue, essentially, that the degree of intrasite plan similarity to Teotihuacan at sites in the basin is correlated with both site type and settlement zone. This would be expected since the site type is defined on the basis of settlement data which reflect site function and site complexity. By definition Large and Small Nucleated Villages, although possessing some ceremonial architecture, would lack elaborate and well-developed ceremonial avenues and pyramid/plaza complexes.

Distance from Teotihuacan is also important, since the same site types within a 30 km radius of Teotihuacan have proportionally more intrasite plan features in

Table 15.2   *Teotihuacan influence in intrasite settlement patterns: Middle Horizon settlements, Basin of Mexico and adjacent areas.*

	SITE TYPE	SETTLEMENT ZONE	COMPACT/ NUCLEATED	APARTMENT COMPOUNDS	GRID PLAN	CEREMONIAL AVENUES	PYRAMIDS/ PLAZAS
Teot.	1	1	YES	YES	YES	YES	YES
Prov.							
Cntr.	2	2	YES	YES	YES	YES	YES
"	2	3*	NO	NO	INDET.	INDET.	INDET.
"	2	4	YES	POSS.	NO	NO	NO
Calpulalpan			YES	YES	INDET.	INDET.	YES
Tepeapulco			YES	YES	INDET.	YES	YES
Chingu			YES	YES	YES	YES	YES
San Ignacio (RAS–78)			YES	NO	INDET.	INDET.	YES
Lrge. Nuc.							
Vill.	3	2	YES	YES	YES	YES	YES
"	3	3	No occupations of this type				
"	3	4	No occupations of this type				
Small Nuc.							
Vill.	4	2	YES	YES	YES	YES	YES
"	4	3	YES	INDET.	NO	NO	NO
"	4	4	YES	INDET.	NO	NO	NO

*Notes.**   According to Parsons (1971) the occupation at the only Provincial Center in this area (Portezuelo) is obscured by Early Toltec occupations.

Sources: Basin: Blanton 1972; Charlton 1965, 1972; Kolb 1979; Parsons 1971, 1974; Parsons *et al.* 1982; Sanders 1965, 1967, 1976; Sanders and Santley 1983; Sanders *et al.* 1979.

         Calpulalpan: Brasdefer, 1978; García Cook and Merino C. 1977; García Cook and Trejo 1977; Kolb 1979; Linné 1942.

         Tepeapulco: Kolb 1979; Matos M. *et al.* 1981.

         Chingu: Díaz O. 1980, 1981.

         San Ignacio (RAS–78): Hirth 1980.

common with Teotihuacan than those located outside this radius. Distance, however, is mitigated by site type in some cases. Although directly comparable survey data for areas outside but immediately adjacent to the basin are not available for the complete site hierarchy, enough data have been published for several Provincial Centers of the Middle Horizon to consider them with reference to Teotihuacan's influence on intrasite plans. I have included in Table 15.2 data for the Provincial Centers of Calpulalpan (Las Colinas), approximately 30 km southeast of Teotihuacan, and Tepeapulco, located approximately 30 km northeast of Teotihuacan (Fig. 15.1). These sites share several intrasite plan characteristics with Teotihuacan but differ from each other in overall intrasite patterns. Chingu, about 60 km northwest of

Teotihuacan, also shares numerous site plan characteristics with Teotihuacan but differs from both Calpulalpan and Tepeapulco (Fig 15.1). San Ignacio (RAS 78) (Fig. 15.1), 100 km south of Teotihuacan and the most distant of the Provincial Centers, shares the fewest site characteristics with Teotihuacan. None of these sites is a reflection in miniature of Teotihuacan.

Evaluation of the data

As I mentioned above, none of the data on site plans of Middle Horizon sites outside of Teotihuacan in the Basin of Mexico and adjacent regions is equivalent to those available for the site plan of Teotihuacan. In this section I shall evaluate the data used to support the occurrence of the five selected characteristics of the Teotihuacan site plan at sites outside of Teotihuacan within the Basin and immediately adjacent areas. I shall also discuss the possibility that any of these sites was built in specific imitation of Teotihuacan.

Compact and nucleated

For sites in the Basin of Mexico this is probably the best documented characteristic of Teotihuacan's site plan occurring in other sites. Obviously it is the lowest common denominator since it rests only on artifactual and structural debris densities and does not involve good preservation of structural remains in the intrasite pattern. Although there has been a substantial amount of coordination of the precise meanings of density statements during surveys in the basin, density definitions remain problematic for multicomponent sites (Sanders *et al.* 1979:60–5).

The data for the degree of compactness and nucleation in Middle Horizon sites are restricted to Stage I survey observations in most cases. In one case a detailed plane-table site map was made at a Small Nucleated Village (TC 8) in Zone 2 (Sanders *et al.* 1979:334–353) (Fig. 15.2). This clearly demonstrates the density of structural remains. At Tepeapulco Matos M. *et al.* (1981) set up a grid of squares 60 m to the side to facilitate mapping and collecting. Díaz O. (1980) divided Chingu into four quadrants and then subdivided each quadrant into units of 100 m per side prior to surveying and making collections at the site. Hirth (1980) made a topographic map of the largest mounds at San Ignacio and established reasonably objective measures of ceramic density to calculate population. To the best of my knowledge these four studies represent the only cases in which a start to the objective definition of statements of density and compactness of Middle Horizon sites has been undertaken. In general, and despite the problems involved in objectively defining intrasite density and compactness, I think that the available data do show that during the Middle Horizon people lived closer together not only at Teotihuacan but also in the Provincial Centers and in the Nucleated Villages of Zone 2. I suspect that in most cases the density and compactness of the remains are directly related to the presence of apartment compounds, a type of residence unique to Middle Horizon Teotihuacan (Millon 1981).

Apartment compounds

Apartment compounds similar to those at Teotihuacan have been reported for some Zone 2 sites on the basis of excavations. The detailed mapping and excavations at TC 8 have confirmed the presence of apartment com-

pounds (Sanders 1965, 1967; Sanders *et al.* 1979:334–53). Since TC 8 is located 5 km west of the Pyramid of the Sun at the end of the projected prolongation of the West Avenue it is not surprising that excavations there yielded apartment compounds. Recent excavations by Monzón F. (1982), Lara D. (1982), and Quintanilla M. (1982) have exposed similar structures on the northern, southeastern, and western peripheries of the city (Zone 1). Rattray (1981) excavated a portion of a Teotihuacan apartment compound on the East Avenue near the Hacienda Metepec (Fig. 15.2). This structure had been reoccupied during the Coyotlatelco period. At TC 302, 4.5 km east of the Ciudadela on the extension of the East Avenue (Zone 1), I encountered structural remains similar to those of apartment compounds but did not clear an entire structure (Charlton 1972:110–17) (Fig. 15.2).

Further away, within the TC 87, 88, 89 site complex at the end of the East Avenue extension (Zone 2), I found similar structural remains (Charlton 1972: 56–7, 74–80) (Fig. 15.2). I mapped one large structure measuring about 130 m by 80 m and carried out small-scale excavations in areas which had been pitted. Later road building in the same area revealed a stratified series of floors in this structure. The structure (Tl. 484) probably represents an apartment compound. Other excavations I carried out as part of Sanders' Teotihuacan Valley Project at TC 46, north of Cerro Gordo (Zone 2), revealed structural remains indicative of apartment compounds although not always as well constructed nor as formally planned as those in the city or TC 8 (Charlton 1965, 1976; Sanders *et al.* 1979: 354–6).

In the far southwestern corner of Zone 2 Tozzer (1921) excavated part of a Teotihuacan apartment compound in Santiago Ahuitzotla (Fig. 15.1). This had been reused during the Coyotlatelco period. More recently Cepeda C. (1978) reported on the excavation of apartment compounds in nearby San Miguel Amantla (Fig. 15.1). He claims these are identical to those found at Teotihuacan. Outside the basin the partial clearing of a residential structure at Calpulalpan (Linné 1942; Brasdefer 1978) (Fig. 15.1) suggests an apartment compound. At all other sites where apartment compounds have been claimed, to the best of my knowledge, their presence is inferred on the basis of the occurrence of large, low mounds, associated with structural and artifactual debris (Charlton 1965: 52–71; Díaz O. 1980; Kolb 1979:367–555; Matos M. *et al.* 1981; Sanders *et al.* 1979:108–29, 355).

Obviously, with the exception of the excavations of residences near Teotihuacan, such as those at TC 8, we lack detailed information on the type of residential structure present at Middle Horizon sites. On the basis of the surveys, mapping, and excavations that have been carried out it is certainly reasonable to infer that at the very least a variant of the Teotihuacan apartment compound was present at Provincial Centers and Nucleated Villages within 30 km of Teotihuacan and probably present at Provincial Centers as far away as 60 km, although not as far away as 100 km. Outside of these cases we have little information on residence type. Sanders *et al.* (1979:355) speculate that "the small site size, dispersed occupation, and near absence of any architectural remains in [the] more distant areas are strongly suggestive of significant differences in residential patterns, economic roles, and societal composition relative to the urban-suburban core of the Middle Horizon settlement system." Since the apartment compound is of restricted spatial and temporal duration (Millon 1981) further survey and excavations in Middle Horizon sites would be of great value in determining the extent to which the apartment compound (and presumably its associated social and economic organization) occurs at sites outside of Teotihuacan.

Grid plans

Grid or quadrangular intrasite plans analogous to that at Teotihuacan have been defined for those sites where preservation was good. "Wherever we were able to define the specific community plan [intrasite plan], all of the larger settlements were laid out on a grid comparable to that of the city" (Sanders *et al.* 1979:125). This certainly was the case at TC 8, a Small Nucleated Village in Zone 2, where detailed mapping accompanied the excavations (Sanders *et al.* 1979:355). Similarly Díaz O. (1980) makes a good case for the arrangement of structures at Chingu on a grid aligned to Teotihuacan's. Cepeda C. (1978) infers that the structures at Amantla were also aligned with streets between them but does not detail the possible plan.

At other sites in Zone 2 the data used to support the presence of a grid or quadrangular plan are derived only from the Stage I surveys. I included in my dissertation (Charlton 1965:52–71) plans of two sites (TC 40 and TC 42) on the north side of Cerro Gordo (Zone 2) showing the grid plan (and also the ceremonial avenues and plaza and pyramid complexes) with an orientation similar to that of Teotihuacan (Fig. 15.2). J. Marino had reconstructed these plans on the basis of his surveys (Kolb 1979:435–6, 440–2). Marino also described similar plans on the basis of comparable data for two other sites, TC

73, north of Cerro Gordo, and TC 83, in the eastern Teotihuacan valley. Of the four sites mentioned, Sanders *et al.* 1979: Maps 14 and 24 classify three (TC 40, TC 73, and TC 83) as Provincial Centers and one (TC 42) as a Small Nucleated Village. (See Kolb 1979 for details of the problems of classifying many of these sites.) My review of the survey data in the site reports from which the TC 40, TC 42, and TC 73 plans were constructed suggests to me now that the definition of such plans in multicomponent sites on the basis of the initial survey data might have been a little optimistic. A visit to TC 73 in 1974 and the resurvey of TC 83 in 1975 (Charlton 1975b) support this conclusion. It is possible in these last two sites, however, that agricultural expansion and house building might have destroyed relevant data. Nevertheless I think we were too ambitious in trying to apply Teotihuacan's master plan to all sites where significant numbers of mounds survived without carrying out additional Stage II surveys.

Grid or quadrangular plans are not apparent at the three Provincial Centers of Tepeapulco, Calpulalpan, and San Ignacio, nor are they claimed for the sites by those who have investigated them (Brasdefer 1978; Hirth 1980; Kolb 1979; Linné 1942; Matos M. *et al.* 1981). The question of the intrasite organization of residences and ceremonial structures according to a grid plan based on Teotihuacan's plan is still open. With two possible exceptions, TC 8 and Chingu, no such plan has been clearly demonstrated through intensive surveys and excavations for any Middle Horizon site.

Ceremonial avenues

There is only one Provincial Center for which a ceremonial avenue has been clearly and unequivocally defined. This is Tepeapulco (Matos M. *et al.* 1981) (Fig. 15.1). A ceremonial avenue flanked by low mounds begins at a small pyramid complex (which faces northwest) and runs to the northwest. It is between 40 and 50 m in width and between 300 and 350 m in length (Matos M. *et al.* 1981:123). This is the best example of a site constructed in part to emulate Teotihuacan and it deviates substantially from Teotihuacan's orientation, Chingu may have similar ceremonial avenues but they are not as clearly defined (Díaz O. 1980). Although some localized mound alignments at San Ignacio suggest the presence of a ceremonial avenue this may simply be a result of the long narrow structure of the site itself (Hirth 1980:75).

The ceremonial avenues defined by Marino for TC 40, TC 42, TC 73, and possibly for TC 83, are subject to the same problems that affected the grid plans. No ceremonial avenues have been defined for Calpulalpan and none appears obvious from the plans and aerial photographs of the site. To the best of my knowledge no ceremonial avenues have been attributed to other Middle Horizon sites. If detailed maps were developed for those sites with relatively well-preserved architecture the questions of both the grid plan and the ceremonial avenue could be addressed.

Pyramid plaza complexes

This complex has been defined at all of the Provincial Centers and at some Large and Small Nucleated Villages in Zone 2. The extent, elaboration, and location of the complex varies even at the Provincial Centers. As I noted above, Tepeapulco has a single small pyramid with a plaza on the northwest side enclosed by low flanking mounds similar to those bordering the ceremonial avenue which begins at the pyramid/plaza complex (Matos M. *et al.* 1981). At Calpulalpan the apparent pyramid mounds, some with associated plazas, cluster in the center of the site (Brasdefer 1978:148; Linné 1942). At Chingu Díaz O. (1980:21–3) reports a series of open and enclosed plazas in association with pyramid mounds aligned along the eastern axis of the site. Hirth's map of San Ignacio (1980:75) depicts one open and two enclosed plazas associated with pyramid mounds.

Several pyramid/plaza complexes have been attributed to the Provincial Centers of TC 40 and TC 73. A single pyramid, possibly with an associated plaza, was present in TC 83. The Small Nucleated Village of TC 8 had a single pyramid/plaza complex. At least three pyramid/plaza complexes have been attributed to TC 42 (Charlton 1965, 1975b; Kolb 1979; Sanders 1965; Sanders *et al.* 1979). I should note that, with the exception of TC 8, the problems of identifying ceremonial avenues at these sites apply to a lesser degree to the identification of pyramid/plaza complexes. Undoubtedly some of the mounds and open spaces may have functioned as temple bases and plazas. However, additional survey and excavation data are needed to resolve these questions.

Summary and conclusions

My examination of Teotihuacan's influence on road systems outside the city proper suggests that the only roads were possible extensions of the city's main axes to areas where the topography precluded further extension. Only the East Avenue extended any distance from the city and served as a main entry and exit route for both people and goods moving from or to the southeast.

In my consideration of Teotihuacan's impact on the intrasite plans of contemporary sites I suggested that sites within Zones 1 and 2 were most affected but that Provincial Centers as far away as 100 km were similarly influenced, albeit to varying degrees. No site, on the basis of the data I have examined, was a true replica of Teotihuacan. Tepeapulco comes closest with its well-defined ceremonial avenue and pyramid/plaza complex. However, the orientation of the structures at Tepeapulco does not even approximate that of Teotihuacan. In addition the ceremonial avenue and pyramid/plaza complex is not centrally located as it is at Teotihuacan.

Our knowledge of the intrasite plans of Middle Horizon sites apart from Teotihuacan and TC 8 is extremely limited with respect to the five components I have examined. The data base consists primarily of excavations with very limited exposures of structures and Stage I survey impressions. I can conclude first that it appears that both distance and site type figure in the presence of the five elements of Teotihuacan's plan in other sites, and second that no sites have plans identical to Teotihuacan. Even the Provincial Centers exhibit a significant degree of variability suggesting that Teotihuacan either was not emulated or was not in control of all aspects of the planning of those centers.

The legacy

What was Teotihuacan's legacy in the areas of regional roads and urban planning? I do not know, but I do suspect that any direct and immediate legacy will be found in the Coyotlatelco states which I have called "Teotihuacan writ small" (Charlton 1975a). Unfortunately information on the intrasite plans of Coyotlatelco sites is so limited that I can only engage in speculation about such impact. It is possible that the particular combination of elements making up the intrasite plan of Teotihuacan may have had as limited an impact as a complex on succeeding cultures as it did on sites contemporary with Teotihuacan. Selected aspects of Teotihuacan's plan occur in various combinations and intensities at sites of the Middle Horizon in and near the Basin of Mexico. I expect that when Coyotlatelco sites are fully explored we will find that in addition to compactness and nucleation (Charlton 1973, 1975a) other elements of Teotihuacan's plan will occur, such as apartment compounds (Rattray 1981), ceremonial avenues, and pyramid/plaza complexes (Parsons 1971, 1974; Parsons *et al.* 1982). None, however, will duplicate Teotihuacan. Teotihuacan's legacy in regional routes and intrasite planning will be as diffuse in later periods as it was during the Middle Horizon.

References

Blanton, Richard E.
1972 *Prehispanic Settlement Patterns of the Ixtapalapa Peninsula Region, Mexico.* Occasional Papers in Anthropology 6, Department of Anthropology, Pennsylvania State University, University Park

Braniff, Beatriz
1972 Secuencias arqueológicas en Guanajuato y la Cuenca de México: intento de correlación. In *Teotihuacán, XI Mesa Redonda*, edited by Alberto Ruz Lhuiller, pp. 273–323. Sociedad Mexicana de Antropología, Mexico

Brasdefer, Fernando C. de
1978 *Asentamientos humanos: un análisis del patrón en el area de Calpulalpan, Tlaxcala.* 2 vols. Tesis profesional, Escuela Nacional de Antropología e Historia, Mexico

Cepeda C., Gerardo
1978 Atzcapotzalco. In *Los Procesos de cambio en Mesoamerica y areas circunvecinas, XV Mesa Redonda*, edited by Noémi Castillo T. pp. 403–11. Sociedad Mexicana de Antropología, Mexico

Charlton, Thomas H.
1965 *Archaeological Settlement Patterns: An Interpretation.* Ph.D. dissertation, Tulane University. University Microfilms, Ann Arbor
1970 El Valle de Teotihuacán: cerámica y patrones de asentamiento, 1520–1969. *Boletín* 41:15–23. I.N.A.H., Mexico
1972 *Post-Conquest Developments in the Teotihuacan Valley, Mexico.* Part I. *Excavations.* Office of the State Archaeologist Report 5. University of Iowa, Iowa City
1973 Texcoco Region Archaeology and the Codex Xolotl. *American Antiquity* 38:412–23
1975a From Teotihuacán to Tenochtitlán: The Early Period Revisited. *American Antiquity* 40:231–5
1975b Reconocimientos superficiales de rutas de intercambio prehispánico, Segunda Parte. Informe submitted to the Departamento de Monumentos Prehispánicos, Instituto Nacional de Antropología e Historia, Mexico. Multilithed
1976 Report on Excavations at Santa María Maquixco el Alto, Estado de México, October and November, 1963. In *Teotihuacán Valley Project Final Report* (Teotihuacán volume), edited by W. T. Sanders, in press
1978 Teotihuacán, Tepeapulco, and Obsidian Exploitation. *Science* 200:1,227–36
1984 Urban Growth and Cultural Evolution from a Oaxacan Perspective. *Reviews in Anthropology* 11:197–207
1987 Teotihuacán Non-Urban Settlements: Functional and Evolutionary Implications. In *Teotihuacán: nuevos datos, nuevas síntesis, nuevos problemas*, edited by Emily McLung de Tapia and Evelyn Childs Rattray, pp. 473–88. Instituto de Investigaciones Antropológicas, Serie Antropológica 72. Universidad Nacional Autónoma de México, Mexico

Coe, William R.
1972 Cultural Contact between the Lowland Maya and Teotihuacán as seen from Tikal, Petén, Guatemala. In *Teotihuacán, XI Mesa Redonda*, edited by Alberto Ruz Lhuiller, pp. 257–71. Sociedad Mexicana de Antropología, Mexico

Corona Núñez, José
1972 Los Teotihuacanos en el occidente de México. In *Teotihuacán, XI Mesa Redonda*, edited by Alberto Ruz Lhuiller, pp. 253–71. Sociedad Mexicana de Antropología, Mexico

Díaz O., Clara L.
1980 *Chingú: un sitio clásico del area de Tula, Hidalgo.* Colección Científica 90, I.N.A.H.-S.E.P., Mexico
1981 Chingú y la expansión teotihuacana. In *Interacción cultural en México central*, edited by Evelyn C. Rattray, Jaime Litvak King, and Clara Díaz Oyarzábal, pp. 107–12. Serie Antropológica 41, Instituto de Investigaciones Antropológicas, Universidad Nacional Autónoma de México, Mexico

Drewitt, Bruce
1967 Planeación en la antigua ciudad de Teotihuacán. In *Teotihuacán, XI Mesa Redonda*, edited by Alberto Ruz Lhuiller, pp. 79–95. Sociedad Mexicana de Antropología, Mexico

García Cook, Angel, and B. Leonor Merino Carrión
1977 Notas sobre caminos y rutas de intercambio al este de la Cuenca de México. *Comunicaciones* 14, Proyecto Puebla-Tlaxcala, pp. 71–82. Fundación Alemana para la Investigación Científica, Puebla, Mexico

García Cook, Angel, and Elia Del Carmen Trejo
1977 Lo Teotihuacano el Tlaxcala. *Comunicaciones* 14, Proyecto Puebla-Tlaxcala, pp. 57–69. Fundación Alemana para la Investigación Científica, Puebla, Mexico

Hirth, Kenneth G.
1980 *Eastern Morelos and Teotihuacan: A Settlement Survey.* Vanderbilt University Publications in Anthropology 25, Nashville, TN

Kolb, Charles C.
1979 Classic Teotihuacán Period Settlement Patterns

in the Teotihuacán Valley, Mexico. Ph.D. dissertation, Pennsylvania State University. University Microfilms, Ann Arbor

Lara D., Eugenia
1981 Asentamientos teotihuacano y azteca externos al centro urbano. In *Memoria del Proyecto Arqueológico Teotihuacán 80–82*, coordinated by Rubén Cabrera Castro, Ignacio Rodriguez G. and Noel Morelos G., pp. 329–39. Colección Científica 132, I.N.A.H.-S.E.P., Mexico

Linné, Sigvald
1942 *Mexican Highland Cultures: Archaeological Researches at Teotihuacán, Calpulalpan, and Chalchicomula in 1934–35*. Ethnographic Museum of Sweden, new series, Publication 7, Stockholm

Lorenzo, José L.
1968 Clima y agricultura en Teotihuacán. In *Materiales para la arqueología de Teotihuacán*, edited by José L. Lorenzo, pp. 51–72. Serie Investigaciones 17, Instituto Nacional de Antropología e Historia, Mexico

Marquina, Ignacio
1972 Influencia de Teotihuacán en Cholula. In *Teotihuacán, XI Mesa Redonda*, edited by Alberto Ruz Lhuiller, pp. 241–51. Sociedad Mexicana de Antropología, Mexico

Matos Moctezuma, Eduardo, María Teresa García García, Fernando Lopez Aquilar, and Ignacio Rodriguez García
1981 Proyecto Tepeapulco: resumen preliminar de las actividades realizadas en la primera temporada de trabajo. In *Interacción cultural en México central*, edited by Evelyn C. Rattray, Jaime Litvak King, and Clara Díaz Oyarzábal, pp. 113–48. Serie Antropológica 41, Instituto de Investigaciones Antropológicas, Universidad Nacional Autónoma de México, Mexico

Millon, René
1970 Teotihuacán: Completion of Map of Giant Ancient City in the Valley of Mexico. *Science* 170:1,077–82
1973 *Urbanization at Teotihuacán, Mexico Vol. 1: The Teotihuacán Map*, part 1, Text. University of Texas Press, Austin
1981 Teotihuacán: City, State, and Civilization. In *Archaeology*, edited by J. Sabloff, pp. 198–243. Supplement to the *Handbook of Middle American Indians*, Vol. I, general editor Victoria R. Bricker. University of Texas Press, Austin

Millon, René, R. Bruce Drewitt, and George L. Cowgill
1973 *Urbanization at Teotihuacán, Mexico, Vol. I: The Teotihuacán Map, part 2, Maps*. University of Texas Press, Austin

Monzón Flores, Martha
1982 Exploración de Dos Casas–Habitación. In *Memoria del Proyecto Arqueológico Teotihuacán 80–82*, coordinated by Rubén Cabrera Castro, Ignacio Rodriguez Garcia, and Noel Morelos Garcia, pp. 321–7. Colección Científica 132, I.N.A.H.-S.E.P., Mexico

Paddock, John
1972a Relaciones de la sección sobre extensión de la cultura teotihuacana. In *Teotihuacán, XI Mesa Redonda*, edited by Alberto Ruz Lhuiller, pp. 325–7. Sociedad Mexicana de Antropología, Mexico
1972b Distribución de rasgos teotihuacanos en Mesoamérica. In *Teotihuacán, XI Mesa Redonda*, edited by Alberto Ruz Lhuiller, pp. 223–39. Sociedad Mexicana de Antropología, Mexico

Parsons, Jeffrey R.
1971 *Prehispanic Settlement Patterns in the Texcoco Region, Mexico*. Memoir 3, Museum of Anthropology, University of Michigan, Ann Arbor
1974 Patrones de asentamiento prehispánicos en el noroeste del Valle de México, Región de Zumpango. Informe submitted to the Departamento de Monumentos Prehispánicos, I.N.A.H., Mexico, and the National Science Foundation. MS on file, Museum of Anthropology, University of Michigan, Ann Arbor

Parsons, Jeffrey R., Elizabeth Brumfiel, Mary H. Parsons, and David J. Wilson
1982 *Prehispanic Settlement Patterns in the Southern Valley of Mexico, the Chalco-Xochimilco Region*. Memoir 14, Museum of Anthropology, University of Michigan, Ann Arbor

Porter Weaver, Muriel
1981 *The Aztecs, Maya, and Their Predecessors: Archaeology of Mesoamerica*. Second edition. Academic Press, New York

Quintanilla M., Patricia E.
1982 Estructura 69. In *Memoria del Proyecto Arqueológico Teotihuacán 80–82*, coordinated by Rubén Cabrera Castro, Ignacio Rodriguez García and Noel Morelos García, pp. 355–60. Colección Científica 132, I.N.A.H.-S.E.P., Mexico

Rattray, Evelyn C.
1981 Un Taller de bifaciales de obsidiana del período Coyotlatelco en la Hacienda Metepec, Teotihuacán. Paper presented at the symposium La Obsidiana en Mesoamérica, Centro Regional Hidalgo, I.N.A.H., Pachuca, Hidalgo, Mexico

Sanders, William T.
1965 The Cultural Ecology of the Teotihuacán Valley.

MS on file, Department of Sociology and Anthropology, Pennsylvania State University, University Park
1967 Life in a Classic Village. In *Teotihuacán, XI Mesa Redonda*, edited by Alberto Ruz Lhuiller, pp. 123–48. Sociedad Mexicana de Antropología, Mexico
1976 Final Field Report: Cuauhtitlán-Temascalapa Survey Project. MS on file, Department of Anthropology, Pennsylvania State University, University Park

Sanders, William T., and Robert S. Santley
1983 A Tale of Three Cities: Energetics and Urbanization in Pre-Hispanic Central Mexico. In *Prehistoric Settlement Patterns: Essays in Honor of Gordon R. Willey*, edited by E. Z. Vogt and R. M. Leventhal, pp. 243–91. University of New Mexico Press and Peabody Museum of Archaeology and Ethnology, Harvard University, Cambridge, MA

Sanders, William T., Jeffrey R. Parsons, and Robert S. Santley
1979 *The Basin of Mexico: Ecological Processes in the Evolution of a Civilization*. Academic Press, New York

Snow, Dean R.
1972 Classic Teotihuacán Influences in North-Central Tlaxcala. In *Teotihuacán, XI Mesa Redonda*, edited by Alberto Ruz Lhuiller, pp. 245–51. Sociedad Mexicana de Antropología, Mexico

Tozzer, Alfred M.
1921 *Excavations at a Site at Santiago Ahuitzotla, Mexico D.F.* Bureau of American Ethnology Bulletin 74, Smithsonian Institution, Washington, DC

16 The structure of the Aztec transport network

ROBERT S. SANTLEY

Economies are open systems that extract, convert, and distribute matter, energy, and information from the environment for use by human populations. All economies contain elements, and in complex societies those elements are hierarchically organized. The day-to-day functioning of state economies also requires facilities such as offices, factories, warehouses, and roads, but these physical forms in themselves are not the economy. Rather, they are the structural residue, the material artifacts of human behavior. What binds the system together into a coherent whole are sets of interrelationships between the objects. An interesting aspect of state economies is that they exhibit variability in structure. This variability in structure determines the placement of facilities so that the system can operate efficiently. Knowledge about the location of facilities, then, should allow for specification of the structure which determines the generic form a particular economy has adopted.

Two models have been advanced in recent years describing the organization of Aztec economy. Michael Smith (1979), for example, has argued that the distribution of Aztec centers exhibits a close fit to the $K = 3$ central-place model as originally developed by Christaller (1966). In $K = 3$ central-place systems commercial factors predominate in structuring settlement location, with lower-order marketing centers situated equidistant between three higher-order centers (Lloyd and Dicken 1972). $K = 3$ economies represent a least-effort solution to packing the maximum number of commercial places in a landscape consistent with minimization of transport costs. This system, Smith submits, is the most efficient way for integrating largely rural landscapes and for facilitating rural–urban exchange. Susan Evans (1980), in contrast, suggests that environmental and political factors outweighed marketing in shaping the organization of Aztec economy. A hybrid K = 4/K = 7 model, in other words, probably provides a much better characterization of economic structure. In K = 4 economies lower-ranking centers are placed equidistant between two higher-ranking centers, owing to the effect of the exchange of goods between them. Settlement location, then, is dictated by transport considerations. In K = 7 systems, on the other hand, administrative considerations override marketing and transport factors such that higher-order centers exert a gravitation effect, pulling smaller communities closer to centers of regional decision-making.

Network analysis is a method for describing aspects of system economic organization. Network analysis may be employed to isolate elements of system structure *only if* system vertices and linkages are known (Kansky 1963). In this case, the system is composed of a hierarchy of centers and dependent communities connected to one another by a net of roadways designed to facilitate the movement of goods, people, and information across the landscape (Gonzalez A. 1973; Sanders *et al.* 1979). Graph theory allows one to describe the relative position of points and the pattern of accessibility within the network. When one wishes to know the overall accessibility of a network, the concept one measures is connectivity (Taylor 1977). Inaccessible systems are ones in which the region is divided up into a set of spatially bounded units that are rarely connected to one another (Fig. 16.1 – upper left). Well-connected networks, in contrast, are systems that permit movement both horizontally and vertically between a hierarchy of centers on a regional landscape (Fig. 16.1 – upper right). Such systems have been called complex, interlocking central-place economies, of which the K = 3 and K = 4 models are fundamental subtypes (Smith 1976). Sandwiched in between these two extremes are several different kinds of partly connected networks, of which solar central-place and dendritic economies are two outstanding examples (Fig. 16.1 – lower left and right). In dendritically organized economies vertical linkages between nodes predominate, and there is little articulation between centers of equivalent rank (E. A. J. Johnson 1970; Kelley 1976). On the other hand, solar central-place systems encourage some horizontal movement, although the direction of many matter and information flows is still up the economic hierarchy (Smith 1976). Solar and dendritic central-place systems have been described as "administered economies." This is because political and economic elites are one and the same, and political decisions are frequently made to safeguard elite economic interests. This leads to only partial commercialization and to the incomplete development of a hierarchy of centers.

Fig. 16.1. Models of economic system structure (after Smith 1976).

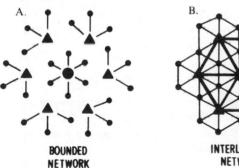

A.

BOUNDED NETWORK

B.

INTERLOCKING NETWORK

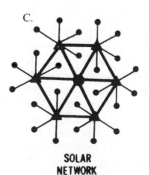

C.

SOLAR NETWORK

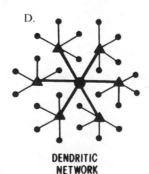

D.

DENDRITIC NETWORK

The Aztec settlement system

At the time of the Spanish Conquest the Aztecs were the dominant political force in Mesoamerica (Gibson 1971; Davies 1973; Collier *et al.* 1982). The seat of Aztec imperial power was the Basin of Mexico, a great upland plain situated near the southern end of the Meseta Central (Sanders *et al.* 1979). Because the basin is surrounded on four sides by mountain ranges of various heights, it is a closed hydrographic unit. Until recently, a substantial part of the floor of the basin was covered by a series of large, shallow lakes, and during the Aztec Period (A.D. 1150–1522) large sections of this lacustrine zone, especially Lake Chalco-Xochimilco, were converted into raised fields, agricultural plots that the Mexica called *chinampas* (Fig. 16.2) (Armillas 1971; Parsons 1976). Indeed, *chinampa* agriculture was so successful that it became a major determinant of settlement

Fig. 16.2. Distribution of Late Aztec period settlements in the Basin of Mexico (after Sanders, Parsons and Santley 1979).

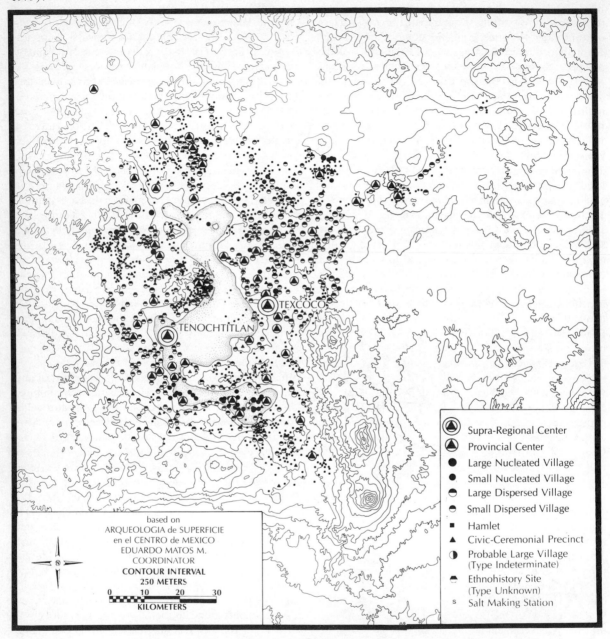

Legend:
- Supra-Regional Center
- Provincial Center
- Large Nucleated Village
- Small Nucleated Village
- Large Dispersed Village
- Small Dispersed Village
- Hamlet
- Civic-Ceremonial Precinct
- Probable Large Village (Type Indeterminate)
- Ethnohistory Site (Type Unknown)
- s Salt Making Station

based on
ARQUEOLOGIA de SUPERFICIE
en el CENTRO de MEXICO
EDUARDO MATOS M.
COORDINATOR
CONTOUR INTERVAL
250 METERS
0   10   20   30
KILOMETERS

TEXCOCO
TENOCHTITLAN

location (Sanders *et al.* 1979; Parsons *et al.* 1982). The Aztec capital of Tenochtitlan, located on an island in Lake Texcoco, was one such *chinampa* settlement (Calneck 1972, 1982). The *chinampa* district around Tenochtitlan was protected by the great dike of Nezahualcoyotl, which ran from Atzacualco 13 km south to Ixtapalapa (Sanders *et al.* 1979). The capital, with a population of 150,000–220,000, was connected to the mainland by a series of large masonry causeways, which in turn were linked to a network of roads that permitted traffic throughout the Basin of Mexico (Gonzalez A. 1973; Sanders and Santley 1983). These facilities provided the basis for regional economic organization. That organization involved a hierarchy of central places, local specialization in craft and subsistence production, and an imperial tribute system (Smith 1979; Berdan 1982).

The basic unit of Aztec political organization was the territorial state, each with its local hereditary nobility (*pipiltin*) and ruler (*tlatoani*). Each territorial state covered 150–200 km^2 and consisted of a central town, with its core of urban occupation, and a number of dependent villages and hamlets whose subsistence base derived principally from agriculture. At the time of the Spanish Conquest there were forty-four such entities, including Tenochtitlan, its sister city, Tlatelolco, and Texcoco (Sanders *et al.* 1979). Territorial states, moreover, could be ranked in a hierarchy. At the base were towns like Ecatepec, Huexotla, Teotihuacan, or Mixquic that had populations of 1,000–5,000 and held markets periodically. Above these towns were larger centers such as Chalco, Xochimilco, Azcapotzalco, and Cuauhtitlan, with populations numbering 8,000–10,000, that often extracted tribute from smaller states (Gibson 1964). In several instances markets were held several times a week. At the top were the members of the Triple Alliance: Tenochtitlan, Texcoco, and Tlacopan. These centers received tribute not only from local states but also from the empire at large, and in two instances, Tenochtitlan and Texcoco, the central place was an urban center containing great numbers of craftsmen and other specialists. Markets were held every day, and in the case of Tenochtitlan-Tlatelolco the marketplace was a state-constructed facility, with exchange monitored directly by government administrators.

Two classes were present in Aztec society. The *pipiltin* or elite class comprised that segment of society from which political decision-makers were drawn. These individuals paid taxes to the state but were exempt from labor service. The noble stratum itself was internally differentiated with respect to authority and wealth. The

dominant member of the nobility functioned as heads of patrimonial estates over which they were granted hereditary rights by the Triple Alliance to the produce of certain lands and services of serfs in return for their administrative services within the larger state organization (Sanders *et al.* 1979). This elite also had rights to agricultural produce and labor services of local free commoners for whom they provided certain local-level administrative and redistributional functions.

At the base of the social hierarchy was the great majority of the population. This population was divided into two groups: the *macehualtin*, free commoners with direct access to corporately held land; and the *mayeque*, serfs or landless tenants who resided on patrimonial or private estates (Sanders *et al.* 1979). Both groups paid taxes in kind and were required to perform military service and corvée labor for the state. The basic unit of organization for free commoners was the *calpulli*, which was internally subdivided into small units called *barrios pequeños*. Each *calpulli* was a large segmentary lineage, probably with a patri-bias in terms of descent reckoning and inheritance. The *calpulli* functioned as a land-holding unit, paid taxes, had important religious and educational functions, and in war served as a military unit. Status positions within the *calpulli* were internally differentiated, with heads selected from the highest-ranking lineage. In rural areas most *calpulli* members specialized in certain crafts and lived in specific portions of the city. These *calpulli* were aggregated into *huecalpultin* or *tlaxilcalli*, the four major wards of Tenochtitlan. *Calpultin* in rural areas were also sometimes economically specialized. These specializations reflected variability in the distribution of key raw materials or natural resources. The town of Ecatepec, for example, contained several *barrios* of salt makers, while several communities in the northern basin specialized in lime slaking (Sanders *et al.* 1979; Sanders and Santley 1983). Even farmers who lived in suburban Tenochtitlan grew special products like flowers and vegetables, not maize, for sale in the urban market (Calnek 1972).

Above this local system was the empire. In reality, the term empire is a misnomer, as the empire was merely a collection of tributary provinces over which the Aztecs exercised little administrative control (Gibson 1971). According to Calnek (1982), each province was under the authority of a high steward (*huecalpixqui*) who supervised the activities of local tribute collectors (*calpixque*). Accounts of tribute paid were kept in pictoglyphic form, and the material was stored in warehouses in Tenochtitlan and other Triple Alliance capitals for later use. The entire tribute system was coordinated by a

Fig. 16.3. Map of the Aztec roadway network in the Basin of Mexico (after Gonzalez A. 1973).

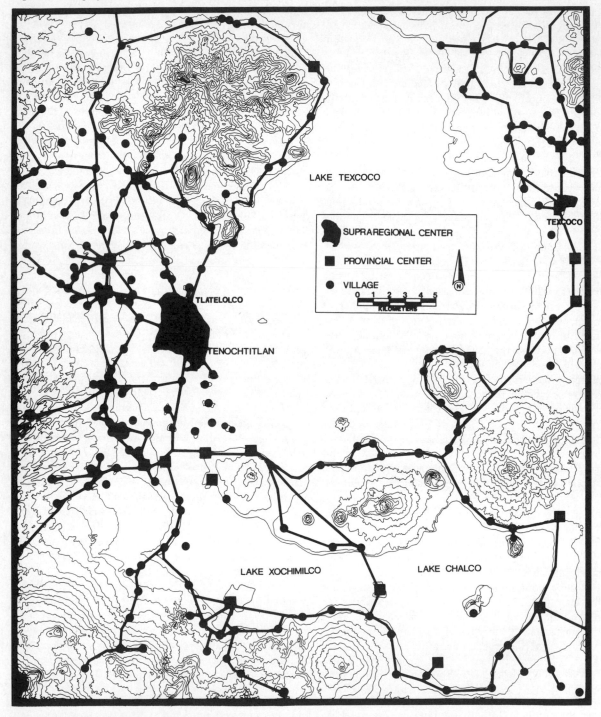

single official holding the title of *petlacalcatl* (Calnek 1982). Provinces within a 150 km radius paid their tribute in agricultural products such as maize, beans, amaranth, fruits, and vegetables, supplemented with some elite goods; distant provinces, in contrast, provided largely non-agricultural products or special foods for the exclusive use of the nobility (Bedoian 1973). This tribute was used for a variety of important system-serving functions, including support of the royal palace, gifts and commissions to distinguished warriors, political underlings, merchants, and artisans, subsidy of state administrative and military activities, elite long-distance trade, emergency storage, and maintenance of urban populations (Berdan 1982).

The empire was linked together by a series of roadways over which state messengers, the Aztec military, pilgrims, and caravans carrying goods traveled (Rees 1975). This roadway network attained its most evolved expression in the immediate vicinity of Tenochtitlan (Fig. 16.3) (Gonzalez A. 1973). Four major causeway systems permitted entry to the capital. Each causeway was a large earthen construction with a masonry veneer. Bridges were also placed at intervals to control water level and facilitate canoe traffic. These causeways were state constructions built with corvée labor late in the history of the Aztec state. Each causeway in turn was connected to a series of roadways that linked major centers on the mainland. Many of these were also paved with tabular limestone and occasionally flanked with balustrades. The documentary sources are not very specific concerning whether major mainland roads too were state-built, though the larger ones linking Tenochtitlan with its tributary domain probably were. Rural villages were also connected to local towns. Many of these roads were probably footpaths, built and maintained by each local territorial state. There was also much trafficking by canoe (Sanders and Santley 1983). This provided an efficient link with the *chinampa* districts immediately around Tenochtitlan and to the south in Lake Chalco-Xochimilco.

Topological analysis of the Aztec network

Topology is a branch of geometry that reduces empirical reality to its bare essentials. In topology distance, direction, and all other Euclidean concepts are ignored. In graph theory only four types of basic structure are identified: isolated points, paths, trees, and circuits. Isolated points occur in systems in which there are no connections. A path is a series of one of more lines connecting points such that each point is connected to only one or two other points. In trees or dendritic

systems one vertex is connected to several points, but there are no loops. Thus, one cannot get back to the starting point without retracing steps. In circuits one or more loops occur such that movement around the network to the starting point is possible without retracing steps.

Three properties of network structure must be known in order to measure network connectivity: e, the number of lines, edges, or roads between points in the system; v, the number of vertices, points, or settlements in a region; and p, the number of separate subgraphs, including isolated points (Kansky 1963). All other indices of network geometry are derivative measures.

The simplest way of measuring network connectivity is to calculate the cyclomatic number. The cyclomatic number is defined by the expression

$$u = e - v + p$$

This index specifies how many basic circuits there are in the network. Values range from 0 in totally unconnected systems to much larger numbers in more complex networks. This index is not a very useful comparative measure because the score derived is dependent on the number of points in the system.

A better estimate of system connectivity is given by the alpha index. Alpha is the ratio of number of circuits, the cyclomatic number, to the maximum number of circuits that could occur given the number of points. The equation for alpha is

$$\text{alpha} = \frac{u}{2v - 5}$$

Values for alpha rank from 0 to 1. Although the alpha index is a relative measure, all isolated networks, simple paths, or dendritic systems automatically score 0 on its scale because they have no circuits by definition. As Taylor (1977:62) has pointed out, "We would normally expect a tree to be more connected than a path, which in turn is more connected than a pattern of no links between points ..."

This ambiguity is remedied by the beta index. Beta avoids use of the cyclomatic number or the alpha index. Instead, beta utilizes the ratio of the number of lines to the number of points to measure accessibility. The formula for beta is

$$\text{beta} = \frac{e}{v}$$

In this case unconnected systems still score 0, but paths and trees vary between 0 and 1. All networks with one or more circuits have an index of 1 or more. Beta, however, is an absolute measure of linkage connectivity. Thus its maximum value also varies with the number of points.

This problem is overcome by computing the gamma index. Gamma is defined as the ratio of the number of observed lines to the total number of lines possible given the number of points. The expression for gamma is

$$\text{gamma} = \frac{e}{3(v-2)}$$

Since the number of lines cannot be greater than its maximum, values for gamma also range from 0 to 1. This index allows for discrimination between points, paths, trees, and circuits, all of which are normalized to a relative number.

Occasionally, different graphs, networks connected in fundamentally different ways, score identically using gamma (James *et al.* 1970). This problem can be resolved through use of the *S–I* index (Ord 1967). Computation of the *S–I* index involves the construction of a shortest-path matrix. All points are numbered sequentially and listed as column and row headings beginning with 1. The number of links that one has to pass from point 1 to reach point 1 is 0. This number is placed in the appropriate cell in the matrix. This operation is repeated for all other points and for all possible pairs of points, each time taking the shortest path. The first moment, or mean, $\mu_1{}'$ is given by

$$\mu_1{}' = \bar{l} = \frac{1}{N}\sum_{1=0}^{\sigma} f_l l$$

where *n* is the number of points, *l* is the number passed, and f_l is the frequency the same number of links were passed, as indicated by the cells in the matrix. The second and third moments are computed by

$$\mu_2 = \frac{1}{N}\sum_{1=0}^{\sigma} f_l (l - \bar{l})^2$$

and $\mu_3 = \frac{1}{N}\sum_{1=0}^{\sigma} f_l (l - \bar{l})^3.$

The *S–I* index, then, is defined as

$$S = \mu_3/\mu_2$$
$$\text{and } I = \mu_2/\mu'_{1-}$$

The data utilized derive from a recent study, *Plano Reconstructivo de la Región de Tenochtitlán* (Gonzalez A. 1973). They consist of 222 centers and villages connected by 229 roadway segments (Fig. 16.3). Two sites, Tenochtitlan and Texcoco, are major urban centers, twenty-one are provincial centers, settlements with resident *tlatoani*,

that formerly served as capitals of small autonomous city-states, and the remainder are agricultural or craft-specialty villages. The roadway links are artificial constructions, frequently built of masonry and of substantial size, that provide connections between settlements. The data are also separated into three zonal strata: the region immediately around Tenochtitlan (Sector 1); the Southern Basin, Ixtapalapa peninsula, and Tenayuca region (Section 2); and the Eastern Basin (Sector 3). This was done to see if patterning in network accessibility varied systematically as a function of distance from the capital. I have refrained from applying data collected by the Basin of Mexico Project (Sanders *et al.* 1979), as the sample of communities around Tenochtitlan is incomplete. The settlements plotted, however, include all larger communities known to have been occupied during the Conquest period.

Table 16.1 presents basic data on Aztec sites as well as indices of network structure. Mean roadway length is 1.8 ± 1.7 km. Sites, however, are more dispersed with greater distance from Tenochtitlan, as reflected by mean distance and standard deviation. Settlements near Tenochtitlan, then, are more closely spaced, and the distribution of sites is more regular. Cyclomatic numbers vary

Table 16.1 *Parameters and indices for the Aztec roadway network.*

Variable	a. *All sites*			
	All sites	*Sector 1*	*Sector 2*	*Sector 3*
Mean distance between sites	1.799	1.445	2.036	2.062
Standard deviation	1.716	1.195	1.632	2.209
No. of sites	222	96	60	66
No. of edges	229	101	65	73
No. of graphs	32	15	8	9
Cyclomatic No.	39	20	13	16
Alpha index	0.089	0.107	0.113	0.126
Beta index	1.032	1.052	1.083	1.106
Gamma index	0.347	0.358	0.374	0.380
	b. *Centers*			
Mean distance between sites	8.010	3.800	16.980	7.120
Standard deviation	37.652	3.342	37.363	22.008
No. of sites	23	9	4	10
No. of edges	33	18	5	15
No. of graphs	2	2	1	1
Cyclomatic No.	12	11	2	6
Alpha index	0.293	0.846	0.667	0.400
Beta index	1.435	2.000	1.250	1.500
Gamma index	0.524	0.857	0.833	0.626

considerably. Correlation with point frequency indicates that much of this variability is tied to site number, as discussed earlier ($r = 0.997$, $p < .05$). Alpha values range from 0.107 to 0.126, with a score of 0.089 for the entire network. Betas, in contrast, fluctuate from 1.052 to 1.106, with a value of 1.032 for all sites. Gammas likewise exhibit little spatial variability; the index for all sites is 0.347, for different sectors, from 0.358 to 0.380. Curiously, Sector 3, the eastern Basin around Texcoco, is somewhat better connected than Sectors 1 and 2, regions closer to the capital. Apparently, this is a function of the number of isolated points, for if the seven sites connected to the network by water-borne traffic are removed from the computation of gamma, Sector 1 scores 0.387. Thus, sectors that contain urban centers are somewhat better connected than sectors that do not, and Tenochtitlan, the political capital, is slightly more accessible than Texcoco, the rank 2 community. Gammas were also calculated for centers only. Predictably, all scores are higher, frequently by significant margins. The relative amount of increase in score is 0.177 for all centers, 0.245 to 0.499 for centers in different sectors. In particular, the network of centers around Tenochtitlan is well connected. Overall, however, the Aztec roadway system is not highly accessible. Scores are consistently below those one would expect for a system containing multiple circuitry (Kansky 1963: Taylor 1977). In fact, the only multiple circuits in the

system occur near Tenochtitlan and Texcoco, the region's principal central places.

Parameters and indices were also computed for the graphs illustrated in Fig. 16.1. These are given in Table 16.2. The number of points is held constant to observe directional patterning in network accessibility. The gamma index ranges from 0.276 for the highly bounded graph to 0.931 for complex interlocking systems of the classical central-place type. Solar systems score 0.414, dendritic systems 0.345, when all sites are included. Not surprisingly, centers are more accessible than all sites. This is particularly the case for solar systems where the amount of gain in relative connectivity is 0.386. Alphas and betas behave similarly. In all cases, there is an increase in scores as the number of network connections rises. Kansky (1963) has demonstrated that this variability is closely related to the degree of system economic development. Immature systems are defined by few links, little commercialization, and only a vague tendency for hierarchical development. Mature systems, in contrast, support complex transportation networks, are more highly commercialized, and contain well-developed hierarchies of central places.

Table 16.2 *Parameters and indices for different economic systems.*

a. *All sites economic system*

	Bounded	Dendritic	Solar	Interlocking
No. of sites	31	31	31	31
No. of edges	24	30	36	31
No. of graphs	7	1	1	1
Cyclomatic No.	0	0	6	51
Alpha index	0	0	0.105	0.895
Beta index	0.774	0.968	1.161	2.613
Gamma index	0.276	0.345	0.414	0.931

b. *Centers*

	Bounded	Dendritic	Solar	Interlocking
No. of sites	7	7	7	7
No. of edges	0	6	12	15
No. of graphs	7	1	1	1
Cyclomatic No.	0	0	6	9
Alpha index	0	0	0.667	1.000
Beta index	0	0.357	1.714	2.143
Gamma index	0	0.400	0.800	1.000

Table 16.3 *Shortest-path matrix for Aztec centers.*

	1	2	3	4	5	6	7	8	9	10	11	12	13	14	15	16	17	18	19	20	21	22
1	0	1	1	1	1	1	1	1	0	2	2	2	2	2	3	3	3	4	5	6	7	6
2	1	0	2	2	3	3	3	3	0	3	3	3	3	3	4	4	4	5	6	7	8	7
3	1	1	0	2	2	2	2	2	0	3	3	3	3	3	4	4	4	5	6	7	8	7
4	1	1	2	0	1	2	2	2	0	3	3	3	3	3	4	4	4	5	6	7	8	7
5	1	2	2	1	0	1	1	1	0	2	2	2	2	2	3	3	3	4	5	6	7	6
6	2	3	3	2	1	0	1	1	0	2	2	2	2	2	3	3	4	5	6	7	8	7
7	1	2	2	2	1	1	0	1	0	2	1	1	1	1	2	2	3	4	5	6	7	6
8	1	2	2	2	1	1	1	0	0	1	2	2	2	2	2	2	3	4	5	6	5
9	0	0	0	0	0	0	0	0	0	0	0	0	0	0	0	0	0	0	0	0	0	0
10	2	3	3	3	2	3	2	1	0	0	2	1	2	2	1	1	1	2	3	4	5	4
11	2	3	3	3	2	2	1	2	0	2	0	1	1	1	2	2	3	4	5	6	5
12	2	3	3	3	2	2	1	2	0	1	1	0	1	1	2	1	1	2	3	4	5	4
13	2	3	3	3	2	2	1	2	0	2	1	1	0	1	2	2	2	3	4	5	6	5
14	3	3	3	3	2	2	1	2	0	2	1	1	1	0	1	1	2	3	4	5	6	5
15	3	4	4	4	3	3	2	2	0	1	2	1	2	1	0	1	1	2	3	4	5	4
16	3	4	4	4	3	4	3	2	0	1	2	1	2	2	1	0	1	2	3	4	5	4
17	3	4	4	4	3	4	3	2	0	1	2	1	2	2	1	1	0	1	2	3	4	3
18	4	5	5	5	4	5	4	3	0	2	3	2	3	3	2	2	1	0	1	2	3	2
19	5	6	6	6	5	6	5	4	0	3	4	3	4	4	3	3	2	1	0	1	2	1
20	6	7	7	7	6	7	6	5	0	4	5	4	5	5	4	4	3	2	1	0	1	1
21	7	8	8	8	7	8	7	6	0	5	6	5	6	6	5	5	4	3	2	1	0	1
22	6	7	7	7	6	7	6	5	0	4	5	4	5	5	4	4	3	2	1	1	1	0

l	0	1	2	3	4	5	6	7	8
f_l	64	89	108	74	53	38	28	22	8

The *S–I* index was also applied to measure network structure. Owing to the sheer number of sites, the shortest-path matrix was constructed for centers only (Table 16.3). The index for centers is $S = -7.509$, $I = 2.135$. Scores were also computed for the different graphs illustrated in Fig. 16.1, again only using centers. These values were as follows: bounded systems, $S = 0.000$, $I = 0.000$; solar and interlocking systems, $S = 0.440$, $I = 0.417$; and dendritic systems, $S = -0.622$, $I = 0.514$. The scores for the Aztec network are considerably higher than the indices for the different models of economy. This is because the *S–I* index, an absolute measure, is sensitive to the number of points given in the graph. Index values can therefore be greater than 1. James *et al.* (1970) compute indices for graphs with different structures. Multiple-circuit systems generally have positive indices, with *I* greater than *S* and *S* scoring near 0. For paths and simple circuits *I* is also larger than *S*, with the values of *S* ranging from -0.6 to -0.3 and 0.3 to 0.6. Dendritic systems, in contrast, have negative *S* scores, with values of *S* that are considerably less than *I*. Perhaps a better measure is the *S/I* ratio. The *S/I* ratio for different dendrographs presented by James *et al.* varies from -1.433 to -2.223. The *S/I* ratio for the Aztec network is -3.517. *S/I* ratios for other types of graphs are always greater than -1.000.

The Aztec roadway network clearly has a dendritic structure. The observed gamma (0.347) closely approximates the score expected for a totally dendritically connected system. The *S/I* index yielded similar results; the *S* value is negative, as is the *S/I* ratio, and the value for *S* is significantly less than the *I* score, precisely what one would expect under conditions of dendritic linkage. Nevertheless, there is variability in network connectivity. This is especially the case for the heart of the system where the scores, for centers in particular, correspond to values expected under conditions of solar marketing. This structure does not accord well with the proposition that interlocking marketing factors were the primary determinant of regional economic organization, for the only multiple circuits in the system occur within a short radius of the top-ranking central place. A dendritic structure, however, is precisely what one would expect if bulking considerations were a major impetus behind road building (Kelley 1976; Santley n.d.a.). Indeed, this is precisely what the ethnohistoric record indicates. Sanders (1965), for example, has pointed out that certain Aztec towns rose in economic importance because of their key positions along major routes of transit leading *into and out of* the Basin of Mexico. More recently, Parsons (1976) has suggested that much of the pro-

duction of the *chinampa* zone in Lake Chalco-Xochimilco was destined for consumption by urban dwellers in Tenochtitlan. Brumfiel (1980) also feels that many commodities were channeled up the settlement hierarchy rather than distributed through local markets, judging from data from the Aztec town of Huexotla. Carrasco (1978, 1982) comes to a similar conclusion: that marketing and exchange were highly administered and that commercial factors played a subordinate role in structuring regional economic organization.

Aztec regional economic organization

How then was the Aztec economy organized? I suggest that bulking considerations and large-scale production for export had evolved as factors of primary importance in conditioning regional politicoeconomic organization. The Aztec politicoeconomy, I submit, bears an exceedingly close resemblance to the dendritic central-place model. In dendritic politicoeconomies the size of the principal central place is typically quite large, there are at least four levels in the site-size hierarchy, with second- and/or third-order centers absent and those centers present lacking interstitial placement. The distribution of rural bulking sites is size-sequential, with larger sites located near the largest center, and the rank-size plot of centers within the political unit is primate in configuration (Smith 1976; Kelley 1976; Santley n.d.a.). Moreover, those marketing facilities and craft specializations that are present are generally confined to the primate center, though some local facilities and specialists may exist in the countryside, and the economic climate of the largest central place is dominated by large-scale export–import enterprises frequently involving industrial production and wholesale vending abroad (E. A. J. Johnson 1970; Vance 1970). In addition, stratification systems are ethnically defined and culturally plural, with great lifestyle differences and little socioeconomic mobility between strata (Smith 1976). Elites tend to be concentrated in the largest central places where they monopolistically dominate both economy and polity. Rural communities are open yet isolated economically, non-corporate and egalitarian in structure, and integrated by patron–client relationships.

Three lines of evidence support this characterization. First, it appears that a substantial part of the population of Tenochtitlan was engaged in craft production of one form or another (Sanders and Santley 1983). Many of these craftsmen lived in specific barrios of the city and, in the case of artisans producing luxury goods, featherworkers, lapidaries, and metalworkers, they were organized into large hereditary guilds which limited membership, had internal control over education and ranking, and worshipped their own patron deities (Berdan 1982). Downtown Tenochtitlan in turn was surrounded by suburbs of *chinampa* farmers who grew special crops for sale in the urban market. Much of this craft activity was not for local use but for exchange abroad. The great market at Tlatelolco, then, serviced not only the Basin of Mexico but also the empire at large. Production for export also conditioned the politicoeconomy of Tula and Totihuacan, two earlier urban centers in the Basin of Mexico (Spence 1981; Healan, Kerley, and Bey 1983; Sanders and Santley 1983; Santley n.d.a., n.d.b.). Tula and Teotihuacan were not as large as Tenochtitlan, and the proportion of the population who were craftsmen appears to have been less. Tenochtitlan, therefore, probably controled a marketing hinterland of considerably greater size, at least demographically.

There is also strong evidence that the Aztecs dominated long-distance trade throughout the most densely settled parts of Mesoamerica (Chapman 1957; Sanders 1977; Bittman and Sullivan 1978). During the Aztec period long-distance trade was controlled by the *pochteca*, professional merchants who were organized into ranked kindreds, each of which maintained its own religious cult and legal code. These professional merchants "dealt in relatively large lots of goods ... and conducted economic exchanges in both marketplaces and neutral ports of trade beyond the bounds of the empire" (Berdan 1982:31). Caravans, sometimes involving thousands of burden bearers, were outfitted in Tenochtitlan and other Central Plateau cities. Although many trade items were highly valued luxury goods for use by the nobility, there was also much trafficking in basic utilitarian goods, particularly obsidian and salt. Virtually all of the obsidian traded to the Valley of Oaxaca during Late Postclassic times came from the Basin of Mexico (Appel n.d.), and there is evidence that the Aztecs also provided the Tuxtlas Region of the South Gulf Coast with significant quantities of Basin of Mexico obsidian (Santley n.d.b.). In fact, I suspect that most of the obsidian traded long distances during the Conquest period either came from the Aztec heartland or was exchanged by the *pochteca*. This long-distance trade in luxury and domestic goods was so vigorous that the *pochteca* established permanent colonies at strategic points to act as local agents for the merchants (Chapman 1957).

The *pochteca* also functioned as factors of the Aztec state, as spies and as tribute collectors. The amount of tribute that entered Tenochtitlan was extraordinary, amounting literally to thousands of tons of material annually (Codex Mendoza 1938). As Berdan (1982:36) has pointed out, the yearly tribute tally from only one province, Tochtepec on the Gulf Coast, involved the following: "9600 decorated cloaks, 1600 women's tunics, 1 warrior's costume and shield, 1 gold shield, 1 feather standard, 1 gold diadem, 1 gold headband, 2 strings of gold beads, 3 large jades and 7 strings of jades, 40 lip plugs, 16,000 rubber balls, 80 handfuls of quetzal feathers, 4 bunches of green and yellow feathers, 24,000 little bunches of feather, 100 pots of liquid amber, and 200 loads of cacao." The annual requirement of all thirty-eight tributary provinces thus must have been staggering. Both luxury and subsistence goods were extracted as tribute. Agricultural products were collected predominantly by nearby provinces, whereas more distant parts of the empire such as Tochtepec met their annual levy with sumptuary goods (Bedoian 1973). Virtually all these goods entered Tenochtitlan before use by the imperial establishment. Tribute was also converted into other goods that were later traded abroad. In the words of Frances Berdan (1982:40):

> In one event during Ahuitzotl's reign (1486–1502), professional merchants from Tenochtitlan were given 1600 large cotton cloaks, which they took to Tlatelolco. These cloaks were then divided equally between the merchants of Tenochtitlan and Tlatelolco and traded for other goods. These goods were then carried to the Gulf and Pacific coastal trading centers, where they were exchanged for still other goods. Throughout all these exchanges, the goods always belonged to the state. This same, or similar, pattern of the use of state goods for trade probably persisted until the Spanish conquest.

Etzioni (1961) has observed that all empire-building involves three phases of development, each of which involves a different power relationship. In the first the state exerts coercive power in empire-building and the establishment of a tributary domain. Coercion, however, frequently alienates the governed, so power must be based in other terms. This is provided by remunerative power, the rewarding of constituents both materially and by according them substantial autonomy over local affairs (Collier 1982). The amount of remuneration is size and density dependent. Remunerative power is commonly differentially apportioned. First comes the imperial heartland, the regime's home constituency, then the nobility of conquered provinces, and finally the vast majority of the citizenry, the population of the empire. Normative power is the third means by which empires achieve integration. Here state ideologies are fostered,

Robert S. Santley   208

which subverts local loyalties and promotes a more cosmopolitan, transregional association with the state, particularly in the nobility. It is clear that coercive force built the Aztec empire. It is also clear that the empire used remunerative power as a basis for concreting its hold on its citizenry, a power basis that was also reflected in the structure of the transportation network.

In my opinion, the structure of the Aztec roadway network and the organization of regional economy cannot be divorced from the imperial system of which it was obviously an integral part. The heartland of the empire, Tenochtitlan and its immediate environs, was characterized by an enormous amount of trafficking in goods up and down the settlement hierarchy. This trafficking required an efficient transportation network to facilitate the movement of goods *to and from* Tenochtitlan. A dendritic system is the most efficient way of servicing a central point once bulking considerations pass critical thresholds. A dendritic structure, however, does not preclude the operation of other marketing arrangements. For example, there is evidence that rural markets were held periodically on different days of the week and that these markets were serviced by itinerant merchants who moved goods locally from one center to the next (Smith 1979). This system of solar markets appears to have had little effect on roadway structure, for the system was not designed to permit efficient transit between centers of equivalent rank. Lateral movement was possible nonetheless, but this was feasible only within a short radius of Tenochtitlan and Texcoco, the principal urban centers.

Concluding remarks

In this paper I have employed graph theory as a means of investigating aspects of Aztec regional economic organization. That analysis indicates that the roadway network was dendritically organized; that is, that it facilitated trafficking up and down the settlement hierarchy. I have also argued that the Aztec politicoeconomy exhibits many of the characteristics of a dendritic central-place system. The demonstration that system linkages were dendritically structured need not always imply the presence of a dendritic central-place economy. Ebert and Hitchcock (1980) have recently shown that the Chacoan road system also had a dendritic structure. This structure, however, does not associate with any of the properties of a dendritic central-place system. Primate cities are lacking as is any firm evidence of large-scale bulking or production for export, despite occasional claims to the contrary. I have also assumed that overland traffic was the only transport mode available to the Aztecs.

This assumption cannot be upheld, for the lakes provided an alternative mode of transit. Water-borne traffic, however, probably effectively linked sites only in that part of the lake system where *chinampa* agriculture was widespread: Lake Chalco-Xochimilco and the area around Tenochtitlan, in other words. Elsewhere lake levels would have fluctuated dramatically both annually and from season to season. In fact, during the winter months Lake Texcoco, the largest, was probably nothing more than a series of shallow, unconnected lagoons. Finally, the presence of a dendritic network does not mean that more complex economic arrangements were not in the process of developing. Indeed, the existence of multiple circuitry in the immediate vicinity of Tenochtitlan suggests a drift toward greater complexity.

References

Appel, Jill
   n.d.Obsidian Production and Distribution in Periods IIIA through V. In Monte Alban's Hinterland, Part I: The Prehispanic Settlement Patterns of the Central and Southern Parts of the Valley of Oaxaca, Mexico, edited by Richard E. Blanton. MS, Purdue University, West Lafayette

Armillas, Pedro
   1971 Gardens on Swamps. *Science* 174:653–61

Bedoian, William G.
   1973 Oro y Maiz: The Economic Structure of the Mexica Empire and its Effects on Social Stratification and Political Power. M.A. thesis, The Pennsylvania State University, University Park

Berdan, Frances F.
   1982 *The Aztecs of Central Mexico: An Imperial Society*. Holt, Rinehart and Winston, New York

Bittman, Bente, and Thelma D. Sullivan
   1978 The Pochteca. In *Mesoamerican Communication Routes and Cultural Contacts*, edited by Thomas A. Lee, Jr. and Carlos Navarrete, pp. 211–18. Papers of the New World Archaeological Foundation 40. Brigham Young University, Provo

Brumfiel, Elizabeth M.
   1980 Specialization, Market Exchange, and the Aztec State: A View from Huexotla. *Current Anthropology* 21:459–78

Calnek, Edward
   1972 Settlement Pattern and Chinampa Agriculture at Tenochtitlan. *American Antiquity* 37:104–15
   1976 The Internal Structure of Tenochtitlan. In *The Valley of Mexico: Studies in Prehispanic Ecology and Society*, edited by Eric R. Wolf, pp. 287–302. University of New Mexico Press, Albuquerque

1982 Patterns of Empire Formation in the Valley of Mexico, Late Post-Classic Period, 1200–1521. In *The Inca and Aztec States 1400–1800: Anthropology and History*, edited by George A. Collier, Renato I. Rosaldo and John D. Wirth, pp. 43–62. Academic Press, New York

Carrasco, Pedro
1978 La Economía del México prehispánico. In Economía Política e Ideología en el México prehispánico, edited by Pedro Carrasco and J. Broda, pp. 15–76. Editorial Nuevo Imagen, Mexico City
1982 The Political Economy of the Aztec and Inca States. In Collier, Rosaldo and Wirth 1982: 23–40

Chapman, Anne H.
1957 Port of Trade Enclaves in Aztec and Maya Civilizations. In *Trade and Market in Early Empires*, edited by Karl Polanyi, Conrad M. Arensberg, and Harry W. Pearson, pp. 114–50. Henry Regnery Co., Chicago

Christaller, Walter
1966 *Central Places in Southern Germany*, Prentice-Hall, Englewood Cliffs, NJ

Codex Mendoza
1938 *Codex Mendoza*, edited by James Cooper Clark. Waterlow and Sons, London

Collier, George A.
1982 In the Shadow of Empire: New Directions in Mesoamerican and Andean Ethnohistory. In Collier, Rosaldo and Wirth 1982: 1–20

Collier, George A., Renato I. Rosaldo, and John D. Wirth (eds.)
1982 *The Inca and Aztec States 1400–1800: Anthropology and History*. Academic Press, New York

Davies, Nigel
1973 *The Aztecs: A History*. Putnam, New York

Ebert, James I. and Robert K. Hitchcock
1980 Locational Modeling in the Analysis of the Prehistoric Roadway System at and around Chaco Canyon, New Mexico. In *Cultural Resources Remote Sensing*, edited by Thomas R. Lyons and Frances Joan Mathien, pp. 169–207. National Park Service, Washington, DC

Etzioni, Amatai
1961 *A Comparative Analysis of Complex Organizations: On Power, Involvement, and Their Correlates*. The Free Press, New York

Evans, Susan T.
1980 Spatial Analysis of Basin of Mexico Settlement: Problems with the Use of the Central Place Model. *American Antiquity* 45:866–75

Gibson, Charles
1964 *The Aztecs Under Spanish Rule: A History of the Indians of the Valley of Mexico, 1519–1810*. Stanford University Press, Stanford
1971 Structure of the Aztec Empire. In *Handbook of Middle American Indians*, Vol. X, pp. 376–94. University of Texas Press, Austin

Gonzalez A., Luis
1973 *Plano reconstructivo de la región de Tenochtitlán*. Instituto Nacional de Antropología e Historia, Mexico

Healan, Dan M., Janet M. Kerley and George G. Bey, III
1983 Excavation and Preliminary Analysis of an Obsidian Workshop in Tula, Hidalgo, Mexico. *Journal of Field Archaeology* 10:127–45

James, G. A., A. D. Cliff, P. Haggett, and J. K. Ord
1970 Some Discrete Distributions for Graphs with Applications to Regional Transport Networks. *Geografiska Annaler* 52:14–21

Johnson, E. A. J.
1970 *The Organization of Space in Developing Countries*. Harvard University Press, Cambridge, MA

Kansky, S. J.
1963 *Structure of Transport Networks: Relationship Between Network Geometry and Regional Characteristics*. Research Paper 84. Department of Geography, University of Chicago, Chicago

Kelley, Klara B.
1976 Dendritic Central Place Systems and the Regional Organization of Navaho Trading Posts. In *Regional Analysis, Vol. I, Economic Systems*, edited by Carol A. Smith. Academic Press, New York

Lloyd, Peter, and Peter Dicken
1972 *Location in Space: A Theoretical Approach to Economic Geography*. Harper and Row, New York

Ord, J. K.
1967 On a System of Discrete Distributions. *Biometrika* 54:649–56

Parsons, Jeffrey R.
1976 The Role of Chinampa Agriculture in the Food Supply of Aztec Tenochtitlan. In *Cultural Change and Continuity*, edited by Charles Cleland, pp. 233–57. Academic Press, New York

Parsons, Jeffrey R., Elizabeth Brumfiel, Mary H. Parsons, and David J. Wilson
1982 *Prehispanic Settlement Patterns in the Southern Valley of Mexico: The Chalco-Xochimilco Region*. Memoir 14, Museum of Anthropology, University of Michigan, Ann Arbor

Rees, Peter W.
1975 Origins of Colonial Transportation in Mexico. *Geographical Review* 65:323–34

Sanders, William T.
1965 *The Cultural Ecology of the Teotihuacan Valley.* Department of Sociology and Anthropology, The Pennsylvania State University, University Park
1977 Ethnographic Analogy and the Teotihuacan Horizon Style. In *Teotihuacan and Kaminaljuyu: A Study in Prehistoric Culture Contact*, edited by William T. Sanders and Joseph W. Michels. The Pennsylvania State University Press, University Park
Sanders, William T., Jeffrey R. Parsons, and Robert S. Santley
1979 *The Basin of Mexico: Ecological Processes in the Evolution of a Civilization.* Academic Press, New York
Sanders, William T. and Robert S. Santley
1983 A Tale of Three Cities: Energetics and Urbanization in Prehispanic Central Mexico. In *Prehistoric Settlement Patterns*, edited by Evon Vogt and Richard Leventhal, pp. 243–91. University of New Mexico Press, Albuquerque, in press
Santley, Robert S.
n.d.a. The Politico-Economic Organization of Ancient Teotihuacan. In *New Models of the Political Economy of Pre-Columbian Polities*, edited by Patricia Netherly and David Freidel. In preparation
n.d.b. Final Field Report, Matacapan project: 1982 season. Report to the National Science Foundation, in preparation
Smith, Carol A.
1976 Regional Economic Systems: Linking Geographical Models and Socioeconomic Problems. In *Regional Analysis, Vol. I, Economic Systems*, edited by Carol A. Smith. Academic Press, New York
Smith, Michael E.
1979 The Aztec Marketing System and Settlement Pattern in the Valley of Mexico: A Central Place Analysis. *American Antiquity* 44:110–25
Spence, Michael W.
1981 Obsidian Production and the State in Teotihuacan. *American Antiquity* 46:769–88
Taylor, Peter J.
1977 *Quantitative Methods in Geography: An Introduction to Spatial Analysis.* Houghton Mifflin, Boston
Vance, James E.
1970 *The Merchant's World.* Prentice-Hall, Englewood Cliffs, NJ

17 Roads, thoroughfares, and avenues of power at Xochicalco, Mexico

KENNETH HIRTH

Introduction

The study of transportation networks is important because it provides insight into the structural organization of populations across space. Roads provide visible linkages between communities, supplying clues about the social, political, and economic interaction between groups. The scale of transportation architecture also functions as a symbol of power and prestige for both the central government and its ruling elite. Although all of these topics are of interest to archaeologists working in Mesoamerica, few in-depth studies have been conducted which discuss the role and importance of transportation networks in the development of precolumbian civilizations.

The reason for this is quite simple. Roads did not have as important an economic role in Mesoamerica as they did in many other parts of the world. All goods were transported by human porters, who do not require well-constructed roads to move products. Without wheeled vehicles and pack animals there were few economies of scale to warrant the construction of rapid transportation networks. Similarly, roads did not figure prominently in the formation and control of military empires as they did among the Romans and the Inka.

I am not implying that interregional communication was unimportant for the development of Mesoamerican society. The available data on both economic and information systems show that areas widely removed in space were part of a mutually interacting exchange network (Flannery 1968; Parsons and Price 1971; Hirth 1984a; Sharp 1978). Interregional communication, however, was not dependent upon the construction and maintenance of large-scale road systems. Prehispanic transportation routes frequently escape detection because they lack architectural characteristics which can be identified using archaeological methods. Although regional roads have been reported and studied throughout the Maya region (Villa Rojas 1934; Garza Tarazona de Gonzalez and Kurjack 1980; Kurjack and Andrews 1976) and in Northern Mexico (Kelley 1971; Trombold 1976), few corollary networks have been reported from any of Mesoamerica's major highland regions. In Central Mexico the earliest evidence for regional roads comes from Teotihuacan where intensive mapping and reconnaissance work suggest that the city's main streets were part of a regional transportation network which extended out into the surrounding countryside (Millon 1973; Sanders 1965:121; Charlton, this volume). Most other references to Central Mexican transportation systems are based on ethnohistoric documentation (Ball and Brockington 1978; Feldman 1978; Santley, this volume).

It was therefore exciting to find that intensive surface reconnaissance in 1978 around the large urban center of Xochicalco (Fig. 17.1) confirmed the presence of an Epiclassic road system in western Morelos (Hirth 1982). This research was conducted as part of the Xochicalco Mapping Project which was interested in collecting information on the growth and development of the site's urban configuration and to investigate its relationship with Teotihuacan after A.D. 650.[1] Stone-surfaced pavements were identified which run throughout the site and extend into the surrounding countryside. These pavements appear to have been part of a regional communication network connected with Xochicalco's role as a prominent social, religious, and political center in western Morelos.

This paper has two objectives. First, it will describe and date the Xochicalco road system. Since data on preconquest communication networks are difficult to obtain in Central Mexico it is important to document the form and organization of Xochicalco's transportation architecture. Secondly it will discuss the role and significance of transportation architecture in the organization of Epiclassic society. These interpretations do not include a structural analysis of site linkages with Xochicalco since the data are too fragmentary to define precisely the size and extent of the road system.

The character of Mesoamerican roads

Throughout history the importance of land and water transportation routes has been proportional to the need for rapid communication between groups and the interregional shipment of large quantities of bulk commodities. Reliance on human porters as the primary means of transportation throughout Mesoamerica limited the ability to transport bulky commodities over long distances. As a result, staple commodities such as corn and beans rarely moved beyond a 200 km radius of where they were produced even during the Late Horizon when transportation costs could be deferred as part of a broad-based tribute system (Drennan 1984a, 1984b).

Fray Bernardino de Sahagun (1963:266–9) provides an interesting classification of precolumbian roads in Volume XI of the Florentine Codex. Sahagun identifies seven types of roads, two of which, the main road (Ochpantli) and the Oquetzalli or royal road, are of interest here.[2] The Ochpantli is identified as the main transportation artery and is equated by Sahagun with paved Spanish highways. Despite their important transportation functions his description indicates that main roads were poorly constructed and never well maintained. In describing main roads he says, "It is clean, smooth, slick; very stony, full of holes. It is full of holes. It is pitted. It has gullies, a gorge, crags, rough. It becomes rough" (Sahagun 1963:266) and "It is a hardened place, a rocky road, choked with trees, full of stones; an old road, an old main road; a new road, a new main road" (Sahagun 1963:267).

Sahagun is suggesting that main roads in central Mexico were not things of beauty. Rather, they were simply communication routes between places and degeneration of the road by erosion or use did not impede travel by human porters. From an archaeological perspective main roads of this sort, no matter how well traveled, would not leave traces readily detectable using available techniques.

Sahagun's description, however, of the Oquetzalli or royal road is categorically different. He describes this road as follows: "It means the new road. It is clean, a cleaned place, very smooth. It is smoothed, decorated, arrayed, new, a road which is the privilege of the rulers. It is preciously good, a preciously good place, completely clean, made good, smoothed. Nothing lies cast away" (Sahagun 1963:268).

This type of road is described as something special. Unfortunately, Sahagun does not elaborate on whether it was limited in size or only located in special areas. It is, however, the only road which he describes as being specially prepared and is the one most likely to be identified using archaeological techniques. From his description one might assume that if any road was to have been paved with stones or surfaced with lime plaster it would have been the Oquetzalli. What is interesting about Sahagun's account is that good roads are associated with the rights and privileges of the political elite. It is

Fig. 17.1. Location of Xochicalco in Mesoamerica (inset). Regional roads in the area surrounding Xochicalco.

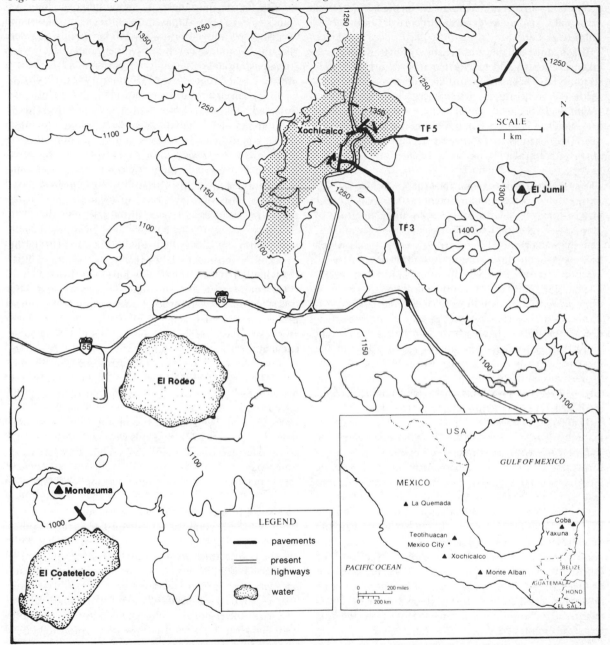

possible that roads were only maintained through state sponsorship and were so rare in central Mexico that they were automatically associated with rulers as symbols of political power.

When thinking about Mesoamerican transportation networks we should also remember that there never seems to have been a need for all-weather roads intended for heavy use throughout the entire year. Interregional communication was somewhat seasonal throughout Mesoamerica with both military and mercantile expeditions frequently planned for the fall and winter months after agricultural activities were finished.

The early reports of regional roads at Xochicalco

References to roads and pavements at Xochicalco occur in two forms: 1. in the early exploration literature of traveling eighteenth- and nineteenth-century naturalists, and 2. in a series of literary travelogs or novels which became popular during the later half of the nineteenth century. These accounts often contain much useful information because many of the colonial roads in central Mexico followed established prehispanic transportation routes (Rees 1975). Travelers paid close attention to the routes they used during the eighteenth and nineteenth centuries so as not to get lost and, in the process, occasionally mention vestiges of ancient roads. While many of these references are less specific than one might like, they nevertheless provide valuable clues to reconstructing the extent of regional roadways.

The earliest reference to pavements at Xochicalco is made by Alzate y Ramirez (1791) who first visited the site in 1777. Alzate was impressed by the site's military fortifications and internal organization. Although he incorrectly characterized the site as a spiraling ramp (1791:10), he cogently observed the use of ramps as a means for structuring population movement within the site. He alludes to the presence of regional roads when he says "restan algunos vestigios de quatro Calzadas, que por los quatro vientos principales se dirigían al Castillo o fábrica de Xochicalco" (1791:23). Since he does not include distance measures we cannot be sure whether he is discussing streets within the site as the term *calzada* might suggest or roads entering the site from the surrounding countryside.

Guillaume Dupaix was the first visitor to mention a specific pavement in the site. His statement, "se sube a la plaza en la que se halla el Monumento por una antiqua calzada con bastante declive" (1834:222), is possibly a reference to the main southern thoroughfare (TF–1) which was also cited by Manuel Gama (1897).

Confirmation of regional roads comes from two closely spaced but independent visits by Charles Latrobe in 1834 and Renato de Pedreauville in 1835 who took routes to the site different from their predecessors. Instead of traveling southwest from Cuernavaca through Tetlama, both took a more southerly and circuitous route passing near Xochitepec. Latrobe first reports the presence of a road east of the Arroyo de los Sabinos when he states, "For many miles previously we had observed and repeatedly crossed an ancient paved causeway, about eight feet in breadth composed of large stones tightly wedged together, and running directly over plain and barranca towards the hill of Xochicalco" (1836:184). Upon reaching the site he also mentions pavements leading to the Pyramid of the Plumed Serpent from four different directions but gives the impression that these are internal aspects of the site.

Latrobe's road (Thoroughfare TF–5) was noted again in the following year by Pedreauville (1835) as part of the Mexican government's first official site visitation. Pedreauville apparently traced this pavement from Xochicalco out into the surrounding countryside. He described the pavement as "una calzada de piedras planas, que comenzaba en el monte, se estendía a muchas leguas acia la dirección del Este, y todavía se encuentran algunas partes muy bien conservadas sobre las faldas mas escarpadas de los cerros que atraviesan el país" (Pedreauville 1835:548). Shortly thereafter, Brantz Mayer (1844:187) visited the site and reported an ancient paved road leading north from the site toward Cuernavaca. Edward Tylor visited the site in a later visit and noted that, "on neighboring hills we could discern traces of more terrace-roads" (1861:184). While his reference is somewhat unclear I believe he is referring to terraces rather than pavements ascending the slopes of hills.

The Xochicalco transportation architecture

In 1978 the Mapping Project confirmed earlier reports that roads and paved streets were part of Xochicalco's overall architectural design.[3] In studying the site's transportation architecture it is useful to differentiate between regional and site-level phenomena. The term "road" will be used specifically to refer to transportation arteries at the regional level which connect two or more spatially separated sites. I use the term "thoroughfare" to refer to streets and other communication corridors which organize space and/or direct traffic flow within the community. The regional sacbes of the Maya and the transportation systems associated with La Quemada represent our best-documented examples of early roadways in Mesoamerica (Folan 1977; Villa Rojas 1934; Trombold 1976). Street-thoroughfares are much more

Fig. 17.2. The location of Epiclassic roads and thoroughfares at Xochicalco, Morelos, Mexico.

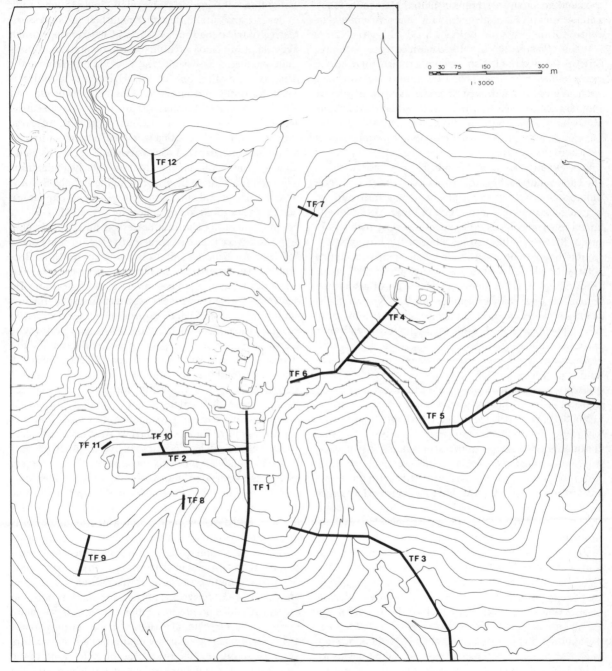

common and are found at a number of large sites north of the Maya area including Teotihuacan (Drewitt 1967), Monte Alban (Blanton 1978), and Tenochtitlan (Marquina 1964; Lombardo de Ruiz 1973). The Xochicalco transportation network fulfilled both of these functions.

Thus far twelve major and minor thoroughfares have been located at Xochicalco (Fig. 17.2). These thoroughfares vary between 3 and 5 m in width and are paved with a mosaic of rough-cut stones ranging between 25 and 50 cm in diameter. The sides of the pavements were edged with cut-stone masonry blocks although most of these have been removed and recycled into later construction at the site. The pavement surfaces do not appear to have been stuccoed except on their flanking masonry edging. Pavements are flush with the surfaces they traverse although ramps were occasionally constructed on slopes to even out abrupt inclines. In some cases step-like stone abutments interrupt the smooth ascents of these ramps. The ramps facilitated vertical movement within the site, beautified plaza-temple groups, and minimized the effects of erosion on pavements over sharply sloping surfaces. Several of the pavements were flanked or enclosed by lateral masonry walls which certainly helped channel population movement throughout the site.

Entrance points into the site were guarded by large flanking mounds. In one instance we know where a small bridge, presumably of wood, was built along thoroughfare TF–5 to span a defensive moat on Cerro de la Bodega. At least three of these thoroughfares (TF–1, TF–3, TF–5) extended beyond the limits of the site, continuing as roads into the surrounding countryside (Fig. 17.1). Outside of the site roads averaged between 2 and 3 m wide and were surfaced with a rough, uncut mosaic of flat stone without lateral edging.[4] The surface of these roads was generally flush with the ground although elevated ramps were constructed where inclines and irregular terrain were crossed.

Two of the most important thoroughfares on Cerro Xochicalco were TF–1 and TF–2. These pavements provided the major baselines used in orientating adjacent civic and residential architecture (Hardoy 1973:98). Thoroughfare TF–1 appears to have been one of the main accessways onto Cerro Xochicalco. At the base of the South Hill, TF–1 passes between large flanking platform mounds and through a narrow walled enclosure which acted as a gateway controling access to the site.[5] Thoroughfare TF–2 provided access to such important structures as the Malinche Pyramid and the West Ballcourt. Perhaps the most interesting aspect of TF–2 is that it was not constructed as a continuous pavement but

was interrupted like a stairway by three vertical risers about 2 m in height.

Several other important thoroughfares are located on Cerro Xochicalco. Thoroughfare TF–9 is located on the West Hill and may have linked the main body of residents on Cerro Xochicalco with the hilltop precincts of Temascal, La Silla, and El Limón. Access to Xochicalco from the north was more problematical. Thoroughfare TF–12 traverses the area between the La Maqueta mound group and the base of the North Hill. Access to the top of Cerro Xochicalco would have been possible by following the artificial defensive ditch (DF–9) which climbs the hill in a southeasterly direction. Thoroughfare TF–3 is located on the South Hill and descends the hillside in a southeasterly direction where it leaves the site and continues into the surrounding countryside. It is the best-preserved and longest continuously traceable pavement in the region and can be followed for roughly 2.5 km before it disappears under modern construction.

Several pavements (TF–4, TF–5, and TF–7) were also found on Cerro de la Bodega. The longest of these is thoroughfare TF–5 which crosses the eastern defensive moat between Cerro de la Bodega before continuing to Cerro Xochicalco's upper ceremonial zone. TF–5 descends the east side of Cerro de la Bodega and continues as a road into the fields below. Segments of TF–5 were traced more than 3 km to the east where it crosses the Arroyo de los Sabinos before becoming lost in the fields west of Acatlipa.

Thoroughfare TF–4 ascends the southwestern flank of Cerro de la Bodega, reaching the ceremonial precinct located on its summit. This thoroughfare was enclosed by two tall lateral walls and, although only 240 m long, was one of the best-constructed pavements at the site. Thoroughfare TF–7 is a short, interesting pavement located on the north slope of the hill. It ends abruptly after about 50 m and gives the impression of never having been completed since it does not provide access to any architectural constructions on the hillside.

Latrobe's mention of a road east of the Sabino river and Tylor's reference to stone ramps on the hillsides around Xochicalco are interesting because they suggest the presence of regional roads at an early date. While Tylor was probably referring to the stone-lined terraces of Cerro Jumil, it is important to note that stone-paved ramps similar to those of Xochicalco have been found at several contemporary sites in the region. A stone-faced ramp was discovered by Raul Arana at Cerro Montezuma, 7 km south of Xochicalco (Fig. 17.1). This ramp is well built and links the hilltop residential and elite zones with the lake below. A similar ramp has been reported but not mapped on the hillslope above the town of Cuauchichinola, 18 km south of Xochicalco. I believe these ramps were part of a regional communication network which connected outlying sites to Xochicalco.

The preponderance of data indicates that all of Xochicalco's roads and thoroughfares were constructed during the Epiclassic period (A.D. 650–900) when the site reached its maximum size and influence (Hirth 1984b). These dates are derived primarily from excavations in structures located alongside major thoroughfares. In two instances it is the thoroughfare which provides the orientation for constructing adjacent monuments. Pavements TF–1 and TF–2 were used to establish the orientation of ceremonial buildings on the South and West Hills and must be contemporaneous with the construction of the architectural precinct. Numerous structures have been excavated along both these thoroughfares (Noguera 1945, 1946; Saenz 1962, 1964) which together with systematic mapping and dating of the residential terraces indicate that the Xochicalco pavements were part of a well-integrated site plan designed and built during the early part of the Epiclassic period.

Discussion

Xochicalco's roads and thoroughfares illustrate a number of important characteristics of Epiclassic transportation design. When discussing the function and meaning of Xochicalco's transportation architecture it is important to distinguish between its role at the level of the site and how it may have functioned with respect to the surrounding region. Intrasite pavements at Xochicalco were used to help structure the use of architectural space, facilitate and direct population movement within the site, and emphasize and beautify approachways to important temple precincts. Roads on the other hand fulfilled regional transportation needs and symbolized the power of the central state.

Careful planning went into organizing the site's 2 km^2 central core which sought to fit a conventional symmetrical site plan to the irregular hillside topography. The only way to achieve this was by organizing the site as a series of ascending concentric arcs which connected to form different levels within the site much like a large layer cake. The major problem with this design was that it disarticulated adjacent components of the site located at different elevations on the hillside. A network of ramps and pavements provided a solution and brought vertically separated portions of the site closer together.

The concentric plan had to be modified to construct the site's central administrative and ceremonial precinct at the top of the hill. Long-standing architectural canons in Central Mexico required that important buildings be laid out along orthogonal axes. The site's irregular topography required a compromise which resulted in the use of partial axis arrangements which provided the symmetrical orientations for major buildings. Mounds were arranged in large orthogonal plaza groups only on areas of naturally gentle slope or where the bedrock could be mined and/or artificially leveled. Residential and civic monuments outside of this district conform to terrace orientations or topographic irregularities rather than any master grid plan.

A basic function of Xochicalco's thoroughfares clearly was to direct and facilitate the movement of population within the site. It is significant, therefore, that several of the site's major thoroughfares appear to converge and meet at an architectural compound on the South Hill known as the Plaza Central. This compound is important because it contains Structure E, the largest single platform mound constructed on Cerro Xochicalco. Pavements TF–2 and TF–3 intersect with thoroughfare TF–1 and enter the south end of the Plaza Central while TF–5 appears to have entered the plaza on its northeastern side.

Ease of access into the Plaza Central distinguishes it in an important way from the architectural compound known as the Plaza Ceremonial. This compound is located on the upper acropolis of the North Hill and was removed from easy communication with other portions of the site. The Plaza Ceremonial was a walled precinct which, together with its isolated location, suggests that it was an elite precinct not accessible, or at least symbolically removed, from the general population. This contrasts with the Plaza Central which was generally accessible to the entire population. The location of Structure E at the terminus of roads leading into the site suggests that the temple and its associated ceremonies were the focus of civic and religious life throughout the surrounding countryside.

Xochicalco has long been recognized as a fortified urban center (Armillas 1951) and its thoroughfares were integrated into the site's military defenses. Accessways were the weak links in Xochicalco's defensive perimeter and were bolstered correspondingly by the construction of gates, platforms, ditches, and ramparts. Entranceways into the site from the surrounding countryside were protected by flanking platforms which would have exposed the unshielded sides of intruders to projectile fire in the same way that bent-angle city entrances did in the Old World. Recent excavations by the Instituto Nacional de Antropología e Historia[6] have revealed that the passage between the flanking mounds along TF–1 was constricted by two masonry walls leaving an entranceway into the site less than 2 m in width which could easily have been blocked in times of defense.

Major thoroughfares frequently cut through the major terraces they cross rather than rising to the level of their down-slope edges. The reason for this appears to have been twofold. First, it exposed the unshielded sides of the attackers to defenders on the terraces in the same way as did flanking platforms. Secondly, the thoroughfares helped subdivide the concentric site plan into a series of horizontally distinct and non-communicating sections. Walls were constructed along both sides of TF–1 and TF–4 as a means of further restricting horizontal movement throughout the community which, in the case of the TF–4, also appears to have formed part of the precinct defenses on Cerro de la Bodega. Subdivision of the site into distinct horizontal components was not restricted to the construction of thoroughfares, but was also achieved by digging steep-sided trenches into the bedrock. It is possible that site compartmentalization was a means of emphasizing social boundaries within the site as much as it was for dividing it into mutually exclusive defensive precincts.

The presence of three roads leading to Xochicalco indicates that the site occupied a central role in regional socioeconomic, political and religious interaction. Six km of flat stone pavement have been traced out from the site thus far. Contemporaneous sites with similar stone-faced ramps and pavements are reported both from Cerro Montezuma and Cuauchichinola which may have been linked in a regional communication network similar to those reported for La Quemada and Coba (Trombold 1976; Villa Rojas 1934).

Future field reconnaissance is needed to clarify several aspects of the Xochicalco road network. First, we need to define the limits of the network and determine which communities were linked directly to it by means of roads. We also need to clarify whether this network was designed specifically for transportation purposes and to facilitate population movement or whether it was more important as a symbol of state power and prestige. Maya roads, for example, apparently had broader political or symbolic purposes which may have been more important than transportation functions. For instance, while the Coba causeways connect major centers in eastern Yucatan, few village or ceremonial sites are found at intermediate points even in optimal resource zones which would have attracted human habitation (Folan 1977). Conversely, the Xochicalco system and road TF–5 apparently bypassed the important contempo-

raneous center of El Jumil without providing a visible link with Xochicalco.

From an architectural viewpoint, the regional roads at Xochicalco more closely resemble Sahagun's description of *Oquetzalli* roads than they do the *Ochpantli* which were used primarily for transportation purposes. Although I am not suggesting that these were elite or royal roads in the sense that Sahagun uses the term, they certainly entailed more effort to construct than was required for meeting the transportation needs of the Xochicalco polity. I believe these road systems were constructed to demonstrate the prestige of the ruling elite and were a regional symbol of the site's political and religious importance. The distribution of fortified precincts around Xochicalco suggests that the central state was supported by a league or confederation of regional elites (Hirth 1984b, 1985). If this is substantiated by future work, the extent of the transportation network may provide clues to the size and number of participating regional centers.

The size of the road system provides a direct measure of Xochicalco's political power and indicates the presence of a centralized political unit capable of organizing large-scale public construction. Construction of this system required the mobilization of large quantities of resources which would have required the participation of communities throughout its surrounding hinterland. The Xochicalco elite did not lose an opportunity to underscore their importance and constructed many important monuments in areas where people would be entering the site along regional roads. For instance, most of the small basal platforms used to erect stelae are located in plaza areas traversed or intersected by roads entering the site from the surrounding countryside.

Conclusions

Information on prehistoric transportation networks in Central Mexico prior to Spanish contact is scarce. This study has documented and examined the evidence for transportation architecture found around the large Epiclassic site of Xochicalco. Transportation architecture helped structure the organization of architectural space within the site and at the regional level provided visible linkages between Xochicalco and its surrounding hinterland. Perhaps the most significant aspect of Xochicalco's regional roads is that they provide evidence for the emergence of centralized state authority at a time when political fragmentation was characteristic of the eclipse of Teotihuacan as the dominant political power in Central Mexico.

As a recommendation for future fieldwork we should

remember that prehispanic roads normally did not require special construction simply to achieve interregional transportation functions. This means that many major precolumbian transportation networks will escape detection using most archaeological techniques presently at our disposal. When roads have been identified in Mesoamerica it has been because they were either constructed on elevated roadbeds or surfaced with paving stones which have withstood the ravages of time. We should remember that roads of this sort may have been special-purpose structures meant to symbolize the power and prestige of the ruling political or religious elite. While they still were used as transportation arteries they do not reflect an accurate picture of the *entire* transportation network. This limits the utility of approaches such as graph theory in studying prehistoric road systems until archaeologists are capable of evaluating what the transportation network actually reflects.

Notes

1. For a discussion of Xochicalco's role in Central Mexican prehistory see Hirth (1984b), Porter Weaver (1981:227–31) and Litvak King (1970).
2. The seven types of roads are the main road (*Ochpantli*), trail, short cut, secret road, footpath, *Oquetzalli* and the old road (Sahagun 1963:266–9).
3. Between 1965 and 1966 field exercises by the Escuela Nacional de Antropología e Historia were carried out at Xochicalco to define the site's internal settlement pattern and to develop a regional research design for studying Xochicalco. Reconnaissance and controled surface collections were used to develop measures of site similarity and interaction. A preliminary study of regional communication networks was carried out which confirmed that traces of regional roads could still be identified in the Xochicalco region (Gonzalez Crespo and Garza Tarazona 1966). Unfortunately this study was never published and neither the authors of the report nor the coordinator of the seminar retained a copy of the report.
4. The width and composition of these stone-surfaced roads corresponds well to the description provided by Latrobe for a road presumably extending in a northeasterly direction toward Cuernavaca.
5. Thoroughfare FT–1 very probably extended south as a road beyond the limits of Xochicalco. I believe that this road followed the same path as the modern road leading to the site which passes very close to where TF–1 can be detected at the base of the South Hill. It is possible that all traces of this road were destroyed

early in the twentieth century when Batres first constructed a road leading to Cerro Xochicalco.
6. Excavations along TF–1 were conducted in 1984 under the joint direction of Norberto Gonzalez Crespo and Silvia Garza Tarazona.

References

Alzate y Ramirez, Joseph Antonio
1971 *Descripción de las antigüedades de Xochicalco dedicada a los señores de la actual expedición marítima alrededor del orbe*. Suplemento a la Gazeta de Literatura, Mexico City

Armillas, Pedro
1951 Mesoamerican Fortifications. *Antiquity* 25(8):77–86

Ball, Hugh, and D. Brockington
1978 Trade and Travel in Prehispanic Oaxaca. In *Mesoamerican Communication Routes and Cultural Contacts*, edited by T. Lee and C. Navarrete, pp. 107–14. Papers of the New World Archaeological Foundation 40, Provo, UT

Blanton, Richard
1978 *Monte Alban: Settlement Patterns at an Ancient Zapotec Capital*. Academic Press, New York

Drennan, Robert D.
1984a Long Distance Movement of Goods in the Mesoamerican Formative and Classic. *American Antiquity* 49:27–43
1984b Long-Distance Transport Costs in Pre-Hispanic Mesoamerica. *American Anthropologist* 86:105–12

Drewitt, Bruce
1967 Planación en la antigua ciudad de Teotihuacán. In *Teotihuacán. XI Mesa Redonda*, Vol. I, pp. 79–94. Sociedad Mexicana de Antropología, Mexico

Dupaix, Guillaume
1834 *Antiquités mexicaines. Relation de trois expéditions du Capitaine Dupaix, ordonnées en 1805, 1806, et 1807, pour la recherche des antiquités du pays*. Bureau des Antiquités Mexicaines, Paris

Feldman, Lawrence
1978 Timed Travels in Tarascan Territory: Friar Alonso Ponce in the Old Tarascan Domains 1586–1587. In *Mesoamerican Communication Routes and Cultural Contacts*, edited by T. Lee and C. Navarrete, pp. 123–6. Papers of the New World Archaeological Foundation 40, Provo, UT

Flannery, Kent
1968 The Olmec and the Valley of Oaxaca: A Model for Interregional Interaction in Formative Times. In *Dumbarton Oaks Conference on the Olmec*, edited by

E. Benson, pp. 119–30. Dumbarton Oaks Research Library and Collection, Washington, DC

Folan, William
1977 El sacbe Cobá–Ixíl, un camino Maya del pasado. *Nueva Antropología* 6:31–42

Gama, Manuel
1897 Un monumento prehistórico. *Proceedings of the 11th International Congress of Americanists*, pp. 528–32. Mexico City

Garza Tarazona de Gonzalez, Silvia, and Edward Kurjack
1980 *Atlas arqueológico del estado de Yucatán*. Instituto Nacional de Antropología e Historia, Mexico

Gonzalez Crespo, Norberto, and Silvia Garza Tarazona
1966 Comunicaciones y accesos de Xochicalco. Escuela Nacional de Antropología e Historia, Mexico City, MS

Hardoy, Jorge
1973 *Pre-Columbian Cities*. Walker, New York

Hirth, Kenneth G.
1982 Transportation Architecture at Xochicalco, Morelos, Mexico. *Current Anthropology* 23:322–4
1984a *Trade and Exchange in Early Mesoamerica*. University of New Mexico Press, Albuquerque
1984b Xochicalco: Urban Growth and State Formation in Central Mexico. *Science* 225:579–86

Kelley, J. Charles
1971 Archaeology of the Northern Frontier: Zacatecas and Durango. In *Handbook of Middle American Indians*, Vol. XI, edited by G. Ekholm and I. Bernal, pp. 768–801. University of Texas Press, Austin

Kurjack, Edward, and E. Wyllys Andrews, V.
1976 Early Boundary Maintenance in Northwest Yucatan, Mexico. *American Antiquity* 41:318–25

Latrobe, Charles
1836 *The Rambler in Mexico, 1934*. Harper and Brothers, New York

Litvak King, Jaime
1970 Xochicalco en la caída del clásico: una hipótesis. *Anales de Antropología* 7:131–44. Universidad Nacional Antónoma de México, Mexico

Lombardo de Ruiz, Sonia
1973 *Desarrollo urbano de México-Tenochtitlán*. Instituto Nacional de Antropología e Historia, Mexico

Marquina, Ignacio
1964 *Arquitectura prehispánica*. Instituto Nacional de Antropología e Historia, Mexico

Mayer, Brantz
1844 *Mexico As It Was and As It Is*. New World Press, New York

Millon, René
1973 *Urbanization at Teotihuacan, Mexico: The Teotihuacan Map*, Vol. I, part 1. University of Texas Press, Austin

Noguera, Eduardo
1945 Exploraciones en Xochicalco. *Cuadernos Americanos* 19:119–57
1946 Cultura de Xochicalco. In *México Prehispánico* pp. 185–93. Anthology from *Esta Semana (This Week)*, 1935–46, edited by J. Vivo. Editorial Emma Hurtado, Mexico

Parsons, Lee, and Barbara Price
1971 Mesoamerican Trade and Its Role in the Emergence of Civilization. In *Observations on the Emergence of Civilization in Mesoamerica*, edited by R. Heizer and J. Graham, pp. 169–95. Contributions of the University of California Archaeological Research Facility 11

Pedreauville, Renato de
1835 Viaje a las antigüedades de Xochicalco de orden del gobierno supremo de México, en marzo de 1835. *Revista Mexicana, Periódico Científico y Literario* 1(5):539–50. Mexico

Porter Weaver, Muriel
1981 *The Aztecs, Maya and Their Predecessors*. Academic Press, New York

Rees, Peter
1975 Origins of Colonial Transportation in Mexico. *The Geographical Review* 65:323–34

Saenz, Cesar
1962 *Xochicalco, temporada 1960. Informes* 11, Departamento de Monumentos Prehispánicos, Instituto Nacional de Antropología e Historia, Mexico

Sahagun, Fray Bernardino de
1963 *Florentine Codex. General History of the Things of New Spain. Book 11, Earthly Things*, translated by C. Dibble and A. Anderson. School of American Research and the University of Utah, Sante Fe

Sanders, William
1965 *The Cultural Ecology of the Teotihuacan Valley*. Department of Anthropology, Pennsylvania State University, University Park

Sharp, Rosemary
1978 Architecture as Interelite Communication in Preconquest Oaxaca, Veracruz, and Yucatan. In *Middle Classic Mesoamerica: A.D. 400–700*, edited by E. Pasztory, pp. 158–71. Columbia University Press, New York

Trombold, Charles
1976 Spatial Distribution, Functional Hierarchies and Patterns of Interaction in Prehistoric Communities

around La Quemada, Zacatecas, Mexico. In *Archaeological Frontiers: Papers on New World High Cultures in Honor of J. Charles Kelley*, edited by R. B. Pickering, pp. 149–82. Southern Illinois University Museum, Carbondale

Tylor, Edward Barnett
1861 *Anahuac: Mexico and the Mexicans, Ancient and Modern*. Longman, Green, Longman and Roberts, London
Villa Rojas, Alfonso
1934 The Yaxuna–Coba Causeway. *Carnegie Institution of Washington* 9(2):187–208

18 Sacbes of the northern Maya

WILLIAM J. FOLAN

During the full course of their existence, the Maya of southern Mesoamerica have had need of one type of communication network or another. For reasons of analysis and understanding, this network can be divided into real and mythological routes developed by the Maya to cross and circumnavigate their homeland and its surrounding territories. The real can be further classified into dry and wet routes. Additionally, mythological routes can be separated into both celestial and subterranean features.

Among the real routes developed by the Maya are the surface-level sacbes or roadways (Fig. 18.1). These linear features, ranging in width from 3 to over 20 m, measure from only a few meters up to 99 km in length (Fig. 18.2). They are generally composed of rock-filled roadbeds (i.e., Fig. 18.3) in places such as Coba, Quintana Roo, of packed earth in Calakmul, Campeche (Folan: personal observation), or of tamped earth and oyster shell as in the Rio San Pedro and San Pablo regions of Tabasco (Vargas 1985:102). Stone sacbes are often paved with liberal quantities of lime or *sascab* extended and pounded into place on top of a gravel layer that serves to prepare the larger-stone sacbe fill for surfacing. They are usually raised slightly higher in the middle than at the sides.

One of the commonest features associated with sacbes in Coba is a narrow line of plain, rectangular stones running down the center. Some sacbes have another feature, narrow culverts that facilitate the passage of water from one side to the other. Altars also appear on sacbes from time to time, as do vaulted arches. But the most visible and frequent feature of the Coba sacbe system are the ramps associated with both intra- and inter-urban sacbes. These are of four principal types. 1.

Ramps associated with architecture may have had an administrative function (Fig. 18.4) and are frequently referred to as customs check points around such places as Coba (Folan and Stuart 1974; Folan 1977; Folan *et al.* 1983). 2. There also exist a few huge ramps without additional architectural associations (Fig. 18.5) that are difficult to classify. These are found exclusively at or near the terminal points of various sacbes such as the ones linking Coba and Ixil (Murphy 1968; Folan and Stuart 1974; Folan 1977, Folan *et al.* 1983) and between Coba and Yaxuna (Villa Rojas 1934). 3. Ramps designed to pass over high points along their route or occasionally to provide access to the edge of sinkholes or water. 4. A ramp situated on Sacbe 3 between the junction of Sacbe 1 and the San Pedro terminus in Coba may have had a ceremonial function (Fig. 18.6). Another having prob-

able ceremonial use is a four-way ramp (Fig. 18.7) located at the junction of Sacbe 1 and Sacbe 3 in Coba (Thompson *et al.* 1932). Although its purpose is not thoroughly understood, an associated stela fragment and a small Postclassic shrine may provide some clues.

The above types of sacbes and their associated features linked administrative or combined administrative/ceremonial and residential nodes while longer sacbes served to unite secondary and tertiary cities and towns with a regional capital, as for example the case of Coba–Yaxuna and Coba–Ixil (Fig. 18.8), Izamal–Ake (Lincoln 1980) and Uxmal–Kabah (Victor Segovia Pinto, personal communication).

According to a statement made by Zubrow *et al.* (1974), roads in general represent physical manifestations of social, political, and economic relationships

Fig. 18.1. Yucatan peninsula including some of the major cities associated with sacbes.

that existed in the past between settlements and other nodes. In other terms, one may say that land-level sacbes represent a twenty-four-hour, twelve-month-a-year communication network essential to the maintenance of city and state. They facilitated the movement of its population for sacred, secular, and military purposes including the transportation of goods and services from near and far thereby providing a near-perfect element to any forest-bound communication network. It can be said that Maya sacbes were dedicated at least to those ends as were those water routes located off the coast of the Yucatan peninsula made famous by people such as the Putun Maya canoe traders (Thompson 1976:3).

Moreover, sacbes have at times also served as dikes in Coba (Folan 1982) and in El Mirador, Guatemala (Dahlin *et al.* 1980), thus including them within the water-management systems of the ancient Maya as well as the later Mexica of Tenochtitlan.

In addition to real land-level systems and those of a sea-going nature, local tradition in Coba and its environs relates that Coba and the Cenote Sagrado of Chichen Itza were united by means of a mythological land-level sacbe. The Cenote Sagrado is said to be connected with Mexico by means of a mythological underground sacbe (Folan 1975) as part of the same network. Although not stated by my Maya colleagues from Coba,

Figure 18.2 Coba, Quintana Roo. Plan showing major sacbes. Original plan by George E. Stuart published in Folan (1975).

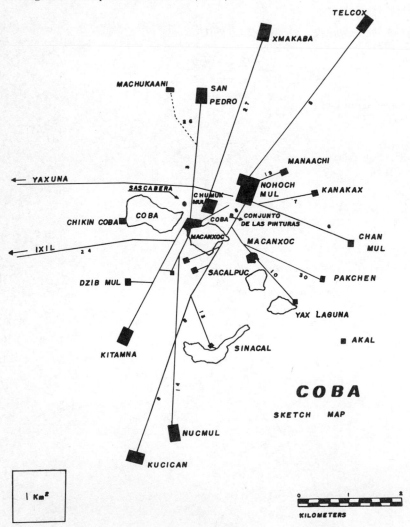

this sacbe may be related to the underground passageway running under the Temple of Kukulcan that local mythology has joining the Cenote Sagrado with the nearby Cenote Xtoloc. This subterranean feature may represent the same passageway that is mentioned in the Popol Vuh as the tortuous mythological route traveled by the Enchanted Twins to the Underworld which,

according to one interpretation (Folan 1980), seems to have been located under the Main Ball Court at Chichen Itza. This association with Xilbalba, according to Florey Folan (1982, personal communication), may also account for the extraordinarily large number of ball courts to be found in this northern Maya/Toltec center.

For those areas around Coba not linked by a real or mythological stone sacbe, local mythology has Coba associated with an aerial route in the form of a blood-filled tube. This is said to have been built by the Itza between Tulum (near Coba's Classic period port of Tancah) and Coba itself, and Zaci (or Valladolid) to the northwest. From Valladolid this Kusam Sum continued on to Ichcansihoo (Merida), another prehispanic Maya city and regional capital of considerable importance

Fig. 18.3. Idealized cross-section of a sacbe.

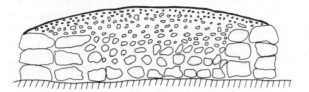

Fig. 18.4. Ramp with associated architecture on sacbe Coba–Ixil. No scale.

Fig. 18.6. Ramp with associated architecture on Sacbe 3 to San Pedro. No scale.

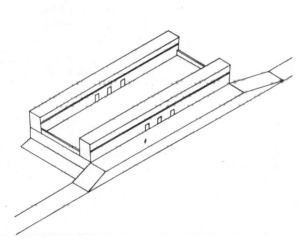

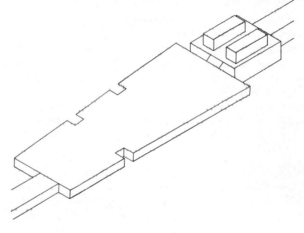

Fig. 18.5. Large ramp without additional architectural associations found at beginning and end of major interurban sacbe in Coba. No scale.

Fig. 18.7. Four-way ramp with oratorio and stela fragment at junction of Sacbe 1 and Sacbe 3. No scale.

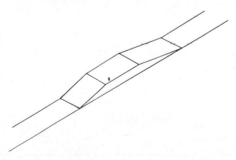

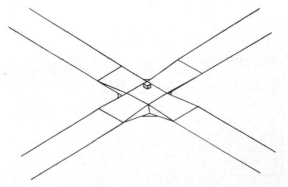

(Tozzer 1907; Miller 1974). This celestial sacbe, wide enough to support armies of horsemen, was reportedly cut by Mexican forces present in Yucatan as an act of war (Folan 1975). There also exists a Kusan Sum between Dzibilchaltun and Izamal, according to local informants.

The above descriptions and interpretations are some of the ideas that have been associated with Maya sacbes for a considerable period of time as represented in the writings of such early investigators as Fray Diego de Landa (1941), John Lloyd Stevens (1843), Teobert Maler (1932), Alfred Marston Tozzer (1907), J. Eric Thompson *et al.* (1932), and Alfonso Villa Rojas (1934) as well as several later writers and investigators such as E. Wyllys Andrews IV (1938), Michael and William Coe (1949), Carlos Navarrete *et al.* (1979), Edward Kurjack and E. Wyllys Andrews V (1976), Arthur Miller (1974), Antonio Benavides (1981a, 1981b) and Fernando Robles (1976).

In this paper, however, I thought I would try to go somewhat beyond these mainly descriptive accounts of Maya sacbe systems in search of something more abstract and far reaching by developing a model that may help to explain the potential represented by these features. One thing is for certain, that virtually none of the sacbe systems with which I am familiar in the Maya area seems to conform to a definite, overall ground pattern. Some are mainly linear, extending between two main intrasite groups as in Copan, Honduras (Leventhal 1981) and in Kabah, Yucatan (Andrews 1975:Fig. 230),

or between a regional center and one of its tributary centers as in the case of Coba and Ixil and Coba and Yaxuna. Others include the ones from San Gervasio to Vista del Mar to the east and San Miguel to the west on the island of Cozumel (Sabloff and Rathje 1980). Other systems, however, are not linear but seem to run off in several different directions at the same time, or in some cases, different times. Some of these systems are represented by sacbes that extend out to at least the four cardinal directions (plus several other directions as in the case of Coba). This is also represented to a certain extent by the sacbe system at Izamal, Yucatan (Lincoln 1980) and El Mirador in the Northern Peten region of Guatemala (Dahlin *et al.* 1980).

Although many of these sacbes could have been easily laid out by the Maya in straight north–south and east–west trajectories, there exists a very good possibility that some sacbes and their associated architecture were oriented specifically to align with astronomical bodies important to them and other Mesoamerican groups. For example, I found it difficult not to believe that at least some of the sacbes of Coba and those of El Mirador, especially the ones forming the Andrews, Bullard, and

Fig. 18.9. Andrews, Bullard and Gifford causeways at El Mirador, Guatemala. No scale. (Redrawn from Dahlin and Chambers [1978] in Dahlin et al. *1980: Fig. 32.)*

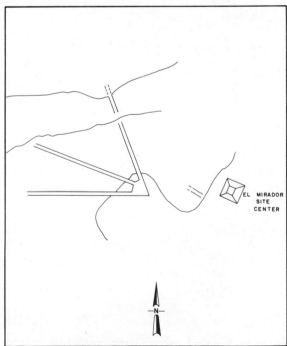

Fig. 18.8. Map showing the relative location of Coba, Yaxuna and Ixil and the approximate trajectory of their intersite sacbes. (Original drawings by Villa Rojas [1934] and a sketch by George E. Stuart drawn in 1974 based on survey data by Caamal Canche, May Hau, Florey Folan and Folan [field notes].)

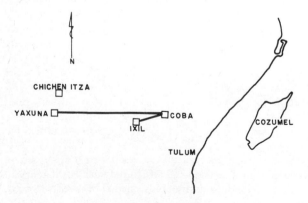

Gifford Causeways (Fig. 18.9), do not represent some type of astronomical alignment in much the same way as the openings in the Caracol Observatory (Fig. 18.10) of Chichen Itza seem to be aligned with the sun and Venus according to studies made by Aveni *et al.* (1975). For example, suggestions made by Jonathan Reyman (1982: letter) from studying our map of Coba indicate that Sacbe 6 leading from the Ixmoja Temple to Chan Mul could have been set in alignment to the rise of Sirius, the brightest star in the sky between A.D. 500 and 1000 as it is now. Furthermore, Sacbe 5, leading from the rear of the Ixmoja Temple to Telcox, could have been set in alignment with Canopus, the second brightest star in the sky during the same period. Sacbe 19, leading from the Ixmoja Temple to Manaachi, could have been set in alignment with the Pleiades, a constellation of much importance in Mesoamerica. The same sacbe could also have been set in alignment with the summer solstice sunrise and winter solstice sunset. Sacbe 7 leading from Ixmoja to Kanakax also may have been set in alignment with the Pleiades, moonrise (northern minimum) and moonset (southern minimum). Other possibilities include Sirius in the constellation Canis Major and Regulus in the constellation Leo, both first-magnitude

Fig. 18.10. Horizontal section through Caracol windows. No scale. (Redrawn from Aveni et al. *1975: Fig. 6.)*

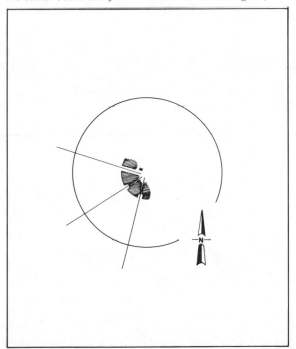

stars. Sacbe 30 leading to Pakchen could also have been set in alignment with the Pleiades and moonrise (southern minimum) and moonset (northern minimum). Sacbe 10 leading to Yax Laguna could have been set to align with Deneb, a first-magnitude star in the constellation Cygnus, especially if this particular sacbe was built around A.D. 500 (Folan *et al.* 1983:81–2).

In addition to astronomical alignments, it has also occurred to me that sacbes and associated architecture in regional centers such as Coba may represent small-scale maps or models of a larger feature. Thus, in addition to their sociopolitical importance and celestial orientation, one could get the idea that the various sacbe termini in Coba could, in reality, represent the relative location of secondary and tertiary centers in its realm. This plan could include the distribution of these centers in respect to each other, with those sacbes leading out to Ixil and Yaxuna representing the limits of the realm to the south-west and west respectively. Additionally the Kusan Sum or celestial sacbes described above could represent, in part, the northern and eastern limits of the regional state.

There also exists the possibility that the so-called free-standing arches at places such as Coba, Chichen Itza, Cozumel, Kabah, and Uxmal may, at least in part, have served as alignments for tracing the movements of heavenly bodies. It is also possible that the Coba sacbes may have served to organize an area into sociopolitical units such as barrios while the Coba and other sacbes could have led in some cases to family shrines or combined residences/shrines.

In conclusion, it seems to me that much more is to be learned from both ground-level, celestial, and underground systems in the Maya area than has so far been offered. If we look at linear features such as sacbes as representing only high-status links and manifestations of high-level social organization without going further afield, we may be limiting our possibilities in the same way that early authors thought of the Nazca lines as only representing pathways, the Inca ceque lines as huaca alignments and Medicine Wheels only as places where Plains people went on vision quests (Folan 1985). On the other hand, however, I am not suggesting a science fiction interpretation but something testable that will take us beyond the limits of what we have already been able to accomplish with these highly sophisticated linear features crisscrossing Mayan towns, cities, and regional states.

It is suggested here that sacbes not only organized an area such as Coba into structured social and political units including households, neighborhoods, barrios, cities and states (Folan 1976, 1977; Folan *et al.* 1983) but that their trajectory and, in some cases, associated features are astronomically aligned and perhaps calendrically significant. They may also have formed models of regional states as well as mirroring star maps. The mythological celestial and subterranean sacbes not only may have formed regional boundaries but also perhaps defined local and long-distance associations, thus linking this great urban center with a good part of mainline Mesoamerica.

Acknowledgments

I would like to thank Karen Olson Bruhns and Lynda Florey-Folan and an anonymous reviewer who made several helpful suggestions on this paper. As always, however, whatever error of fact or judgment made on these pages is the exclusive property of the author. I would also like to thank Cobañeos Nicolas Caamal Canche, Jacinto May Hau, Bernabel Can Canche, Evaristo Aban and Teldoro May Chi who helped Lynda Florey-Folan and myself comprehend their particular understanding of the local and far-flung route network associated with Coba.

References

Andrews, E. Wyllys, IV
1938 Some New Material from Coba, Quintana Roo, Mexico. *Ethnos* 3(2–3):33–47. Statens Etnografiska Museum, Stockholm

Andrews, George F.
1975 *Maya Cities: Placemaking and Urbanization.* The Civilization of the American Indian Series. University of Oklahoma Press, Norman

Aveni, Anthony F., Sharon Gibbs, and Horst Hartung
1975 The Caracol Tower at Chichen Itza. An Ancient Astronomical Observatory? *Science* 188:977–85

Benavides Castillo, Antonio
1981a *Los caminos de Cobá y sus implicaciones sociales (proyecto Cobá).* Instituto Nacional de Antropología e Historia. Centro Regional del Sureste, Mexico

Coe, William R., II and Michael D. Coe
1949 *Some New Discoveries at Cobá.* Notes on Middle American Archaeology and Ethnology 93. Carnegie Institution of Washington

Dahlin, Bruce H., John E. Foss, and Mary Elizabeth Chambers
1980 Project Acalches: Reconstructing the Natural and Cultural History of a Seasonal Swamp at El Mirador, Guatemala; Preliminary Results. In *El Mirador, Peten, Guatemala. An interim report*, edited by Ray T. Matheny, pp. 37–57. Papers of the New

World Archaeological Foundation 45. Brigham Young University, Provo, UT

Folan, William J.
1975 Coba Archaeological Mapping Project, Interim Report 2, August 6, 1975. Xerox. Also in *Boletín de la Escuela de Ciencias Antropológicas de la Universidad de Yucatán* 22, 23:29–51
1976 Coba Archaeological Mapping Project, Interim Report 3, Coba, Quintana Roo, Mexico. Xerox. Also in *Boletín de la Escuela de Ciencias Antropológicas de la Universidad de Yucatán* 22, 23:52–71
1977 El Sacbe Cobá–Ixil: un camino maya del pasado. *Nueva Antropología* 6:39–42
1980 Chichén Itzá, el cenote sagrado y Xibalba; una nueva visión. *Boletín de la Escuela de Ciencias Antropológicas de la Universidad de Yucatán* 44:70–6
1982 Paleoclimatología y prehistoria: el desarrollo cultural y hidrológico de Cobá, Quintana Roo, México. *Información. Boletín del Centro de Estudios Históricos y Sociales de la Universidad Autónoma del Sudeste* 2:9–37
1985 Los derechos de paso de los antiguos mayas, américa del sur y del norte. Accepted for publication in *Información*

Folan, William J., Ellen R. Kintz, and Laraine A. Fletcher
1983 *Coba, A Classic Maya Metropolis.* Studies in Archaeology. Academic Press, New York and London

Folan, William J., and George E. Stuart
1974 Coba Archaeological Mapping Project, Interim Report 1, Quintana Roo, Mexico. June 24 – August 17, 1974, Coba. Xerox. Also published in *Boletín de la Escuela de Ciencias Antropológicas de la Universidad de Yucatán* 22, 23:20–29 in 1977

Kurjack, Edward B., and E. Wyllys Andrews, V
1976 Early Boundary Maintenance in Northwest Yucatan, Mexico. *American Antiquity* 41:318–25

Landa, Fray Diego de
1941 *Relación de las cosas de Yucatán*, translated and edited with notes by Alfred M. Tozzer. Papers of the Peabody Museum 18, Harvard University, Cambridge, MA

Leventhal, Richard M.
1981 Settlement Patterns in the southeast Maya area. In *Lowland Maya Settlement Patterns*, edited by Wendy Ashmore. A School of American Research Book. University of New Mexico Press, Albuquerque

Lincoln, Charles Edward
1980 Izamal, Yucatán, México. Un reconocimiento breve, descripción preliminar y discusión. *Boletín de la*

Escuela de Ciencias Antropológicas de la Universidad de Yucatán 43:24–69

Maler, Teobert
1932 Impresiones de viaje a las ruinas de Cobá y Chichén Itzá (con un prólogo del Lic. D. Santiago Burgos Brito). Merida

Miller, Arthur
1974 The Iconography of the Painting in the Temple of the Divine God. Tulum, Quintana Roo: The Twisted Cords. In *Mesoamerican Archaeology: New Approaches*, edited by Norman Hammond. University of Texas Press, Austin

Murphy, Francis
1968 Searching a Mayan Road to the Sea. In *American Quintana Roo Expedition 1968*, edited by Robert O. Lee. Xerox MS in possession of the author

Navarrete, Carlos, María José Con Uribe, and Alejandro Martínez Muriel
1979 *Observaciones arqueológicas en Cobá, Quintana Roo*. Centro de Estudios Mayas. Universidad Nacional Autónoma de México, Mexico

Robles, Fernando
1976 Ixíl. Centro agrícola de Cobá. *Boletín de la Escuela de Ciencias Antropológicas de la Universidad de Yucatán* 20:13–43

Sabloff, Jeremy A., and William A. Rathje
1980 The Rise of a Maya Merchant Class. Reprinted in *Readings from Scientific American. Pre-Columbian Archaeology* with introductions by Gordon R. Willey and Jeremy A. Sabloff, pp. 139–49. W. H. Freeman and Company, San Francisco

Stephens, John Lloyd
1843 *Incidents of Travel in Yucatan*. 2 vols. New York

Thompson, J. Eric
1976 *Maya History and Religion*. University of Oklahoma Press, Norman

Thompson, J. Eric, Harry E. D. Pollock, and Jean Charlot
1932 *A Preliminary Study of the Ruins of Coba, Quintana Roo, Mexico*. Carnegie Institution of Washington Publication 424, Washington, DC

Tozzer, Alfred Marston
1907 *A Comparative Study of the Mayas and the Lacandones*. Archaeological Institute of America 1902–5, New York

Vargas Pacheco, Ernesto
1985 Arqueología e historia de los Mayas en Tabasco. In *Olmecas y Mayas en Tabasco. Cinco Acercamientos*, edited by Lorenzo Ochoa. Gobierno Del Estado de Tabasco, Villahermosa

Villa Rojas, Alfonso
1934 The Yaxuna–Coba Causeway. *Carnegie Institution of Washington* 9(2):187–208

Zubrow, Ezra B. W., Margaret C. Fritz, and John M. Fritz
1974 The Romantic Vision II. In *Readings from Scientific American New World Archaeology: The Ritual and Cultural Transformations*, pp. 21–5. W. H. Freeman and Company, San Francisco

19 Prehistoric roads and causeways of lowland tropical America

WILLIAM M. DENEVAN

Introduction

Somewhere deep in Amazonia, early Spanish explorers encountered Indian roads and were greatly impressed: "betwixt Peru and Bresill ... the waies [are] as much beaten as those betwixt Salamanca and Valladolid" (José de Acosta in 1590; 1880, vol. I:171).

The tropical lowlands of the Americas are not considered likely locales for the discovery of ancient roads. To be sure, aboriginal people had and continue to have large and intricate networks of trails (paths) cut through the forests. However, for the most part these are narrow, temporary, and unimproved by paving or raising, and few have clearly survived from the pre-European past. Posey (1983:241), for example, reports "thousands of kilometers" of trails for the present-day Kayapo in central Brazil.

Lowland roads of prehistoric origin which have survived to the present are primarily causeways (*terraplenes*, *calzadas*); that is, roads which have been elevated with stone or earth for the purpose of drainage, dramatic visibility, or possibly defense. This essay is concerned mainly with surviving causeways, their locations, characteristics, and functions. There are quite a few of them in the tropical lowlands, both in forests and in savannas, particularly in Yucatan, in the Upper Amazon of Bolivia, and in the Orinoco Llanos of Venezuela. First, a survey is provided of early reports of Indian roads and causeways.

Historical accounts
Puerto Rico
Christopher Columbus was the first European to observe an aboriginal road in the New World. On November 20, 1493, on his second voyage, he landed in a

bay (either Boqueron or Añasco) on the west coast of Puerto Rico. At an abandoned village there, his son reported that between the plaza and a watch tower near the sea there was "a wide road leading to the sea and bordered by towers of cane on both sides" (Colón 1959:117). This may have been similar to roads discovered by Rouse (1952:485–7) at the Palo Hincado site in the central interior of Puerto Rico. Three roads lead from a plaza, not causeways but lined on each side by artificial embankments. They range in length from 37 to 1,133 m, in width from 5 to 15 m, and the embankments are from 0.30 to 3.0 m high. Their functions are not clear.

Yucatan

Mayan causeways (sacbes) in Yucatan have been known since the Spanish conquest. Hernando Cortés in 1524 penetrated Tabasco, Campeche, and Peten and reported following or crossing roads which led to or out of Maya towns. Von Hagen (1960:180–1) suggested that some of these were causeways, but in his Fifth Letter Cortés only uses the words "road" (*camino*) and "path" (*caminillo*) (Cortés 1963:242–322). Cortés was given a map drawn on henequén cloth by Indian merchants showing the location of villages and the road or route from the Gulf Coast to either Itzamkanac in Campeche or all the way to Nicaragua (Cortés 1963:243; 1971:340, 344, 365, 514 n 12; López de Gómara 1965:345; Díaz, 1944, vol. III:33). In Itzamkanac he received from Chief Apaspolon another map drawn on cloth showing the main road. These maps (not preserved) were among the earliest maps to show Indian roads, but they were of little help to Cortés who had a terrible time getting through the swamps of Tabasco and Campeche. Bernal Díaz (1944, vol. III:64, 65) in his account of the march mentioned a "direct" and "wide" road from Nito to Naco near the Gulf of Honduras. Diego de Landa (1978:86) later (1566) reported a possible causeway ("fine paved road") from Merida to Izamal.

Stevens (1962, vol. II:77, 220) in 1841 observed stone causeways between Kabah and Uxmal and at Coba. The longest Mayan causeway is that from Coba to Yaxuna, which measures 99 km. A dramatic photo of intersecting causeways just south of Coba was taken in 1930 by the University of Pennsylvania aerial survey of Mayan archaeological sites (see Fig. 11.51 in Morley *et al.* 1983, and in earlier editions). The photo clearly shows the causeways as straight lines etched by the shadows thrown by the higher trees growing on top of the causeways. The Pennsylvania survey was one of the first attempts to use aerial photography in Mesoamerican

archaeology (Deuel 1969:214–18). The causeways of Coba, numbering over fifty, are mapped, described, and discussed by Folan *et al.* (1983). Causeways on Cozumel Island are mapped and described by Freidel and Sabloff (1984:79–84).

The Mayan causeways are of dressed limestone, with rubble between two retaining walls, and the tops covered by lime cement. They are about 4–5 m wide, 0.5–2.5 m high, and of variable length (Morley *et al.* 1983:333–5). There are now a large number of descriptions of specific intersite and intrasite causeways throughout the Maya lowlands in archaeological reports, including at Coba, Tikal, Cozumel, Becan, El Mirador, Uaxactun, Nakum, Yaxha, Seibal, Copan, Uxmal, Dzibilchaltun, Chichen Itza, Labna, Quirigua, Tamanche, and Izamal. Dates of construction and use vary. Linear stone works served other functions besides roads, including boundaries, terraces, and dikes.

The only lengthy general account of the Maya causeways is by von Hagen (1960:179–90), who provided some history, description, and a map of the major intersite causeways in Yucatan. The map is based in part on the map in Morley (1946:Plate 19), with additions by von Hagen, and is far from complete and in places inaccurate. What is needed is an updated map based on air photographic coverage.

The role of Mayan causeways in connecting buildings and sites and probable symbolic and ceremonial functions is discussed by Kurjack and Garza (1981:300–9), Freidel and Sabloff (1984:79–84), and by Folan (this volume).

South America

Possibly the first report of roads in Amazonia is by Friar Gaspar de Carvajal who accompanied the Orellana expedition down the Amazon in 1541. He reported "many roads, and fine highways ... to the inland country ... more like royal highways and wider" (Toribio Medina 1934:202). It is not clear where these roads were, who built them, where they went, or whether they were causeways. Probably they extended from the river to interior villages and may only have been widened and much-used trails.

In the Orinoco Llanos, the Sedeño expedition of 1536 encountered "a great calzada, which was over 100 leagues long and had vestiges of old settlements and ridges of former fields" (on or near?), according to Juan de Castellanos (1955, vol. I:539), writing in 1589. Jacinto de Carvajal (1956:117) reported that the explorer Miguel de Ochogavia told him that on his expedition of 1647 he encountered Caquetio Indians fleeing from Coro who had built earthworks in the Llanos, and these may have included causeways. Later Alexander von Humboldt (1852, vol. II:96) in relation to his journey through the Llanos in 1800 mentioned a causeway: "A fine road is also discovered near Hato de la Calzada, between Varinas and Canagua, five leagues long, made before the conquest, in the most remote times, by the natives." He said it was of earth and 15 feet high. However, Humboldt did not observe the causeway himself, his route through the Llanos lying to the east.

In the Llanos de Mojos of eastern Bolivia, numerous causeways were mentioned by the 1617 Solís Holguín expedition, one of the first to reach Mojos and leave written descriptions. Several members of the expedition reported seeing *calzadas* connecting or entering Mojo villages (Lizarazu 1906:134, 136, 170, 188, 200). Diego Felipe de Alcaya mentioned "clean roads 15 feet wide" and a *calzada* 10 *brazos* long (about 8 m) connecting two plazas. Juan de Limpias told of "entering a village on a street or *calzada* which divided the fields and on which three men could ride side by side." Juan Antonio Justiniano reported using a "wide road" leading to the villages. According to Alonzo Soleto Pernia there were "roads so straight and so wide that they were almost wider than a [Spanish] street; and these roads were so swept up and clean, that it is certain we have never seen such a thing before." There is no doubt, then, that causeways were being used and maintained in conjunction with villages in the area of southeastern Mojos visited by the expedition (Denevan 1966:79).

There are also Jesuit missionary references later to Indian causeways in Mojos. Diego Francisco Altamirano (1891:103) in about 1710 mentioned wide and well-cared-for Baure Indian roads. Francisco Javier Eder (1888:36) in 1791 described old *calzadas* that were large enough for two carts and that stood above water even during the highest floods.

In the Guayas Basin of coastal Ecuador, Cieza de León (1959:299) reported a major Inka road or causeway which crossed or followed the Guayas River (or one of its major tributaries); this has since assumed legendary status as "El Paso de Huaynacapac." It is shown on several old maps, but the actual site and form are debated. Von Hagen (in Cieza de León 1959:304ff.) believed that a river-crossing or bridge was unlikely, and he shows instead a grand highway, clearly conjectural, from Chimbo in the highlands, west along the Rio Alausi, to Guayaquil. Mathewson (1982), who has looked into the matter and examined air photos, found one short stretch of stone causeway extending from a zone of prehistoric raised fields in seasonal swamp along

the west side of Cerrito Sapan to the Rio Los Tintos west of the town of Samborondon. He believes there probably were other causeways in the large backswamps of the Guayas Basin but that they have been destroyed by agricultural activity.

Causeways have been reported but not described in several other lowland regions of South America. One is the Paressi Indian area in the savannas between the upper Rio Guapore and the Serra dos Parecis in Mato Grosso in western Brazil (Métraux 1942:164). The Paressi were an Arawak tribe, now extinct, that had a dense population and impressive farms. Métraux reported that they "were great road builders and connected their villages with broad, straight, and perfectly clean highways"; however he provided no source for this information. In a summary section of the *Handbook of South American Indians*, Wendell Bennett (1949:54) said that the Warrau Indians of the Orinoco delta built "banked roads," but this fact is not mentioned in descriptions of the Warrau elsewhere. Parsons and Bowen (1966) mention reports of a few causeways in the Rio San Jorge region of northern Colombia. Various tribes elsewhere in the tropical lowlands of South America probably built roads with some sections raised as causeways. Finally, there are the roads leading out of the eastern Andes to the edge of the tropical lowlands. Few have been mapped and we know little about them and their role in highland–lowland interactions.

Thus there is a long history of reports of Indian roads in the tropical lowlands, but little detail. It is not always certain that these features are prehistoric, or whether at the time of observation they were still maintained and in use. Recently, scholars have provided more specific information, but few of the surviving causeways have been excavated and none has been systematically described. We know most about the causeways in the Llanos de Mojos, the Orinoco Llanos, and the Maya lowlands. Mayan causeways are discussed elsewhere in this volume (Folan) and so will not be examined further here.

The Llanos de Mojos, Bolivia

The Llanos de Mojos is a large seasonally inundated savanna in the upper Amazon region of northeastern Bolivia, now primarily the Department of the Beni (Fig. 19.1). At the time of initial Spanish contact in the late sixteenth century, it was occupied by several tribes (Mojo, Baure, Cayuvava) categorized by Steward and Faron (1959:252–61) as theocratic tropical-forest chiefdoms. They were associated with large villages and large numbers of earthworks, including mounds, raised fields,

Fig. 19.1. Map of the Llanos de Mojos, Bolivia, showing locations of causeways.

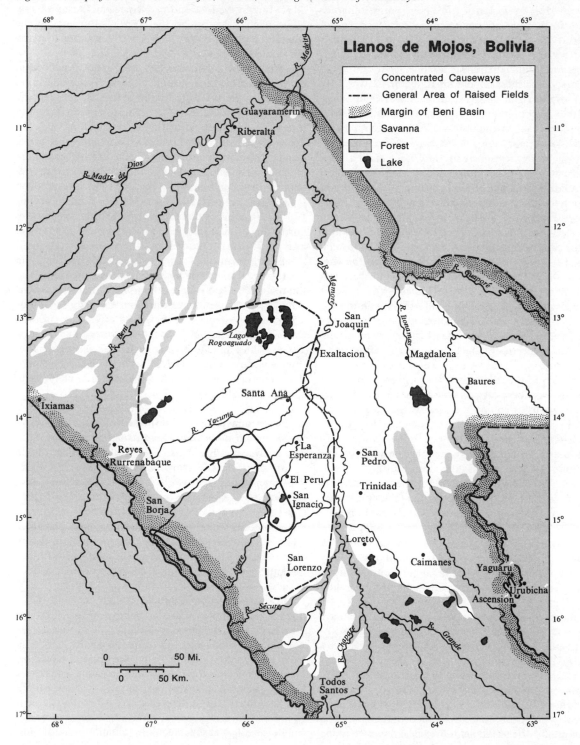

Llanos de Mojos, Bolivia

Concentrated Causeways
General Area of Raised Fields
Margin of Beni Basin
Savanna
Forest
Lake

canals, moats, and causeways. From Jesuit mission data, I estimated a population for the entire Llanos (180,000 km²), much of it marginal for settlement, of at least 100,000 in 1690 and possibly 350,000 at initial contact around 1580 (Denevan 1966:116, 120); other authors support lower figures.

I undertook fieldwork in Mojos in 1961–2, with an interest in aboriginal adaptation to seasonal flooding and particularly raised fields. From Métraux (1942:66) I was already aware of causeways in Mojos. He reported that "Mojo villages were connected by wide causeways, some of which were sufficiently high to remain above water during the flood." However, I was unprepared for the number and extent of the causeways I saw on the ground, from bush planes, and on air photos. I estimate that they total over 1,500 km in Mojos and adjacent areas. They are found throughout the Llanos de Mojos from the Rio Secure north to Lago Rogoaguado and from the Rio Beni to east of Baures nearly to the Rio Guapore. They also occur in the large savannas between the Rio Beni and the Rio Madre de Dios.

Most of the Mojos causeways are short, connecting local settlements, rather than being lengthy cross-country roads. Most are pre-Spanish, but some are probably Jesuit. Some are still in use, and they continue to be built to the present time. A causeway has been built for much of the new road from Trinidad west across the savanna to San Borja. I was able to measure and map (from air photos) many of the causeways, but I did not undertake any excavations. The only archaeologist who previously mentioned the causeways was Erland Nordenskiöld, seventy-five years ago, and then only in passing. Apparently Alfred Métraux, the French anthropologist who wrote a monograph on the Indians of eastern Bolivia (1942), never visited Mojos and relied on Nordenskiöld and others. There has been some survey archaeology since 1962, but only Erickson (1980) comments at any length on causeways. The Mojos causeways have not been dated, nor cultural associations determined.

The following description is from my monograph on Mojos (Denevan 1966, 1980), with only minor modifications.

Following the Jesuits, who were expelled from Mojos in 1767, Mojos causeways were seen and described by many travelers, including Alcides D'Orbigny (1958:756) between Magdalena and Baures; Ciro Bayo (1911:358, 359) southeast of Loreto and in the Pantano de Sayuba between Rurrenabaque and Ixiamas west of the Rio Beni; Erland Nordenskiöld (1913:225) in southeastern Mojos; and more recently by oil-company personnel in southwestern Mojos (Plafker 1963). The causeways are

well known to the Benianos who recognize them as roads built either by the Indians or by the Jesuits. According to Nordenskiöld (1916:148) the *terraplenes* were always mentioned when people "were asked about the curiosities of the region."

I have seen causeways on the ground near San Ignacio, La Esperanza, Caimanes, and Baures and from the air in all parts of the Mojos savannas. The densest concentration is between the Rio Mamore, the Rio Yacuma, and the town of San Lorenzo (Fig. 19.1). In one area of about 3,800 km² near San Ignacio, I counted on aerial photographs and mosaics 564 causeways totaling 505 km in length. Most of these causeways are less than 1.5 km long, but one, 50 km west-northwest of San Ignacio, the longest I know of in the Beni, measures 13.2 km. There is a causeway about 11 km long 55 km northwest of San Borja. Few causeways have been measured east of the Rio Mamore, but Orbigny (1958:756) mentioned one between Magdalena and Baures as being 8 km long, and I saw one between Baures and the Rio Blanco said to be 12 km long. There are also long causeways in the Caimanes area, including a discontinuous one extending east from Caimanes to Yaguaru and another between Caimanes and nearby Tajibo. Thus the Mojos causeways are numerous and some are fairly long; however, I know of no causeways that "continue uninterrupted for tens of miles" as is claimed by Plafker (1963:377).

Causeways were constructed of available earth material, mainly alluvial clays and silts. Most of the causeways that I saw on the ground were from 0.6 to 1.2 m high, with a few as much as 1.5 m high. Widths averaged from 1.8 to 4.5 m. One wide causeway near El Peru, however, is between 6 and 7.5 m wide. Some of the causeways in the vicinity of Caimanes are about 6 m wide. Plafker (1963:377) gives an average of 0.45 to 0.76 m for the height of causeways, but I saw few that were less than 0.6 m high. Nordenskiöld (1913:225) saw several causeways that were about 3 m wide and 0.5 m high. Undoubtedly all the aboriginal causeways in Mojos have been reduced in height by erosion.

Most causeways have sufficient height to stand above flood waters, and because of good drainage they are invariably lined with trees. Because of abrupt relief, vegetation is somewhat protected from fire, and this could be an important factor in tree growth. Common plants include the totai and motacú palms, cacti, and thorny species of mimosa. The causeways are unusually straight except for a few that are smoothly curved. Because of their straightness and tree cover, causeways can be identified easily in open savanna from the air and on aerial photographs, and they are also obvious features on the ground. Even when covered only by grass, causeways stand out clearly, owing to a relatively lighter color in comparison with surrounding grasses. Causeways in forest can sometimes be picked out from the air because the trees on them stand slightly higher than adjacent trees and therefore cast a longer shadow.

It is fairly clear that the aboriginal causeways were built to connect settlements with one another, with areas of cultivation, with ceremonial and burial sites, and with rivers. Causeways occur in conjunction with habitation sites, artificial mounds, canals, and drained fields. The basic purpose of the causeways was not for cross-country travel but for local movement across stretches of low-lying ground subject to flooding. However, some of the causeways, especially the longer and probably more important ones, continue across both high and low ground (for example, in the Caimanes area). The building of raised roads on high ground where there is no drainage problem is probably indicative of the importance that causeways came to have for some of the savanna tribes and is one of many examples of cultures retaining traits in situations where they are no longer utilitarian.

The straightness of most of the causeways is impressive. When they branch off or change direction the angles are sharp, indicating either intentional change in direction or later additions. While the engineering needed to maintain a straight road in flat, open terrain is relatively simple, building a long straight road to a destination that cannot be seen is not easy. The sharp angle jogs appearing in many causeways (Fig. 19.2) may in some instances be compensations for the inaccurate determination of an intended direct line between two points. Causeways frequently continue on the same course after crossing rivers. The long causeway shown in Plate 13 in Denevan (1966) crosses the bends of two meanders, and undoubtedly the meanders cut across the causeway after the causeway was built.

There are no references to the Jesuits building causeways; however, there are causeways leading to mission sites, and undoubtedly some of them were built under the leadership of the padres following the aboriginal examples. The Franciscan padres of the Guarayos missions clearly did build causeways across local depressions. Padre José Cardús (1886:221–2) mentioned *terraplenes* between Ascension and Yaguaru, between Ascension and Urubicha ("a curiche over 1 kilometer long across which the Urubichá converts have built a solid terraplene"), and between Urubicha and Yaguaru ("a terraplene about 2 leagues [about 10 km] long built

by the Franciscans"). Padre Zacarias Ducci (1895:80, 82) also mentioned *terraplenes* built by the Franciscans in the same area, one across a *gran curiche* near Urubicha and another 2 leagues long between Urubicha and Yaguaru.

Today there are postconquest causeways in or near many of the old mission towns of Mojos, including some built in recent years. While causeways are a logical means of providing usable roads and trails during flooding, the idea for their construction cannot be divorced from a tradition in Mojos which is many hundreds of years old. The general attitude in the Beni today, however, is that causeways are too much work and too expensive to be justified. Most roads on the Beni plains are not elevated and are unimproved. They are easily torn up by cattle, oxcarts, and flooding, the usual remedy being the creation of a new trail adjacent to the old one. As a result, most modern trails and roads are seasonal and are constantly changing, and in comparison with the aboriginal causeways they are anything but straight.

Because old causeways are usually short and tend not to lead in directions desired by present travelers, they are seldom utilized by major trails, although local people may use some of them to get across depressions during flooding. Since the introduction of horses, oxen, and oxcarts capable of traversing wet ground, causeways have not had the utility and value, considering the labor involved in building them, that they undoubtedly had in aboriginal times.

Since my own work, there has been a more recent report on the Mojos causeways by archaeologist Clark Erickson (1980). In a survey of the area between the villages of San Ignacio and San Borja, Erickson found large numbers of causeways not only in savannas but in forest zones which are usually on high ground and well drained. He provides a map of causeways at Campo España near San Borja. Most of the causeways are associated with adjacent canals. Erickson believes that the causeways served not only for transportation but for water control for agriculture or fish ponds. Some causeways seem to have been dikes connecting natural levées to form shallow reservoirs (Erickson 1980: Figs. 1 and 2; also Bustos 1978). Such dikes could have served either to impound water or to reduce flooding, or both. Such functions are suggested by narrow gaps in some embankments which could have served as floodgates. Erickson suggests that another possible secondary function of the causeway and canal systems was field demarcation. As for the age of the causeways, to my knowledge neither Erickson nor any other archaeologist who has

Fig. 19.2. Map of sector of causeways in southwestern Mojos (from Denevan 1966:82).

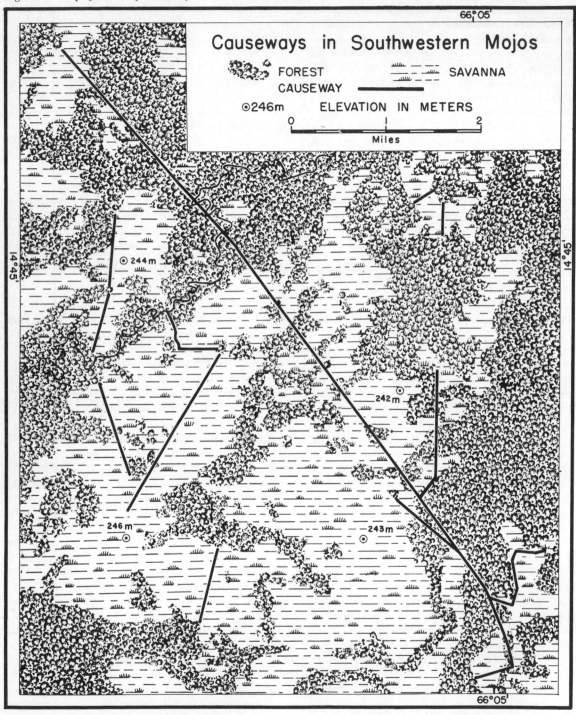

Fig. 19.3. Map of causeways at Hato la Calzada, Barinas, Venezuela (based on Garson 1980:309).

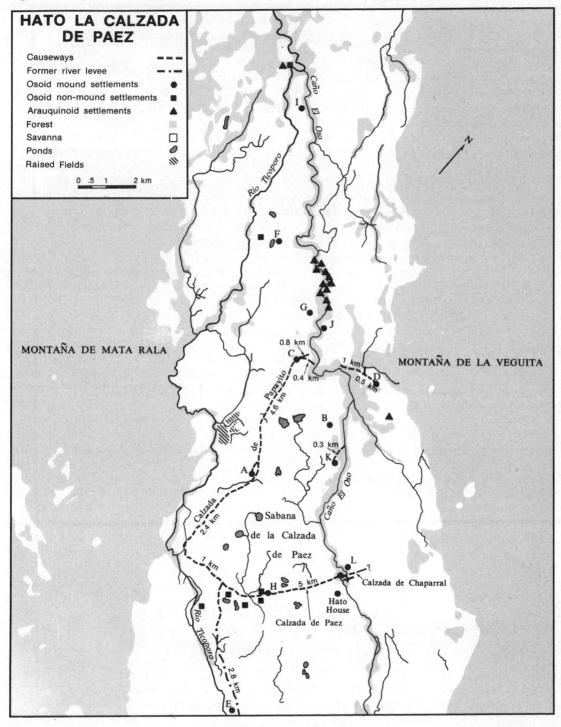

excavated recently in the Beni (Bustos 1978; Dougherty and Calandra 1981) has obtained a date for cultural material in or beneath a causeway.

Western Llanos, Venezuela

In the western Llanos of Venezuela causeways have been observed in poorly drained savannas at a number of locations in the states of Barinas, Portuguesa, and Apure, although never in the quantities found in Mojos. No inventory has been made, but lists of causeways seen or reported (less than twenty) were given by Alvarado (1956:385) in 1904 and by Oramas (1917:142–3). Oramas (1917:140) used dynamite to "excavate" artificial mounds and possibly causeways in order to recover artifacts. Few measurements or other descriptions are provided. Alfredo Jahn (1927:217–22) mentioned some of the same causeways. He believed that the causeways and artificial mounds of Mojos, the Llanos, and elsewhere in South America were all constructed by related Arawak tribes.

The best-known and most-studied causeways in the Orinoco Llanos, or anywhere in the wet tropics of South America, are those at Hato la Calzada de Paez in central Barinas (Fig. 19.3). Hato (cattle ranch) La Calzada was named for a large prehistoric causeway sometime before the hato became the home of General José Antonio Páez in about 1807 (Garson 1980:51). Subsequent to Humboldt there are various mentions of these causeways and a brief description in 1904 by Alvarado (1956:385). More recently they have been described by Cruxent (1952, 1966), Zucchi (1972, 1973), and particularly by Garson (1980), who carried out a major study of the archaeology of the region.

Cruxent (1952, 1966) described four causeways in central Barinas: 1. Calzada de los Mochuelos (near the town of Torunos), which was 1,700 m long, 8–27 m wide, and 0.5 m high; 2. Calzada de Paez, which was 5,000 m long, 13–25 m wide, and 1–2 m high (Figs. 19.4–5); 3. Calzada de Chaparral (an extension of Calzada de Paez), which had main branches of 1,500 and 2,000 m and lesser branches of 60 and 80 m, and was 10 m wide and 1.5–2 m high; and 4. Calzada de Ojo de Agua (near Calzada de Paez), which was 200 m long, of irregular width, and 1.8 m high.

Garson (1980:122–6) did a more complete survey, measuring and mapping most of the Hato La Calzada de Paez causeways (Fig. 19.3). The main section of Calzada de Paez is 5,000 m long, with a 1,000 m branch northwest to the Rio Ticoporo, and a 700 m branch south. The latter extends an additional 2,100 m south along a natural levée to Mound E. The Calzada de Papayito runs 2,400 m from the Rio Ticoporo to near Mound A, with a small unmeasured branch to Mound A, and with a northern branch of 4,600 m to Mound C. There are small causeways of 420 and 780 m from Mound C to Caño el Oso, of 1,000 and 540 m from Mound D, and of 300 m from Mound K to Caño El Oso. Calzada de Chaparral, with its main and minor branches, is only partly mapped by Garson. In all, counting branches, there are fourteen causeways at Hato La Calzada de Paez.

Garson (1980:303) believes that: "Causeways can indicate functional and social interaction and reflect aspects of social and economic organization." Accordingly, he identifies three categories of causeways based on those at la Calzada: 1. causeways that interconnect settlements; 2. causeways that interconnect settlements with non-residential activity areas (such as streams); and 3. intra-settlement causeways. The short causeways are generally straight (rectilinear) and the long ones meandering as a result of being routed through a heterogeneous landscape (Garson 1980:303–5). In Mojos, in contrast, many of the long causeways are quite straight.

The primary function of the Llanos causeways is generally assumed to have been that of roadways across poorly drained or seasonally flooded savanna or marsh (Jahn 1927:219; Alvarado 1956:385; Cruxent 1952, 1966; Garson 1980; 323–4). Cruxent also considered other

Fig. 19.4. Cross-section of Calzada de Paez, Barinas, Venezuela.

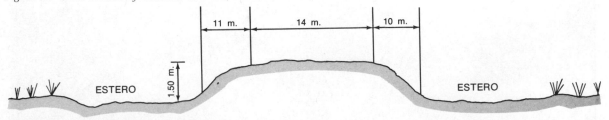

CALZADA DE PAEZ

possible functions such as house platforms, hunting sites, and agricultural fields. None of these would seem primary given the interconnective characteristics of most causeways (Garson 1980:324). Adjacent, excavated canals which may have served for canoe traffic, as in Mojos, are absent, or if once present are now silted in, although there are some shallow depressions (Garson 1980:126).

While Garson did not excavate any causeways, he did excavate closely associated mounds, as did Zucchi. The ceramics indicate that all the causeways are associated with the Osoid series and probably date to *c.* A.D. 500–600, which is pre-Arauquinoid (Garson 1980:122, 301; Zucchi 1973:188). Zucchi (1972) excavated a trench 12.1 m long and 1 m wide from the center of Calzada de Paez to the lateral borrow pit at a point directly north of Hato House (see Fig. 19.3). The causeway consists of yellow clay over an original floor of yellow sandy clay. The original height of the causeway was 2 m and the width was about 12 m. The height has been reduced by

about half by erosion and filling in of the trench. A few sherds were found in the excavation pertaining to La Betania Complex (A.D. 650–1200), possibly intrusive after the causeway was constructed. To my knowledge, this is the only excavation anywhere of a tropical lowland causeway.

Whether there is a cultural connection between the Llanos mounds and causeways and those in Mojos, which are similar in many respects, is speculative (Denevan 1966:25). The Mojos causeways still have not been dated or identified as to cultural origin. Raised fields, which are common in Mojos, occur in one small patch (10.3 ha) at la Calzada, but may be younger than the causeways (Garson 1980:129–30, 327). A larger area of raised fields, dated to *c.* A.D. 1200–1400, in southern Barinas is not associated with causeways (Zucchi and Denevan 1979).

Conclusions
The evidence for prehistoric roads in the tropical lowlands of the Americas consists both of observations

Fig. 19.5. Calzada de Paez, Barinas, Orinoco Llanos, Venezuela; the parallel lines are from modern cultivation (Zucchi 1968).

made in the early sixteenth century, and of improved roads, mainly causeways, which have survived to the present. Because no causeways other than Calzada de Paez have been excavated, and thereby dated directly, we must rely on close association with prehistoric sites in order to date them and confirm them as prehistoric, as has been done in Barinas and in Yucatan where there has been considerable research. There is little historical evidence to indicate that causeways are postconquest in origin, except for a few in Mojos.

In South America, reported lowland causeways outside Mojos number only a few dozen and apparently were not a significant landscape or communication feature. In Mojos, however, they probably number over a thousand and must be considered an important element of prehistoric culture, with a considerable investment in labor and with major interconnective and drainage functions. The Mojos and Barinas causeways are predominantly located in savanna, subject to permanent or periodic flooding or water logging. In Barinas they connect settlement mounds with each other and with streams. In Mojos they connect settlement mounds, settlement sites on forested islands of high ground, raised-field complexes, and streams and lagoons. Archaeology is needed, however, to determine just what kinds of settlement sites are interconnected. Since causeways connect natural or artificial points of high ground in areas of poor drainage, both the Mojos and Barinas causeways would seem to have had a fundamental drainage function, that of facilitating movement across poorly drained terrain. However, some of the Mojos causeways continue over high ground, usually well-drained forest, such as the long causeway shown in Fig. 19.2. Such long causeways and their branches may have connected major settlement sites and acquired a role beyond that of simply keeping people out of mud and water. In both Mojos and Barinas the evidence of archaeology, earthworks, and intensive agriculture indicates the presence of socioculturally complex people and relatively dense populations and settlement patterns (Denevan 1966; Garson 1980).

The Maya situation is somewhat different, involving as it does one of the major New World civilizations, people who built cities and massive monuments. Most of the stone causeways are on well-drained ground where a wide, well-beaten pathway would suffice. The raised, permanent road, then, takes on other significance (Folan, this volume). In all three causeway areas, however, further research is needed which systematically excavates causeways, maps their distribution, and associates their terminals with residential and non-residential human sites, with agricultural and aquatic resource areas, and with other phenomena.

References

Acosta, Joseph [José] de
1880 [1550] *The Natural and Moral History of the Indies*, Vols. LX, LXI. Hakluyt Society, London

Altamirano, Diego Francisco
1891 [*c.* 1710] Historia de la misión de los Mojos. *Documentos históricos de Bolivia: historia de la misión de los Mojos*, edited by Manuel V. Ballivian, Imprenta de El Comercio, La Paz

Alvarado, Lisandro
1956 *Datos etnográficos de Venezuela*, Obras Completas de Lisandro Alvarado, Vol. IV, Ministerio de Educación, Caracas

Bayo, Ciro
1911 *El Peregrino en Indias: En el corazón de la América del Sur*. Librería de los Sucesores de Hernando, Madrid

Bennett, Wendell C.
1949 A Cross-Cultural Survey of South American Indian Tribes: Architecture and Engineering, in *Handbook of South American Indians*, Vol. V, edited by Julian H. Steward, pp. 1–65. Bulletin of the Bureau of American Ethnology 143

Bustos, Víctor
1978 *La arqueología de los Llanos del Beni*, Documentos Internos 32/78, Instituto Nacional de Arqueología de Bolivia, La Paz

Cardús, José
1886 *Las Misiones Franciscanas entre los Infieles de Bolivia: Descripción del Estado de Ellas en 1883 y 1884*. Librería de la Inmaculada Concepción, Barcelona

Carvajal, Jacinto de
1956 [1648] *Relación del Descubrimiento del Río Apure hasta su Ingreso en el Orinoco*. Ediciones Edime, Caracas

Castellanos, Juan de
1955 [1589] *Elegías de varones ilustres de Indias*, 4 vols. Editorial A B C, Bogota

Cieza de León, Pedro de
1959 [1553] *The Incas of Pedro de Cieza de León*, edited by V. W. von Hagen. University of Oklahoma Press, Norman

Colón, Fernando
1959 *The Life of the Admiral Christopher Columbus by His Son Ferdinand*, translated and edited by Benjamin Keen. Rutgers University Press, New Brunswick

Cortés, Hernán
1963 *Cartas y Documentos*. Editorial Porrua, Mexico.

1971. *Letters from Mexico*, translated and edited by A. R. Pagden. Grossman, New York

Cruxent, J. M.
1952 Notes on Venezuelan Archeology. In *Selected Papers of the XXIXth International Congress of Americanists: Indian Tribes of Aboriginal America*, Vol. III, edited by Sol Tax, pp. 280–94, University of Chicago Press, Chicago
1966 Apuntes sobre las calzadas de Barinas, Venezuela. *Boletín Informativo* (Instituto Venezolano de Investigaciones Científicas), 4: 10–22

Denevan, William M.
1966 *The Aboriginal Cultural Geography of the Llanos de Mojos of Bolivia*, Ibero-Americana 48, University of California Press, Berkeley
1980 *La Geografía cultural aborigen de los Llanos de Mojos*. Librería Editorial Juventud, La Paz

Deuel, Leo
1969 *Flights into Yesterday: The Story of Aerial Archaeology*. St. Martin's Press, New York

Díaz del Castillo, Bernal
1944 *Historia verdadera de la conquista de la Nueva España*. 3 vols. Editorial Pedro Robredo, Mexico

Dougherty, Bernard, and Horacio H. Calandra
1981 Nota preliminar sobre investigaciones arqueológicas en los Llanos de Moxos, Departamento del Beni, República de Bolivia. *Revista del Museo de la Plata (Nueva Serie), Sección Antropología* 8 (53): 87–106

Ducci, Zacarias
1895 *Diario de la visita a todas las misiones existentes en la República de Bolivia, América Meridional, praticada por el R.P. Sebastian Pifferi*. Assisi (Italy)

Eder, Ferencz Xaver (Francisco Javier)
1888 [1791] *Descripción de la provincia de los Mojos en el reino del Perú*, translated by Nicolás Armentia, Imprenta de El Siglo Industrial, La Paz

Erickson, Clark L.
1980 Sistemas agrícolas prehispánicos en los Llanos de Mojos, *América Indígena* 40: 731–55

Folan, William J., Ellen R. Kintz, and Laraine A. Fletcher
1983 *Coba: A Classic Maya Metropolis*. Academic Press, New York

Freidel, David A. and Jeremy A. Sabloff, eds.
1984 *Cozumel: Late Maya Settlement Patterns*. Academic Press, Orlando

Garson, Adam G.
1980 Prehistory, Settlement and Food Production in the Savanna Region of La Calzada de Páez, Venezuela. Ph.D. dissertation, Yale University. University Microfilms, Ann Arbor

Humboldt, Alexander von, and Aimé Bonpland
1852 *Personal Narrative of Travels to the Equinoctial Regions of America During the Years 1799–1804*. George Routledge and Sons, London

Jahn, Alfredo
1927 *Los Aborígenes del occidente de Venezuela*. Lit. y Tip. del Comercio, Caracas

Kurjack, Edward B., and Silvia Garza T.
1981 Pre-Columbian Community Form and Distribution in the Northern Maya Area. In *Lowland Maya Settlement Patterns*, edited by Wendy Ashmore, pp. 287–309. University of New Mexico Press, Albuquerque.

Landa, Diego de
1978 [1566] *Yucatán: Before and After the Conquest*. Dover, New York

Lizarazu, Juan de
1906 [1638] Informaciones hechas por Don Juan de Lizarazu sobre el descubrimiento de los Mojos. In *Juicio de límites entre el Perú y Bolivia*, edited by Victor M. Maurtua, Vol. IX, pp. 124–216. M. G. Hernández, Madrid

López de Gómara, Francisco
1965 *Cortés: The Life of the Conqueror*, translated and edited by L. B. Simpson. University of California Press, Berkeley

Mathewson, Kent
1982 Bridging the Guayas River Gap: Legend and Landscape Archaeology in Coastal Ecuador. *Andean Perspective* 4:15–20

Métraux, Alfred
1942 *The Native Tribes of Eastern Bolivia and Western Matto Grosso*, Bulletin of the Bureau of American Ethnology 134

Morley, Sylvanus G.
1946 *The Ancient Maya*. Stanford University Press, Stanford

Morley, Sylvanus G., G. W. Brainerd, and R. J. Sharer
1983 *The Ancient Maya*. Stanford University Press, Stanford

Nordenskiöld, Erland
1913 Urnengräber und Mounds im bolivianischen Flachlande. *Baessler Archiv* [Leipzig and Berlin] 3: 205–55
1916 Die Anpassung der Indianer an die Verhältnisse in den Uberschwemmungsgebieten in Südamerika. *Ymer* [Stockholm] 36: 138–55

Oramas, Luis R.
1917 Apuntes sobre arqueología venezolana. In *Proceedings of the Second Pan American Scientific Congress*, Vol. I, pp. 138–45. Washington, DC

Orbigny, Alcides D'
1958 [1835–1847] Viaje a la América Meridional. In *Biblioteca indiana: viajes y viajeros*, Vol. III, pp. 15–920. Aguilar, Madrid

Parsons, James J., and William A. Bowen
1966 Ancient Ridged Fields of the San Jorge River Floodplain, Colombia. *Geographical Review* 56: 317–43

Plafker, George
1963 Observations on Archaeological Remains in Northeastern Bolivia. *American Antiquity* 28: 372–8

Posey, Darrell A.
1983 Indigenous Ecological Knowledge and Development of the Amazon. In *The Dilemma of Amazonian Development*, edited by Emilio F. Moran, pp. 225–57. Westview Press, Boulder

Rouse, Irving
1952 Porto Rican Prehistory: Excavations in the Interior, South and East; Chronological Implications. In *Scientific Survey of Porto Rico and the Virgin Islands*, Vol. XVIII, part 4, pp. 463–578. The New York Academy of Sciences, New York

Stevens, John Lloyd
1962 [1841] *Incidents of Travel in Yucatán*. 2 vols. University of Oklahoma Press, Norman

Steward, Julian H., and Louis C. Faron
1959 *Native Peoples of South America*. McGraw-Hill, New York

Toribio Medina, José, ed.
1934 *The Discovery of the Amazon According to the Account of Friar Gaspar de Carvajal and Other Documents*. American Geographical Society, Special Publication No. 17, New York

von Hagen, Victor W.
1960 *The World of the Maya*. Mentor, New York

Zucchi, Alberta
1972 Aboriginal Earth Structures of the Western Venezuelan Llanos, *Caribbean Journal of Science* 12: 95–106
1973 Prehistoric Human Occupations of the Western Venezuelan Llanos. *American Antiquity* 38: 182–90

Zucchi, Alberta, and William M. Denevan
1979 Campos elevados e historia cultural prehispánica en los llanos occidentales de Venezuela, *Montalban*, Vol. IX, pp. 565–736. Caracas

20 The association between roads and polities: evidence for Wari roads in Peru

KATHARINA J. SCHREIBER

Introduction

This paper deals with the relationship between roads and complex political organizations. Specifically, it approaches the problem of identifying particular roads that formed portions of formalized, "official" road systems in prehistoric states and empires. This identification is not always obvious when one is dealing with purely archaeological data. Two assumptions underlie much of the following discussion. First, the fact that a polity made use of a road does not necessarily indicate that the road was built by that polity; frequently polities incorporated roads that were already in existence. And second, not all roads in use during a particular political episode were necessarily part of the "official" system; some roads may have functioned in this capacity, while many, if not most, roads existed independently of the political organization.

It is useful to distinguish between roads that were used by a state, and roads that constituted a *formal* road system. A formal road system is one that was established by a state, incorporating existing roads or building new ones, or some combination of these; was maintained by the state; and was used for political purposes. These political purposes may include providing links between administrative centers, channels for long-distance communications, movement of military forces, movement of trade and tribute goods, as well as a variety of other state-level activities. Certainly all polities made use of roads, but not all polities had formal road systems.

This paper begins with a discussion of four lines of evidence that may be followed when using archaeological data to establish the association between particular roads and polities. The second section presents the results of a case study in the south highlands of Peru, revealing evidence for the existence of formalized road systems within both the Wari and Inka Empires. Finally, the data from other parts of Peru supporting the existence of a Wari road system are summarized.

The association of roads with political systems

Several lines of evidence may indicate the association between particular roads and a particular political organization, and hence support the existence of a formalized system of "royal" roads. First, and most obvious, it must be demonstrated that particular roads are *contemporaneous* with the existence of the political system under investigation. This may be accomplished in several ways, the most reliable means being the association of dated sites with a road. Elsewhere in this volume, Beck (chapter 8) suggests using the principle of cross-cutting relationships to estimate the relative date of different roads. The association between roads and features such as agricultural terraces may also indicate relative dating of road use.

The fact that certain roads were *in use* at a particular time is not, in and of itself, sufficient to identify those roads as royal roads. In fact, it is likely that the majority of roads in use had little to do with formal political organization. Further, the initial construction of a road may significantly predate the period of political domination. Although political organizations such as empires certainly built new roads to serve special purposes or to connect new settlements, in many or even most cases they simply formalized roads that were already in existence. And many roads probably continued in use long after the fall of the particular polity, and in some cases may have been used by later polities as well.

Once the contemporaneity of roads and polities can be established, it then remains to ascertain which roads formed part of a formalized system, and which did not. One line of evidence that might be followed here is to consider the *locations* of the roads in question. Within a region, many roads served to provide links between local villages, or between settlements and resource exploitation areas. Other roads, however, may be seen to have connected a discrete region with other regions. These interregional roads are more likely candidates for royal roads, especially in the case of regions located some distance from the political capital. Interregional roads that connected an area with the political core are especially likely to have been part of a formal road system. Within a region it may be more difficult to identify royal roads, since interregional royal roads may connect with and make use of local road systems. And in regions within which are found political capitals or major administrative centers, the density of royal roads may be much higher than in more distant provinces. In these cases roads may form extensive lattices of interconnections between political centers.

A third line of evidence that may support the association of roads with political organization is the *association of sites* with roads. This association can indicate both the contemporaneity and also the cultural affiliation of the road with respect to the site. Here a useful distinction can be drawn between settlements of the local populace and sites representing political authority. Certainly local villages were located along roads, but such local roads need not have had anything to do with the over-arching political organization. However, the association of sites of political function with particular roads suggests that those roads served a political function. Sites may be associated with particular roads by simple physical proximity, consistent topographic position, or direct articulation.

A fourth line of evidence that may indicate construction and/or formalization of roads by a polity is the *detail of construction style* and particular features of the road. Evidence for the planning and engineering of a road, requiring substantial amounts of labor input, may imply that the road was built by some sort of managerial organization. Elsewhere in this volume other authors have distinguished between roads and paths on the basis of evidence of planning and engineering. The fact that a road was engineered does not necessarily imply, however, that its construction was carried out under the direction of a state-level organization. In other words, all state roads probably show evidence of formal planning and engineering, but all engineered roads need not have been built by states. It may be possible in some cases to identify specific construction styles associated with known states; formal elements of road morphology such as paving style may supply such evidence. In addition, other associated features such as bridges may be of distinctive styles, enabling the association of particular roads with a political organization.

To summarize, four lines of evidence may help establish a direct association between roads and polities. First, the contemporaneity of road use and the existence of the polity in question must be demonstrated. Second, the locations of roads, especially interregional ones, may indicate their inclusion within a network of royal roads. Third, sites associated with roads may support the cultural and temporal affiliations of each road. And fourth, particular styles of construction may help to identify a

Fig. 20.1. The Carhuarazo valley.

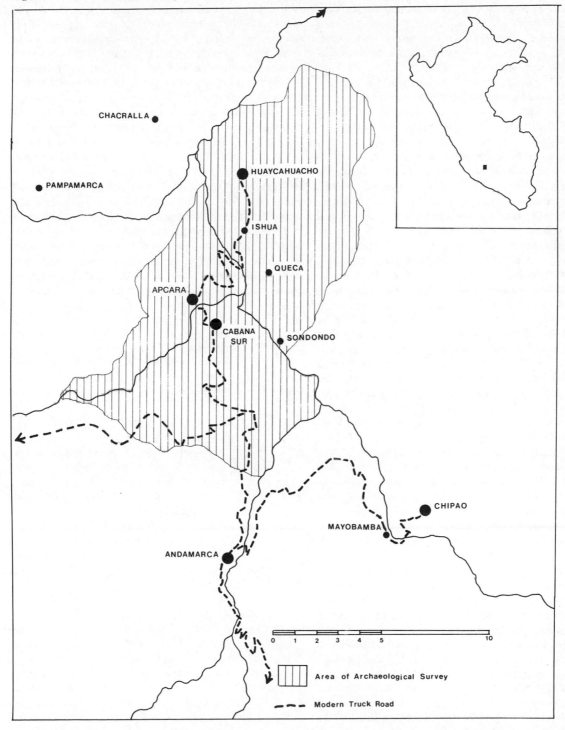

road as the construction of a particular polity. None of these lines of evidence is likely to produce unquestionable interpretations when taken alone. However, when taken together, the convergence of several lines of evidence may produce a stronger association between particular roads and polities.

In the following section a set of archaeological data is analyzed with respect to these lines of evidence in an attempt to identify a road system associated with a pre-Inka polity in the central highlands of Peru.

The evidence of the Carhuarazo valley

The Carhuarazo valley is located in the south highlands of Peru, at a latitude of about 14 degrees south (Fig. 20.1), in the modern Department of Ayacucho. According to historic documents this valley was occupied by a discrete ethnic group, the Andamarca Rucanas, at the time of its incorporation into the Inka Empire about A.D. 1475 (Cock MS). Topographically and ethnically the valley is clearly bounded and isolated from neighboring populated areas. In 1976 archaeological excavations were undertaken at the site of Jincamocco, which was found to be an administrative center of the Middle Horizon Wari Empire (A.D. 600–800) (Schreiber 1978). In 1981 an intensive archaeological survey was completed in most of the valley (Fig. 20.1) in order to provide a regional-level cultural context in which to interpret Jincamocco. The major focus of this study was to evaluate the effect on the local culture of incorporation into the two successive highland Andean empires: the Wari Empire, and the later Inka Empire (Schreiber 1987). One specific focus of this study was the elucidation of prehistoric road networks within the valley (Schreiber 1984), and between the valley and other neighboring regions.

This section discussed the archaeological evidence for the existence of formalized road systems in the Carhuarazo valley, under both the Wari and Inka Empires.

Roads and trails

In this volume a distinction has been drawn between roads and trails. Roads are defined as showing evidence of planning and engineering, including formal features of construction, while trails are more fortuitous, being the result of long-term use. Observations of roads and trails in contemporary use in the Carhuarazo valley suggest this distinction is both valid and useful, and that roads may be further subdivided into two categories.

Two types of roads have been defined in this region: intravalley roads and interregional roads. In the first

case, an extensive network of roads is found within the valley, providing connections between all modern settlements (Fig. 20.2); these are termed intravalley roads. All such roads are found within the cultivated portion of the valley, that is, at elevations less than 3,800 m. All show evidence of planning and intensive labor input. Because of the terrain, portions of the roads are very steep and these sections are always provided with stone steps. Occasionally roads may be cut into hillsides and paved. Intravalley roads are typically bounded by stone walls on either side to keep animals from trampling adjacent agricultural fields. Finally, roads are provided with permanent bridges where they cross the major rivers.

The second type of road may be termed an interregional road. At least eight major interregional roads have been identified that connect the Carhuarazo valley with other regions (Fig. 20.2). The Carhuarazo valley is quite isolated topographically from other regions, the nearest population centers being a three-day walk away. These roads ascend from the network of intravalley roads to the high elevation *puna* zone at altitudes of 4,000–4,800 m,

Fig. 20.2. Contemporary road networks.

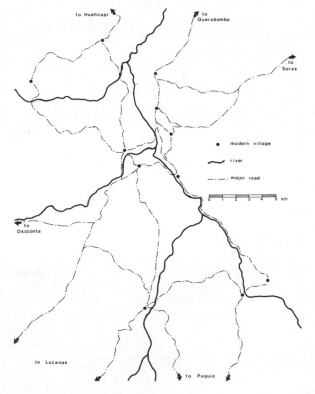

cross this high plateau region, and descend into other populated valleys. Across the high, flat *puna* these roads may show very little evidence of planning and engineering, but they appear quite distinctive on aerial photos. At least two of the roads are said by local informants to be paved their entire distance across the *puna*. As the roads descend into the populated valley they all show clear evidence of labor-intensive construction.

Finally, an extensive network of trails is also found within the valley. These trails serve to connect settlements with agricultural fields and other resource-exploitation areas. Like roads, they generally are walled with stone on either side, but they seldom show major improvements such as paving or stone steps. In this particular example, the width of the trails can be used to distinguish them from intravalley roads, as trails are quite narrow (less than 2m) and roads are relatively wide. In addition, trails tend to follow very circuitous routes among the agricultural fields, while roads take much more direct routes between settlements. Trails are never provided with formal bridges, although many ford small streams. Finally, trails intermittently serve as irrigation channels, temporarily impeding passage.

These types of roads and trails are based on observations of the contemporary culture in the Carhuarazo valley. It is assumed that many if not most of the roads were built and used in prehistoric times. Within the valley, the alignments of intravalley roads and trails may have changed somewhat through time as settlement locations changed. For example, some routes that function only as minor trails today have some of the formal prehistoric roads, but no longer function as such as a result of the abandonment of prehistoric settlements with which they were associated. However, the routes of the interregional roads probably have not changed significantly since they were established, as the most direct and topographically suitable routes from this valley to adjacent valleys have not changed since prehistoric times.

Relative dating of road use

Historical records of road construction in the Carhuarazo valley do not exist, but certain documents do make mention of roads in use during the colonial period and refer, in some cases, to their use in the late prehistoric period. In 1586 a Spanish *visitador* recorded the names and locations of all the local villages, the roads connecting them, and the distances from one to the next. He also mentioned three of the interregional roads, stating that one was the road to Guamanga (the regional capital), and that those to the southwest and the northeast comprised part of the Inka system of royal roads (Monzón 1881:239). The lengthy letter to the king of Spain written at the end of the sixteenth century by Felipe Guaman Poma de Ayala also refers to the Inka road passing through this valley. His list of *tampu* (way stations) along the Inka highways includes one at the town of Apcara, an Inka-period site in this valley (Guaman Poma 1966:424–5). Guaman Poma was born and raised in the Carhuarazo valley, so his descriptions are particularly noteworthy.

As informative as these documents are, they tell us little about non-Inka and pre-Inka roads. A second line of evidence indicating period of road use is the association of particular sites with roads. Roads that are immediately adjacent to sites, roads that go through sites, or roads that terminate at sites can often be demonstrated to be directly associated with those sites. A regional ceramic chronology has been developed for the Carhuarazo valley, spanning the time from the Initial period through the Late Horizon; sites are dated according to this relative scheme. This line of evidence is most effective within the valley, where several sites are found associated with each road. However, outside the valley, along the interregional roads, few sites are known, both because settlements on the *puna* are generally rare, and because the systematic archaeological survey did not extend above elevations of 4,000 m. It may be seen that major intravalley roads are associated with sites from several time periods, indicating that, although some roads may have been built in quite early times, they frequently continued in use for many centuries thereafter. And as mentioned above, some roads associated with prehistoric sites now function as trails, although they do retain the formal characteristics of roads.

A third line of evidence that may serve to indicate the relative date of some roads in this valley is their association with agricultural terraces. Much of the valley below the elevation of 3,300 m is intensively terraced with stone retaining walls. In terraced zones, roads in use at the time of terrace construction were incorporated into the construction. That is, terraces were not built across and through major roads, but rather these roads formed permanent established routes through the system of terraces. On the other hand, traces of earlier roads were probably completely removed by the construction of terraces. Later roads either avoided terraced areas, or used existing routes (usually small trails) through terraced zones. Some later roads may have had to follow trail routes through terraced areas, and hence appear narrow and circuitous.

Although the association between roads and terraces is relatively clear, the dating of terrace construction is not. In the Carhuarazo valley, several convergent lines of evidence suggest that most terraces were built during the Middle Horizon, that is, during the period of Wari domination. Since terracing serves to limit erosion on steep slopes, it also serves to hinder the downslope movement of artifacts. Sites predating the Middle Horizon frequently have extensive scatters of artifacts extending for long distances down slopes below site boundaries, even when those slopes are terraced. On the other hand, terraces below sites dating to the Middle Horizon or later, seldom exhibit artifact scatters beyond the first or second level of terracing. This suggests that terraces were not built before the Middle Horizon.

Most Middle Horizon sites are found immediately adjacent to agricultural terraces, but terraces do not cut into the sites, even in areas without stone architecture. This suggests that the sites and the terraces were in use at the same time. Also, beginning in the Middle Horizon, houses within sites are sometimes built on artificially leveled platforms, built exactly like agricultural terraces, suggesting that this technique became prevalent at this time. Finally, structures built directly on agricultural terraces never pre-date the Middle Horizon. In sum, the evidence of associated sites suggests that the terrces were built during the Middle Horizon.

Another line of evidence supporting a Middle Horizon date for the construction of the terraces is a shift in settlement location that took place in the Middle Horizon. Prior to this time local villages were located at elevations from 3,300 to 3,600 m. During the Middle Horizon, the villages at 3,600 m were abandoned and new villages were established at or below 3,300 m (Schreiber 1987). This implies a change in subsistence strategy involving the introduction of or increased reliance on maize production. Since at high altitudes the ability to grow maize is increased by the construction of terraces, it is likely that the settlement shift and the building of terraces occurred at approximately the same time. Further, the construction of the terraces may have been undertaken by the Wari Empire, at its expense, in order to increase the production of maize to be paid as tribute to the empire, much as maize was collected by the Inkas from subject people (Schreiber 1987).

In sum, the interruption of downslope artifact wash, the association of archaeological sites, and the suggestion of increased maize production, all support the interpretation that most terraces in the Carhuarazo valley were built during the Middle Horizon. If this is so, then major roads incorporated into the terrace system must have been in use at that time. Roads used in later periods frequently followed these same routes.

Associated site types

The association between roads and archaeological sites as a means of determining the relative date of road use was discussed in the previous section. In this section a distinction is made between sites that reflect political authority and sites that represent settlements of the local governed population. In this manner roads that were part of a system of official roads may be distinguished from roads serving local needs.

For the Middle Horizon, the period of domination by the Wari Empire, four sites are found in the Carhuarazo valley that can be identified as representing political authority (Fig. 20.3). All four are characterized by Wari style and/or local ceramics dating to the Middle Horizon, and rectangular compound architecture, a style foreign to this region where local constructions were free-standing small round structures. The largest of the four sites is Jincamocco, some 15 ha in extent, which

Fig. 20.3. Roads of the Middle Horizon.

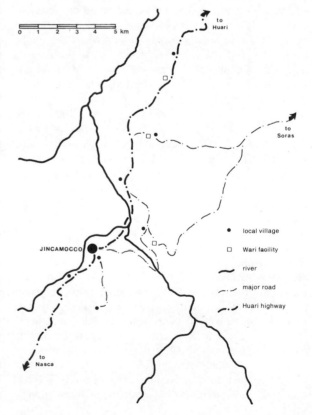

was a major administrative center of the Wari Empire (Schreiber 1978). Centrally located in the valley, it is associated with a major intravalley road that connects directly with one of the interregional roads, the road leading to the southwest and eventually to the Pacific coast at Nasca. The other three Wari sites are small compounds 80 by 100 m each. Two of these are located adjacent to local villages and along intravalley roads; these sites may have functioned as storehouses for agricultural produce. The third site is located immediately adjacent to an interregional road that enters the valley from the north; its topographic position suggests that it functioned to limit access into or out of the valley along this road. The association of this site and Jincamocco with particular interregional roads suggests that those roads were used by the Wari Empire, and perhaps were part of a formal system of official roads.

In the case of the Inka Empire of the Late Horizon, five Inka sites are found within the valley (Fig. 20.4). One structure, a rectangular adobe house, is found within the local town of Apcara, and is thought to be

the house of the Inka governor of this province. (As local centralized authority already existed in the valley at the time of the Inka conquest, no major administrative center was built. Government was achieved through alliance with local leaders [Schreiber 1987].) The town of Apcara, and hence the site of Inka governance, was located on a major intravalley road. A short distance to the southwest along this road is located an Inka structure that probably functioned as a bath or a shrine. Continuing along the same road, one passes a row of Inka storehouses and two Inka buildings, located at the edge of Jincamocco; this Inka site may have been the *tampu* mentioned by Guaman Poma. The road continues through to the southwest. The association of Inka imperial installations with the road would suggest that this was an official royal road. It is especially interesting that this royal Inka road seems to follow the same route as the Middle Horizon Wari road to Nasca.

On the other side of the valley two Inka storage centers are found; both are connected to the local town of Queca by intravalley roads. The historic documents cited above indicate that the royal Inka road passed from Apcara through Queca and out of the valley to the northeast, to Soras and eventually to Cuzco. The exact route between Apcara and Queca certainly followed local intravalley roads, although most of the route can be reconstructed on the basis of construction style and one other associated feature: remains of an Inka suspension bridge.

Construction style and other features

As mentioned above, all roads within the valley show evidence of planning and engineering, in that they are provided with stone steps in steeper areas, are walled on either side, and are sometimes cut into the adjacent hillside. However, now that certain roads have been found to be possible or definite imperial roads, perhaps attributes of construction style can serve to add confirmation to these identifications. In the case of the royal Inka road, clearly defined from Apcara to the southwest, and from Queca to the northeast, it was found that the road is completely paved with stone slabs as it leaves the valley. Paving apparently continues all the way across the *puna*, according to its appearance on aerial photos, and the reports of local informants. The Inka road is probably the only road that continues to be paved for a considerable distance out of the valley. Within the valley, however, this paving does not always distinguish it from other intravalley roads.

Within the valley, between Apcara and Queca, the route of the Inka road is less clear. Fortunately, the

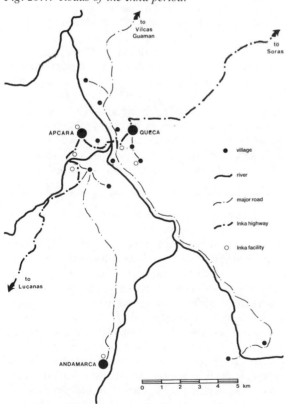

Fig. 20.4. Roads of the Inka period.

remains of an Inka-style suspension bridge were located on either side of the river, so the point at which the road crossed the river is known. Connecting Apcara to this point is a major road, in some sections carved into bedrock cliffs; the extreme lower end of the road has fallen into disrepair, as it is no longer used for bridge access. A modern bridge is located some 2 km downstream, so the road leading from Apcara toward the Inka bridge now turns north toward the modern bridge. In any case, the route of the royal Inka road from Apcara to the old suspension bridge is reasonably clear. It follows a route that avoids, for the most part, terraced areas, so did not have to conform to pre-existing routes between terraced fields.

From the bridge up to Queca is quite a different story. This entire zone is intensively terraced, although a myriad of trails wind through it. The Inka road apparently had to follow these pre-existing routes because there is no evidence of any road that provides direct access between the bridge and Queca. However, at the upper end of the terracing, still several hundred meters from Queca, a major road appears, carved into bedrock and leading to the town. This is probably an Inka construction.

In the case of Wari roads of the Middle Horizon, the situation with regard to construction style is not quite so clear. The road from Jincamocco out of the valley to the southwest was certainly used by the empire, but nothing can be said about paving or construction style because the same route was re-used by the Inka Empire. If it were built in a distinctive Wari style, any trace of this was eliminated by the Inka reconstruction and paving. The Wari road entering the valley from the north, however, does have some unique attributes. As this road descends into the valley, a linear distance of 5 km and a vertical drop of 450 m, stone steps are built along the entire distance, even in relatively level areas. And the road is not paved with stone slabs between steps, as are the Inka roads and most other intravalley roads. Whether or not this constitutes a distinctive Wari style of road construction will have to await future identification of other Wari roads in other regions within the empire.

This road entering the valley from the north, coming ultimately from Wari itself, becomes part of the intravalley road network. Beyond the small Wari compound it continues south, passing a local village occupied during the Middle Horizon, and then leads directly to the location of the Inka bridge. Although suspension bridges are commonly thought to be of Inka origin, it is likely that they originated in the broader Andean tradition, and may have existed for quite some time prior to

the Late Horizon. The example under discussion here strongly suggests that the suspension bridge was in use during the Middle Horizon. The location of the Inka bridge is the only place in the valley suitable for a suspension bridge, and no other type of bridge would have been appropriate here. If the Wari road also crossed the river at this point it is only logical to assume that it, too, used a suspension bridge.

A short distance up from the bridge, on the west side of the valley, the road diverges. One branch is the Inka road to Apcara, discussed above. The other fords a small stream and then continues as a major road up to Jincamocco. Thus, the entire route of the Wari road through the valley may be tentatively identified.

The association of roads and polities in the Carhuarazo valley

In the preceding section, an attempt was made to associate particular roads in the Carhuarazo valley with two prehistoric polities, the Wari Empire and the Inka Empire. This analysis followed four steps. First, different types of roads and trails were defined, based on observation of contemporary routes. Second, the relative dating of roads was discussed, since it must be established that the roads in question were in use at the time of each political domain. This was accomplished with the use of ethnohistoric documents, the association of dated sites with particular roads, and the association between roads and agricultural terraces. Third, once networks of roads were seen to be in use at each time in question, it was necessary to isolate those roads that were used for political purposes; the association between roads and centers of political control provided much of this identification in both cases, although ethnohistoric documents provided confirmation of Inka roads. Finally, attributes of construction style and other associated features were considered in order to help define these roads, and also indicate less obvious details of the routes followed within the valley.

In the case of the Middle Horizon (Fig. 20.3), the construction of the system of agricultural terraces indicates that major roads in those zones were established at that time. The association between Middle Horizon sites and particular intravalley and interregional roads indicates which roads were in use at the time. More importantly, the association of one small Wari site and the large administrative center at Jincamocco with particular interregional roads suggests that these roads formed part of an empire-wide system of long-distance roads. The association of this road with a bridge suggests that suspension bridges were in use during the Middle

Horizon. A style of road construction, unique in this valley, suggests that the road was not a local construction, but rather was a formal maintained Wari road. Whether this style of construction is typical of other Wari roads in other regions of the empire must await further investigation.

On a broader geographical scale, the Carhuarazo valley lies about midway between Wari, the imperial capital, and Nasca, an influential area within the Wari Empire; travel time on foot north to Wari is about six days, southwest to Nasca about the same. The road from the Carhuarazo valley north to Wari may have been known to, and occasionally used by, the Inkas. About two-thirds of the way to Wari its most likely route takes it past the Inka site of Vilcas Guaman. According to Cieza de León (1985:42), there were three or four major roads that joined at Vilcas, two of which formed the main Chinchaysuyu highland road connecting Vilcas with Cuzco to the southeast, and Quito to the north (see also Regal Matienzo [1936:47] and Strube Erdmann [1963:34]). The third road was certainly the road connecting the highland road with the coast road near Pisco. Hyslop has surveyed and documented much of the route of this road, which passed by the important Inka site at Huaytara (Hyslop 1984:103). The possible fourth road may have led south from Vilcas to the Carhuarazo valley, where it joined the Inka connector road at the suspension bridge. Von Hagen (1976:69) states that this road connected Vilcas with the territory of the Soras and Rucanas, meeting the connector road, and continuing from there to Nasca, but he does not cite his sources for this information. In any case, it is possible that the fourth road to Vilcas may be none other than the Wari road identified here.

In the case of the Late Horizon (Fig. 20.4), the association of sites and roads indicates something of the network of intravalley roads in use at the time. The association of Inka facilities with the road to the southwest indicates its use as a royal road; historic documents confirm this and also identify the Inka road to the northeast. A distinctive paving style distinguishes the Inka roads from other interregional roads, but within the intravalley system the identification of the Inka route is less clear. There is no doubt that this road was part of a formalized Inka road system, incorporated and maintained by that empire. The existence of an Inka bridge enables the identification of the probable route of the Inka road on the west side of the valley, but the extensive terracing on the east side precludes a positive identification, at least up to the point at which the road climbs out of the terraced zone.

The evidence for an empire-wide Wari road system

Given the evidence from the Carhuarazo valley, it does appear that the Wari Empire used a system of interregional roads. However, is there any evidence of this from other parts of the empire? A political regime such as that which existed in the Middle Horizon probably needed roads to serve as communications arteries, to move military forces, and to mobilize economic resources, among other things. Following the same lines of evidence used above, but on a macroregional scale, this possibility can be considered. First, can roads be established as contemporaneous with the period of Wari domination? Second, can imperial installations be directly associated with particular roads? Third, do such roads conform to a pattern of interregional road networks?

The evidence to evaluate these lines of inquiry does not yet exist, at least in any coherent body of data. However, certain indications suggest that Wari did, indeed, have an official road system. The primary data are the associations of major Wari sites with the Inka road system. As seen in the case study presented above, there are indications that the Inka re-used certain Wari roads. This does not necessarily argue that Wari built the Inka highway system; on the contrary, in most cases Wari probably also re-used pre-existing routes. The question is not who built the roads, but who used them and maintained them, and were they part of a formal system of state roads?

The association of Wari installations with any major interregional roads would help support the notion that it had a road system. Since the Inka system is the only major prehistoric road system that has received careful study, the association of Wari sites with it is a valid pursuit. Some of these associations have been presented by Lumbreras (1974:162), regarding Middle Horizon sites in general. Here the discussion is limited to sites exhibiting distinctive Wari architecture: large orthogonal compounds, and distinctive arrangements of patios and galleries (cf. Schreiber 1978).

The site of Wari, capital of the empire, is located along the Inka highway. North of Wari, along the main Chinchaysuyu trunk line, are found several other Wari sites, including Azangaro (formerly Incaraqay), Wari Willka, and possibly Viracochapampa. In his survey of Inka roads, John Hyslop also noted a possible Wari site, Yamobamba, immediately adjacent to the Inka road near Cajamarca (Hyslop 1984:273). South and east from Wari along this same trunk line no Wari imperial sites are clearly identified, except Pikillaqta near Cuzco, which is adjacent to the Inka road. As discussed above, Jincamocco is located on the Inka road from Cuzco to

Nasca. On the central coast, Pachacamac was an important site during both the Middle and Late Horizons, and it lies along the Inka coast road. Pachacamac was the center of distribution of a variant of Wari polychrome normally found only on the coast. However, examples of Pachacamac-style Wari ceramics were found at Wari Willka in the central highlands; an Inka road connects these two locations.

From this brief summary it may be seen that there are tantalizing bits of data that suggest that the Wari Empire was using some of the same routes that later became the "royal highway of the Inka." This would imply that the Wari Empire, too, had a system of royal roads. Some might argue that the Wari Empire actually created much of the Inka highway system, but this is probably taking the argument farther than the data warrant. More to the point, it does appear that the Wari sites are located along major interregional routes, and therefore that the Wari probably did have an imperial road system.

On the other hand, there is still no evidence of actual construction of Wari roads, or rebuilding and maintenance of extant roads. Further, there is no evidence of a system of rest houses, *tampu*, like those of the Inka; they must have existed if the analogy with the Inka system is to hold up. Of course, if the Inka system is coterminous with the Wari system in most areas, the Inka rebuilding of the roads may have eliminated obvious traces of Wari features. Thus, at present, it cannot be said with absolute certainty that the Wari Empire established a formal road system. It is clear, however, that its major installations are located on major interregional routes, and that it certainly used these roads during its domination of the central Andes. The evidence from the Carhuarazo valley suggests that Wari undertook the construction and maintenance of particular roads, and that these roads connected political centers within the valley with regions outside the valley. Whether or not this is a general pattern throughout the Wari Empire must await future investigation.

Acknowledgments

The field research on which this paper is based was funded by two grants from the National Science Foundation (SOC75–16865 and BNS80–06121). Permission to undertake fieldwork in the Carhuarazo valley was granted by the Centro de Investigación y Restauración de Bienes Monumentales of the Instituto Nacional de Cultura, Lima, Peru. Facilities for data analysis were provided by the Museo Nacional de Antropología y Arqueología, Pueblo Libre, Lima. The support of all these institutions is gratefully acknowledged. I also thank John Hyslop for his generosity in sharing his expertise with me, and for his comments on an earlier version of this paper.

References

Cieza de León, Pedro de
  1985 *Crónica del Perú, segunda parte*. Edición, prólogo y notas de Francesca Cantú. Pontificia Universidad Católica del Perú, Academia Nacional de la Historia

Cock, Guillermo
  MS Etnia y Etnicidad en Lucanas Andamarcas. Manuscript in possession of author.

Guaman Poma de Ayala, Felipe
  1966 *Nueva crónica y buen gobierno*, Part III. Interpretado por el Tnte. Corl. Luis Bustíos Gálvez. Lima

Hyslop, John
  1984 *The Inka Road System*. Academic Press, Orlando

Lumbreras, Luis G.
  1974 *The People and Cultures of Ancient Peru*. Smithsonian Institution, Washington, DC

Monzón, Luis de
  1881 Descripción de la tierra del repartimiento de los Rucanas Antamarcas de la corona real, jurisdicción de la ciudad de Guamanga (1586). *Relaciones geográficas de Indias*, Vol. I:237–48. Madrid

Regal Matienzo, Alberto
  1936 *Los caminos del Inca en el antiguo Perú*. Sanmarti, Lima

Schreiber, Katharina J.
  1978 Planned Architecture of Middle Horizon Peru: Implications for Social and Political Organization. Doctoral dissertation, State University of New York at Binghamton. University Microfilms, Ann Arbor
  1984 Prehistoric Roads in the Carhuarazo Valley, Peru. In *Current Archaeological Projects in the Central Andes, Some Approaches and Results*, edited by Ann Kendall, pp. 75–94. BAR International Series 210. Oxford
  1987 Conquest and Consolidation: A Comparison of the Wari and Inka Occupations of a Highland Peruvian Valley. *American Antiquity* 52(2):266–84

Strube Erdmann, Leon S.
  1963 *Vialidad imperial de los Incas*. Instituto de Estudios Americanistas, Serie Histórica 33. Universidad Nacional de Córdoba, Argentina

von Hagen, Victor W.
  1976 *The Royal Road of the Inca*. Gordon and Cremonesi, London

21 The Chincha roads: economics and symbolism

DWIGHT T. WALLACE

A road system was identified from aerial photographs of the Chincha valley used during an archaeological survey of this and the Pisco valleys of south-central coastal Peru (Wallace 1971). The ease of discerning these roads can be tested on the photo-mosaic in Fig. 21.1; the two arrows point to ceremonial centers with which the roads are clearly associated. The regular layout of the road system is most obvious for the diagonal roads, since they stand out in contrast from the generally rectilinear pattern of the modern roads and field divisions. The plan of the roads and locations of contemporary archaeological sites are shown in Fig. 21.2.

The regular overall plan of the roads and their alignment with ceremonial sites suggest some ideological function for the system. But the recent discovery of a sixteenth-century document mentioning a precolumbian road in Chincha, along with some distinctive features of the Chincha polity, open up other possibilities. In fact, some of the roads do align with major access routes to the valley, suggesting the function of trafficking of goods. In addition, a distinctive archaeological habitation pattern and some documented occupational differences in habitation location, open up the possibility of the roads functioning in terms of socioeconomic integration with political overtones. Since a multifunctional explanation would be quite acceptable, there are several intriguing possibilities. Although the road system remains the starting and ending points, questions of its possible cultural context will be discussed extensively, despite sketchy data and the question of the validity of ethnohistorical sources. The attempt, then, is to do trial modeling of possible cultural context for understanding this unusual case, a process that does have its value in reminding us of the ultimate purpose of all descriptive work.

Fig. 21.1. *Aerial photo-mosaic of the Chincha Valley. The upper arrow locates the major late south coast pilgrimage center of La Centinela, the lower arrow a secondary ritual/administrative center, La Centinela de San Pedro. Other features are noted in the text.*

Fig. 21.2. Map of Chincha with Late Horizon and Intermediate period sites located; the size of the marks is roughly proportional to site size. The associated road system is shown by the straight solid lines.

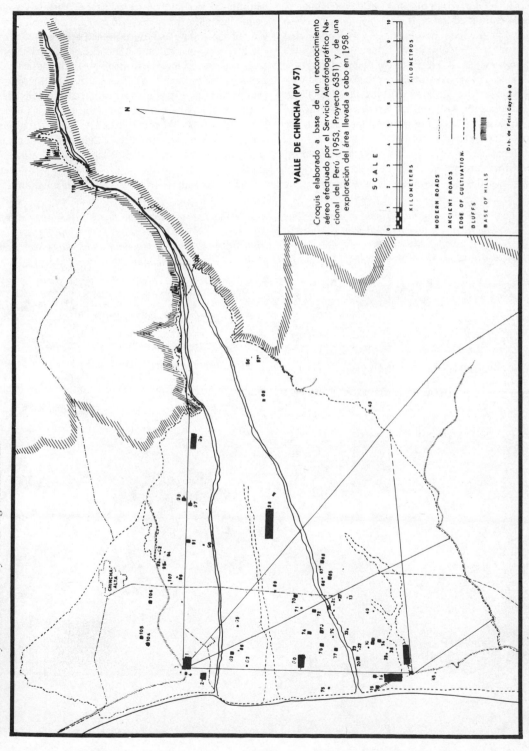

VALLE DE CHINCHA (PV 57)

Croquis elaborado a base de un reconocimiento aéreo efectuado por el Servicio Aerofotográfico Nacional del Perú (1953, Proyecto 6351) y de una exploración del área llevada a cabo en 1958.

SCALE

KILOMETERS

KILOMETROS

MODERN ROADS

ANCIENT ROADS

EDGE OF CULTIVATION.

BLUFFS

BASE OF HILLS

Dib. de Felix Caycho G.

To set the physical scene, Chincha is a compact coastal valley 200 km south of Lima, with approximately 22,000 ha of cultivated fields. It is a triangular area with roughly 25 km of open beach and a very constricted mouth of the gorge from which it emerges from the Andes approximately 20 km from the ocean, slightly off the aerial photograph. The northern area of small properties is Chincha Alta, on a bluff above the river floor; Chincha Alta has grown from the *reducción* established for what little was left of the native population in the latter part of the sixteenth century.

The colonial town of Chincha Baja and its port, Tambo de Mora, are on the valley floor just south of La Centinela. The river has sufficient flow to irrigate the entire valley, which has maintained one of the largest outputs of agricultural products on the coast south of Lima. An older river bed can be noted in the southern part of the valley, its mouth immediately to the north of the arrow pointing to the site of San Pedro. The present river has been channeled into two branches. The area between the branches still shows traces of a major flood that occurred early in this century. Bluffs line both sides of the valley, cut from the fairly flat pampas formed by the uplift of the old ocean floor. A level area along the ocean beach, now continuously cultivated, connects the valley floors of Chincha and Pisco, the next valley to the south.

The roads radiate from the Late Intermediate Period

Fig. 21.3. The main terrace and pyramid of La Centinela, seen from the southeast. The broad basal terrace is 13 m above the surrounding fields, the pyramid proper 20 m above the terrace. The cross to the left is on a small pyramid (La Cumbe) on the bluff of Chincha Alta behind La Centinela; from certain distances, this point could have been used for sighting direction from points where the top of La Centinela itself was not outlined against the sky.

ceremonial center of La Centinela (Fig. 21.3), shown as the most northerly arrow in Fig. 21.1. The only published description of La Centinela beyond brief mention is that of Max Uhle (1924). The outer two of the four major roads radiating from La Centinela are at exact right angles (see Fig. 21.2), one parallel with the beach, the other proceeding straight up-valley. The up-valley road aligns with a notch in the foothill spur into which it runs; this notch or pass still serves as the only path leading up-river past the narrow mouth of the mountain gorge. The other two main diagonal roads are at evenly spaced intervals within this right angle, cutting diagonally across the valley. Of the three angles formed by these arms, two adjacent ones are exactly 25 degrees. The road parallel to the beach leads to a second, much smaller ceremonial center, La Centinela de San Pedro (the lower arrow in Fig. 21.1; Fig. 21.4). At least two additional roads radiate from San Pedro, one up-valley, the other diagonal. The up-valley road probably met the

major diagonal road which continues across the pampas to the Pisco valley; nothing about the topography or alignment with other roads or physiographic features explains why this up-valley road is not at an exact right angle with the road parallel to the beach. The north–south road in the center of the valley on the aerial photographs is the Pan American Highway.

The road parallel to the beach may have extended south to the lower Pisco valley. There are very numerous habitation mounds of the period in this lower valley area, and the aerial photos show a number of diagonal field divisions which contrast with the otherwise rectilinear fields. However, no alignments with sites or an overall pattern has yet been discovered.

The neat plan of the prehistoric roads is by no means evident on the ground. One short stretch does have a road floor over 1 m lower than the surrounding fields, expectable with a well-used dirt road; it also is lined with meter-high *tapia* (puddled adobe) walls on both sides.

Fig. 21.4. The terrace-pyramid of La Centinela de San Pedro, seen from the west. The present summit is approximately 14 m above the fields.

Uhle (1924:61) noted that the west–east road, 5 m wide, between La Centinela and the up-valley pass was also lined with such walls, and he argued that the road was surely precolumbian. One section is now part of the main dirt road up-valley from the Pan American to El Carmen and the old Jesuit hacienda of San Jose; its present tortuous course has been formed by the bordering *acequia*, which has undercut its banks between the trees that line its sides, but nevertheless looks straight as an arrow on the aerial photographs. Elsewhere, the road pattern has been maintained largely by field divisions.

The ethnohistorical and archaeological data on Chincha present somewhat contradictory pictures, creating an interesting context within which to examine possible functions of the road system. The valley was noted in various documents as being one of the richest of Peru and center of an empire, its lord held in highest regard by the Inka, as having its name used by the Inka to refer to the entire northwestern sub-area of their empire, Tawantinsuyu (Hyslop 1984:102), and having the distinction of being kept directly under the administration of the King of Spain after the Spanish conquest.

Archaeologically, La Centinela is quite impressive as a temple mound, but in terms of habitation is at best an elite center, not an urban one. La Centinela de San Pedro even more notably lacks nucleated habitation, although two linear habitation sites are nearby, lining the roads to the north and east. There are close to fifty sizeable habitation mounds in Chincha and Pisco, scattered mainly in small groups. On the valley edges, especially the northern bluffs, there are many rectangular, semi-subterranean, communal, chullpa-like tombs and also innumerable graves on the northern bluffs that date to the period; most have been completely looted, probably not long after the conquest. The pottery style is prosaic (Kroeber and Strong 1924) and has no notable distribution outside of Chincha and Pisco. Of the various local southern coastal styles, the Ica ceramics have been judged as the prestige style of the region until a flood of Chincha style traits shortly before the Inka conquest (Menzel and Rowe 1966).

In short, the archaeological data would seem to contradict the ethnohistorical data, or the documents simply present exaggerated or otherwise inaccurate evidence. Also, Late Intermediate period architecture and settlement patterns for the south coast do not suggest the types of sociopolitical units which are normally associated with powerful and prestigious groups. The only clear exception to this characterization is the monumentality of the La Centinela temple mound, with its inferred religious function. However, in a sixteenth-century document published by Rostworowski (1970), Chincha is claimed to have been the center of a long-distance economic interchange system, new information which has led directly to the present reassessment both of the Late Chincha polity and of the road system.

The data and interpretations

The question of dating should first be clarified. A major Inka administrative center was built on the platform below the main pyramid at La Centinela, the different temporal and ethnic source obvious from the construction techniques used: rectangular adobes for the Inka construction and puddled adobe or *tapia* for the local construction. The main platform at San Pedro also shows some signs of Inka occupation; in addition, the hacienda just across an ancient riverbed from the site is called Lurinchincha, strongly suggesting that the site was the center of a typical Inkaic moietal division, La Centinela then presumably being *Hatun* Chincha. Dating the road system solely to the period of Inka occupation has been ruled out by the lack of evidence for roads in such a pattern ever having been constructed by the Inka. To superimpose such a road system on an already established field layout within a heavily populated valley seems equally unlikely. That the Inkas took over the system, however, is quite obvious.

The ceramic style which marks the later prehistory of the valley begins after the disruptions of the Middle Horizon in a very distinguishable form which shows clear continuity up to the Spanish conquest (Kroeber and Strong 1924; Menzel 1976). The present survey also established a distinct temporal difference between the adobes of earlier periods (various specific shapes, none rectangular) and the consistent use of puddled adobe for the period in question. As far as could be determined, all the sites of the Late Intermediate period were occupied up to the Spanish conquest, hardly surprising for habitation sites which were taking up space right in the areas of easily irrigated farmland.

La Centinela is the furthest south of the known coastal pilgrimage centers south of Pachacamac (Patterson 1985:164) and in size has no rival except the Pachacamac temple itself. The convergence of such an extensive and regular road layout on this important ceremonial center could then be explained as an extension of the monumentality and symbolism of the site as a pilgrimage center for populations far beyond the inhabitants of Chincha alone. Roads undoubtedly also approached it from the north, by both the coast and the inland route through Topara. But roads to the north do not seem likely to have been part of the regular layout, unless at their near approach to the site, now obliterated by the postconquest occupation of the Chincha Alta heights. A series of spaced concentrations of stones, with some sherds, was recorded by John Hyslop (1984:314; Fig. 21.5) in a survey along one arm of the road system as it crosses the pampas to the Pisco valley to the north. As a negative note – but one of obvious importance – no astronomical orientation is apparent for the roads.

While this ceremonial function may provide a sufficient explanation for the road system, the documentary claim for Chincha as an important center for economic interchange highlights another obvious feature of the roads. The coastal road, if extended, leads directly to the lower Pisco valley and then south to the base of the Paracas bay over a straight and level path. Roads to the middle Ica valley, then south to Nasca and beyond, could have led off this road at various points. The diagonal road crossing the pampas leads to the point where the Pisco valley enters the mountains: it would then join the major up-valley road to the highlands, the importance of which is indicated by the later construction of Inkaic Tambo Colorado along this road somewhat farther up-river. In addition, from a point across the river from this junction, a road still identified as being used within memory follows the base of the foothills to the upper Ica valley. The road up-valley from San Pedro would also join this road to Pisco. Only the two remaining diagonal roads, one from each of the ceremonial centers, lead to the bluffs bordering the south side of the valley and seem to lead no further.

The road system, therefore, provides direct access to all the important routes leading east and south, including a major highland road. A dual function for both pilgrims and merchants would then seem most likely. Since the long-distance trade in such ritually important materials as spondylus shell is well documented, a strong distinction between religious ritual and secular economic trafficking should not be made. The offerings of the pilgrims and the goods transported by the merchants may well have been similar and the two activities may have developed in tandem. In this view, the road system funnels all such materials and their bearers to the major center in the valley.

It is conceivable that the architecture of the center of such a road system could be monumental, but not religious. The typical pyramidal form of La Centinela is presumed, at present, to indicate a primary religious function in the central Andes. However, pyramidal form cannot in itself be presumed to indicate religious function in the Chincha valley. Many of the Late Intermediate period sites in the valley are closer to pyramidal than

flat-topped mounds, with up to sixteen in a group. In addition, the main La Centinela pyramid has rooms on three of its sides, quite like habitation mounds. However, its fourth side has a sheer drop of 20 m to the major terrace and an additional sheer drop of about 15 m from terrace to plaza.

Another possibility of combined religious and economic functions would be integrated temple/storage-room complexes such as the early Mesopotamian temple centers and possibly also the Harappan citadel. With the Inka practice of "tithing" for the religious sector, the potential for such sites does exist in the Andes. However, I know of only one Inka site of mainly religious and storage function and that is the highland site of San Pedro de Cacha, also unique for its very monumental main gabled structure. With excavations such as those by Craig Morris, La Centinela could well prove to be of salient religious function with closely associated storage complexes. But as yet there is no central Andean prototype to bolster such an interpretation.

The possibility that habitation sites were missed in the survey should never be ruled out, particularly since almost all sites were within the areas farmed both prehistorically and presently. Moderately mounded habitation sites might have been covered by the tightly clustered houses and small fields of postconquest Chincha Alta. Recent work by Daniel Sandweiss has located late habitation sites on the ocean side of the bluffs of Chincha Alta, but it is very clear that none occurred elsewhere on or near the edges of the valley floor.

The question then arises of how ceremonial sites such as La Centinela can be distinguished from pyramidal habitation sites. A clue was taken from the two La Centinelas, namely that temples took the form of large high rectangular platforms on top of which the pyramidal mounds were constructed. La Centinela de San Pedro very clearly fits this description (Fig. 21.4); the platform is quite impressive in its height and sheer sides, while the pyramid on top is very small and not at all impressive. The main section of La Centinela itself also follows this form.

Only one other site in the valley would fit this terrace-mound construction form, and that is La Saliteria (PV57–97), next to the up-valley road from La Centinela. This site also had some rectangular adobes along with the usual *tapia*, indicating that it dated, at least in part, to the Late Horizon or period of Inka occupation. The site also had fragments of a deep-relief adobe frieze, known elsewhere only for La Centinela. The Inkaic adobes and the relief are both associated with pre-Inkaic sites of ritual or sociopolitical importance. Since this possibly ceremonial site is on one of the outer roads, with the platform mound of San Pedro on the other outer arm of the road system, a potential symmetry in religious–civic architecture is suggested in respect of the road system. Nevertheless, it should be noted that the San Pedro mound is associated with two large nearby habitation sites, while La Saliteria is not. If it were possible to distinguish artifacts from such a site from those of purely habitation sites, work such as that done here by Patrick Carmichael could help answer this question.

This point leads to another important one: none of the proposed ceremonial centers is the nucleus for extensive habitation areas, as would be expected from the classic model of urban centers. The smaller proposed ceremonial centers of San Pedro and La Saliteria have only minor possible residential areas, although the former does have the two habitation sites less than 1 km away. La Centinela itself has moderately extensive areas which certainly could have served as habitations for a not inconsequential number of people. But the number of people involved would most probably fit the dignitaries, their retainers, and those necessary to manage the pilgrims at the site, rather than the range of social and economic differences expected from the urban model. At most these might be seen as elite centers, that is, centers both of ceremonial activity and also of elite habitation, with concomitant economic functions. And if habitation proves to have been more extensive around these sites than it now seems to have been – if, for example, the Tambo de Moro site (PV57–2) can be shown to have been connected with La Centinela – these ceremonial sites still seem unlikely to have been urban sites in the normal sense of the term.

Of the other, presumably mainly habitational sites, site size has been roughly indicated in Fig. 21.2 by the size of the markings for each site. Six sites stand out in size, all being over 10 ha. Five of these larger sites are along arms of the road system. However, the largest, the Las Huacas site (PV57–38) in the upper center of the valley, is not particularly close to any road. Las Huacas consists of thirty mounds, covering an area of 80 ha, including the areas between the mounds. There is no question whether the Las Huacas site was occupied when the road system was in use. With this curious exception, then, the settlement pattern and the road system can be said to be associated with and presumably served habitation concentrations, although the remaining sites, thirty-one of which are less than 4 ha in area, have no strong orientation to the road system. However, the absolute size of the total area should be kept in mind; the main

area of settlements of the period is only about 12 × 8 km, so that distances between settlements themselves and also the road system are not very great.

To summarize the settlement data, at least two ceremonial sites are focal points in the layout of the road system, with a third possible temple mound in addition. Four out of five large habitation sites, lacking evidence of having temple mounds within their boundaries, are also orientated to the road system; the fifth, which is rather far from any arm of the road system, happens also to be the largest in area and in number of habitation mounds. Six of these sites are between 10 and 80 ha in area. Only the main ceremonial site of La Centinela falls within this group, and then as the smallest.

Therefore, ceremonial centers and some large habitation agglutinations are in orientation to the road system, but the apparent ceremonial centers are separate from the larger, apparently mainly habitational centers. It is also clear that a large part of the population lived in many additional settlements ranging from small hamlet to large village in size. There is, if anything, a negative correlation between the location of La Centinela and these various habitation sites; they would seem to cluster in the lower part of the valley, although it should be noted that those that might have existed in the central east–west axis of the valley could well have been wiped out by a flood that occurred in the area earlier in this century.

The main data still to be considered are those of the ethnohistorical sources. Rostworowski (1970) has published a document, along with extensive analysis, which she convincingly establishes as written by Fray Pablo de Castro, one of the Dominicans who established the convent of Santo Tomás de Aquino in Chincha around 1542. In this document, fishermen are described as living along (and, when relaxing, dancing in) a "beautiful" straight road which began 2 leagues (probably about 8 km) before reaching the valley and extended for 3 leagues (12 km) within the valley; the 12 km would fit the distance between La Centinela and La Centinela de San Pedro, while the "beginning" 8 km could be either to the south or north along the beach. This documentary verification of at least one arm of the road system is obviously welcome.

Both of the major components of this document concern occupational and economic factors of the native Chincha polity. Pablo de Castro claims that 8,000 of a total of 30,000 tribute payers were merchants, 12,000 were farmers, and 10,000 were solely occupied in fishing. Since the total population would be a multiple of the total tribute payers, the figures suggest a sizeable population for the valley, with an average of 500 tribute payers per occupation site, or a more conservative 300–400 if it is assumed that there were originally up to 50 percent more sites than were recorded in the survey.

The total of 8,000 merchants, or 20 percent of the tribute payers, may seem an unusually high proportion for a preindustrial society. However, Pablo de Castro makes it clear that Chincha was the center of a major economic system of interchange, in which the Chincha merchants exchanged goods from as far north as Ecuador with ones from the central and south highlands. The author makes it clear that this was the basis for the renown of Chincha.

In addition, the 10,000 tribute payers occupied exclusively with fishing is an unusually high proportion. There are no rocky outcrops on the shores north of the ocean side of the Paracas peninsula or south of Cañete, so shellfishing is restricted. However, Chincha and Pisco, including Paracas Bay, share one notably long stretch of open beach which would be (and presently is) excellent for various types of net fishing. In addition, this beach is directly adjacent to the arable fields, so that distance between locations of subsistence activity is not a problem, eliminating a major rationale for differentiation of full-time specialization in farming or fishing.

Both the number of these fishermen – a full third of the tribute payers – and their purported exclusionary habitational pattern strongly support the presence of a major fishing specialization. There is little reason to believe the valley, even including nearby ones, could consume enough fish to support such a high proportion of fishermen. It seems more likely that fish, probably dried, might well have been entered into the exchange system, quite possibly as the only locally produced good in the system, aside from the knowledge and experience of the merchants themselves.

As a last point, the mention of the fishermen as being the only inhabitants of the coastal road indicates a segmentation or localization of habitation by occupation which seems unusual, given the close proximity of the fishing beaches and arable fields. The possibility of occupational localization being associated with one arm of the road introduces another dimension in the possible functions of the road system. In addition, this occupational localization may also contribute to the fairly dispersed nature of occupation sites.

Discussion

The seeming contradiction between the modest archaeological remains and the ethnohistoric claims of great wealth, power, and prestige accorded Chincha has been puzzling. The restricted distribution of artifacts clearly produced in Chincha or copied in the Chincha styles does not follow the pattern of militant expansion known for the Inka, Chimu, or Wari states. The archaeological and documentary data on the late preconquest Chincha polity now suggests the possibility of a societal system which might not be quite like any of the models for Central Andean societies as yet proposed. Although there is still little good excavational data for Chincha or Pisco, there is sufficient information covering a variety of cultural aspects to propose a preliminary societal model. Speculation is cheap, but preliminary models can direct the continuing work towards expansion, continual checking, and making alterations in the model.

The road system can be seen as a physical expression of an integration of ideological, economic, and sociopolitical factors, and thus mirror a series of features central in understanding the Chincha polity. It provides an efficient system for moving goods and also pilgrims between the valley and the highlands and coastal valleys to the south. It enhances the centrality of the major religious pilgrimage center south of Pachacamac. It can also be seen as a counterforce to the dispersed, multicentric habitation centers that dot the valley.

Features of a model for Chincha can be derived by partial analogy with the classic, Polanyi-school port-of-trade concept, one in which politically neutral trade centers are established to help avoid the collapse of trade networks during political disputes. Since these classic cases of ports of trade were not independent polities, the commercial specialization of Switzerland, coupled with the political neutrality, provides an even closer analogy.

Applied to the case of Chincha, such an apolitical, non-militaristic stance would go far in explaining the lack of fortification and defensible location of sites, the lack of population concentration for easier defense, and, in particular, the lack of evidence for a state presence outside the home territory. In short, the "power" of Chincha in material terms would be strictly economic, while the success of its long-distance interchange activities would be augmented by its non-militant posture. While it may well be carrying the argument too far, an intentional locational decentralization might have been carried out to deemphasize, physically, the size of the population of the valley. In any case, the lack of any claim in the documents for Chincha being a militaristic power does fit this interpretation.

An implication of military efficiency has undoubtedly been read into the ethnohistorical report of the partially successful resistance by Chincha to a political take-over by the Inka. This interpretation could well be an ethnocentric one. Resistance may have been quite real, but at least in part by vocal threat of breakdown in the interchange network, in addition to any physical resistance. The Inka may have been well aware of the value of the intangible trading ties and experience of the Chincha merchants and traffickers. They may also have realized that the network did not ultimately depend on any organizational body or physical location in Chincha; the heart of the network was with a highly mobile group of specialists.

In terms of the economic interchange network attributed to Chincha, precious metals and gems are specified in the document, including emeralds from the northern Andes. Such goods need not be transported in large quantities to be profitable. More bulky goods could be constantly trans-shipped, thereby requiring minimal warehousing. Again, no development of large centers is required. In addition, with the part exception of the fishermen, no notable centralization for economic maximization of locally produced goods is required by this mode, for either economic activity or habitation of specialists. In fact, many of those directly involved in the interchange of goods would be away from the valley at any given time.

Although the documentary source does not mention markets in Chincha itself, it seems likely that at the very least some exchange between local sources and the pilgrims did occur at or near La Centinela. But, if preoccupied with the trafficking of goods, few being produced in the valley, it seems possible that the inhabitants of Chincha would have been quite content to let the potters of Ica do the work of producing the "prestige" ware of the region, as Menzel has termed Late Ica pottery, bringing it to Chincha for sale to pilgrims. The flood of Chincha-style features on the immediately pre-Inka ceramics of Ica, as noted by Menzel and Rowe (1966), would fit the claim for Chincha's pre-eminence. However, the prosaic nature of both the Ica and Chincha style features makes it a somewhat difficult basis for determining the directions of influence; the Chincha style features may indeed have been borrowed under the shadow of Chincha's general prestige, but reflected merely the frequency of pilgrimages by the people of Ica to Chincha, rather than being a good measure of differential in prestige.

In a related vein, there is also a passage in the Pablo de Castro document claiming the use of a type of copper money by the Chincha merchants. The subject of whether this would involve "true" money or some intermediate medium of exchange is then raised, plus the

obvious question of whether the statement is accurate. More importantly, Rostworowski discusses whether a true market-place system is involved, the main alternative being the integrated political-economic system of the Inka, lacking any evidence of economic redistribution through merchants or markets. These questions are beyond the scope of the present data, unfortunately, although important enough to call attention to.

Assuming the acceptability of this model of specialization in management of an extensive economic interchange system, coupled with studied political neutrality, the contrast would be all the more notable between this model and those covering the political centralization of the Chimu cities or the political solutions to control of long-distance exchange by the Inka. Such contrasting approaches may themselves have been solutions to competition arising from the replication of eco-zones between the many coastal river valleys.

The focus of this article is the road system, so it is appropriate to draw to a conclusion by pointing out that the road system can be taken as establishing a tangible paradigm of the structure of the late Chincha polity. In the view from the outside and as entry to the valley, the roads emphasize the centrality and enhance the monumentality of a major ritual pilgrimage center. When viewed from this center, the roads lead outward to join the major egress routes to the highlands and valleys to the south, fitting both for a ritual center that serves pilgrims from afar, as well as for a physical center of an economic system that depends on contacts far outside the valley. La Centinela becomes both an abstract and a material center of power – providing the efficacy of ritual on the one hand and the material symbols of status on the other.

The other side of the coin would be that the system would provide the people of Chincha itself with their own abstract and material power, through the operation of a neatly integrated system of economic activities, social class, and the political trappings of the state. Particularly when a neutral stance towards outside power plays is added, the resultant mix can be claimed to be more than just a convenient fit of the various factors. The presence of an oracular service for pilgrims from the outside can be seen as a Madison Avenue dream for conveying the image of Chincha as a non-militant, politically benign center for certain economic goods, especially those goods used in the rituals themselves. And this mutual support can be stated for all items in the mix, indicating the presence of a well-integrated system.

One additional function can be suggested, one that

can be derived from the apparent internal decentralization of the Chincha polity itself, with only La Centinela as a symbolically powerful center. Whether a loosely organized polity or one with strong organizational control, but lacking an elaborated physical center of government, a place for the role of some symbol of valley-wide unity is apparent. The road system could then have functioned as such a symbol of the integration of the sociopolitical unit, as much for the inhabitants of the valley and the perpetuation of their system as – again in a non-threatening way – for those from the outside.

Acknowledgments

The survey of Chincha was funded by a Fulbright postdoctoral fellowship. The head of the Fulbright Commission in Lima at that time, Dr. Eduardo Indacochea, deserves special thanks, as do Luis Lumbreras and Isabel Flores, at that time doctoral students who were assigned as field assistants.

References

Hyslop, John
  1984 *The Inka Road System*. Academic Press, Orlando
Kroeber, Alfred Louis, and William Duncan Strong
  1924 The Uhle Collections from Chincha. *University of California Publications in American Archaeology and Ethnology* 21 (1):95–133. Berkeley
Menzel, Dorothy
  1976 *Pottery Style and Society in Ancient Peru*. University of California Press, Berkeley
Menzel, Dorothy, and John H. Rowe
  1966 The Role of Chincha in Late Pre-Spanish Peru. *Ñawpa Pacha* 4:63–76. Berkeley
Patterson, Thomas C.
  1985 An Andean Oracle under Inca Rule. In *Recent Studies in Andean Prehistory and Protohistory*, edited by D. Peter Kvietok and Daniel Sandweiss, pp. 159–76. Latin American Studies Program, Cornell University
Rostworowski de Diez Canseco, María
  1970 Mercaderes del valle de Chincha en la época prehispánica: un documento y unos comentarios. *Revista española de antropología americana* 5:135–77, Facultad de Geografía e Historia, Universidad Complutense, Madrid. (Reprinted in Rostworowski de Diez Canseco 1977.)
  1977 Mercaderes del valle de Chincha en la época prehispánica: un documento y unos comentarios. In *Etnía y sociedad: costa peruana prehispánica*, pp. 97–140. Instituto de Estudios Peruanos, Lima
Uhle, Max
  1924 Explorations in Chincha. *University of California Publications in American Archaeology and Ethnology*, 21 (2):55–94. Berkeley
Wallace, Dwight T.
  1971 *Sitios arqueológicos del Perú: valles de Chincha y de Pisco*. Arqueológicas 13. Lima

Index